P9-CQM-427

U.S. History For Dummies

Cheat Sheet

50 Key Dates in U.S. History

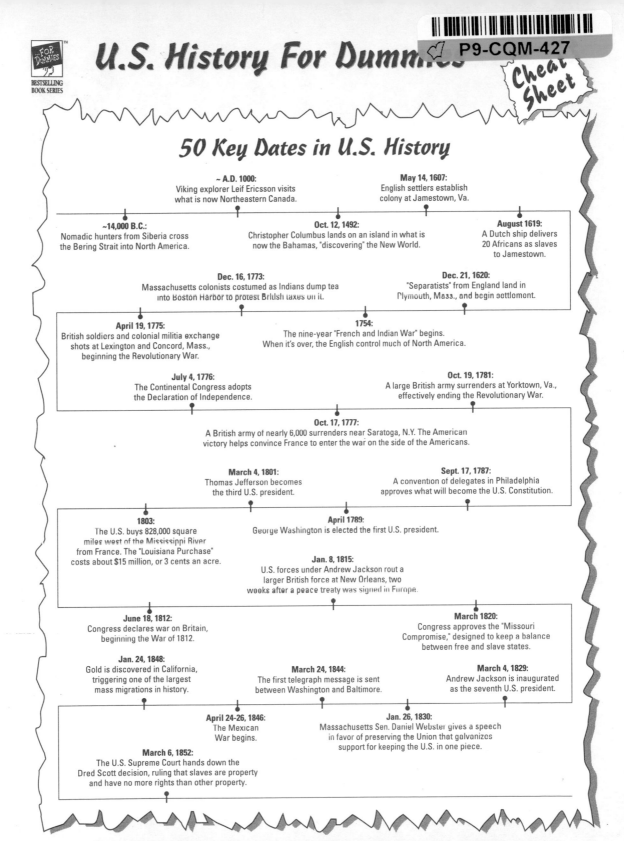

~ A.D. 1000:
Viking explorer Leif Ericsson visits
what is now Northeastern Canada.

May 14, 1607:
English settlers establish
colony at Jamestown, Va.

~14,000 B.C.:
Nomadic hunters from Siberia cross
the Bering Strait into North America.

Oct. 12, 1492:
Christopher Columbus lands on an island in what is
now the Bahamas, "discovering" the New World.

August 1619:
A Dutch ship delivers
20 Africans as slaves
to Jamestown.

Dec. 16, 1773:
Massachusetts colonists costumed as Indians dump tea
into Boston Harbor to protest British taxes on it.

Dec. 21, 1620:
"Separatists" from England land in
Plymouth, Mass., and begin settlement.

April 19, 1775:
British soldiers and colonial militia exchange
shots at Lexington and Concord, Mass.,
beginning the Revolutionary War.

1754:
The nine-year "French and Indian War" begins.
When it's over, the English control much of North America.

July 4, 1776:
The Continental Congress adopts
the Declaration of Independence.

Oct. 19, 1781:
A large British army surrenders at Yorktown, Va.,
effectively ending the Revolutionary War.

Oct. 17, 1777:
A British army of nearly 6,000 surrenders near Saratoga, N.Y. The American
victory helps convince France to enter the war on the side of the Americans.

March 4, 1801:
Thomas Jefferson becomes
the third U.S. president.

Sept. 17, 1787:
A convention of delegates in Philadelphia
approves what will become the U.S. Constitution.

1803:
The U.S. buys 828,000 square
miles west of the Mississippi River
from France. The "Louisiana Purchase"
costs about $15 million, or 3 cents an acre.

April 1789:
George Washington is elected the first U.S. president.

Jan. 8, 1815:
U.S. forces under Andrew Jackson rout a
larger British force at New Orleans, two
weeks after a peace treaty was signed in Europe.

June 18, 1812:
Congress declares war on Britain,
beginning the War of 1812.

March 1820:
Congress approves the "Missouri
Compromise," designed to keep a balance
between free and slave states.

Jan. 24, 1848:
Gold is discovered in California,
triggering one of the largest
mass migrations in history.

March 24, 1844:
The first telegraph message is sent
between Washington and Baltimore.

March 4, 1829:
Andrew Jackson is inaugurated
as the seventh U.S. president.

April 24-26, 1846:
The Mexican
War begins.

Jan. 26, 1830:
Massachusetts Sen. Daniel Webster gives a speech
in favor of preserving the Union that galvanizes
support for keeping the U.S. in one piece.

March 6, 1852:
The U.S. Supreme Court hands down the
Dred Scott decision, ruling that slaves are property
and have no more rights than other property.

U.S. History For Dummies®

Cheat Sheet

April 12, 1861:
Southern forces fire on the federal Fort Sumter at Charleston, S.C., beginning the Civil War.

April 14, 1865:
Abraham Lincoln is shot while attending a play in Washington, D.C. He dies the next day.

Nov. 6, 1860:
Abraham Lincoln is elected the sixteenth U.S. president.

July 2-4, 1863:
In a massive battle near Gettysburg, Pa., Union forces defeat a Confederate army in perhaps the most pivotal battle of the war.

June 25, 1876:
A force of U.S. cavalry under Col. George A. Custer is wiped out by American Indian forces at the Little Big Horn River in South Dakota.

May 16, 1868:
The Senate votes 35-19 to remove President Andrew Johnson from office, one vote short of the two-thirds needed to do so.

May 6, 1896:
The U.S. Supreme Court, in Plessy v. Ferguson, rules that states have the right to legally segregate public facilities if they are "equal" in quality.

July 1868:
The Fourteenth Amendment to the U.S. Constitution is ratified, entitling all people born or naturalized in the United States to U.S. citizenship and equal rights under the law.

Feb. 15, 1898:
The U.S. battleship Maine mysteriously explodes in Havana Harbor, triggering a war with Spain.

April 6, 1917:
The U.S. enters World War I.

Oct. 24, 1929:
The New York Stock Exchange collapses on what becomes known as "Black Thursday."

Dec. 17, 1903:
Wilbur and Orville Wright complete the first successful flights in a heavier-than-air machine at Kitty Hawk, North Carolina.

1920:
The first U.S. commercial radio station is established in Pittsburgh.

June 24, 1950:
North Korean troops invade South Korea. Within a week, U.S. troops are involved in the fighting.

Dec. 7, 1941:
U.S. forces are attacked by a Japanese armada at Pearl Harbor, Hawaii, drawing the U.S. into World War II.

Nov. 8, 1932:
Franklin Delano Roosevelt is elected the thirty-second U.S. president.

Aug. 6, 1945:
A U.S. plane drops an atomic bomb on the city of Hiroshima, Japan, effectively ending World War II.

Aug. 14, 1935:
Roosevelt signs the Social Security Act, creating a federal pension system.

May 17, 1954:
In Brown v. Board of Education, the U.S. Supreme Court rules that segregation of public schools is unconstitutional.

April 4, 1968:
Civil rights leader Martin Luther King, Jr., is assassinated while on a motel balcony in Memphis.

Nov. 22, 1963:
President John F. Kennedy is assassinated while riding in a motorcade in Dallas.

Aug. 8, 1974:
President Richard M. Nixon resigns the presidency in the wake of the Watergate scandal.

Feb. 12, 1999:
The Senate votes to acquit President Bill Clinton of impeachment charges stemming from the "Monicagate" scandal.

Jan. 16, 1991:
U.S. and allied forces launch a giant aerial attack on Iraq, four months after Iraq invaded neighboring Kuwait.

Nov. 8, 1980:
Ronald Reagan is elected the fortieth U.S. president.

The IDG Books Worldwide logo is a registered trademark under exclusive license to IDG Books Worldwide, Inc., from International Data Group, Inc. The ...For Dummies logo and For Dummies are trademarks of IDG Books Worldwide, Inc. All other trademarks are the property of their respective owners.

IDG BOOKS WORLDWIDE

Copyright © 2001 IDG Books Worldwide, Inc. All rights reserved.

Cheat Sheet $2.95 value. Item 5249-X.

For more information about IDG Books, call 1-800-762-2974.

For Dummies™: Bestselling Book Series for Beginners

 ™

References for the Rest of Us ™

BESTSELLING BOOK SERIES

Do you find that traditional reference books are overloaded with technical details and advice you'll never use? Do you postpone important life decisions because you just don't want to deal with them? Then our *...For Dummies®* business and general reference book series is for you.

...For Dummies business and general reference books are written for those frustrated and hard-working souls who know they aren't dumb, but find that the myriad of personal and business issues and the accompanying horror stories make them feel helpless. *...For Dummies* books use a lighthearted approach, a down-to-earth style, and even cartoons and humorous icons to dispel fears and build confidence. Lighthearted but not lightweight, these books are perfect survival guides to solve your everyday personal and business problems.

> "More than a publishing phenomenon, 'Dummies' is a sign of the times."
> — *The New York Times*

> "...you won't go wrong buying them."
> — *Walter Mossberg, Wall Street Journal, on IDG Books' ...For Dummies books*

> "A world of detailed and authoritative information is packed into them..."
> — *U.S. News and World Report*

Already, millions of satisfied readers agree. They have made *...For Dummies* the #1 introductory level computer book series and a best-selling business book series. They have written asking for more. So, if you're looking for the best and easiest way to learn about business and other general reference topics, look to *...For Dummies* to give you a helping hand.

IDG BOOKS WORLDWIDE

U.S. History FOR DUMMIES®

by Steve Wiegand

IDG Books Worldwide, Inc.
An International Data Group Company

Foster City, CA ◆ Chicago, IL ◆ Indianapolis, IN ◆ New York, NY

U.S. History For Dummies®

Published by
IDG Books Worldwide, Inc.
An International Data Group Company
909 3rd Avenue, 21st Floor
New York, NY 10022

www.idgbooks.com (IDG Books Worldwide Web Site)
www.dummies.com (Dummies Press Web Site)

Copyright © 2001 IDG Books Worldwide, Inc. All rights reserved. No part of this book, including interior design, cover design, and icons, may be reproduced or transmitted in any form, by any means (electronic, photocopying, recording, or otherwise) without the prior written permission of the publisher.

Library of Congress Control Number: 00-110910

ISBN: 0-7645-5249-X

Printed in the United States of America

10 9 8 7 6 5 4 3 2 1

1O/RT/QS/QR/IN

Distributed in the United States by IDG Books Worldwide, Inc.

Distributed by CDG Books Canada Inc. for Canada; by Transworld Publishers Limited in the United Kingdom; by IDG Norge Books for Norway; by IDG Sweden Books for Sweden; by IDG Books Australia Publishing Corporation Pty. Ltd. for Australia and New Zealand; by TransQuest Publishers Pte Ltd. for Singapore, Malaysia, Thailand, Indonesia, and Hong Kong; by Gotop Information Inc. for Taiwan; by ICG Muse, Inc. for Japan; by Intersoft for South Africa; by Eyrolles for France; by International Thomson Publishing for Germany, Austria and Switzerland; by Distribuidora Cuspide for Argentina; by LR International for Brazil; by Galileo Libros for Chile; by Ediciones ZETA S.C.R. Ltda. for Peru; by WS Computer Publishing Corporation, Inc., for the Philippines; by Contemporanea de Ediciones for Venezuela; by Express Computer Distributors for the Caribbean and West Indies; by Micronesia Media Distributor, Inc. for Micronesia; by Chips Computadoras S.A. de C.V. for Mexico; by Editorial Norma de Panama S.A. for Panama; by American Bookshops for Finland.

For general information on IDG Books Worldwide's books in the U.S., please call our Consumer Customer Service department at **800-762-2974**. For reseller information, including discounts and premium sales, please call our Reseller Customer Service department at **800-434-3422**.

For information on where to purchase IDG Books Worldwide's books outside the U.S., please contact our International Sales department at **317-572-3993** or fax **317-572-4002**.

For consumer information on foreign language translations, please contact our Customer Service department at **1-800-434-3422**, fax **317-572-4002**, or e-mail rights@idgbooks.com.

For information on licensing foreign or domestic rights, please phone **+1-650-653-7098**.

For sales inquiries and special prices for bulk quantities, please contact our Order Services department at **800-434-4322** or write to the address above.

For information on using IDG Books Worldwide's books in the classroom or for ordering examination copies, please contact our Educational Sales department at **800-434-2086** or fax **317-572-4005**.

For press review copies, author interviews, or other publicity information, please contact our Public Relations department at **650-653-7000** or fax **650-653-7500**.

For authorization to photocopy items for corporate, personal, or educational use, please contact Copyright Clearance Center, 222 Rosewood Drive, Danvers, MA 01923, or fax **978-750-4470**.

LIMIT OF LIABILITY/DISCLAIMER OF WARRANTY: THE PUBLISHER AND AUTHOR HAVE USED THEIR BEST EFFORTS IN PREPARING THIS BOOK. THE PUBLISHER AND AUTHOR MAKE NO REPRESENTATIONS OR WARRANTIES WITH RESPECT TO THE ACCURACY OR COMPLETENESS OF THE CONTENTS OF THIS BOOK AND SPECIFICALLY DISCLAIM ANY IMPLIED WARRANTIES OF MERCHANTABILITY OR FITNESS FOR A PARTICULAR PURPOSE. THERE ARE NO WARRANTIES WHICH EXTEND BEYOND THE DESCRIPTIONS CONTAINED IN THIS PARAGRAPH. NO WARRANTY MAY BE CREATED OR EXTENDED BY SALES REPRESENTATIVES OR WRITTEN SALES MATERIALS. THE ACCURACY AND COMPLETENESS OF THE INFORMATION PROVIDED HEREIN AND THE OPINIONS STATED HEREIN ARE NOT GUARANTEED OR WARRANTED TO PRODUCE ANY PARTICULAR RESULTS, AND THE ADVICE AND STRATEGIES CONTAINED HEREIN MAY NOT BE SUITABLE FOR EVERY INDIVIDUAL. NEITHER THE PUBLISHER NOR AUTHOR SHALL BE LIABLE FOR ANY LOSS OF PROFIT OR ANY OTHER COMMERCIAL DAMAGES, INCLUDING BUT NOT LIMITED TO SPECIAL, INCIDENTAL, CONSEQUENTIAL, OR OTHER DAMAGES.

Trademarks: For Dummies, Dummies Man, A Reference for the Rest of Us!, The Dummies Way, Dummies Daily, and related trade dress are registered trademarks or trademarks of IDG Books Worldwide, Inc. in the United States and other countries, and may not be used without written permission. All other trademarks are the property of their respective owners. IDG Books Worldwide is not associated with any product or vendor mentioned in this book.

is a registered trademark under exclusive license to IDG Books Worldwide, Inc., from International Data Group, Inc.

About the Author

Steve Wiegand has not only written about U.S. history, he's been around for about 22 percent of it since the country formally began. An award-winning journalist for 25 years, Wiegand has covered everything from mass murders to massive earthquakes to six presidential campaigns and has written extensively on contemporary and historical American politics and social issues.

Wiegand is a graduate of Santa Clara University, where he majored in American literature and U.S. history. He also holds a Master of Science degree in Mass Communications from California State University, San Jose. Wiegand has won numerous journalism awards during his career as a writer and columnist at the *San Diego Evening Tribune, San Francisco Chronicle,* and *Sacramento Bee,* and is the author of a book on California's capital, *Sacramento Tapestry* (Towery Books).

He lives in Northern California.

ABOUT IDG BOOKS WORLDWIDE

Welcome to the world of IDG Books Worldwide.

IDG Books Worldwide, Inc., is a subsidiary of International Data Group, the world's largest publisher of computer-related information and the leading global provider of information services on information technology. IDG was founded more than 30 years ago by Patrick J. McGovern and now employs more than 9,000 people worldwide. IDG publishes more than 290 computer publications in over 75 countries. More than 90 million people read one or more IDG publications each month.

Launched in 1990, IDG Books Worldwide is today the #1 publisher of best-selling computer books in the United States. We are proud to have received eight awards from the Computer Press Association in recognition of editorial excellence and three from Computer Currents' First Annual Readers' Choice Awards. Our best-selling ...*For Dummies*® series has more than 50 million copies in print with translations in 31 languages. IDG Books Worldwide, through a joint venture with IDG's Hi-Tech Beijing, became the first U.S. publisher to publish a computer book in the People's Republic of China. In record time, IDG Books Worldwide has become the first choice for millions of readers around the world who want to learn how to better manage their businesses.

Our mission is simple: Every one of our books is designed to bring extra value and skill-building instructions to the reader. Our books are written by experts who understand and care about our readers. The knowledge base of our editorial staff comes from years of experience in publishing, education, and journalism — experience we use to produce books to carry us into the new millennium. In short, we care about books, so we attract the best people. We devote special attention to details such as audience, interior design, use of icons, and illustrations. And because we use an efficient process of authoring, editing, and desktop publishing our books electronically, we can spend more time ensuring superior content and less time on the technicalities of making books.

You can count on our commitment to deliver high-quality books at competitive prices on topics you want to read about. At IDG Books Worldwide, we continue in the IDG tradition of delivering quality for more than 30 years. You'll find no better book on a subject than one from IDG Books Worldwide.

John J. Kilcullen

John Kilcullen
Chairman and CEO
IDG Books Worldwide, Inc.

Eighth Annual
Computer Press
Awards ➢ 1992

Ninth Annual
Computer Press
Awards ➢ 1993

Tenth Annual
Computer Press
Awards ➢ 1994

Eleventh Annual
Computer Press
Awards ➢ 1995

IDG is the world's leading IT media, research and exposition company. Founded in 1964, IDG had 1997 revenues of $2.05 billion and has more than 9,000 employees worldwide. IDG offers the widest range of media options that reach IT buyers in 75 countries representing 95% of worldwide IT spending. IDG's diverse product and services portfolio spans six key areas including print publishing, online publishing, expositions and conferences, market research, education and training, and global marketing services. More than 90 million people read one or more of IDG's 290 magazines and newspapers, including IDG's leading global brands — Computerworld, PC World, Network World, Macworld and the Channel World family of publications. IDG Books Worldwide is one of the fastest-growing computer book publishers in the world, with more than 700 titles in 36 languages. The "...For Dummies®" series alone has more than 50 million copies in print. IDG offers online users the largest network of technology-specific Web sites around the world through IDG.net (http://www.idg.net), which comprises more than 225 targeted Web sites in 55 countries worldwide. International Data Corporation (IDC) is the world's largest provider of information technology data, analysis and consulting, with research centers in over 41 countries and more than 400 research analysts worldwide. IDG World Expo is a leading producer of more than 168 globally branded conferences and expositions in 35 countries including E3 (Electronic Entertainment Expo), Macworld Expo, ComNet, Windows World Expo, ICE (Internet Commerce Expo), Agenda, DEMO, and Spotlight. IDG's training subsidiary, ExecuTrain, is the world's largest computer training company, with more than 230 locations worldwide and 785 training courses. IDG Marketing Services helps industry-leading IT companies build international brand recognition by developing global integrated marketing programs via IDG's print, online and exposition products worldwide. Further information about the company can be found at www.idg.com.   1/26/00

Dedication

To Ceil, for all my pasts, and to Erin, for all our futures.

Author's Acknowledgments

Thanks first to my friends and colleagues John D. Cox, for getting me the chance to do this book, and Bill Enfield, for his interest and encouragement.

Thanks also to my literary agent, Skip Barker of the Wilson Devereux Company, for knowing when to push and when to pull, and for knowing his business. To Linda Brandon, my project editor at IDG Books Worldwide, Inc., thanks for her enthusiasm and pragmatism. And thanks to copy editor Rowena Rappaport for her thoughtful editing.

Finally, thanks to my mom for giving me the determination to do it, and to my dad for giving me the sense of humor not to take it too seriously along the way.

Publisher's Acknowledgments

We're proud of this book; please register your comments through our IDG Books Worldwide Online Registration Form located at http://my2cents.dummies.com.

Some of the people who helped bring this book to market include the following:

Acquisitions, Editorial, and Media Development

Project Editor: Linda Brandon

Acquisitions Editor: Susan Decker

Copy Editor: Rowena Rappaport

Technical Editor: Diane Lindstrom

Media Development Specialist: Megan Decraene

Editorial Manager: Christine Beck

Editorial Assistant: Jennifer Young

Cover Photos: © Joseph Nettis/Stock, Boston/PictureQuest

Production

Project Coordinator: Nancee Reeves

Layout and Graphics: Amy Adrian, Jackie Nicholas, Jill Piscitelli, Heather Pope, Jacque Schneider, Jeremey Unger, Erin Zeltner

Proofreaders: Laura Albert, Nancy Price, York Production Services

Indexer: York Production Services

Special Help
Robert Annis

General and Administrative

IDG Books Worldwide, Inc.: John Kilcullen, CEO; Bill Barry, President and COO

IDG Books Consumer Reference Group

Business: Kathleen A. Welton, Vice President and Publisher; Kevin Thornton, Acquisitions Manager

Cooking/Gardening: Jennifer Feldman, Associate Vice President and Publisher

Education/Reference: Diane Graves Steele, Vice President and Publisher; Greg Tubach, Publishing Director

Lifestyles: Kathleen Nebenhaus, Vice President and Publisher; Tracy Boggier, Managing Editor

Pets: Dominique De Vito, Associate Vice President and Publisher; Tracy Boggier, Managing Editor

Travel: Michael Spring, Vice President and Publisher; Suzanne Jannetta, Editorial Director; Brice Gosnell, Managing Editor

IDG Books Consumer Editorial Services: Kathleen Nebenhaus, Vice President and Publisher; Kristin A. Cocks, Editorial Director; Cindy Kitchel, Editorial Director

IDG Books Consumer Production: Debbie Stailey, Production Director

IDG Books Packaging: Marc J. Mikulich, Vice President, Brand Strategy and Research

◆

The publisher would like to give special thanks to Patrick J. McGovern, without whom this book would not have been possible.

◆

Contents at a Glance

Introduction *1*

Part 1: Getting There, Getting Settled, and Getting Free ... *7*

Chapter 1: Before the Beginning: 14,000 B.C.–A.D. 1492 9
Chapter 2: Columbus Discovers the Bahamas: 1492–1607 21
Chapter 3: Pilgrims' Progress: The English Colonies, 1607–1700 33
Chapter 4: Old Grudges in a New World: 1700–1763 47
Chapter 5: Revolting Developments: 1763–1775 57
Chapter 6: Yankee Doodlin': 1775–1783 69
Chapter 7: Blueprints and Birth Pains: 1783–1800 85

Part 11: Growing Pains *97*

Chapter 8: "Long Tom" Becomes President: 1800–1809 99
Chapter 9: One Weird War: 1809–1815 111
Chapter 10: The Good, the Bad, and the Very Ugly: 1815–1828 119
Chapter 11: The Influences of Andrew Jackson: 1829–1844 133
Chapter 12: War, Gold, and a Gathering Storm: 1845–1860 147
Chapter 13: A Most Uncivil War: 1861–1865 165
Chapter 14: Putting It Back Together: 1865–1876 181

Part 111: Coming of Age *193*

Chapter 15: Growing Up: 1876–1898 195
Chapter 16: Growing Out: 1899–1918 215
Chapter 17: Bathtub Gin, Jazz, and Lucky Lindy: 1919–1929 229
Chapter 18: Uncle Sam's Depressed: 1930–1940 245
Chapter 19: The World at War: 1941–1945 261

Part 1V: America in Adulthood *277*

Chapter 20: The Fast Fifties: 1946–1960 279
Chapter 21: Camelot to Watergate: 1961–1974 295
Chapter 22: Hold the Malaise, or Ayatollah So: 1975–1992 311
Chapter 23: The Future is Now: 1993–2000 327

Part V: The Part of Tens 343

Chapter 24: The 10 Best — and 10 Worst — Presidents 345
Chapter 25: Ten Historical Events That Probably Never Happened 347
Chapter 26: Ten Inventions That Changed Life as We Know It 351
Chapter 27: Ten Events That Defined American Culture 355

Part VI: Appendixes 359

Appendix A: Preamble to the United States Constitution 361
Appendix B: The Bill of Rights: Amendments 1–10 of the Constitution 363
Appendix C: The Declaration of Independence 365
Appendix D: The Gettysburg Address 369

Index 371

Book Registration Information.......................Back of Book

Cartoons at a Glance

By Rich Tennant

page 359

page 7

page 277

page 193

page 343

page 97

Cartoon Information:
Fax: 978-546-7747
E-Mail: richtennant@the5thwave.com
World Wide Web: www.the5thwave.com

Table of Contents

Introduction *1*

   About This Book 1

   How This Book Is Organized 2

      Part I: Getting There, Getting Settled, and Getting Free 2

      Part II: Growing Pains 3

      Part III: Coming of Age 3

      Part IV: America in Adulthood 3

      Part V: The Part of Tens 4

      Part VI: Appendixes 4

   Icons Used in This Book 4

   Where to Go from Here 5

Part 1: Getting There, Getting Settled, and Getting Free ...7

   Chapter 1: Before the Beginning: 14,000 B.C.–A.D. 1492 9

      Coming to America 9

      Exploring Early Civilizations 11

         The Anasazi 12

         The Mound Builders 12

      Too Many Tribes, Not Enough Indians 13

         In the Northwest 13

         In the Southwest 14

         On the Great Plains 14

         In the Northeast 14

         In the Southeast 15

      De-stereotyping the American Indians 15

      Discovering America the Viking Way 16

      Determining Who Else Came to America 18

      Gee, Grandpa, What Else Happened? 19

   Chapter 2: Columbus Discovers the Bahamas: 1492–1607 21

      Spicing Up Life 21

      Christopher Columbus: Dream Salesman 22

      Discovering a Dozen Other People Who Dropped By 25

      Getting Rid of the Indians: The Sword, the Cross, and the Measles 27

         Indian slavery 27

         The men in the brown robes 28

         Destruction through disease 29

      Arriving Late for the Party 30

         France 30

         England 31

      Gee, Grandpa, What Else Happened? 32

Chapter 3: Pilgrims' Progress: The English Colonies, 1607–1700   . . .33

Go West, Old Chap, Go West 33
Starting It All in Jamestown 34
    Early troubles 34
    Making Indian friends 35
    Finding a cash crop 35
Setting Up Slavery 37
Colonizing: Pilgrims and Puritans 38
    The Mayflower Compact — a Dutch pilgrimage 38
    The Massachusetts Bay Colony — a pure haven 40
Bringing Religious Freedom: Dissidents, Catholics, and Quakers 41
    Settling in Rhode Island 42
    Beginning in Maryland 43
    Starting Pennsylvania 43
Going Dutch Treat 44
Dealing with Indian Troubles 44
Gee, Grandpa, What Else Happened? 46

Chapter 4: Old Grudges in a New World: 1700–1763 47

1700 America Gets a Facelift 47
Colonizing New France 48
The First True World Wars 49
    King William's War 49
    Queen Anne's War 50
    King George's War 50
The Great Awakening 52
The French and Indians: At It Again 53
    Unifying the Colonies 53
    Holding back the British 54
    Outfighting the French 54
Gee, Grandpa, What Else Happened? 55

Chapter 5: Revolting Developments: 1763–1775 57

Seeing a Growth Spurt 57
Looking at the Brits' Point of View 59
England and America: Heading Toward Divorce 60
    The Proclamation of 1763 61
    The Revenue Acts (1764) 61
    The Stamp Act (1765) 61
    The Townshend Act (1767) 62
    The Boston Massacre (1770) 63
    The Boston Tea Party (1773) 64
    The "Intolerable" Acts (1774) 64
Congressing and Cocktails 65
Mr. Revere, Your Horse Is Ready 66
Gee, Grandpa, What Else Happened? 67

Chapter 6: Yankee Doodlin': 1775–1783 69

In This Corner, the Brits 69
In This Corner, the Yanks 70
Mr. Washington Goes to War 72
    Choosing a leader 72
    Finding faults 72
    Commanding a country 73
Declaring Independence 74
    Sparking an interest 74
    Writing history 75
French Kissing-up 76
Changing Lives 77
    Loyalists 77
    Slaves 78
Winning a War 79
    Fort Ticonderoga 79
    Bunker Hill 79
    The Canada Campaign 81
    New York 81
    Trenton and Princeton 81
    Saratoga 81
    Bonhomme Richard versus Serapis 82
    Charleston 82
    Guilford Courthouse 82
    Yorktown 83
Gee, Grandpa, What Else Happened? 83

Chapter 7: Blueprints and Birth Pains: 1783–1800 85

Making the Rules 85
    Going back to Philly 87
    Selling It 88
Dishing Up Politics, American Style 89
Raising the Dough 92
Earning Respect 93
    The Whiskey Rebellion 93
    Speak no evil 93
Finding Foreign Friction 94
Gee, Grandpa, What Else Happened? 95

Part II: Growing Pains 97

Chapter 8: "Long Tom" Becomes President: 1800–1809 99

Jefferson Gets a Job 99
Disorder in the Court 101
Growing by Leaps and Bounds 102
    Napoleon has a going-out-of-business sale 103
    Lewis, Clark, and the woman on the dollar coin 105

Fighting Pirates and Passing an Embargo 106

"To the shores of Tripoli . . . " 107

No one likes a bloodless war 108

Gee, Grandpa, What Else Happened? 109

Chapter 9: One Weird War: 1809–1815 111

Bringing Madison to Term 111

Gaining control 112

Looking for a war 112

Fighting the Indians — again 112

Invading Canada 113

Three Strikes and the Brits Are Out 115

Let's Call It Even 116

Gee, Grandpa, What Else Happened? 117

Chapter 10: The Good, the Bad, and the Very Ugly: 1815–1828 119

Pulling Together 119

Taking it to the bank 120

A "tariffic" idea 121

This land is my land, but for how much? 121

Orders from the court 123

Increasing Industry 123

A Cancer Grows 125

The cotton boom means more slaves 125

A political issue 127

Compromising over Missouri 128

Mind Your Own Hemisphere 129

Mud Wrestling to the White House 130

Gee, Grandpa, What Else Happened? 132

Chapter 11: The Influences of Andrew Jackson: 1829–1844 133

Old Hickory 133

Nullify This 136

The speech that helped win a war 137

A "tarrible" idea 138

Creating Inventions to Improve American Life 138

Making a withdrawal 138

Riding the train 140

Reaping what you sow 140

Communicating across America and the Atlantic 141

Removing the Indians 141

Claiming Independence for Texas 143

Remembering the Alamo 143

Becoming a state 144

Fighting for the Presidency 144

Gee Grandpa, What Else Happened? 146

Chapter 12: War, Gold, and a Gathering Storm: 1845–1860 147

Heading South of the Border 147
    Starting a war 148
    Capturing California and the West 149
Rushing for Gold 150
    Going West 151
    The Compromise of 1850 153
Coming Over and Spreading Out 155
    Living dangerously 155
    Trailing the Mormons 157
    Wagons ho! 157
    The women's movement 158
The Beginning of the End 159
    Factoring a slave's life 159
    Shedding blood in Kansas 160
    Making a "dredful" decision 161
Squaring Off for a Showdown: The Lincoln–Douglas Debate 162
    Spark No. 1: John Brown 162
    Spark No. 2: Lincoln's election 162
Gee, Grandpa, What Else Happened? 163

Chapter 13: A Most Uncivil War: 1861–1865 165

A Man Called Lincoln 165
    What makes a president 166
    Views on slavery states and the state of the Union 167
North versus South: The Tale of the Tape 169
Freeing the Slaves 171
    Announcing the Emancipation Proclamation 172
    Fighting a just fight 172
Who Won What Where 172
    Meet the generals 174
    On the seas 174
    The land war 174
Two More Reasons Why the North Won 178
Losing a Hero 179
Gee, Grandpa, What Else Happened? 179

Chapter 14: Putting It Back Together: 1865–1876 181

A Southern-fried Mess 181
    Starting life anew 182
    Becoming sharecroppers 183
Finding Bitter Solutions 183
    Piecing the Union back together 184
    Using violence to keep blacks down 186
The Tailor-made President 186
    Taking control of Congress 187
    Attempting impeachment 188

Growing Corruption in Politics 189
    Taking a cue from the White House 190
    Trying to change the tides 190
    Fixing a presidency 191
Gee, Grandpa, What Else Happened? 192

Part III: Coming of Age 193

Chapter 15: Growing Up: 1876–1898 195

Spreading to the West 195
    Mining for money 195
    Ranching cattle 196
    Farming the land 198
Ousting "Undesirables" 199
    Putting up a fight 200
    Legalizing discrimination 201
Populating the East 203
Inventing Big Business 205
    Building the railroads 206
    Manufacturing steel 207
    Drilling and refining oil 208
    Producing the telephone and light bulb 209
    Creating trusts 209
Electing a String of Forgettable Presidents 210
The Rise of Populism 211
Declaring War with Spain 212
Gee, Grandpa, What Else Happened? 213

Chapter 16: Growing Out: 1899–1918 215

Here Today, Guam Tomorrow 215
Making a Lot of Noise and Carrying a Big Stick 217
Progressing Toward Reform 218
Contracting Labor Pains 219
Transporting America 221
Suffering for Suffrage 222
Migrating to Cities as the Promised Land 223
The War to End All Chapters 225
Gee, Grandpa, What Else Happened? 227

Chapter 17: Bathtub Gin, Jazz, and Lucky Lindy: 1919–1929 229

Trying to Keep the Peace 229
Restricting Immigration and Challenging the Natives 231
    Closing the gate 231
    Return of the Klan 232
    Darwin versus God 232
Keeping Republicans in the White House:
    Harding, Coolidge, and Hoover 233

Spending Money Made for Good Times: Or Did It? 235
    Helping the rich 235
    Increasing American spending habits 236
    Making it difficult on the poor 236
Ain't We Got Fun? 237
    Going to the movies 237
    Listening to the radio 238
    Listening to music and writing literature 239
    Playing games 239
Drying Out America: Prohibition 240
Changing Morals 241
Ushering in an Age of Heroes 242
Gee, Grandpa, What Else Happened? 243

Chapter 18: Uncle Sam's Depressed: 1930–1940 ....**245**
Analyzing the Causes and Consequences of the Great Depression 245
Even Worse Off. 248
    Shoving aside African Americans, Mexicans,
        and Native American Indians 248
    Keeping women at home — or work 250
    Developing organized labor 250
FDR: Making Alphabet Soup 251
    Electing a reformer 252
    Giving hope for better lives with New Deal programs 253
    Implementing court-packing tactics 255
Critics, Crooks, and Crimefighters 256
    Huey Long 256
    Frances E. Townsend 257
    Charles E. Coughlin 257
    Bad guys and G-men 258
Gee, Grandpa, What Else Happened? 260

Chapter 19: The World at War: 1941–1945 ....**261**
Trying to Avoid War — Again 261
Gearing Up For War 264
    Getting industry and the economy in shape
        for the World War 264
    Working with labor unions during war times 265
    Employing women for the war effort 266
    Making strides — African Americans help out
        with the work shortage 267
    Returning for work after being kicked out — Latinos 268
    Treating the Japanese Americans poorly 269
Dealing With the War in Europe 270
Dealing With the War in the Pacific 272
Dropping the Bomb 274
Gee, Grandpa, What Else Happened? 275

Part IV: America in Adulthood 277

Chapter 20: The Fast Fifties: 1946–1960 279

Starting a Cold War and Hot "Police Action" 279
    The United Nations 280
    The world as a chess board 280
    The Berlin airlift 281
    The "miracle of '48" 282
    The Korean War 282
    Uncle Sam's big stick 283
Finding Commies under the Bed 284
    Hiss and Chambers 284
    The Rosenbergs 285
    Federal worker loyalty 285
    "Tail-Gunner Joe" 286
Having It All 287
    A booming economy 287
    The burbs 288
    The tube 289
    Rock 'n roll 290
    An American king 290
Riding at the Back of the Bus 291
    Brown against the board 291
    Boycotting the bus 292
Gee, Grandpa, What Else Happened? 293

Chapter 21: Camelot to Watergate: 1961–1974 295

Electing an Icon 295
    The Bay of Pigs 296
    The October crisis 296
    Dark day in Dallas 297
Sending Troops to Vietnam 298
    The Gulf of Tonkin 299
    The Tet Offensive 299
Increasing Pressure in 'Nam and Escalating Fears at Home 299
Climbing the Mountain to Racial Freedom 301
    Enforcing their rights — African Americans 301
    Challenging the system — La Raza 303
    Maintaining their culture — Native Americans 303
Entering a Generation in Revolt 305
    Draft dodging, drugs, and demonstrations 305
    Feminism 305
    Gay days 306
Problems in the White House 307
    The Nixon Administration 307
    Watergate 308
Gee, Grandpa, What Else Happened? 309

Chapter 22: Hold the Malaise, or Ayatollah So: 1975–1992 311
   Wearing Someone Else's Shoes 311
     Doing the best he could 312
     Whipping inflation 312
   Good Intentions, Bad Results 313
     Measuring misery 314
     Befriending the enemy 315
   There's a First Time for Everything 316
     Buying into the "Reagan Revolution" 317
     Paying for "Reaganomics" 318
     Dealing with foreign affairs 319
   Warming Up after the Cold War 321
     The Gulf War 323
     Back on the home front 324
   Gee, Grandpa, What Else Happened? .325

Chapter 23: The Future is Now: 1993–2000 327
   Testing America: The Clinton Administration 327
     Presiding over a nation 328
     Pushing the "Contract with America" 329
     Judging a president 330
   Terrorism at Home 331
     Ruby Ridge 331
     Waco 332
     Oklahoma City 333
     The Unabomber 334
   Making Ourselves Sick 335
     Suffering from AIDS 335
     Dealing with drugs 337
   Creating a World of Change 337
     Entering the e-mail revolution 338
     Trading under a global economy 339
   Getting a New Look 340
   Gee, Grandpa, What Else Happened? .340

Part V: The Part of Tens *343*

Chapter 24: The 10 Best — and 10 Worst — Presidents 345

Chapter 25: Ten Historical Events That Probably Never Happened . . .347

Chapter 26: Ten Inventions That Changed Life as We Know It 351

Chapter 27: Ten Events That Defined American Culture 355

Part VI: Appendixes *359*

   Appendix A: Preamble to the United States Constitution 361

   Appendix B: The Bill of Rights: Amendments 1–10
   of the Constitution 363

   Appendix C: The Declaration of Independence 365

   Appendix D: The Gettysburg Address 369

Index...*371*

Book Registration Information ....*Back of Book*

Introduction

● ●

"*T*hose who cannot remember the past," said American philosopher George Santayana, "are condemned to repeat it." Generally in the twelfth grade.

Lots of people think learning U.S. history is a punishment. It's a subject you had to take in school. You memorized a bewildering array of dates, absorbed definitions for terms like *Manifest Destiny,* and wondered if America really needed two presidents named Harrison. Historical figures were presented to you as if they were characters in a junior high school costume pageant. Their blemishes were airbrushed out, and their personalities were drained away. Sure, you were taught George Washington warned the country about foreign entanglements in his "Farewell Address." But wouldn't it have been more interesting if you'd learned he never actually gave that speech? (It was printed in the newspapers. It may have been fun to find out that one of the reasons he didn't like to speak publicly was because of his false teeth, which were made not of wood but of hippopotamus ivory.)

Alas, textbooks often overlook the fascinating moments of history. They present U.S. history as something dry and distant, all events and facts, and don't focus on what it really is: the story of Americans. It's the story of people: what they thought, did, and tried to do; what they ate, drank, and slept in and on; what made them angry and what made them laugh.

About This Book

This book isn't a textbook. It focuses on people: famous, infamous, and obscure. It gives you a basic foundation of information about U.S. history. You can also use it as a handy reference. Haul it off the shelf to look up a fact, to settle an argument, or to store up ammunition for that next conversation with your know-it-all brother-in-law.

This book is also not completely objective. Although I've tried to stick to the facts — or at least the most widely accepted historical interpretations of the facts — the bottom line is that my own thoughts and biases may sneak in from time to time. Sorry. Just ignore them. Because U.S. history hasn't always been bright and shining, especially when it comes to a topic such as slavery or the treatment of American Indians, this book doesn't always deal with pleasant subjects. Some of what you read may anger you, sadden you, or even make you feel a little ashamed. But this book has a generally optimistic tone, and anyone who knows me will tell you it's not because I'm a naturally cheery guy. Twenty-five years as a journalist has caused me to grow a pretty thick and skeptical shell. But the truth is that overall, America's story is a positive one.

I've also included some things you may not find in most overviews of U.S. history. Although they may be of little importance in the long-term scheme of things, these facts are kind of fun to know about. Some examples: the Civil War general whose name helped to popularize a common term for prostitutes (Joseph Hooker); the Old West gunfighter who ended up a New York City sportswriter (Bat Masterson); and the kids' toy that came about as a result of efforts to invent a rubber substitute during World War II (Silly Putty).

And if you're a history purist, I think there's a mention of Manifest Destiny in here somewhere.

How This Book Is Organized

Here's some good news: You don't have to consume this book in one big gulp, or even from start to finish. Each chapter is written so you can read it out of order if you want, without worrying about there being stuff in it that you had to know from the chapters in front of it. (Told you it wasn't a textbook.) So, if you can't wait to see how the Spanish-American War came out, go straight to Chapter 15. You can always go back and read about Manifest Destiny in Chapter 12 later. And at the end of each chapter, at no extra cost, are 10 additional things that also happened during the period covered by that chapter. Think of them as little information bonuses.

If you stopped by the Table of Contents before wandering through the Introduction, you may have noticed this book is divided into six major parts. You can read the parts in any order you choose. The following sections describe what's in each part.

Part 1: Getting There, Getting Settled, and Getting Free

Someone had to be the first person to come to America, but your guess as to who that was is as good as mine. Nobody knows. This part looks at one group of people who were in America pretty early, the American Indians. It also examines the lives of the first non-Indians to explore the New World, from the Vikings to people like Henry Hudson. Part I also considers the first efforts of the Europeans to create an actual settlement in America.

Chapters 3, 4, and 5 cover the development of the English colonies, as well as the start of two scourges that still haunt the United States — slavery and the treatment of American Indians. The last chapter of this first part deals with the American Revolution: from its roots in rum and other issues, through the actual fighting, and into the difficult process of drawing up a blueprint for a new country.

Part II: Growing Pains

Remember how I said this book is about people? Well, Part II begins by focusing on one of the most important people in the early days of the United States, Thomas Jefferson. It ends by showing you one of the most influential people during the country's adolescence, Abraham Lincoln.

In between these two great men, wars are fought against pirates, England, Indians, and Mexico. The United States then spends a lot of time and effort futilely trying to prevent a war between its own North and South. Gold is discovered, and California is invented. This part ends with the Civil War and the struggles that followed in trying to put the country back together. You can find Manifest Destiny in this part, too.

Part III: Coming of Age

Here's where America grows up. This part begins with the conquering of the West, the inventions of things like the light bulb and the telephone, and the country's accelerating change from a nation of farms to a nation of cities.

It moves through the Spanish-American War, the development of a U.S. empire, and World War I. It talks about a whole lot of changes, ranging from growing racial and labor unrest to Prohibition and the development of the mass media. This part also looks at some of the most interesting Americans ever, from gangsters to sports heroes.

The country goes broke in Part III and sees much of its farmland blown away. You also get to know an aristocratic New Yorker named Franklin Delano Roosevelt, who has some pretty ambitious ideas on how to fix things. This section ends with World War II, certainly the most epochal event of the twentieth century. It also examines the development of a particular weapon and its effects, which would be felt all over the world for half a century.

Part IV: America in Adulthood

Part IV begins by examining the Cold War with communism and the hot war in Korea. It then takes you through the fascinating '50s and explores the most dominant medium of our age, the boob tube. Television allowed most of

America to watch the birth of John F. Kennedy's "New Frontier," witness a terrifying game of diplomacy over missiles in Cuba, and see Kennedy killed by an assassin's (or assassins'?) bullets.

This part traces the events leading up to and including the war in Vietnam, and it also explores the culture-shaking effects of this war. It talks about hippies, Richard Nixon, Gerald Ford (remember him?), and a former Hollywood actor who became president.

The section ends with a look at the 1990s, especially the end of the Cold War and the development of the microchip and computer.

Part V: The Part of Tens

You may want to trot out Part V when the party is getting a little slow or when you just want to irritate that uncle who has a loud opinion on everything. This section starts with a list of the ten best and ten worst presidents. It's based strictly on my assessments, so don't get too worked up if you disagree. You can always make your own list. Besides, it gives you and your uncle something to argue about.

Then Part V moves to ten events people believe to be true but never actually happened — or at least didn't happen the way people think they happened. Take a look and you will see what I mean. Next, I give you a list of ten inventions that changed the way Americans live. Obviously, lots more inventions exist; this list just gets you thinking about them. Part V ends with a list of ten events that affected American culture or the way Americans act and think of themselves.

Part VI: Appendixes

Well, I told you it was a reference book. In the Appendixes, I've included some of the most important documents in American history: the Preamble to the U.S. Constitution, the Bill of Rights, the Declaration of Independence, and the Gettysburg Address. Yeah, I know. It seems a bit silly to leave the best writing in the book until the end.

Icons Used in This Book

Throughout the book, you can find icons in the margins that alert you to particular aspects or features of history. Think of them as path markers or footnotes that you don't have to go all the way to the bottom of the page to find. Here's what they mean:

This icon provides a little information on interesting events just off the main historical route.

 This icon calls your attention to mini-profiles of those people who made an impact on American history or who are just fun to read about.

 This icon points out quotes from letters, speeches, documents, and advertisements of the past.

 You can find origins of customs, events, phrases, and other aspects of American life wherever this icon is located.

 The names, numbers, and other stats behind the news are the focus of this icon.

 This icon alerts you to a fact or idea that you may want to stash in your memory bank.

Where to Go from Here

Congratulations! By reading this far, you've already learned something about U.S. history: It doesn't bite, induce deep comas, or poke you in the eye with a sharp stick. Read a few pages, however, and it may give you an itch to read a few more. As I said before, history is the story of people. And people are the most interesting story of all.

Part I
Getting There, Getting Settled, and Getting Free

The 5th Wave   By Rich Tennant

"Obviously they know we're home now, thanks to Running Elk's decision to STAND UP!! Alright, we'll have one quick cup of coffee and send them on their way."

In this part . . .

*E*very story needs a setting, and the story of America takes place on a stage that was empty until relatively recently in world history. When people did show up, they came in all shapes and colors, from a lot of different places. Most of them came voluntarily. Some of them were forced.

Those who arrived of their own free will had a lot of different reasons for coming to America, from looking for a better place to live, to seeking freedom from religious persecution, to pure greed. Many died on the way or shortly after getting here. Some persevered. A few prospered.

Eventually, all these different elements combined into a people unique in the world. These people, in turn, created a unique style of government around a different way of looking at things. They had an idea and called it America.

In this part, we cover the arrival of people to the North American continent, their struggles to establish themselves here, and the events leading up to and through the American Revolution and the creation of the country.

Chapter 1

Before the Beginning: 14,000 B.C.–A.D. 1492

In This Chapter

▶ The first tourists

▶ Early civilizations

▶ Understanding American Indian tribes

▶ The Vikings and other possible visitors

▶ Who else was here?

▶ Timeline

*F*or the most part, the descendants of Europeans (me included) have written the history of America. Because of that, historians have been criticized — often quite fairly — for over-emphasizing the experiences and contributions of European settlers and their descendants to the formation of the United States. Historians have also been criticized for not paying enough attention to others who came over (American Indians included).

In the case of the Indians, however, tracking what they did is difficult because they left no written records of their activities. Researchers are left to make educated guesses based on what physical evidence they can find. This chapter covers some of those guesses about the first Americans.

Coming to America

Once upon a time, about 14,000 years ago, some people from what is now Siberia walked across what was then a land bridge but is now the Bering Strait, and into what is now Alaska. They were hunters in search of ground sloths the size of hippopotamuses, armadillos the size of Volkswagens, mammoth-sized wooly mammoths, and other *really* big game. Figure 1-1 shows the possible route taken by these first visitors.

They weren't in any kind of a hurry. Their descendants kept walking south for 4,000 or 5,000 years — not stopping until they got to Patagonia, at the tip of South America. Along the way, they split up and spread out until people could be found in all parts of the continents and islands of North and South America.

Maybe.

Actually, no one knows when humans first showed up in the New World. For most of this century, the most widely accepted view among scholars has been the one told in the preceding paragraphs: People got to the Americas by walking across a land bridge during the Ice Age, when there was more ice and the water level of the world's oceans was lower than it is today.

Figure 1-1:
The possible route of nomadic peoples from what is now Siberia, across the Bering Strait, into Alaska, and down into the Americas.

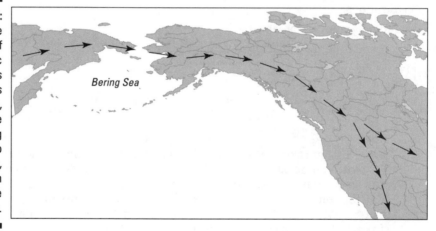

Bering Sea

Scientists formed that theory by working backwards (which you do a lot in history). Some obviously man-made artifacts were found among the bones of mammoths and other giant mammals. This finding proved that people got here during the late Ice Age or before all of the animals died out. By estimating how long it might take a big game-hunting group to walk that far from Alaska, scientists figured that no one was in the Americas until about 12,000 B.C.

But recent discoveries have caused many scientists to think that Americans, in one form or another, have been around a lot longer than 14,000 years. Archeological sites in California, Pennsylvania, Peru, and other places have yielded clues, such as footprints, cooking fires, and artifacts, which indicate humans may have been in the Americas for as much as 20,000 to even 40,000 years. If that's the case, they may very well have come some other way, such as by water, and from some place (or places) other than Siberia. But where is anybody's guess.

TECHNICAL STUFF

Getting the point

In the early 1930s, researchers near Clovis, New Mexico, found long spearheads made of chert, obsidian, and other stone materials. The spearheads, which were found with the bones of dead animals, had grooves in their base where they could be attached to wooden shafts and hurled with great force by using a throwing stick.

These spearheads have since been found in a wide area of North America. Scientists call them *Clovis points* and offer them as proof man was here during the Ice Age. Many scientists now believe the hunters using the spearheads were so efficient they helped hasten the extinction of most of the period's giant mammals.

The sites also yielded evidence that the first Americans didn't rely exclusively on hunting giant animals but also on gathering and eating plants, small game, and even shellfish. Imagine being the first guy in your tribe to be talked into putting an oyster or a lobster into your mouth.

Other puzzles are popping up to cause scientists to look hard at the Bering Strait theory. One study of human blood types, for example, found that although the predominant blood type in Asia is B, the blood types of American Indians tested is almost exclusively A or O. This finding means that at least some of their ancestors came from somewhere else.

Exploring Early Civilizations

Although it's unclear who got here first and when, it is known that the forerunners of American Indians were beginning to settle down by about 1000 B.C. They cultivated crops, most notably *maize,* a hearty variety of corn that took less time to grow than other grains and could also grow in many different climates. Beans and squash made up the other two of the "three sisters" of early American agriculture.

Growing their own food enabled the groups to stay in one place for long periods of time. Consequently, they could make and acquire things and build settlements, which allowed them to trade with other groups. Trading resulted in groups becoming covetous of other groups' things, which eventually led to wars over these things. Ah, civilization.

The Anasazi

One of the earliest cultures to emerge in what is now the United States was the Anasazi. The group's name comes from a Navajo word that has been translated to mean ancient people or ancient enemies. Although they were around the Southwestern U.S. for hundreds of years, they flourished from about A.D. 1100 to 1300.

At their peak, the Anasazi built adobe-walled towns in nearly inaccessible areas, which made the communities easy to defend. The towns featured apartment houses, community courts, and buildings for religious ceremonies. The Anasazi made highly artistic pottery and tightly woven baskets. The baskets were so good that the culture is sometimes referred to as "The Basket Makers."

Because of the region's arid conditions, the Anasazi people could not support a large population and were never numerous. But just why their culture died out so suddenly around the beginning of the fourteenth century is a puzzle to archaeologists. One theory is that a prolonged drought simply made life unsustainable in the region. A much more controversial theory, which has won some backing in archaeological circles, is that marauding Indians from Mexico, who had a most unpleasant habit of eating those they captured or killed in battle, plagued the Anasazi. According to the theory, these cannibals literally absorbed the Anasazi or drove them off. But just who the cannibals might have been has not been determined. However their demise came about, the Anasazi culture was developed enough to continue, in many ways unchanged, and is evident in some of the Southwest tribes of today.

The Mound Builders

East of the Anasazi were groups of early Americans who became known as Mound Builders, after their habit of erecting large earthworks that served as tombs and foundations for temples and other public buildings. One group, known as the Woodland Culture, was centered in Ohio and spread east. Their mounds, which took decades to build, reached more than seven stories in height and were surrounded by earthwork walls as long as 500 yards. The largest of these mounds was near what's now the southern Ohio town of Hopewell.

The largest Mound Builder settlement was on the Illinois side of the Mississippi River, about eight miles from what is now St. Louis. It was called Cahokia. At its zenith, around A.D. 1100, Cahokia covered six square miles and may have been home to as many as 30,000 people. To put that in perspective: Cahokia was about the same size as London was in 1100, and no other city in America grew to that size until Philadelphia did, 700 years later.

TECHNICAL STUFF

How many Indians?

Just as no one knows who got here first and when, no one knows just how many American Indians there were. Estimates of the number at the time of Christopher Columbus's arrival in 1492 range from 8 million to more than 60 million; all but 1 million to 1.5 million of them lived in Mexico, the Caribbean, and Central and South America. In 1824, the newly formed Bureau of Indian Affairs put the number of Indians in the U.S. at 471,000. By 1890, the first time Indians were included in the U.S. census, the number was 274,000. The 1990 census counted 1.95 million Indians, 739,000 of them inhabitants of reservations.

The residents of Cahokia had no written language, but they had a knack for astronomy and for building. Their largest mounds, like the pyramids of cultures in Mexico, were four-sided, had a flat top, and covered as much ground as the biggest pyramids of Egypt. The Cahokia Mound Builders also had a penchant for constructing stout, wooden stockades around their city. In doing so, however, they apparently cut down most of the trees in the area, which reduced the amount of game in the region and caused silt to build up in nearby waterways. The city also may have suffered from nasty air pollution because of the wood fires that were constantly burning.

By 1200, people were leaving Cahokia and its suburbs in large numbers. By 1400, the city was abandoned, an early victim of the ills of urban growth.

Too Many Tribes, Not Enough Indians

Although there weren't a whole lot of Indians in what is now the United States — maybe 1 million to 1.5 million or so at the time of Christopher Columbus's arrival in 1492 — there was certainly a wide variety. Historians estimate at least 250 different tribal groups lived in America at that time. They spoke at least 300 languages, and many of them were as different from each other as Chinese is from English. None of them were written languages. Some estimates have put the number of distinct societies as high as 1,200.

In the Northwest . . .

Tribes such as the Chinook, the Salishan, and the Makah lived in well-organized permanent villages of 100 or more. An abundance of fish and a mild climate made many of the tribes relatively prosperous, especially because they dried fish to save for the times of year when food was less available.

The Northwest Indians were avid traders. Acquisitions of material goods — including slaves — resulted in higher status, and gift giving in ceremonies called *potlatches* marked public displays of wealth. The Northwest cultures carved elaborate and intricate totem poles, which represented their ancestral heritage.

In the Southwest . . .

The arid conditions made life tougher for tribes in the Southwest. Tribes such as the Apache were foragers, scrounging for everything from bison to grasshoppers, while tribes such as the Hopi scratched out an existence as farmers. In what is now California, most of the scores of different tribes were pretty laidback. They lived in villages and off the land as hunters and gatherers.

On the Great Plains . . .

Game, especially bison, was plentiful on the plains, but few people hunted them. Hunting was pretty tough anyway, because the Plains Indians — someday to become expert horsemen — didn't have horses until the middle of the sixteenth century. Eventually, Plains tribes, like the Cheyenne and Lakota, would domesticate the wild offspring of animals that Spanish soldiers and explorers had brought over.

In the meantime, the Plains tribes made do by stalking, ambushing, and occasionally stampeding a herd of bison over a cliff. The tribes were semi-nomadic; they packed up their teepees and moved on when the local food got scarce.

In the Northeast . . .

Tribes fell into two large language groups in the Northeast: the Iroquoian and the Algonquian. Because history shows that human beings divided into two groups in the same area tend to not get along, guess what? The Iroquois tribes and the Algonquin fought a lot. They often used tools and weapons made of copper or slate, which they traded back and forth when they weren't fighting. The Northeast Indians lived in communal longhouses and invented a light, maneuverable canoe made out of birch bark.

A remarkable event involving the Northeast tribes occurred around 1450, when five tribes — the Cayugas, Mohawks, Oneidas, Onondagas, and Senecas — formed the Iroquois League. The purpose of this league was to form an alliance against the Algonquin, and settle disputes among themselves. Some scholars believe the uniting of individual tribes for a common cause may have been looked at by the country's founding fathers when they were putting together the federalist form of government after the American Revolution.

Indian gifts

American Indian contributions to modern culture are plentiful, varied, and often overlooked. They include the names of 27 states and thousands of rivers, lakes, mountains, cities, and towns; foods such as potatoes, sweet potatoes, artichokes, squash, turkey, tomatoes, vanilla, cacao (which is used to make chocolate), and maple sugar; medicines such as coca (used to make Novocain), quinine, curare, and ipecac; other items such as hammocks, toboggans, parkas, ponchos, and snowshoes — oh yeah, and tobacco, too.

In the Southeast . . .

The dominant tribes in the Southeast included the Cherokees, the Choctaws, the Chickasaws, the Creeks, and the Seminoles. These tribes got by through a mix of hunting, gathering, and farming. Europeans would later refer to them as the *Five Civilized Tribes,* in part because they developed codes of law and judicial systems, but also because they readily adapted the European customs of running plantations, slaveholding, and raising cattle. They also often intermarried with Europeans. However, despite European admiration for the Southeast tribes' abilities to adapt, the Indians still were exploited, exterminated, or evacuated.

De-stereotyping the American Indians

Both historians and Hollywood have often stereotyped pre-Colombian American Indians as either noble people who lived in constant harmony with nature or mindless knuckleheads who sat around in the dirt when they weren't brutally killing each other. The truth is somewhere in between. Like people everywhere else, American Indians had both virtues and faults. They often showed remarkable ingenuity in areas like astronomy and architecture yet lacked important cultural advances like the plow, the wheel, and sailing ships. Some tribes had no clue what a war was; others lived and died for little else.

Although different tribes and cultures sometimes traded with each other for necessities, the general rule was that they kept to themselves — unless they were fighting with each other. Each group referred to itself as "human beings" or "the people" and referred to other groups as simply "others" or something else less flattering.

Some Indians acted as environmental caretakers, at least to the extent that they took care not to overuse natural resources. Others engaged in environmentally tortuous acts such as clear-cutting forests or setting fires to catch game or clear land.

But it wasn't character traits, good or bad, that ultimately hurt the American Indian. Instead, it was a conspiracy of other elements: an unwillingness or inability to unite against the European invader, a sheer lack of numbers, the lack of any biological defenses against European diseases, and the unfortunate tendency of many newcomers to see the Indians not as human beings but as just another exotic species in a strange New World.

Discovering America the Viking Way

All Vikings were Norsemen, but not all Norsemen were Vikings. *Viking* meant to go raiding, pirating, or exploring. Although some of the Scandinavians of 1,000 years ago surely did all of those things, most of them stayed in Scandinavia and fished or farmed.

For about 300 years, the Norsemen who were Vikings conquered or looted much of western Europe and Russia. In the ninth and tenth centuries, sailing in ships was made speedy and stable by the addition of keels. Consequently, the Vikings journeyed west, not so much for loot as for new lands to settle.

Hopscotching from the British Isles to the Shetland Islands to the Faroe Islands, the Vikings arrived in Iceland about A.D. 870. But Iceland didn't offer a whole lot of good land, and it got crowded pretty quickly. Slightly more than 100 years later, a colorful character known as Eric the Red, who was in exile from Iceland for killing a man, discovered Greenland and led settlers there around 985.

Like many things in human history, the Vikings' first visits to the North American continent were by accident. The first sighting of the New World by a European probably came around 987, when a Viking named Bjarni Herjolfsson sailed from Iceland to hook up with his dad and missed Greenland. Herjolfsson wasn't impressed by what he saw from the ship, and he never actually set foot on land before heading back to Greenland.

Herjolfsson was followed about 15 years later by the son of Eric the Red. His name was Leif Ericsson, also known as Leif the Lucky. Leif landed in what is now Labrador, a part of Newfoundland, Canada. Mistaking seasonal berries for grapes, Leif called the area Vinland. Leif spent the winter in the new land, and he then left to take over the family business, which was running Greenland.

IN THEIR WORDS
"Four score and seven..."

Got milk, Paleface?

"The (Indians) unslung their bales, untied them, and proffered their wares, and above all wanted weapons in exchange. Karlsefni, though, forbade them the sale of weapons. And now he hit on this idea; he told the women to carry out milk to them, and the moment they saw the milk, that was the one thing they wanted to buy, nothing else."   — from a medieval Viking saga

His brother Thorvald visited Vinland the next year. Thorvald got into a fight with the local inhabitants, and he thus gained the distinction of being the first European to be killed by the natives in North America. (Vikings called the natives *skraelings,* a contemptuous term meaning dwarves.) After his death, Thorvald's crew went back to Greenland.

The next Viking visit was meant to be permanent. Led by a brother-in-law of Leif's named Thorfinn Karlsefni, an expedition of three ships, some cattle, and about 160 people — including some women — created a settlement and settled in.

The Karlsefni settlement lasted three years. Chronic troubles with the natives, who had a large numerical advantage, as well as weapons and fighting abilities that were equal to the Vikings', and squabbles arising from too many males and not enough females in the settlement, eventually wore the Vikings down. They sailed back to Greenland. By 1020, most scholars agree, the Vikings had given up on North America. Supply lines to the homelands were long, the voyages back and forth were dangerous, and the natives were unfriendly. The Norsemen apparently felt that the new land was not worth the trouble. By 1400, the Vikings were no longer even in Greenland; they fell victim to troubles with the Eskimos, the area's earlier residents, and a climate becoming colder.

IN THEIR WORDS
"Four score and seven..."

Freydis Eriksdottir

In a world of pretty macho guys, Freydis stood out — and not just because she was Leif Ericsson's half-sister. According to Viking sagas, Freydis was part of the Karlsefni settlement. She reportedly stopped one Indian attack when "she pulled her breast from her dress and slapped her sword on it." She also allegedly ended a trading voyage to the New World by having her partners — who happened to be her brothers — murdered. Then she killed five women that her men refused to do in. Her half-brother, Leif, however, declined to punish her. The Vikings were tough businessmen, especially when they were businesswomen!

The Vikings' forays to the North American continent were relatively brief and had no lasting impact. The main evidence that they were even here is fairly limited: two long sagas written in the Middle Ages and the scattered ruins of three housing clusters and forge at a place called L'Anse aux Meadows, on the northern tip of Newfoundland. But tales of their voyages were well reported around Europe, and they probably served to whet the exploration appetites of people in other places. Other nations, however, plagued by troubles like, well, plagues, were not ready to follow them west for almost 500 years.

Determining Who Else Came to America

So if we know that the Vikings were here and the American Indians — or at least their ancestors — were here before the Vikings, did anyone else get here before Columbus? Well, since I start this chapter with a maybe, I end it with another one. Maybe.

For decades, scholars, researchers, and more than a few crackpots have sought proof that someone other than the Indians and Vikings visited the New World in pre-Colombian times. The theories and suppositions have ranged from a Jewish hermit named Maba, who supposedly lived in a cave in eastern Oklahoma about the time of Christ, to Prince Madoc, an exiled Welsh nobleman who, story has it, established a colony in what is now Georgia and Tennessee in about A.D. 900. The prince also managed to teach the locals to speak Welsh and build burial mounds. Other stories abound: Buddhist monks who toured California, Egyptians who visited the Southeast, and, of course, extra-terrestrials who built landing strips in Peru.

Sure and 'tis a fine day for a boat ride

If frequent flyer miles had existed when St. Brendan the Navigator was alive, he surely would have acquired enough to own his own airline. Or so the stories go. Brendan was born toward the end of the sixth century in Ireland. According to a ninth-century account, he and some other monks sailed in a wood-framed boat covered with skins, called a *curragh,* to lands far to the west, including the Faroe Islands, Iceland, and what may have been the Azores, Jamaica, and the Bahamas. In 1977, a fellow named Tim Severin sailed in a replica of a curragh from Ireland to Newfoundland in an effort to prove that it could be done. Whether Severin actually duplicated the voyage made by the seventh-century Irish saint, however, has not been proved.

The "evidence" for these visits includes petroglyphs, or rock carvings, that no one has been able to figure out. Voyages made in replicas of ancient sailing crafts supposedly demonstrate that making such voyages would have been possible, and stories and legends of the Indians that talk about long-ago visits from beings with white skin or abundant facial hair also add some "proof." But none of the supposed evidence for any of these cases has so far proved conclusive, at least not to most historians. And even if other people did travel to the New World, they, like the Vikings, had no substantial impact on what was to come in America.

Gee, Grandpa, What Else Happened?

3000 B.C.: The world's population reaches approximately 100 million.

A.D. 1066: William the Conqueror, backed by Norsemen, wins the Battle of Hastings and seals the Norman conquest of England.

1075: Acoma, an adobe city high atop a mesa in what is now New Mexico, is founded. At its peak, the settlement has 5,000 inhabitants.

1099: Jerusalem, held by Islamic Arabs, falls to Christian crusaders after a siege of one month.

1271: Marco Polo, a 17-year-old Venetian, joins his father and uncle on a journey to India and the Far East. He returns to Venice in 1295 with fabulous tales of the Orient.

1312: Sailors from Portugal visit the Canary Islands.

1348: The Black Death (bubonic plague) reaches Florence in Italy and begins its march across Europe and back. By the time it runs its course, one-third of the continent's population is dead.

1419: Portuguese explorers land in the Madeira Islands, off the coast of North Africa.

1432: Mariner Gonzalo Cabral claims the Azores Islands for Portugal.

1480: Epidemics and famine decimate the once-mighty Maya empire.

Chapter 2

Columbus Discovers the Bahamas: 1492–1607

- -

In This Chapter

▶ Exploring the Americas

▶ Discovering Christopher Columbus

▶ Looking at a dozen other people who dropped by

▶ Ending empires

▶ Timeline

- -

The New World sat around for a long time waiting for the Old World to come looking for it. Contrary to popular belief, a whole lot of people in Europe and Asia knew the earth was round, and many of them suspected there were vast unexplored lands on the other side of the planet.

This chapter shows you how the colonizing of America progressed: By the end of the fifteenth century, Europeans were ready to come looking for the New World. By the end of the sixteenth century, they had started making it their own.

Spicing Up Life

Say you're walking along the street one day when a stranger stops you and shouts, "Quick! Give me a two-word summary of why Christopher Columbus and all those other people came nosing around North, Central, and South America in the sixteenth century?"

Now, you could answer with "garage sales" or even "Manifest Destiny." But a far better answer would be "rancid meat."

For centuries, people in Europe had no way of preserving food other than salting it, which doesn't make it very palatable. When Europeans were fighting in the Middle East during the Crusades, however, they established overland trading routes that supplied a whole condiment-shelf of spices: cinnamon from Ceylon, pepper from India, and cloves and nutmeg from the Moluccan Islands. They also developed a taste for silks from China and Japan, and they already liked the gold and precious metals of the East.

But in 1453, the Turkish Empire conquered Constantinople (now Istanbul), which had been the capital of the Eastern Roman Empire and the crossroads of the overland supply routes. The Turks closed the routes, and Europeans had to begin thinking about finding a sea route to reopen the trade.

More reasons explain the explosion of interest in exploration as the 1400s came to a close. Countries were putting aside the feudal disputes of the Middle Ages and unifying. In Spain, for example, 700 years of war between the Spaniards and the Moors (Arabs from North Africa) were finally over in 1492. The marriage of Ferdinand of Castile and Isabella of Aragon had united the country's two major realms.

Europe was also stepping briskly toward the Renaissance. People were beginning to believe in the power of the individual to change things, and were more willing to take chances.

The Portuguese, the best navigators and sailors in the world at that time (except for the Polynesians), were pushing farther into the Atlantic and down the coast of Africa. When he reached what he named the Cape of Good Hope in 1488, Portuguese explorer Bartelmo Diaz verified that a sea route to India around the tip of Africa did exist.

Meanwhile, other explorers who knew the earth was a sphere were thinking about reaching the Indies and the East by sailing west across the Atlantic. One of them was named Columbus.

Christopher Columbus: Dream Salesman

According to many accounts, Christopher Columbus was obsessive, deeply religious, stubborn, arrogant, charming, dictatorial, and egotistical. He was physically striking, with reddish-blonde hair that had turned white by the time he was 30, and he stood 6 feet tall at a time when most adult males were about 5'6". He was also one heck of a salesman.

Christopher Columbus was born in Genoa, Italy in 1451 the son of a weaver. In addition to running a successful map-making business with his brother, Bartholomew, Columbus became a first-class sailor. He also became convinced his ticket to fame and fortune depended on finding a western route to the Indies.

IN THEIR WORDS
"Four score and seven..."

Columbus meets the natives

"In order to win the friendship and affection of that people, and because I was convinced that their conversion to our Holy Faith would be better promoted through love than through force, I presented some of them with red caps and some strings of glass beads and with other trifles of insignificant worth. They must be good servants and very intelligent, because I see that they repeat very quickly what I tell them, and it is my conviction they would easily become Christians, for they seem not to have any sect . . . with fifty men, all can be kept in subjection, and made to do whatever you desire."

— From the diary of Christopher Columbus as reported by contemporary biographer Bartolome de las Casas.

Starting in the 1470s, Columbus and his brother began making the rounds of European capitals, looking for ships and financial backing for his idea. His demands were exorbitant. In return for his services, Columbus wanted the title of Admiral of the Oceans, 10 percent of all the loot he found, and the ability to pass governorship of every country he discovered to his heirs.

The rulers of England and France said no thanks, and the king of Portugal also told him to take a hike. So in 1486, Columbus went to Spain. Queen Isabella listened to the pitch, and she, like the other European rulers, said no. But she did appoint a commission to look into the idea and decided to put Columbus on the payroll in the meantime.

The meantime stretched out for six years. Finally, convinced she wasn't really risking much because chances were he wouldn't return, Isabella gave her approval in January 1492. Columbus was on his way.

Partly due to error and partly due to wishful thinking, Columbus estimated the distance to the Indies at approximately 2,500 miles, which was about 7,500 miles short. But after a voyage of about five weeks, he and his crews, totaling 90 men, did find land at around 2 a.m. on October 12, 1492. It was an island in the Bahamas, which he called San Salvador. The timing of the discovery was good; it came even as the crews of the *Nina, Pinta,* and *Santa Maria* were muttering about a mutiny.

Columbus sailed next to Cuba, where he found few spices and little gold. Sailing on to an island he called Hispaniola (today's Dominican Republic and Haiti), the *Santa Maria* hit a reef on Christmas Eve, 1492. Columbus abandoned the ship, set up a trading outpost he called Navidad, left some men to operate it, and sailed back to Spain in his other two ships.

So enthusiastically did people greet the news of his return that on his second voyage, Columbus had 17 ships and more than 1,200 men. But this time he ran into more than a little disappointment. Natives had wiped out his trading post after his men became too grabby with the local gold and the local women. Worse, most of the men he brought with him had come only for gold and other riches, and they didn't care about setting up a permanent colony. Because of the lack of treasures, they soon wanted to go home. And the natives lost interest in the newcomers once the novelty of the Spanish trinkets wore off.

Consequently, Columbus took harsh measures. He demanded tribute in gold, which the Indians didn't have. He also divided up the land and enslaved the natives, thousands of whom died. And he hanged some of the "settlers" for rebelling against his authority.

The third and fourth voyages by Columbus also failed to produce the fabulous riches he had hoped for. When he died in 1506, he was largely considered a failure. But even if Columbus was unaware that he never reached the Orient, he knew he had not failed.

"By the Divine will," he said shortly before his death, "I have placed under the sovereignty of the king and queen an 'other world,' whereby Spain, which was considered poor, is to become the richest of all countries."

A cigar a day keeps the doctor away

Of all the fabulous tales Columbus's men brought back to Europe, one of the strangest was actually true. Many Indians had this weird habit of taking a leafy vegetable, drying it, putting it in a slingshot-shaped pipe called a tabaco, and lighting it on fire. They then put two ends of the pipe into their noses and inhaled the smoke. Another method was to roll the dried leaves into big tubes, put one end in the mouth, and light the other end. The natives praised it as a great medicine.

Sir John Hawkins, an English explorer and part-time pirate, observed that Indians in what is now South Carolina "do suck through the cane the smoke thereof, which smoke satisfieth their hunger and therewith they live for four or five days without meat or drink."

Although Columbus's men brought some of the plant's seeds, which they called tobacco, back to Europe with them, Hawkins is often credited with introducing it to England. In France, the honor went to Jean Nicot, who obtained some seeds from a Portuguese sailor (hence the word *nicotine* to describe the key ingredient in tobacco).

Europe soon marveled at the miracle herb whose raw leaves, it was believed, could help heal sword wounds and whose smoke was good for warding off the plague and clearing congested lungs.

Of course, even then not everyone was in love with tobacco. "Smoking tobacco is loathsome to the eye, hateful to the nose, harmful to the brain, dangerous to the lungs," fumed King James I of England in 1604, " . . . and in the black stinking fumes thereof, most nearly resembles the horrible Stygian smoke of the pit that is bottomless."

Discovering a Dozen Other People Who Dropped By

Remember in school when your history teacher gave you a sheet with a list of a bunch of fifteenth-century explorers' names on one side and a list of the things that they did on the other side, and you had to match them? Well, here's that list again. But before I sum up these people in a paragraph each, it may be a good idea to marvel at what they did. They sailed across hostile and unknown stretches of water in cramped, leaky ships no longer than a tennis court, were provisioned with food that would gag a starving pig, and had crews who were more than willing to cut the throats of their leaders if things went wrong.

When they reached the Americas, they wandered for months (sometimes years) through strange lands populated by people who, though not always hostile, were certainly unpredictable. And then they had to try to get home again to tell someone about what they'd found. Although their motives were rarely pure, they displayed a lot of courage and determination.

Here are a dozen of these daring explorers:

- **John Cabot (England).** An Italian by birth, Cabot was commissioned by King Henry VII to see what he could find in the New World. Using the northern route that the Vikings used 500 years before, Cabot sailed to Newfoundland in 1497, saw lots of fish, claimed the area for England, and sailed back. In 1498, he took a second trip with five ships, but only one ever returned to England. The other ships and their crews, including Cabot, disappeared and were apparently lost at sea. Even so, Cabot is credited with giving England its first real claim on America.

- **Vasco Nunez de Balboa (Spain).** Balboa is credited with being the first European to see the South Seas from the New World. He named it the Pacific because it appeared to be so calm. He was later beheaded by his successor to the governorship of Panama.

- **Ferdinand Magellan (Spain).** Magellan, a Portuguese explorer who was one of the greatest sailors of his or anyone's time, led a Spanish expedition of five ships in 1519. He was looking for a quick passage to the East from Europe. He sailed around the tip of South America and into the Pacific. Magellan was killed during a battle with natives in the Philippines, but one of his five ships made it back to Spain in 1522 — the first to sail around the world.

- **Giovanni Verranzano (France).** Although born in Italy, Verranzano, an expert navigator, was hired by the French to find a quicker passage to the East than Magellan's. In 1524, he sailed along the east coast of America from what is now the Carolinas to what is now Maine, and he decided that the landmass was probably just a narrow strip separating the Atlantic from the Pacific. On a second voyage to the Caribbean, Verranzano was killed and eaten by Indians. See Figure 2-1 to see the routes of great explorers like Verranzano.

✔ **Jacques Cartier (France).** He made two trips to the New World in 1534 and 1535, sailing up the St, Lawrence River. On the second trip, he made it to the site of present-day Montreal. He went back in 1541 with a sizeable expedition to look for gold and precious stones but returned to France with what turned out to be just a bunch of quartz. Still, his trips helped France establish a claim for much of what is now Canada.

✔ **Francisco Coronado (Spain).** This guy led an incredible expedition in 1540 that went looking for the "Seven Cities of Cibola," which were supposedly dripping with riches. Instead, in two years of looking for the elusive cities, Coronado's group explored the Gulf of California, Arizona, Texas, New Mexico, and Kansas and discovered the Grand Canyon. But they never found gold.

✔ **Hernando de Soto (Spain).** He marched around what is now the Gulf states before discovering the Mississippi River in 1541. He died of a fever on its banks.

✔ **Sir Francis Drake (England).** One of the most famous swashbucklers in history, Drake sailed around the world from 1578 to 1580. During his trip, he explored up the west coasts of South and North America as far as present-day Washington, stopping to claim present-day California before heading for the South Seas, and eventually home to England. He returned with more than $9 million in gold and spices, most of it plundered from Spanish ships and cities. Queen Elizabeth I knighted him for it.

✔ **Sir Walter Raleigh (England).** Raleigh inherited the right to establish an English colony from Gilbert, his half-brother. In 1584, Raleigh established a colony in what is now Virginia, and he was knighted by Elizabeth I for his efforts. Unfortunately, 30 years later he was executed on the orders of Elizabeth's successor, James I, for disobeying royal orders.

✔ **Juan de Onate (Spain).** A conquistador (conqueror) who conquered the Pueblo tribes of the Southwest and established the territory of New Mexico in 1599. Onate was one cruel guy — even by conquistador standards. In one conquered village, he ordered a foot be cut off every male adult, and in others he required 25 years "personal services" from all the inhabitants. But he did introduce the horse to the American Southwest: Mounts that escaped or were turned loose by his troops bred in the wild and were eventually domesticated by various Indian tribes.

✔ **Samuel de Champlain (France).** A mapmaker by trade, Champlain landed in the New World in 1603 and explored extensively in the northeastern part of the continent. He founded the colony of Quebec in 1608.

✔ **Henry Hudson (Netherlands).** Hudson sailed up the bay and river that now bear his name in present-day New York in 1609. He was looking for a northwest passage to the Indies. Instead, he found an area rich in fur-bearing mammals and helped the Dutch lay claim to a piece of the continent. He was cast adrift by his crew in a mutiny in 1611 and was never heard from again.

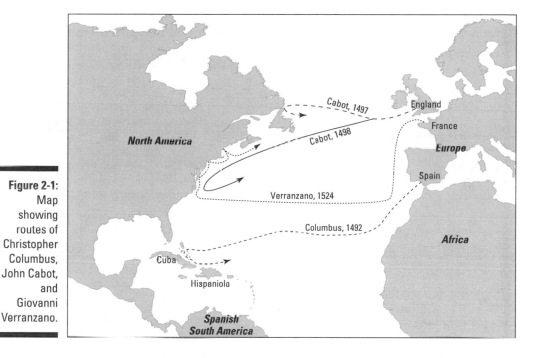

Figure 2-1:
Map
showing
routes of
Christopher
Columbus,
John Cabot,
and
Giovanni
Verranzano.

Getting Rid of the Indians: The Sword, the Cross, and the Measles

One of the problems in discovering a new land that is already inhabited is fig-uring out what to do with the people who got there first. When it came to the Indian populations of the New World, the Europeans generally solved that problem by killing or enslaving them.

Indian slavery

It started with Columbus. By his second voyage to Hispaniola, he set up a system, called the *encomienda,* which amounted to slavery. Under it, a colonist who was given a piece of land had the right to the labor of all the natives who lived on that land — whether they were interested in a job or not. Columbus also imposed a gold tax on the Indians and sometimes cut the hands off of those who could not or would not pay it. Between slavery, killings, and diseases, the population of Hispaniola's natives plummeted from an estimated 250,000 to 300,000 at the time of Columbus's arrival in 1492, to perhaps 60,000 by 1510, to near zero by 1550.

And for the serious sweet tooth. . . .

On his second trip to the Americas in 1493, Columbus stopped by the Canary Islands and picked up some sugarcane cuttings. He planted them in Hispaniola, and they thrived. In 1516, the first sugar grown in the New World was presented to King Carlos I of Spain. By 1531, it was as commercially important to the Spanish colonial economy as gold.

Planters soon discovered a by-product as well. The juice left over after the sugar was pressed out of the cane and crystallized was called *melasas* by the Spanish (and *molasses* by the English). Mixing this juice with water and leaving it out in the sun created a potent and tasty fermented drink. They called it *rum* — perhaps after the Latin word for sugarcane, *saccharum officinarum.* The stuff was great for long sea voyages because it didn't go bad.

Sugar and rum became so popular that sugar plantations mushroomed all over the Caribbean.

As the Indians on the main islands died off, the Spanish settlers in the Caribbean simply raided other smaller islands and kidnapped the residents there. A historian at the time wrote that you could navigate between islands "without compass or chart . . . simply by following the trail of dead Indians who have been thrown from ships."

When even the populations of the little islands waned, the Spanish looked for other cheap labor sources. They found them in Africa. African slaves were first imported to the New World within a few years after Columbus's first trip. By 1513, King Carlos I of Spain had given his royal assent to the African slave trade. He made his decision in part, he said, to improve the lot of the Indians. Of course, the fact that many Spanish landholders in the New World were beginning to prefer African slaves made his decision easier. They believed the Africans had better immunity to European diseases and were more used to hard agricultural labor because they came from agricultural cultures.

The men in the brown robes

Whatever his other motives, the king and his successors did have their consciences regularly pricked by some church leaders and missionaries who accompanied the early voyagers. In 1514, Pope Leo X declared that "not only the Christian religion but Nature cries out against the slavery and the slave trade." Likewise, in 1537, Pope Paul III declared that Indians were not to be enslaved.

With twenty-first century hindsight, it's tempting to shrug off the work of the early European missionaries as a sort of public relations effort designed to make the nastier things the conquerors did look less nasty.

Although there is some truth to the idea that the cross was used to justify bad treatment of the "heathens" (a 1513 proclamation required natives to convert or be enslaved or executed), most of the people who committed the worst atrocities apparently didn't much care who knew about their violent actions. Thus, they didn't need an excuse.

The horrendous actions of some of their fellow Europeans certainly didn't make the missionaries' jobs easier. One American Indian chief, who was being burned at the stake — by government officials not missionaries — for refusing to convert, reportedly replied that he feared if he did join the religion, he "might go to Heaven and meet only Christians."

Destruction through disease

If they survived slavery, the sword, and the excesses committed in the name of the cross, the New World's natives were then likely candidates to die from the Europeans' most formidable weapon: disease. Because they had never been exposed to them as a culture, the Indians' immune systems had no defense when faced with diseases such as measles and smallpox.

AMERICAN FACES

Bartolome de las Casas

Bartolome de las Casas was a scholar, an historian, and — if you had been a sixteenth century American Indian — a true friend. He was born in 1474, the son of a Spanish merchant who had sailed with Columbus's second voyage and made a pretty good sum of money doing it. Las Casas himself went to the New World in 1502. In 1512, he became the first priest to be ordained in the New World. Although he published a classic three-volume contemporary history of the Americas, las Casas is most remembered for being the leading European defender of Indian rights. His arguments were based on experience: After accompanying a "pacification" mission in Cuba, he reported that so many American Indians were killed that "there was a river of blood, as if a multitude of cows had been slaughtered." Returning to Spain, las Casas argued ceaselessly on behalf of the Indians. At first, las Casas argued that Indian slaves should

be replaced with African slaves, because the Africans had no claim to the lands of the New World. Later, he changed his mind and argued against enslaving anyone.

Finally, in 1542, Carlos V signed new laws that las Casas had drafted. The rules were supposed to throw out the old system of virtual slavery. But most of the Spanish colonies ignored the rules, and they were rescinded a few years later.

Undaunted, las Casas continued his fight, publishing a book in 1552 called *Brief Relations of the Destruction of the Indies*. The book excoriated Spanish leaders in the Americas for their barbarism toward the natives. His efforts, while mostly in vain, earned las Casas the title Protector of the Indies. He died in 1566 at the age of 92, and he is considered a national hero in Cuba and Nicaragua.

The first major smallpox epidemic started in 1518 after the disease arrived at Hispaniola via a shipload of colonists. From there, it gradually and sporadically spread through North, Central, and South America by following the trade and travel routes of the Indians. Sometimes disease spread so fast that it decimated tribes before they ever saw a European.

What is certain is that over the next 400 years, smallpox, measles, whooping cough, typhus, and scarlet fever killed thousands of times more Indians than guns or swords.

Arriving Late for the Party

Spain's early explorations of the New World gave that country a great head start over its European rivals. Spanish conquerors defeated mighty empires in Mexico and Peru — the Aztecs and Incas. Both empires had huge caches of gold and silver. Both had sophisticated cultures with built-in labor classes. All the Spanish had to do was kill the old bosses and become the new bosses, so they didn't have to import slaves as they had done in the Caribbean. Moreover, the conquests spawned a herd of *adelantadaos* (or "advancers"), who roamed all over the lower half of America in search of the next big empire.

But Spain's position of preeminence was short-lived. In 1588, Spanish plans to invade England with an armada of ships blew up when the fleet was scattered by the English navy and a fierce storm. Within 30 years, both England and France had established colonies in the New World. Eventually, a growing spirit of independence would strip Spain of its New World Empire. Early on, it was pretty clear that war-weary Europe would soon be fighting again over the spoils of the New World. In an effort to head that off — and also find a way to put his mark of authority over matters in the Americas — Pope Alexander VI divided the area between Spain and Portugal by drawing a line on the map.

This decision left Portugal with what is now Brazil, Spain with everything else, and the rest of Europe pretty peeved. King Henry VII of England declared that he would ignore the papal edict. King Francis I of France sniffed, "We fail to find this clause in Adam's will." Of course, the countries left empty-handed by the Pope's decree got over it in part by picking off Spanish ships laden with treasure on their way home.

France

Throughout much of the sixteenth century, France's efforts to get its share of the Americas were marred by civil wars and inept leadership. The French forays to the New World were limited to fishermen who came each year to mine the cod-rich banks off Newfoundland and explorations of areas that are now New England and eastern Canada.

SIDETRIP

A pox on you

New World Indians may have gathered a measure of revenge in the disease department by giving Europeans syphilis. Many researchers believe Columbus's sailors brought the disease back to Spain from the Americas, where it was relatively common among different Indian groups. The argument is that although indications of syphilis have shown up in Indian skeletons thousands of years old, none has been found in European skeletons dated before Columbus's voyages.

In 1495, after Columbus returned from his first voyage, the rulers of Spain and France sent large armies to besiege the Italian city of Naples. After the city was captured, the soldiers returned and helped to spread a new venereal disease. The French called it "the Neapolitan disease," and the Spanish called it "the French disease." They proved that there are some new things for which no nation wants credit.

Moreover, while the Spanish were in it for the loot and the English for the land, the French weren't quite sure what they wanted. They eventually settled on a little of both. Fur franchises were awarded private companies with the condition that they also start permanent colonies. But the companies didn't try very hard, and as the 1500s came to a close, the French had little more than a tenuous hold on its New World dominion.

England

Despite early explorations by John Cabot, just on the heels of Columbus's voyages, England lagged behind Spain when it came to exploring and exploiting the New World. Part of the problem was that the English were broke, and part of it was that it feared Spain's military might.

By the end of the sixteenth century, however, the British were encouraged by the success of raids against Spanish American cities and ships by *privateers* (a cross between patriots and pirates) like John Hawkins and Francis Drake. The defeat of the Spanish Armada, the invasion fleet that met with disaster off the coast of England in 1588, encouraged England even more.

In 1587, Walter Raleigh, who had the royal right to colonize in the Americas, sent a group that consisted of 89 men, seven women, and 11 children to what is now Virginia. They called their colony Roanoke.

Unfortunately, the looming threat of the Spanish invasion meant the little colony got no support from the homeland. In 1590, when a relief expedition finally arrived, the colonists had vanished. They left behind only rotting and rummaged junk and a single word carved in a tree: *Croatoan*.

The word referred to an island about 100 miles south of Roanoke. No one knows the meaning behind the word. And no one knows exactly what happened to the first English colony in the New World.

Gee, Grandpa, What Else Happened?

1493: Peppers brought back by Columbus from the Indies are used as medicine to treat Queen Isabella.

1513: The Spanish explorer Ponce de Leon plants oranges in Florida.

1520: Chocolate is introduced to Spain.

1543: Oil is found in what is now Texas by Spanish explorer Luis de Moscoso.

1550: The Spanish bring beef cattle, the first in North America, to Florida.

1576: British explorer Martin Frobisher arrives in England with 200 tons of ore he believes contains gold. It doesn't.

1576: A smallpox epidemic kills an estimated 40 percent of all the native inhabitants of Mexico.

1597: The British Parliament okays the deportation of convicted criminals to its colonies.

1602: England launches a final, futile search for survivors of the lost colony of Roanoke.

1605: English man of letters, Ben Jonson, and others publish *Eastward Ho!,* a satirical book about efforts to promote Virginia as a great place to settle in.

Chapter 3

Pilgrims' Progress: The English Colonies, 1607–1700

● ●

In This Chapter

▶ Heading west

▶ The beginnings of slavery

▶ Settling New England

▶ Handling the Indians

● ●

With the defeat of the Spanish naval armada off the coast of England in 1588, Spain seemed to lose interest in expanding its empire in the New World.

England, on the other hand, was eager to make up for lost time. In this chapter, England establishes its colonies in the Americas and two very different — and very key — elements of America's history are planted: slavery and the desire for independence from the Old World.

Go West, Old Chap, Go West

For most of the sixteenth century, England was too poor and too timid to do much about the opportunities presented by the opening of two new continents. By 1604, however, when England and Spain signed a tenuous peace treaty, the English had several good reasons to think about branching out to the new lands of the West. Here are the four main reasons:

✔ **Wool:** England's woolen industry was booming in the late 1500s and early 1600s. Farms were turned into pastures for more and more sheep, and the tenant farmers on the former farms were forced off, with no particular place to go, unless it was the New World.

✔ **Overpopulation:** Even though the entire population of about 4 million was less than half that of modern-day London, many Englishmen pined for a less-crowded land.

- ✔ **Religious dissent:** Protestantism, a rival Christian religion to the one led by the Pope in Rome, had developed in the sixteenth century and become firmly rooted in England. Even though the country had its own state — and Protestant — church, many English Protestants felt it wasn't different enough than the Roman Catholic faith they had left. Religiously restless, they looked to America as a place to plant the seeds of their own version of Christianity.

- ✔ **Economic incentive:** A middle class of merchants, speculators, and entrepreneurs had formed. By pooling their resources in "joint-stock companies," these capitalists could invest in schemes to make money in the New World by backing colonists who would produce goods England and the rest of Europe wanted. They could also harvest resources, such as timber, for which England had to depend on other Old World countries.

Starting It All in Jamestown

It's pretty safe to say the first permanent English colony in America was put together about as well as a soup sandwich. Its organizers weren't sure where they were going, and weren't sure what to do when they got there either.

A group of investors known as the Virginia Company of London were given a charter by King James I to settle somewhere in the southern part of the New World area known as Virginia. After a voyage on which roughly 27 percent of the original 144 settlers died, three ships arrived at the mouth of a river they ingratiatingly named the James, after the king. On May 14, 1607, they began the settlement of Jamestown.

Early troubles

Some of the settlers were indentured servants who had traded seven years of their labor for passage to America. Others were upper-crust types who didn't have a clue how to farm or hunt or do anything remotely useful in the wilderness. As one historian has put it, "it was a colony of people who wouldn't work, or couldn't."

Worse, the site they had chosen for a settlement was in a malaria-ridden swamp, and the local inhabitants were both suspicious and unfriendly. In fact, the Indians launched their first attack against the newcomers within two weeks of their arrival. Within six months, half of the 105 settlers who had survived the trip were dead of disease or starvation.

IN THEIR WORDS

"Four score and seven..."

Between a rock and a hard place

"Having feasted him after their best barbarous manner they could, a long consultation was held, but the conclusion was, two great stones were brought before Powhatan; then as many as could lay hands on him (John Smith), dragged him to them and thereon laid his head, and being ready with their clubs to beat out his brains, Pocahontas, the king's dearest daughter, when no entreaty could prevail, got his head in her arms, and laid her own upon his to save him from death; whereat the emperor was contented he should live...."

— John Smith's third-person account of his rescue by Pocahontas, recounted in a 1524 history.

Those that survived did so largely because of a character named John Smith. An experienced and courageous adventurer, Smith was also a shameless self-promoter and a world-class liar, with a knack for getting into trouble. On the voyage over, for example, he was charged with mutiny, although he was eventually acquitted.

Making Indian friends

But whatever his faults, Smith was both gutsy and diplomatic. He managed to make friends with Powhatan, the chief of the local Indians, and the tribe provided the colonists with enough food to hold on. It's questionable whether Smith's dramatic story of how Powhatan's daughter, Pocahontas, saved Smith's life actually happened (see sidebar "Between a rock and a hard place" in this chapter). But it is undeniable that without his leadership — "he that will not work neither shall he eat," Smith declared — Jamestown would have failed.

As it was, Jamestown came pretty close to disaster. In the winter of 1609, called "the starving time," things got so bad colonists resorted to eating anything they could get — including each other. One man was executed after eating the body of his dead wife. In 1610, the survivors were actually on a ship and ready to head home when a military relief expedition showed up and took charge.

Finding a cash crop

One of the biggest problems the colony faced was that the New World had nothing anyone in England wanted, so there was no basis for a profitable economy. But that began to change in 1613, when a fellow named John Rolfe, who had married the Indian princess Pocahontas, came up with a variety of tobacco that was a huge hit in the mother country. Within a few years, Jamestown had a thriving cash crop.

Pocahontas

Whether or not she actually saved John Smith's life is debatable, since some historians think he simply elaborated on what was an Indian initiation ceremony. But Pocahontas was a remarkable woman in other ways. Her real name was Matowaka. "Pocahontas" was a nickname, meaning "frisky" or "lively one," a nickname she apparently lived up to. Unlike many of her tribe, Pocahontas seemed to be fascinated with the newcomers. At the age of 17, she was kidnapped by Jamestown colonists and held as a hostage to discourage Indian attacks. She eventually married colonist John Rolfe and went to England. She was baptized a Christian, took the name Lady Rebecca and became a big hit in London society. She died of smallpox at the age of 22, just as she was getting ready to return to America. Her son, Thomas, was educated in England and later returned to America as a colonist.

In 1619, three things happened in the Virginia colony that were to have a large impact on the British in America. One was the arrival of 90 women, who became the brides of settlers who paid for their passage at a cost of 120 pounds of tobacco each.

The second was the meeting of the first legislative body of colonists on the continent. Known as the House of Burgesses, it met for about a week, passed laws against gambling and idleness and decreed all colonists must attend two church services each Sunday — and bring their weapons with them. Then the legislators adjourned because it was too hot to keep meeting.

The third event — three weeks after the House of Burgesses had become a symbol of representative government in the New World — was the arrival of a Dutch ship. From its cargo, Jamestown settlers bought 20 human beings from Africa to work in the tobacco fields (see Figure 3-1).

Figure 3-1:
The arrival of slaves in Jamestown: one of the key elements in America's history.

Setting Up Slavery

While it was a Dutch ship that brought the first slaves to Virginia, no European nation had a monopoly on the practice. The Portuguese were the first Europeans to raid the African coast for slaves, in the mid-fifteenth century. They were quickly followed by the Spanish, who used Africans to supplant the New World Indians who had either been killed or died of diseases. By the mid-sixteenth century, the English sea dog John Hawkins was operating a thriving slave trade between Africa and the Caribbean.

Most slaves were seized from tribes in the interior of the continent and sold from ports in West Africa to the New World. Some were hunted down by European and Arab slave traders. Many were sold by rival tribes after being captured in wars or on raids. And some were sold by their own tribes when they failed to make good on personal debts or got on the wrong side of their leaders.

Although the use of African slaves in the tobacco fields proved successful and more slaves were gradually imported, the practice of slavery was by no means a strictly Southern colony phenomenon. While the Northern colonies had less use for slaves as agricultural workers, Africans were used as domestic servants.

 Not everyone in the colonies was enamored by slavery. In 1688, a radical Protestant group in Pennsylvania known as the Mennonites became the first American religious group to formally oppose the practice. In 1700, a New England judge named Samuel Sewall published a three-page tract called "The Selling of Joseph," in which he compared slavery to what Joseph's brothers did to him in the biblical story and called for the abolition of slavery in the colonies.

But voices such as Sewall's were few and far between. Although the total population of slaves was relatively low through most of the 1600s, colonial governments took steps to institutionalize the institution. In 1662, Virginia passed a law that automatically made slaves of slaves' children. In 1664, Maryland's assembly declared that any black person in the colony was a slave for life, whether they converted to Christianity or not. And in 1684, New York's legislators recognized slavery as a legitimate practice.

As the seventeenth century closed, it was clear that African slaves were a much better bargain, in terms of costs, than European servants, and the numbers of slaves began to swell. In 1670, Virginia had a population of about 2,000 slaves. By 1708, the number was 12,000. Slavery had not only taken root, it was sprouting.

Colonizing: Pilgrims and Puritans

While Virginia was being settled by gentlemen farmers, servants, slaves, and some people you wouldn't trust with your car keys, a very different kind of people were putting together England's second colony in America.

These people who settled New England came to America for the wealth of another type. They were spurred by their deep religious beliefs and their zeal to find a haven for the freedom to practice their faith — although not necessarily for anyone else to practice theirs.

The Mayflower Compact — a Dutch pilgrimage

The Pilgrims (actually, they called themselves "the Saints," and everyone else "the Strangers," and weren't dubbed Pilgrims until much later by one of their leaders) were mostly lower-class farmers and craftsmen who had decided the Church of England was still too Catholic for their tastes. So they separated themselves from the Church (thus resulting in everyone else calling them "Separatists"). This did not please King James I, who suggested rather forcefully that they rejoin or separate themselves from England.

The Separatists we're concerned with did just that, settling in Holland in 1608. But after a decade of watching their children become "Dutchified," the English expatriates longed for someplace they could live as English subjects and still worship the way they wanted. The answer was America.

After going back to England and negotiating a charter to establish a colony, taking out a few loans, and forming a company, a group of 102 men, women, and children left England on Sept. 16, 1620, in a ship called the *Mayflower.* (A second ship, the *Speedwell,* also started out, but sprang a leak and had to turn back). The *Mayflower* was usually used for shipping wine between France and England. Its cargo for this trip was decidedly more varied than usual. Although the Pilgrims didn't really pack any smarter than had the Jamestown colonists, they did show some imagination. Among the things they took to the wilderness of North America were musical instruments, all kinds of furniture, and even books on the history of Turkey (the country, not the bird). One guy even brought 139 pairs of shoes and boots.

Despite a rough crossing that took 65 days, only one passenger and four crewmen died, and one child was born. After some preliminary scouting, they dropped anchor in a broad, shallow bay we know as Plymouth. (There is no evidence they landed on any kind of rock.)

Squanto

His real name was Tisquantum, and he was a member of the Pawtuxet tribe. In 1605, Squanto was taken to England, possibly as a slave, by a passing explorer named George Weymouth. In 1613, he returned to the New World as a guide for Capt. John Smith, and remained there. A short time later, however, Squanto was abducted by yet another English expedition and sold as a slave in Spain. This time he escaped, made his way to England and eventually onto a 1619 expedition to New England, only to find his tribe had been exterminated by disease most probably brought by the white newcomers.

So, when the Pilgrims arrived, Squanto spoke fluent English, a little Spanish, and was essentially rootless. He was also apparently extremely tolerant. Until he died a little more than a year after their arrival, Squanto stayed with the Pilgrims, acting as their interpreter and advisor. Talk about a good sport!

Two important things happened on the way over. The first was the Pilgrims missed the turnoff and did not land within the borders laid out by their charter. That meant they were essentially squatters and did not fall under the direct governance of anyone in England. The second thing occurred before they landed. Concerned by mutterings from some members of the group that they should go home, the colony's leaders drew up a compact, or set of rules by which they all agreed to abide.

The Mayflower Compact was remarkable in that it was drawn up by people who were essentially equal to each other and were looking for a way to establish laws that all could live under. Although it certainly left out equal rights for women, slaves, Indians, and indentured servants, it was still a key early step in the colonists' journey toward self-rule and independence from England.

Despite their planning, the Plymouth colony had a very rough first winter. Just like the Jamestown colonists, half the Plymouth settlers died in the first six months. But unlike the Jamestown colonists, the Pilgrims were hard workers. They had an extremely able leader in William Bradford, who was to be governor of the colony for more than 30 years, and an able, although diminutive, military leader in Miles Standish (his nickname was "Captain Shrimpe"). They were also extremely lucky, because the local Indians proved not only to be great neighbors, but had one among them who spoke English (see the sidebar "Squanto" in this chapter).

The locals showed the newcomers some planting techniques and then traded the colonists' furs for corn, which gave the Pilgrims something to send back to England. By the fall of 1622, the Plymouth colonists had much to be thankful about.

The Plymouth colony never got all that big, and by 1691 it was absorbed by the larger Massachusetts Bay colony. But the impact of its approach to government and its impact on the American psyche far outstripped its size or longevity. For generations to come, the Pilgrims dominated most Americans' images of the country's earliest settlers.

The Massachusetts Bay Colony — a pure haven

It's easy to confuse the Pilgrims and the Puritans. Both groups were moved to journey to America for religious reasons. Both were remarkably intolerant of other people's religious beliefs. And neither were much fun at parties.

But there were differences. The Puritans were less radical and were less interested in leaving the Church of England than in "purifying" it. Their leader was a well-to-do lawyer named John Winthrop. Winthrop was the first truly great American leader. He had a lot of the qualities that came to be part of the stereotypical New England Yankee. He was deeply religious, but a practical businessman. He advocated — and put into practice — such egalitarian principles as trial by jury, yet regarded democracy as "the meanest and worst" of all forms of government. He loved his fellow man, as long as his fellow man had exactly the same morals and beliefs as he did.

Armed with a charter that gave the colonists extraordinary independence in making their own rules, Winthrop led an impressive wave of about 500 Puritans to the Massachusetts Bay Colony in New England in 1630, establishing the city of Boston later that year. An even larger group of Puritans had settled at Salem, in another part of the colony, the year before, and by 1642, as many as 20,000 Puritans had left England for America.

The Puritans established fur, fishing, and shipbuilding industries. They set up a system of compulsory free education, institutions of higher learning, and a model for what would eventually become a typical two-house state government in America. They developed crafts such as silver-smithing and printed their own books.

They were also pretty puritanical. Religious dissidents, especially Quakers, were routinely banished and beaten, and sometimes hanged. "If they beat the gospel black and blue," one Puritan minister said in explaining this treatment, "it is but just to beat them black and blue." Adultery was punishable by death until 1632, when the penalty was reduced to a public whipping and the forced wearing of the letters "AD" sewed onto the clothing. The Puritans were also tough on suspected witches.

Which is witch?

Witch hunting started with three kids fooling around. It ended with 20 executions and a wave of hysteria that swept through New England. In early 1692, three young girls in Salem, Massachusetts, began to throw fits and claimed they had been bewitched by a West Indian slave and two other local women.

The accusations begat more accusations as the girls and their friends basked in the attention they were getting. By the time they admitted they had made it up, however, no one was paying attention. Witchcraft accusations were used to settle all sorts of petty personal and political scores.

And by the time Governor William Phips (whose own wife was accused) had put an end to it, 150 people had been charged with consorting with Satan. Of that number, 28 were convicted: 5 confessed and were released; 2 escaped; 1 was pardoned; and 20 — 14 women and 6 men — were executed. All of the women and five of the men were hanged. One man, who was particularly reluctant to speak at his trial, was pressed to death under heavy stones. Despite the widespread belief to the contrary, none of them were burned at the stake, as witches were commonly dealt with in Europe. That may or may not have been some consolation to those who were executed.

The impact of the Puritan society of New England was huge. In it were the roots of the modern corporation system, the representative form of state and federal government, the American legal system, and, the moral conflict between wanting the freedom to think and act as we please and the authority to control how others think and act.

Bringing Religious Freedom: Dissidents, Catholics, and Quakers

The Massachusetts and Jamestown colonies were only the beginning. Throughout the rest of the eighteenth century, English settlers of all kinds moved to America. Some of those didn't like where they landed — or the place they landed didn't like them. But it was a big country, so they began the American tradition of moving on.

Some of the colonies — Maine, New Hampshire, Connecticut, North and South Carolina — were either privately founded or offshoots of the Massachusetts and Virginia colonies (see Figure 3-2). But three of them had very different beginnings.

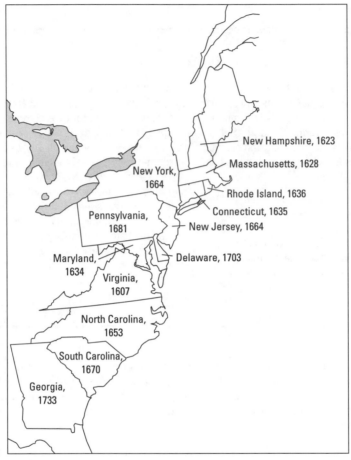

Figure 3-2:
The original
13 colonies
and their
dates of
establish-
ment.

Settling in Rhode Island

Roger Williams was a unique minister. Smart and sociable, he became minister in Salem, Massachusetts in 1633. He also became an expert in Indian languages and was troubled by the way his fellow settlers treated the natives. Williams argued that land should not be taken from the Indians unless it had been the subject of valid treaty negotiations. Even more troubling to his neighbors was Williams's insistence that there had to be a separation between the institutions of church and state. So troubling was this latter idea to the governing Puritan leaders that they decided to ship the troublemaker back to England.

But Williams was tipped off to the plan by John Winthrop, and with the help of friendly Indians, Williams and his family slipped off in 1636 to an unsettled area. By 1644, it had become the colony of Rhode Island. Small and disliked by its neighbors, Rhode Island became a haven for those seeking religious freedom — or those who just plain didn't like it in the rest of Puritan New England.

Anne Hutchinson

She was almost certainly not the first European woman to cause trouble in America, but she was probably the first famous one. Or infamous, if you were a Puritan official.

The mother of 14 children, Anne Hutchinson had the temerity to believe women could interpret the will of God as well as men. This she did, preaching in both private and public. Unfortunately for her, Hutchinson's version — that people could be saved by just recognizing the good within them — was at odds with the version put out by Puritan leaders. So they banished her from the Massachusetts colony in 1638.

Hutchinson went to Rhode Island for awhile and then settled in New York. She and her family were killed by Indians in 1643. Puritan officials attributed it to divine providence.

"No person in this country shall be molested or questioned for the matters of his conscience to God, so he be loyal and keep the civil peace," Williams said. "Forced worship stinks in God's nostrils."

Beginning in Maryland

While the Puritans may have had some religious differences among themselves, they did agree on one thing: They didn't like Roman Catholics. Undaunted, Catholics established a colony north of Virginia in 1634. Called Maryland, it was the result of a grant given by King James I to his former secretary, George Calvert, who had converted to Catholicism.

The colony prospered as a tobacco exporter. It also allowed in so many Protestants that its Catholic founders were threatened with the prospect of being persecuted in their own colony. So they struck a compromise in 1649, which recognized all Christian religions — and decreed the death penalty for Jews and atheists.

Starting Pennsylvania

If Puritans didn't like Catholics, they *really* didn't like Quakers. Quakers were steadfast pacifists who had no paid clergy, refused to use titles or take oaths of allegiance, and were said to "quake" from deep religious emotion.

In 1681, a wealthy Quaker named William Penn got a charter to start a colony in America. He advertised it honestly and exhaustively, attracted a diverse group of settlers, and founded Pennsylvania. Penn treated the Indians fairly, set up a relatively liberal system of laws, and made it easy for just about anyone to settle in his colony. By 1700, Pennsylvania's leading city, Philadelphia, was, after Boston, the colonies' leading cultural center.

Penn died in poverty and in social and political disrepute. But more than any other colony, Pennsylvania was truly tolerant of differing religions, cultures, and national backgrounds.

Going Dutch Treat

While the English, French, and Spanish were noisily tromping all over the New World, the Dutch were establishing themselves as the most successful maritime traders in the Old World. Intent on getting their share of the American trade, they formed the Dutch West Indies Company and in 1626 established a colony at the mouth of the Hudson River, calling it New Amsterdam. Three other settlements added up to a colony the Dutch called New Netherland.

New Amsterdam was different from the New England settlements in that it wasn't founded for religious reasons, and so had a more relaxed attitude when it came to things like drinking and gambling. In addition, land for the colonists wasn't an issue, since it was basically a company town, run for the benefit of the Dutch West Indies stockholders.

After awhile, this began to chafe on the settlers. So in 1664, when English ships and troops showed up to attack the settlement, it surrendered without firing a shot. New Amsterdam became New York, named after its new owner, James, the Duke of York. The Duke gave some of his new colony to a couple of friends, who thus began the colony of New Jersey. Despite its new English ownership, New York kept much of its Dutch flavor for decades.

Dealing with Indian Troubles

When it came to the Indians, English colonists had varying opinions. Some thought they should be treated as pets; others as pests. Some thought the Indians should be treated with respect. Others thought they should be exterminated, and still others thought they should be tricked out of their lands and then exterminated.

For their part, the Indians were not sure what to make of their uninvited guests. The newcomers had some pretty clever possessions, but they seemed awfully helpless at times. The English had a strange god, strange customs, and a fixation with other people's things.

In the Southern colonies, troubles between the two groups started almost as soon as the English got off the ships. The first English attempt at a colony, at Roanoke, was probably wiped out by Indians, although its exact fate is unknown.

What is known is that in 1642, Indians under Chief Opechencanough attacked settlers over a large area of the Virginia colony and killed about 350 of them. The settlers counterattacked a few months later and killed hundreds of Indians.

In New Netherland, the Dutch settlers treacherously murdered nearly 100 Indians in their sleep, cut off their heads, and kicked them around the streets of New Amsterdam. That launched a nasty war that ended when 150 Dutch soldiers killed about 700 Indians at a battle near present-day Stamford, Connecticut.

In New England, thanks in part to the good initial relations between the Pilgrims and local tribes, war was averted until 1634, when a rowdy pirate named John Stone and seven of his crew were murdered by Indians that the settlers decided were from a tribe called the Pequot. After an uneasy two-year truce, New Englanders went on the attack. In 1637, Puritan soldiers and their Indian allies attacked a Pequot fort near Mystic River, Connecticut. In about an hour, they burned the village and slaughtered 600 men, women, and children.

In September 1638, the Pequots surrendered. As many as 2,000 of them were sold as slaves in the West Indies or given to rival tribes. The Pequots were all but exterminated, and the Indian wars in New England were over for nearly 40 years.

In 1675, an Indian chief named Metacom, but called King Philip by the settlers because he liked English customs and dress, decided it was time to push the white invaders out once and for all. The result was King Philip's War

This time, the Indians used guns too, and attacked everywhere. By the time the two-year war was over, half the settlements in New England had been destroyed, and the English were on the edge of being driven into the sea. Finally, however, the colonies united while the Indians did not, and the tide began to turn. King Philip was killed in August 1676, and the war finally ended. It would be 40 years before the area recovered enough to begin expanding its boundaries into the frontier again.

SIDETRIP

Getting even

One of the conditions of the Pequots' surrender was that the name "Pequot" would no longer be mentioned. A derivation of it, however, popped up in the novel "Moby Dick," when author Herman Melville named Captain Ahab's ill-fated whaling ship the "Pequod."

Fast-forward to 1992. The Pequots have been struggling for more than 20 years to stave off efforts by the state to take their last 200 acres of Connecticut countryside. Using loans from an Indonesian oil company, they opened a casino and called it Foxwoods. Today it is the largest casino in the world, having generated more than $2.5 billion in revenue. "Pequot" is not a dirty word in New England anymore — unless the slots have been unkind to you.

Gee, Grandpa, What Else Happened?

December 1610: Spanish officials establish Santa Fe as the new provincial capital of New Mexico.

1618: The governor of Virginia decrees that anyone missing church on Sunday will be put in jail overnight and then forced to work as a slave for a week.

June 29, 1620: The Crown bars the growing of tobacco in England so the Virginia colony's monopoly will be safe.

March 4, 1634: Boston's first tavern is opened by a man named Samuel Cole. (His first customer was probably named "Norm.")

Sept. 4, 1634: The Massachusetts General Court passes a law that bans the drinking of toasts.

March 3, 1639: A 3-year-old college near the Charles River in Boston is renamed Harvard, after John Harvard, a minister who has left half his estate and his 400-volume library to the school.

1664: Horse racing becomes the first established sport in America when a track is opened on Long Island.

1680: Facing starvation, Maryland settlers are forced to eat oysters from Chesapeake Bay.

1697: Spanish missionaries establish a mission at Loreto, in Baja California, the first of many such places that will stretch all the way to Northern California over the next century.

1699: Captain William Kidd, a former English naval hero who was commissioned to hunt down pirates off the American coast, is arrested and charged — with piracy. Kidd pleads not guilty, but is hanged two years later.

Chapter 4

Old Grudges in a New World: 1700–1763

. . . .

In This Chapter

▶ Changing the face of America

▶ Settling New France

▶ Fighting the first world wars

▶ Awakening to relaxed religious attitudes

▶ Removing the French

▶ Timeline

. . . .

*B*y the beginning of the eighteenth century, European powers had been alternately exploring the New World and sparring over what they found for the previous 200 years. It was time for the main event: a showdown among the European countries for control of the American continent.

Actually, it was time for a series of main events. As this chapter unfolds, Europe engages in a seemingly endless succession of wars in which America is not only a pawn but also a battleground. England comes out on top, but her relationship with the American colonies will be dramatically changed.

1700 America Gets a Facelift

The English colonies in America had filled in the gaps between the first two settlements in Virginia and Massachusetts by 1700, and in fact gone beyond them. They now stretched from Maine to South Carolina. But they were a pretty skinny bunch, as colonies go. Few settlers lived more than 75 miles from the Atlantic coast, and vast stretches of land lay unsettled by any nation, although claimed by more than one.

The population had reached 275,000 to 300,000, including 25,000 African slaves. Most people — as many as 90 percent — lived in small communities or farms. The population of New York City was about 5,000; Charlestown about 2,000.

Many of the newcomers were not English, as people from other Western European regions such as Ireland, France, Scotland, and Germany, as well as the Scandinavian countries arrived.

The colonies were maturing in other ways as well. Boston and Philadelphia were major publishing centers. Small manufacturing firms were turning out goods such as furniture and clothing that lessened the colonies' dependence on goods from England. And increasing secularism was loosening the hold of religious authority on everyday life. In fact, things were going along okay, except for all that fighting in Europe.

Colonizing New France

While New England had been filling up with Puritans and the Southern colonies with tobacco growers, the area of North America dominated by the French had been progressing more slowly.

By 1663, when Canada officially became a French crown colony, Quebec had only about 550 people, and the entire region had fewer than 80,000 Europeans by 1750.

One reason for the lack of settlers was the colony was strictly Catholic, and Protestants from France were banned. Many of these thus settled in the English colonies. Another was a looney-tunes system held over from the Middle Ages that awarded vast tracts of the best land to just a few people. A third was the emphasis on fur-trading — conducted by men called *courers de bois* (runners of the woods) — instead of on agriculture, for which people must settle down.

AMERICAN FACES

Sieur de La Salle

He was haughty, overbearing, smart, and extremely brave. Also a good walker and paddler. At the age of 23, La Salle came to the New World with plans not only to be a successful fur trader, but also to found an empire. He learned a dozen Indian dialects, and after three reconnaissance trips of more than 1,000 miles each by foot and canoe, La Salle set off in December, 1681, from what is now Illinois, down the Mississippi River.

By April 1682, La Salle's party had reached the mouth of the Mississippi, and had claimed the entire watershed for France, naming it Louisiana. In 1684, La Salle led another expedition to build a fort where the Mississippi meets the Gulf of Mexico. But the group got lost and ended up wandering around Texas. After three years, the 45 men left out of the 400 he started with killed La Salle, 350 miles from the river he had been looking for. Despite his failure, La Salle's expedition gave France at least a tenuous claim to a vast part of the North American continent.

French officials did what they could to increase the population. Bachelors were censured, and fathers of unwed 16-year-old girls were fined. Despite such efforts, the population remained low, especially compared to the English colonies.

Although few in number, the French were daring explorers, roaming as far south as present-day New Orleans and as far west as the Rocky Mountains.

But the lack of permanent settlements by the French in the vast areas they explored, coupled with their small numbers, spelled trouble for their efforts to hold on to what they had when the wars in Europe spilled over to America.

The First True World Wars

Eighteenth-century royalty didn't need much of an excuse to start a war, from who should be the next king of Spain to the lopping-off of a sea captain's ear. Part of their willingness to fight was based on greed for more territory and the wealth they could bring, and part on their fear that other countries would beat them to it and become more powerful.

What made these wars different from their predecessors was that they were global in scope, fought all over Europe, India, North and South America, and the Caribbean. The main combatants were the French and English, although the Spanish, Dutch, and Austrians did their share of fighting.

France and England were a pretty even match. England had a better navy and France had a better army. In North America, England's colonies had a much larger population: 1.5 million compared to the French colonies' 80,000 in 1750. England's colonies had a much more varied economy, the protection of the English navy, and the support of the Iroquois Confederacy, a six-tribe alliance of Indians who hated the French. The French colonists, on the other hand, had better military leaders, did less quarreling among themselves than the English colonists, and had Indian allies of their own.

So, here's what happened in the first three true world wars.

King William's War

This was the warm-up bout. After a revolution by Protestants in England, James II, a Catholic, was tossed out. Protestant William III and his wife Mary were brought in from the Netherlands and put on the throne in 1689. This did not sit well with the French king, Louis XIV, a Catholic. After William III sided with other countries against France in a territorial dispute, a war was on in Europe that lasted until 1697.

Keeping a not-too-tight ship

While it was customary to give sailors a daily ration of rum in the British Navy, it was sometimes not a great idea in hot climates, because it made some of them tipsy. So on an otherwise unsuccessful expedition to seize the Spanish stronghold of Cartagena in what is now Colombia, in 1741, a British Admiral named Edward Vernon diluted the rum with water. The sailors dubbed the watered-down drink after Vernon's nickname, which was "Old Grog."

The eminent historian Samuel Eliot Morrison attaches two postscripts to the story. One is that for the first time on the Vernon expedition, colonial fighters were referred to as "Americans" by the British, rather than "provincials." The second is that Vernon's surname was also adopted for the family estate of an American captain on the trip named Lawrence Washington. Washington had a half-brother named George who also made some contributions to history.

In America, the war went back and forth. The French led Indian raiding parties into New York, and practiced a kind of warfare that was to become known as "guerilla" fighting: ambushes and hit-and-run attacks. The English outlasted the attacks, but botched attempts to conquer Quebec and Montreal. The war ended in pretty much of a draw.

Queen Anne's War

After King William's War ended, Europe took all of four years to catch its breath. Then in 1701, Louis XIV of France tried to put his grandson on the throne of Spain. Queen Anne, who had succeeded William in England, objected, and they were back at it again.

This time the English colonists found themselves fighting the Spanish in the south and the French in the north. As with the previous war, there were few big battles and lots of raids and counter-raids, with both sides employing Indian allies.

When the war finally ended in 1713, Louis XIV got to put his grandson on the Spanish throne, but England got Nova Scotia, Newfoundland, and the Hudson River Valley, which put it in a good position to take over even more of Canada in future wars.

King George's War

Most wars have more than one cause, but historians with a whimsical turn like to start this one with an English smuggler named Edward Jenkins. Spanish revenue agents caught Jenkins in 1739, and in the course of being interrogated, he involuntarily had one of his ears removed. "Take this back to the king, your master," a Spanish official was said to have said, "whom, if he were present, I would serve in the same fashion."

Jenkins did take his ear back to England, and a new war was on. It eventually merged with a larger war that broke out in Europe. In America, there was the same kind of fighting that had taken place in the earlier wars. The English colonists took a key port called Louisbourg, which commanded the Gulf of St. Lawrence, but they had to give it back as part of the 1748 treaty that settled the war.

To see what land holdings Britain, France, and Spain maintained in the mid-eighteenth century, take a look at Figure 4-1.

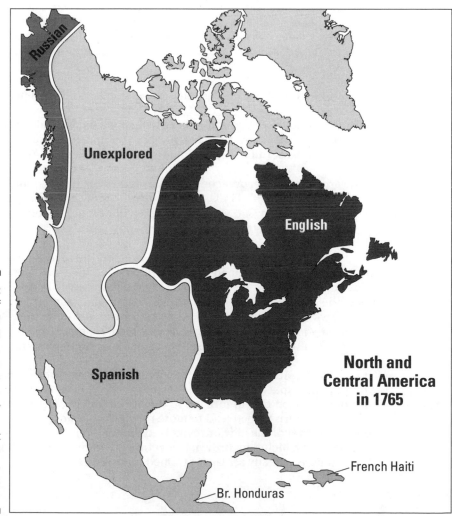

Figure 4-1:
Map of North and Central America during the mid-eighteenth century showing what belonged to Britain, France, and Spain.

The Great Awakening

Despite the nagging presence of almost-continual war, the American colonies were doing pretty well. And as the colonists did better economically, they began to loosen up in terms of their religious beliefs too. "Pennsylvania," said a German observer, by way of example, "is heaven for farmers, paradise for artisans, and hell for officials and preachers."

It wasn't so much that Americans were becoming less devout, but more a function of them becoming less rigid and more likely to question the practice of most clergy to dictate exactly what they were to think and believe.

In the 1730s, a reaction to this shifting of religious attitudes resulted in what came to be known as the Great Awakening. Its catalyst was a genius named Jonathan Edwards. Tall and delicately built, Edwards entered Yale at the age of 13. By the time he was 21, he was the school's head tutor. He wrote papers on insects that are still respected in entomological circles and was a brilliant theologian.

He was also — you should excuse the expression — a hell of a public speaker.

"The God that holds you over the pit of hell, much as one holds a spider or some loathsome insect over the fire, abhors you and is dreadfully provoked," he thundered in a sermon called "Sinners in the Hands of an Angry God."

But Edwards's message, preached to mass audiences throughout New England in the 1730s and 1740s, was not just fire-and-brimstone yelling. Edwards believed that God was to be loved and not just feared, and that internal goodness was the best way to be happy on this earth.

Edwards was joined, and eventually surpassed, on the revival circuit by a Georgia-based minister named George Whitefield. Called the "Great Itinerant" because of his constant traveling, Whitefield drew crowds in the thousands. On one crusade, he traveled 800 miles in 75 days and gave 175 sermons. Equipped with an amazing voice and a flair for the melodramatic, Whitefield quite literally made members of his crowds wild. He made seven continental tours from 1740 to 1770, and it's safe to say he was America's first superstar.

Although the Great Awakening had run its course by the time of the American Revolution, its impact was deep and lasting. It sparked widespread discussions about religion that in turn led to the development of new denominations, which in turn helped lead to more religious tolerance among the colonists. Several of the new or revitalized denominations were encouraged to start colleges, including Brown, Princeton, Dartmouth, and Columbia, in order to ensure a steady stream of trained ministers.

It also helped to break down barriers between the colonies and unify them through their common experience with it. And as the first spontaneous mass movement in America, it heightened the individual's sense of his power, when it was combined with that of others.

The French and Indians: At It Again

Filled with the divine spirit of the Great Awakening, American colonists were ready by 1750 to once more start killing some French and Indians. The first to do so were led by a tall, 22-year-old Virginia militia captain named George Washington.

This time the world war started in America. English speculators had secured the rights to 500,000 acres in the Ohio River Valley. At about the same time, the French had built a series of forts in the same area, as a way to keep lines of communication and supply open between Canada and Louisiana.

In 1754, a year after he had conducted a diplomat/spy mission, Washington was sent to the Ohio Country with 150 men. They ran into a French detachment, the Virginians fired, and the French fled.

"I heard the bullets whistle," Washington wrote later, "and, believe me, there is something charming in the sound."

The French quickly set out to charm Washington by counterattacking a hastily-erected fort the young Virginian had put up (and aptly named "Fort Necessity") and forced Washington to surrender — on July 4. Then in a stroke of luck for a nation yet unborn, the French let Washington lead his men home.

Unifying the Colonies

While Washington was savoring his first taste of battle, representatives of 8 of the 13 colonies were meeting in Albany, New York, at the request of the British government. The purpose was to see if the colonies could be more unified. The British wanted more unity because they figured it would make it easier to fight the French, and also to govern the colonies.

But a few far-seeing colonists — most notably a Philadelphia printer, inventor, scientist, and man-about-town named Benjamin Franklin — saw it as an opportunity to increase the colonies' economic and political clout.

Franklin engineered a sound plan for a colonial union, and it was approved by the gathered representatives. But the assemblies in the individual colonies rejected it, mostly because they felt they would give up too much of their independence.

Holding back the British

On the battlefield, meanwhile, the English had sent two of their worst regiments to the colonies and given command to a general named Edward Braddock. Though undeniably brave (he had five horses shot from under him in one battle), Braddock was arrogant and a plodding bozo when it came to military strategy. He was also contemptuous of the American militia under his command.

In 1755, Braddock and a force of about 1,400 men, including Washington, marched on French forts in the Ohio Country. The British force was surprised by a force of French and Indians. Braddock was killed, along with almost a thousand of his men.

Braddock's defeat was just one of a bunch of losses the British suffered over the next two years. The war in America merged with a war in Europe that involved all of the major European powers. It went badly for the British in both theaters.

Outfighting the French

In 1757, however, things began looking up. An able administrator named William Pitt became head of the London government. Pitt skillfully used the superior British navy and appointed good military leaders.

Among them were James Wolfe and Jeffrey Amherst. Wolfe and Amherst led a British force against the French fortress-city of Quebec in 1759. In one of the most important battles fought in North America, the British took the city. Montreal fell in the following year, and the French were finished in the New World.

The war was formally settled by the Treaty of Paris in 1763. The English got all of Canada, all of America east of the Mississippi, Florida, and some Caribbean islands.

The American colonists got rid of the decades-old threat from the French. More than in previous wars, men from different colonies fought alongside each other, helping to break down barriers between the colonies. Future leaders matured. And the animosity and friction that sprang up between British military leaders and the Americans lingered long after the war was over.

SIDETRIP

Pontiac and Pox

Pontiac was a chief of the Ottawa tribe, which had historically sided with the French in the wars against the British. An able leader and outstanding orator, Pontiac realized early on that his tribe couldn't trust the French or the British, and he worked quietly to unite tribes in the area in a common cause. When English settlers hanged several Indians after a dispute among Indians that did not involve white settlers, a war started.

The resultant fighting was nasty and prolonged, and eight British forts fell to Pontiac's troops. So in July, 1763, when a Colonel Henry Boquet suggested distributing smallpox-infected blankets to the Indians, British military leader Jeffrey Amherst agreed, writing to Boquet that he should also "try every other method that can serve to extirpate [wipe out] this excrable race."

Whether this form of biological warfare was ever followed through on is unclear. But smallpox did break out among the Indians. By 1765, decimated by disease, outnumbered and running low on supplies, Pontiac and his allies sued for peace. The Indian leader was killed by another Indian in 1769 and eventually had a car named after him. Amherst lived to the ripe old age of 80. A Massachusetts town and a college were named after him.

Gee, Grandpa, What Else Happened?

October 1705: Virginia passes a new law that reclassifies slaves as real estate, rather than as a form of servant.

April 1706: The governor of New Mexico, Francisco Cuervo y Vades, founds a new settlement, and calls it Albuquerque.

1709: Quakers establish the first colonial center for the treatment of mental illness, in Philadelphia.

1714: Tea is introduced in the colonies, and quickly becomes all the rage.

1721: A Boston doctor named Zabdiel Boylston inoculates 243 people against smallpox when an epidemic breaks out. All but six survive. Other doctors criticize the practice as simply spreading the disease more.

1741: A man named Andrew Bradford starts the colonies' first magazine, called "American Magazine." It folds after two issues.

1748: The prayer "Now I lay me down to sleep" first appears in a New England textbook.

July 1749: George Washington becomes official surveyor for Culpepper County in Virginia. He is 16 years old.

1755: An English army surgeon named Richard Schuckburg writes a satirical set of lyrics that portrays American colonials as uncouth bumpkins, puts it to a popular tune of the time and calls it "Yankee Doodle."

November 1762: France gives all its North American land west of the Mississippi to Spain. The area, known as Upper Louisiana, is to repay Spain for Caribbean territory it lost to the British.

Chapter 5

Revolting Developments: 1763–1775

In This Chapter

▶ Dealing with America's growing pains

▶ Getting the colonists to pay their dues

▶ Beginning of separation beween England and the colonies

▶ Boycotting trade with Britain

▶ Timeline

America was founded by people who wanted more. Some wanted more religious freedom, others more economic opportunity. There were malcontents, dreamers, idealists, and schemers. What many of them had in common was a dislike of being told what to do by people who stayed home and were thousands of miles away.

But England viewed her colonies as basically economic enterprises. They existed to provide stuff the mother country needed or wanted — tobacco, timber, naval supplies, and other goods — and to act as consumers for the goods England itself produced. Colonists were to simultaneously be employees and good customers.

In this chapter, these two differing perspectives begin to clash more and more — until England finally gets popped in the snoot.

Seeing a Growth Spurt

If there was one inarguable fact about the American colonies in the mid to late eighteenth century, it was that they were growing like crazy. In 1730, the population of the 13 colonies was about 655,000. Boston was the biggest city, with a population of about 13,000, while New York and Philadelphia were home to about 8,500 people each.

The "other" arrivals

One of the fastest growing segments of the eighteenth-century American population wasn't growing voluntarily. In 1725, there were an estimated 75,000 African slaves in the colonies. By 1790, the number was 700,000. The 1790 census reported there were slaves in all but three states: Maine, Massachusetts, and Vermont. In South Carolina, 43 percent of the people living there belonged to other people; in Virginia, 39 percent were slaves.

More than a few colonists raised their voices in alarm at the increasing number of slaves. Some protested for humanitarian reasons. Benjamin Franklin argued the slave system did not make sense from an economic perspective. And even the most ardent proslavery apostles had their doubts. Some were afraid of slave uprisings if the numbers continued to grow, while others wanted to stop the importation of slaves so the value of the ones here would increase. But the British government refused to allow bans on slave importation by the colonies, for fear of damaging the lucrative trade. This refusal became another sore spot between England and America.

By 1760, the population had reached 1.6 million, not including African slaves, and by 1775, the White population stood at 2.5 million. Philadelphia was the largest city in that year, with a populace of about 34,000.

The population explosion was due to two things. One was the natural birth rate of the colonists. Partly because of the time-honored farm family tradition that large families meant more people to work (and maybe because there wasn't much else to do on those long winter nights in the country), the size of many American families was astounding. Benjamin Franklin wrote of a Philadelphia woman who had 14 children, 82 grandchildren, and 110 great-grandchildren by the time she died at the age of 100. The growth rate was even more astounding when you consider the high infant mortality rate. One woman was reported to have lost 20 children at birth or soon thereafter, and the average woman who reached menopause had seven or eight surviving children.

But the growth was by no means all from within the colonies. Immigration continued at a brisk pace, not only from England, but also from other Western European countries. A 1909 population study estimated that at the time of the American Revolution, about 82 percent of the White population were from England and Wales; 5 percent from Scotland; 6 percent from the German states; and about 7 percent from Holland, Ireland, and other countries.

Despite the rapid growth, the colonies suffered a postwar recession after the years of fighting with the French stopped in 1763. Still, they were on a fairly sound economic foundation. About 90 percent of the colonists were involved with agriculture — tobacco, corn, rice, indigo, and wheat being the main crops. Fishing and whaling were big in New England. Timber was the number one manufacturing product, and because trees were plentiful and cheap, shipbuilding boomed. By the time of the American Revolution, one-third of the British Navy had been built in America.

Although the colonists shared problems common to people all over the world in the eighteenth century, such as nasty epidemics, they generally ate better, lived longer, and were more prosperous than any of their European counterparts. Land was cheap and had to sustain fewer people because the population was smaller. Because labor was often in short supply, wages were higher, which raised the standard of living.

While enjoying the protections of the formidable British Empire's military, the average American colonist, if he paid any taxes at all, paid far less than his English cousin. And the argument against British taxes, put forth by the eloquent Boston lawyer James Otis that "taxation without representation is tyranny" rang a little hollow, since more than a few Americans who had to pay local taxes still couldn't vote or didn't have a representative in the colonial assemblies.

Moreover, for the most part, Britain did not interfere in the colonies's internal affairs. Mostly the mother country concerned itself with defense and trade issues, and many of the trade laws were mutually beneficial to both sides of the water (unless one happened to be a big-time smuggler like John Hancock, who later became the first to sign the Declaration of Independence and was Public Enemy No. 1 as far as the British were concerned).

So, most Americans in the 1760s and early 1770s had no interest in independence from England. What they wanted was what they had: protection by the world's mightiest navy, generally cozy trade rules, and freedoms and rights unequalled in the rest of the world.

But Britain could not afford to maintain the status quo.

Looking at the Brits' Point of View

For more than six decades, the British had been in a state of almost continual warfare, mostly against the French and Spanish, their major rivals in the New World. After all that fighting, England had established itself as *the* major power in the Western World, with perhaps the most far-flung holdings since the Roman Empire.

But it didn't come cheap. Before the last French and Indian war, which lasted from 1755 to 1763, the English national debt stood at the equivalent of about $120 million. After the war, it was more than double that. Because a lot of the debt had come about by defending Americans against the French and Indians in America, the British government quite reasonably concluded it was only fair that the Americans pay for part of it.

But they didn't even ask the colonists for their fair share. In fact, all the British government wanted was that the Americans pay for a measly one-third of the future costs of stationing 10,000 British troops in the colonies to protect them.

At the same time, British officials wanted to find a way to prevent friction among the colonists, the American Indians, and the French traders who were now English subjects. The easiest way to do that, the British reasoned, was to keep the groups apart. By limiting western expansion by the American colonists, the British felt they could placate the Indians, who were feeling a bit edgy by the ever-broadening presence of the colonists. And the British also wanted to do something about all the smuggling that was going on in the colonies, and that meant conducting surprise raids and inspections of suspected smugglers's homes.

In the hands of an adroit diplomat, it may have been possible to make all this acceptable to the colonists. After all, the overwhelming majority of them were loyal subjects of Mother England. Unfortunately for Mother England, however, most of her political leaders between 1763 and 1775 were stubborn, stupid, arrogant, or all three. One of them even went insane for a while, yet remained prime minister for two years. The king, George III, was a popular, hard-working fellow with oodles of personal integrity. But he was more politician than statesman, and he chose his advisors and ministers more on their willingness to agree with him than their abilities to lead.

In addition, there was a fundamental disagreement between the English and the Americans on what role Parliament, the English governing body, should play in the colonists' lives. For England, it was simple: Parliament made the rules for England and all its colonies. For America, however, the role of Parliament was negligible. The colonists wanted to come up with their own rules in their own mini-parliaments and deal directly with the king. In the end, it came down to a fight over who should tell whom what to do.

England and America: Heading Toward Divorce

Starting in 1763, England and her American colonies began to irritate each other almost incessantly. Like an impatient parent with an unruly child, England tried different methods to instill discipline. Only America wasn't such a kid anymore, or as Ben Franklin put it: "We have an old mother that peevish is grown; / She snubs us like children that scarce walk alone; / She forgets we're grown up and have sense of our own." The following set of irritants led to a revolution.

The Proclamation of 1763

One of the first things Britain wanted to do after finally whipping the French was to calm down the American Indians, who were understandably upset by the generally pushy, and often genocidal, actions of the colonists. So King George III decided that as of October 7, 1763, no colonist could settle beyond the crest of the Appalachian Mountains. That decision meant America would remain basically a collection of coastal colonies.

The idea was to give everyone a sort of timeout after all the fighting. But even if it was well intentioned, it was impractical. For one thing, a bunch of colonials were already living west of the dividing line, and weren't about to move just because some potentate thousands of miles away said so.

Worse, the decree was a slap in the face to those who had fought against the French and Indians with the expectation that winning meant they could move west to vast tracts of free land. In the end, it was an unenforceable law that did nothing but anger the colonists and vex British officials when it wasn't obeyed.

The Revenue Acts (1764)

On the other side of the sea, there were more than a few Brits who were peeved that their colonial cousins paid next to nothing when it came to taxes, while the British were among the highest taxed people in the world. So British Prime Minister George Grenville pushed a bill through Parliament that was explicitly designed to raise money from the colonists to pay for their defense.

The law actually lowered the tax on molasses, but raised or imposed taxes on other things like sugar, wine, linen, and silk. Colonists objected, asserting that Parliament had no right to impose taxes on them without their assent. They also organized boycotts of the taxed goods and increased their already booming smuggling enterprises.

The Stamp Act (1765)

Unsatisfied with the revenue from the Revenue Acts, Parliament imposed a new levy on 50 items, including dice, playing cards, newspapers, marriage licenses, college degrees, and just about every kind of legal document. Some of the taxes doubled the cost of the item. Not only that, the items had to be stamped or have a stamped receipt showing the tax had been paid.

English citizens had been paying similar taxes for years, at even higher rates. But American colonists saw the Stamp Act taxes as only the beginning. Paying anything, they argued, was an invitation to be milked dry later.

In reaction to the tax, nine colonies sent 27 delegates to a meeting in New York City. The group drew up a petition and sent it to England, where it was ignored. But the colonies also began a boycott of British goods, and that was not ignored. Groups calling themselves the "Sons of Liberty" encouraged and bullied their fellow colleagues to wear "homespun" clothing instead of English wool. They also tarred and feathered more than a few would-be tax collectors (see Figure 5-1).

Figure 5-1:
This cartoon shows a tarred and feathered John Malcolm, a Boston customs official, being paraded through the streets.

The boycott had its desired effect. In 1766, under pressure from English manufacturers, Parliament repealed the taxes. But it also tried to save face by declaring that henceforth it had the right to pass any laws it wanted to govern the colonies. Americans rejoiced at the tax repeal. They praised "Good King George." In New York, they even erected a statue of him in his honor. And they blithely ignored the warning from Parliament.

The Townshend Act (1767)

British Prime Minister William Pitt was a capable leader. But when he had a mental breakdown in 1766, he handed over the government to one of his lieutenants, named Charles Townshend, also known as "Champagne Charley" because he was quite eloquent when drunk. A cocky sort, Townshend vowed to squeeze some money out of the obstinate American colonies, and he got Parliament to impose taxes on a number of goods, including glass, paper, paint — and tea. The revenues were to be used to pay the salaries of royal judges and governors in the colonies. To be fair, Townshend also dropped import duties on some American products entering England, thus making their export more profitable for the colonies.

It was too small a gesture as far as many colonists were concerned. For one thing, many of them had grown extremely fond of tea and were not keen on paying any tax on it. For another, they didn't like the idea of the money going to pay judges and governors. Up until that point, the officials' salaries had been controlled by colonial legislatures, which gave them a fair amount of influence over their policies.

Eager to show he meant business, Townshend sent two regiments of red-coated English troops — sneeringly dubbed "lobsterbacks" by the locals — to Boston in 1768. That set up the next confrontation.

The Boston Massacre (1770)

Because the soldiers sent to Boston were poorly paid, some of them tried to find part-time work, a practice that did not sit well with many Bostonians. So it wasn't unusual for fights to break out between soldiers and groups of colonists.

On the night of March 5, a small mob of lowlifes began throwing rocks and snowballs at a British sentry outside the customs house. Another 20 British soldiers appeared with fixed bayonets, the crowd grew to about 100 boys and men, and after about 30 minutes of being taunted and pelted with rocks and sticks, one of the soldiers opened fire. A few minutes later, 11 members of the mob were dead or wounded.

AMERICAN FACES

Samuel Adams

He was a flop at business and a crummy public speaker — and perhaps America's first truly great politician. More than any of his contemporaries, Sam Adams kept the colonies on the road to independence.

Born to a prosperous family, Adams graduated from Harvard. After failing at a business of his own, he took over a bustling family brewery and managed to run it into the ground. Then he became a tax collector and narrowly avoided jail for mismanaging funds.

But Adams was a success at backroom maneuvering. He helped organize the Sons of Liberty, the Boston Tea Party, and the minutemen. He wrote tirelessly for colonial newspapers on the urge to stand up to Britain, and his letters urging action were circulated throughout America. When the movement seemed to be sputtering, Adams kept it alive almost single-handedly with his writings and organizing.

He attended both continental congresses as a delegate and was a signer of the Declaration of Independence. But once independence was won, there was no need for a rabble-rouser. Although elected governor of Massachusetts for one four-year term in 1794, Adams had dropped from national prominence by the time of his death in 1803, at the age of 81.

At a subsequent trial, the soldiers were ably defended by a Boston lawyer named John Adams, and all but two were acquitted. The two soldiers found guilty were branded on the hand and then let go. But the radicals among the colonists milked the incident for all it was worth. A highly exaggerated engraving of the "massacre" was made by a silversmith named Paul Revere, and copies of it circulated all over the colonies.

Ironically, on the day of the incident, the Townshend Acts were repealed by Parliament — except for the tax on tea.

The Boston Tea Party (1773)

Despite the widespread publicity surrounding the tragedy in Boston, cooler heads prevailed for the next year or two. Moderates on both sides of the Atlantic argued that compromises could still be reached.

Then the powerful but poorly run British East India Company found it had 17 million pounds of tea on its hands. So the British government gave the company a monopoly on the American tea business. With a monopoly, the company could lower its prices enough to undercut the smuggled tea the colonists drank rather than pay the British tax. But even with lower prices, the colonists still didn't like the arrangement. It was the principle of the tax itself, not the cost of the tea. Shipments of English tea were destroyed or prevented from being unloaded or sold.

On December 16, 1773, colonists poorly disguised as Indians boarded three ships in Boston Harbor, smashed in 342 chests of tea, and dumped the whole mess in the harbor, where according to one eyewitness "it piled up in the low tide like haystacks." No one was seriously hurt, although one colonist was reportedly roughed up a bit for trying to stuff some of the tea in his coat instead of throwing it overboard.

King George III was not amused by the colonists' lack of respect. "The die is now cast," he wrote to his latest prime minister, Lord North, who had succeeded Townshend, who had died suddenly. "The colonies must either submit or triumph."

The "Intolerable" Acts (1774)

In response to the tea terrorism, Parliament passed a series of laws designed to teach the upstarts a thing or two. They were called the "Repressive Acts" in England, but to Americans, they were "Intolerable." The new laws closed Boston Harbor until the colonists paid back the damage they had wrought, thus cutting the city off from sources of food, medical supplies, and other goods. The laws also installed a British general as governor of Massachusetts and repealed liberties, such as the right to hold town meetings.

At the same time, the Brits passed the Quebec Act, a law that gave more freedom to conquered French subjects in Canada, including the right to continue customs such as non-jury trials in civil cases. Though a sensible thing to do from an English perspective, it incensed Americans, especially at a time when they felt their own freedoms were being messed with. The act also pushed the borders of the Quebec province well into the Ohio Valley, which infuriated colonials who had fought several wars to keep the French out of that same valley.

The acts galvanized the colonies into a show of unity that had only occasionally been shown before. Food and supplies poured in by land to Boston from all over America. And in Virginia, the colonial legislature decided to try to get representatives from all the colonies together for a meeting.

Congressing and Cocktails

On September 5, 1774, leaders from all of the colonies but Georgia gathered in Philadelphia to talk things over. There were 56 delegates, all of them men and about half of them lawyers. Some, such as New York's John Jay, were politically conservative. Others, such as Virginia's Patrick Henry, were fire-breathing radicals. Despite their differences and the serious state of events, all of them apparently managed to have a pretty good time over the seven-week meeting — except for Massachusetts' Sam Adams, who had an ulcer, and stuck to bread and milk.

His cousin John Adams had no such problem. He dined on "Flummery, [a sweet dessert], jellies, sweetmeats of 20 sorts, trifles and . . . I drank Madeira [a wine] at a great rate, and found no inconvenience in it."

But the delegates to what is called the First Continental Congress did more than party, even though they had no real power except the power of persuasion. Several wrote essays that suggested the colonies stay under the supervision of the king, but have nothing to do with Parliament. They petitioned Parliament to rescind the offending laws. The group also proclaimed that colonists should have all the rights other English subjects had, such as electing representatives to make the laws they were governed by, and that all trade with England should cease until the "Intolerable Acts" were repealed.

The Congress also resolved that if one of the colonies was attacked, all the rest would defend it. And, probably much to the dismay of some members, Congress also resolved to abstain from tea and wine (but not rum), and to swear off recreational pursuits like horseracing and cock fighting until the troubles with England were resolved. The meeting also served to draw the colonies closer together than ever before, as shown in this quote by one colonist:

> "The distinctions between New Englanders and Virginians are no more," declared Patrick Henry. "I am not a Virginian, but an American."

They adjourned on October 26, pledging to come back in May if things didn't get better by then. Things didn't.

Mr. Revere, Your Horse Is Ready

The Congress's decision to boycott all trade with Britain was embraced with enthusiasm almost everywhere. Lists of suspected "traitors" who continued to trade were published, and tar and feathers were vigorously applied to those who ignored the boycott.

While businessmen in England fretted, the colonists's actions were met with disdain by a majority of the members of Parliament. Lord North, the prime minister, resolved to isolate the troublemakers in Massachusetts and thus stifle dissent in other areas.

But some British knew better. General Thomas Gage, the English commander in chief in America, reported that things were coming to a head. "If you think ten thousand men are enough," he wrote North, "send twenty; if a million [pounds] is thought to be enough, give two. You will save both blood and treasure in the end."

In April 1775, Gage decided to make a surprise march from his headquarters in Boston to nearby Concord, where he hoped to seize a storehouse of rebel guns and ammunition and maybe arrest some of their leaders.

But the colonists knew they were coming, thanks to a network of spies and militia called the "minutemen," aptly named because they were supposed to be ready to quickly spring into action. One of these was Paul Revere, the son of a French immigrant.

In addition to being a master silversmith, Revere also made false teeth and surgical tools, and was pretty good on a horse too. So when word came on the night of April 18 that the British were marching on Concord, Revere and two other men, William Dawes and Doctor Samuel Prescott, rode out to warn that the British were coming. After rousing the town of Lexington, Revere and Dawes were captured and briefly detained. But Prescott escaped and made it to Concord. (Revere became the most famous of the three, however, because a poet named Henry Wadsworth Longfellow made him the star of a wildly popular poem in 1863.)

When the 700 British soldiers marched through Lexington, on the morning of April 19, on the way to Concord, they encountered 77 colonials. "Don't fire unless fired upon," said the minutemen's leader, John Parker. "But if they mean to have a war, let it begin here."

Shots were fired, and eight of the minutemen were killed. By the time the British reached Concord, however, resistance had been better organized. At a bridge near one of the entrances to the town, British soldiers were attacked, and the fighting began in earnest.

Now facing hundreds of colonists who prudently stood behind trees and in houses and fired at the redcoats, the British soldiers beat a disorganized retreat to Boston. More than 250 British were dead, missing, or wounded, compared to about 90 Americans killed or wounded. The war of words was over. The war of blood and death had begun.

Gee, Grandpa, What Else Happened?

1764: The Baptist School of Rhode Island is founded. In 1804, it becomes Brown University.

1766: A trader named Benjamin Cutbird travels far into the west, eventually going down the Mississippi to trade furs at New Orleans. His travels take place a full year before the first journey to the region by a man named Daniel Boone, but Boone gets all the publicity. No one ever makes a television series about Benjamin Cutbird.

1766: A stagecoach called "Flying Machine" travels from Camden, New Jersey, to Jersey City, a distance of 90 miles, in a record-breaking two days.

1766: The first permanent theater in the colonies, the Southwark, opens on the outskirts of Philadelphia. The first play is "Katherine and Petruchio," based on Shakespeare's "Taming of the Shrew." It's a big hit.

1769: Father Junipero Serra, a Franciscan priest, establishes the Mission San Diego de Alcala, the first of a series of Spanish outposts in what is now California, and the beginning of a half-hearted effort by Spain to strengthen its grip on its holdings in the Southwest.

1769: A newly elected Virginia legislator named Thomas Jefferson proposes a law to free the colony's slaves. The idea is rejected.

1772: In a trial known as "the Sommersett case," the chief justice of Britain's high court rules that a slave is free from the moment he touches English soil. The ruling is ignored in America.

1773: The president of Yale, Ezra Stiles, and famous clergyman Samuel Hopkins suggest setting up a colony in West Africa for freed slaves.

1775: After eight years of exploring on the western frontier, Daniel Boone establishes a settlement and fort on the Kentucky River called Boonesborough.

1775: American iron ore production has increased to the point that the colonies produce about 15 percent of the world's supply.

Chapter 6

Yankee Doodlin': 1775–1783

In This Chapter

▶ Detailing the British and American forces

▶ Working with George Washington

▶ Creating an independent country

▶ Siding with the French

▶ Impacting Loyalists and slaves

▶ Fighting a war

▶ Timeline

*O*nce blood was spilled at Lexington and Concord, war between Britain and her American colonies was inevitable, even though there were some efforts on both sides to avoid it. British leaders weren't too worried about quelling the disturbance. One English general suggested it wasn't anything that "a capable sheepherder" couldn't handle.

But there's an old saying that it's good to be good, better to be lucky, and best to be both. In this chapter, the American colonists are good when they need to be — and really lucky much of the rest of the time — and win their independence. They also lay out their reasons for doing so in a remarkable declaration.

In This Corner, the Brits . . .

The first thing the British had going for them in a fight with the Americans was a whole bunch of fighters. The English army consisted of about 50,000 men. In addition, they had the best navy in the world. They also had the money to buy stuff with which to fight, including 30,000 mercenary German soldiers. And the people the Brits were fighting, the colonists, had no regular army, no navy at all, and few real resources to assemble them.

But, as America itself was to learn about two centuries later in Vietnam, having the best army and navy doesn't always mean that much. For one thing, the British people were by no means united in a desire to rein in the colonies. When war broke out, several leading British military leaders refused to take part. Some English leaders also recognized the difficulty of winning a war by fighting on the enemy's turf thousands of miles from England, especially when the enemy was fighting for a cause.

"You may spread fire, sword, and desolation, but that will not be government," warned the Duke of Richmond. "No people can ever be made to submit to a form of government they say they will not receive."

Three factors contributed to England's ultimate downfall:

- ✔ **The British political leaders who did support the war were generally inept.** Lord North, the prime minister, was a decent bureaucrat but no leader, and basically did what King George III wanted. (The two of them looked amazingly alike, and both of them looked like bullfrogs.) And some of the British generals were nincompoops. One of them, leaving for duty in early 1777, boastfully bet a fair sum of money that he would be back in England "victorious from America by Christmas Day, 1777." (By Christmas Day, he had surrendered his entire army.)

- ✔ **Britain could not commit all its military resources to putting down the rebellion.** Because of unrest in Ireland and the potential for trouble with the French, who were still smarting from their defeats by the British in the New World, Britain had to keep many of its forces in Europe.

- ✔ **Since the Brits didn't take their opponents seriously, they had no real plan for winning the war.** That meant they fooled around long enough to give the Americans hope. And that gave the French a reason to believe the colonials might just win, so they provided the Americans with what proved to be indispensable arms, money, ships, and troops.

In This Corner, the Yanks . . .

When you look at the disadvantages the British had, and then look at the disadvantages the Americans had, it's no wonder the war took eight years — and a wonder that anyone won at all.

In the early years at least, probably only a third of Americans supported the revolution; a third, called loyalists or "Tories," after the ruling political party in England, were loyal to the crown; and the rest didn't care much one way or another.

Because they weren't professional soldiers, many of those who fought in the American army had peculiar notions of soldiering. They often elected their officers, and when the officers gave orders they didn't like, they just elected new ones. The soldiers signed up for a year or two, and when their time was up, they simply went home, no matter how the war — or even the battle — was going. At one point, the colonial army under George Washington was down to 3,000 soldiers. They also weren't big at sticking around when faced with a British bayonet charge. Many, if not most, battles ended with the Americans running away, so often that Washington once observed in exasperation that "they run from their own shadows."

Regional jealousies often surfaced when soldiers from one colony were given orders by officers from others, and there was at least one mutiny that had to be put down by other American units. The American troops were ill fed, ill housed, and so poorly clothed that in some battles colonial soldiers fought nearly naked. About 10,000 troops spent a bitter winter at Valley Forge, Pennsylvania, literally barefoot in the snow, and about 2,800 of them died. "The long and great sufferings of this army is unexampled in history," wrote the army's commander, George Washington.

They were also paid in currency called "continentals," which became so worthless the phrase "not worth a continental" became a common American saying for decades after the Revolution. Because the money was so worthless, unpatriotic American merchants often sold their goods to the British Army instead, even while American troops wore rags and starved. Others cornered the markets on goods such as food and clothing, stockpiling them until the prices rose higher and higher. Desperate army leaders then were forced to confiscate goods from private citizens to survive.

"We begin to hate the country for its neglect of us," wrote Alexander Hamilton, an aide to Washington. "The country begins to hate us for our oppressions of them."

About the best thing the Americans had going for them was a cause, because men who are fighting for something often fight better. Indeed, as the war wore on, the American soldier became more competent. By the end of 1777, an English officer wrote home that "though it was once the tone of this [English] army to treat them in a most contemptible light, they are now become a formidable enemy."

The fact that there were 13 colonies was also an advantage, because it meant there was no single nerve center for which the British could aim. They conquered New York; they took Philadelphia, and still the colonies fought on. America also had rapid growth in its favor. "Britain, at the expense of 3 million [pounds] has killed 150 Yankees in this campaign, which is 20,000 pounds a head," observed Ben Franklin early during the fighting. "During the same time, 60,000 children have been born in America."

But maybe most important, the Americans were lucky enough to choose an extraordinary leader, and smart enough to stick with him. Not only that, he looks good on the dollar bill.

Mr. Washington Goes to War

George Washington has become so mythic a figure that many people think his importance has been blown out of proportion. That's too bad, because Washington was truly one of the most remarkable people in American history.

Choosing a leader

At the time of the revolution, Washington was 43 years old. He was one of the wealthiest men in the colonies, having inherited a lot of land and money, and married into more. Although he had been a soldier in the wars against the French and Indians, Washington had never commanded more than 1,200 men at any one time. There were other colonists who had more military command experience.

But the Second Continental Congress, which had convened in May 1775 and taken over the running of the Revolution (even though no one had actually asked it to), decided on Washington as the Continental Army's commander in chief. Their choice was based more on political reasons than military ones. New England leaders figured that putting a Virginian in charge would increase the enthusiasm of the Southern colonies to fight; the Southern leaders agreed. Washington was not so sure, and said so with his characteristic modesty.

"I declare with the utmost sincerity, I do not think myself equal to the command I am honored with," he told Congress, and then refused to take any salary for the job.

Finding faults

Washington had his faults. He was not a military genius, and he lost a lot more than he won on the battlefield. In fact, his greatest military gifts were in organizing retreats and avoiding devastating losses. He had no discernable sense of humor, and was a snob when it came to mixing with what he considered the lower classes.

He also had a terrible temper. At one point he was so angry with the lack of discipline and acts of cowardice in the American army that he unsuccessfully asked Congress to increase the allowable number of lashes for punishing soldiers from 39 to 500. Once he was so angry at a subordinate, he broke his personal rule against swearing. "He swore that day till the leaves shook on the trees," recalled an admiring onlooker. "Charming! Delightful! . . . sir, on that memorable day, he swore like an angel from heaven."

Commanding a country

But Washington was a born leader, one of those men who raised spirits and expectations simply by showing up. He was tall and athletic, an expert horseman and a good dancer. He wasn't particularly handsome — his teeth were bad, and he wasn't proud of his hippopotamus ivory and gold dentures, so he seldom smiled. But he had a commanding presence, and his troops felt they could depend on him. He was also a bit of an actor. Once while reading something to his troops, he donned his spectacles, and then apologized, explaining his eyes had grown dim in the service of his country. Some of his audience wept.

He also had an indomitable spirit. His army was ragged, undisciplined, and undependable, with a staggering average desertion rate of 20 percent. His bosses in Congress were often indecisive, quarrelsome, and indifferent. But Washington simply refused to give up. Just as important, he refused the temptation to try and become a military dictator, which he might easily have done.

One of the reasons his men loved him was that Washington was personally brave, often on the frontlines of battles, and always among the last to retreat. He was also incredibly lucky: In one battle, Washington rode unexpectedly into a group of British soldiers, most of whom fired at him at short range. They all missed.

AMERICAN FACES

Benedict Arnold

It's tempting to portray Benedict Arnold as a tragic figure, a hero who took a wrong turn. Sorry. This guy was a scumbag. Yes, he was a brave and daring — and sometimes reckless — soldier. But he was also petulant, arrogant, and greedy.

Born in 1741, Arnold ran away at age 14 to fight the French and Indians, but deserted when he got bored with army life. He became a druggist, a bookseller, and an overseas merchant before forming a militia unit when the Revolution broke out. Arnold was wounded twice and played key roles in battles in New York, Connecticut, and Canada.

In 1780, Arnold entered secret negotiations with the British to turn over the fortress at West Point, New York, where he had been appointed commander. His motives have been described as ranging from revenge for being slighted by his superiors, to his ambitious wife, to the big money the Brits promised him. The plot was thwarted when a British spy was captured with papers outlining Arnold's role in the plot, and the traitor was forced to flee. In 1781, he led two brutal raids against his former comrades, and then left for England.

There he was scorned by his "employers," failed at businesses in Canada and the West Indies, and died in 1801, already reviled as one of the sleaziest figures in American history.

Above all, Washington was a survivor. He drove the British army crazy (they called him "the old fox" even though he wasn't all that old), never staying to fight battles he was losing, and never fully retreating. He bought his new country time, time to find allies and wear down the British will to keep fighting.

Declaring Independence

Despite the fact that fighting had actually started, there were many in the Continental Congress, and throughout the colonies, who were still not all that keen on breaking away completely from Britain. The radicals who were ready for a break needed a spark to light a fire under those who were still reluctant to act. They got two sparks.

Sparking an interest

The first motivator was a political blunder by the English government. The Brits needed more fighters, but English citizens did not fall all over themselves trying to sign up, since being an English soldier often meant brutal treatment, poor pay and food, and the chance someone might kill you.

So British officials hired the services of the soldiers who worked for a half-dozen German princes. Eventually, they rented about 30,000 of these soldiers, called "Hessians," after the principality of Hesse-Kassal, where many of them came from.

The Americans were outraged at this. It was one thing for the mother country and her daughters to fight, but it was a real affront for Mom to go out and hire foreigners to do her killing for her. (Eventually, about 12,000 Hessians deserted and remained in America after the war as citizens of the new country.)

The second spark came from the pen of a 38-year-old tomato-faced Englishman with a big nose. Thomas Paine arrived in the colonies in November 1774. He had been a seaman, a schoolmaster, a corset maker, and a customs officer, and wasn't too successful at any of these occupations. With the help of Benjamin Franklin, Paine got a job as editor of a Philadelphia magazine.

On Jan. 10, 1776, Paine anonymously published a little pamphlet in which he set forth his views on the need for American independence from England. He called it "Common Sense."

It was straightforward, clear, and simple in its prose. Basically, it said the king was a brute, with no reasonable mandate to rule in England, let alone America; that England was a leech feeding off the back of American enterprise; and that it was time for the colonies to stand up on their own and become a beacon of freedom for the world.

The pamphlet electrified the country. It sold 120,000 copies within a few months, and eventually sold a staggering 500,000 copies, or one for every five people in America, including slaves. (Paine never made a dime from it, having patriotically signed over royalties to Congress.) It was read by soldiers and politicians alike, and it shifted the emphasis of the fight to a struggle for total independence, and not just for a new relationship with England.

Writing history

On June 7, 1776, Congress began to deal with the issue in earnest. A delegate from Virginia, Richard Henry Lee, prepared a resolution that the colonies "are, and of a right ought to be, free and independent states." A few days later, the representatives appointed a committee of five to draft a formal declaration backing Lee's resolution, just in case Congress decided to adopt it.

The committee consisted of Benjamin Franklin, John Adams, a Connecticut lawyer named Roger Sherman, a New York iron mine owner named Robert Livingston, and a 33-year-old red-haired lawyer from Virginia named Thomas Jefferson. (The committee got on well enough, although Sherman apparently had a habit of picking his teeth, which provoked Franklin into warning that if he didn't stop it, Franklin would play his harmonica.)

Jefferson was selected to be the chief writer. Why? As Adams explained it to him when Jefferson tried to decline, "Reason first: You are a Virginian, and a Virginian ought to appear at the head of this business. Reason second: I am obnoxious, suspect, and unpopular. You are very much otherwise. Reason third: You can write 10 times better than I can." "Well," replied Jefferson, "if you are determined, I will do as well as I can."

Jefferson set to work at a portable desk he had designed himself, and a few weeks later produced a document that has come to be regarded as one of the most eloquent political statements in human history. (See for yourself in the appendixes in Part VI of this book.) True, he exaggerated some of the grievances the colonists had against the king. True, he rather hypocritically declared that "all men are created equal," ignoring the fact that he and hundreds of other Americans owned slaves, whom they certainly did not regard as having been created equal.

Wanted: Freedom asylum

"O ye that love mankind! Ye that dare oppose not only the tyranny, but the tyrant, stand forth! Every spot of the Old World is overrun with oppression. Freedom hath been hunted around the globe . . . O receive the fugitive, and prepare in time an asylum for mankind."

— Thomas Paine in "Common Sense," 1776.

Overall though, it was a magnificent document that set forth all the reasons America wanted to go its own way — and why all people who wanted to do the same thing should be allowed to do so. A bit of tinkering by Franklin and the document was presented to Congress on June 28.

At the demand of some Southern representatives, a section blaming the king for American slavery was taken out. Then, on July 2, Congress adopted the resolution submitted by Lee. "The second day of July, 1776, will be the most memorable epoch [instant of time] in the history of America," predicted John Adams. He missed it by two days, because America has chosen to remember July 4 instead. That's the day Congress formally adopted the Declaration of Independence, or as one member put it, "Mr. Jefferson's explanation of Mr. Lee's resolution."

With Independence declared, Congress now had to find a substitute form of government. Starting in August 1776, and continuing into 1777, members finally came up with something they called the Articles of Confederation. Basically, it called for a weak central government with a virtually powerless president and congress. Most powers to do key things, such as impose taxes, were left to the states. Even so, it took the states until 1781 to finish ratifying the articles, so reluctant were they to give up any of their power. It was a poor excuse for a new government, but it was a start. In the meantime, the new country was looking for a few foreign friends.

French Kissing-up

Still smarting from its defeats by Britain in a series of wars, France was more than a little happy when war broke out between her archenemy and the American colonies, and almost immediately started sending the rebels supplies and money. By the end of the war, France had provided nearly $20 million in aid of various kinds, and it's estimated as much as 90 percent of the gunpowder used by the Americans in the first part of the Revolution was supplied or paid for by the French.

Who signed what when

Although Jefferson's declaration was adopted and printed on July 4, it was signed immediately only by the Congress's president, John Hancock, and its secretary, Charles Thomson. Hancock signed it big and bold, noting cockily "There! I guess King George will be able to read that!" Most of the other 54 who signed it did so at an August 2 ceremony, although it took delegate Thomas Mckean of Delaware until 1781 to do so. Signers were so afraid of their fate if America lost the war that the names of those who signed weren't made public until 1777.

In December 1776, Congress sent Benjamin Franklin to Paris to see if he could entice even more aid from the French. Personally, he was a big hit with most of France, especially the ladies (and had such a good time that his personal wine cellar reportedly had 1,200 bottles in it by the time he left France). But King Louis XVI was not overly impressed (he is reported to have given one of Franklin's lady friends a chamber pot with Franklin's picture on the bottom), and the king took a wait-and-see attitude before committing the country to a more entangling alliance.

News of a great American victory at the Battle of Saratoga, however, caused Louis and his ministers to think the rebels just might win. On February 6, 1778, France formally recognized America as an independent nation, and agreed to a military alliance. Two different fleets and thousands of French soldiers were sent to the war, and played key roles in the deciding battles. The French entry also caused Britain to have to worry about being invaded by a French army, and to fight the French Navy in the West Indies.

Changing Lives

Before we get to who fought whom where and how it all came out, let's take a look at the war's impact on two very different sets of the American population.

Loyalists

Slightly less than one of every three white colonists didn't side with the Revolution and remained loyal to the crown. Many, but by no means all, were from the aristocracy or had jobs they owed to the British government. Some of these Loyalists, or Tories, kept quiet about their allegiances, but many acted as spies or guides for the British forces. As many as 30,000 actually fought against their rebel neighbors, and some battles were purely American versus American affairs. One of the Tories, Banastre Tarleton, rose to a major command in the British Army and was feared and hated for his savagery and reputation for executing prisoners.

In some areas, such as New York City and parts of North and South Carolina, Loyalists were dominant, but in areas where they weren't, they paid a heavy price for their loyalty. Their taxes were sometimes doubled, their property trashed, and their businesses shunned.

When the war ended, things got even worse. A new verse was added to "Yankee Doodle" by victorious rebels: "Now Tories all what can you say / Come — is this not a griper? / That while your hopes are drained away / 'Tis you must pay the piper." Tory property was confiscated, and as many as 80,000 Loyalists eventually left America for Canada, England, and the West Indies.

Patriots with accents

There were a whole lot of unemployed soldiers in Europe at the time of the American Revolution, and many of them came to America looking for an officer's rank in the rebel army and a piece of the action. Some of them turned out to be valuable additions: Baron Johann de Kalb, a German soldier of fortune who was an able commander and was killed at the Battle of Camden; Count Casimir Pulaski, a Polish cavalryman who was killed at the Battle of Savannah; and Baron Frederick Von Stueben, a Prussian army expert who helped Washington reorganize the army into more efficient fighting units and taught American soldiers what a bayonet was for.

But the most famous was a 19-year-old French aristocrat named Marie Joseph Paul, the Marquis de Lafayette. Lafayette was a godsend to the Americans. He not only contributed about $200,000 of his own money to the cause, but helped convince the French government to aid America and proved to be an able battlefield leader and one of Washington's most trusted aides. After the war, Lafayette helped smooth over sometimes-rocky relations between France and America and remained America's favorite Frenchman for decades.

Slaves

One of the thorniest, and most embarrassing, problems Congress was confronted with during the Revolutionary War was what to do about slaves. At first, Congress declared that no Africans, freed or not, could fight in the Continental Army. But when Washington pointed out they might end up fighting for the British, Congress relented and allowed freed slaves to enlist.

Southern states were not anxious to put guns in the hands of those they held in bondage, while the British were offering them freedom if they turned on their masters. More than a few American leaders were also red-faced about fighting for freedom while owning slaves — a hypocrisy not lost on their critics. "How is it that we hear the loudest yelps for liberty among the drivers of Negroes?" sneered the British writer Dr. Samuel Johnson.

In the end, some slaves fought for the American cause, and some fled to the British. The issue of slavery, meanwhile, grew as a divisive issue between North and South. In most of the Northern states during the war, the slave trade was outlawed. In the South, the number of slaves actually grew, mostly because of the birthrates among slaves already here. And slavery spread as Southerners moved west, into Kentucky and Tennessee.

Winning a War

Okay, here's pretty much how the actual fighting unfolded: The Americans started off pretty promisingly — winning an early battle in New York and holding their own at a big battle outside Boston — mostly because the British were slow to recognize they had a real war on their hands. But then the Americans launched an invasion of Canada, which proved to be a really bad idea. Shortly after the Canada failure, Washington got his tail kicked in New York, and escaped total disaster only through great luck.

But Washington learned a valuable lesson, which was that he could not possibly win by fighting the British in a series of open-field, European-style major battles. The trick, the Continental Army learned, was to be a moving target. "We fight, get beat, rise, and fight again," noted General Nathanael Greene.

Washington did win a couple of smaller victories, which was great for morale, but he also suffered through a couple of hideous winters at Valley Forge, Pennsylvania, and Morristown, New Jersey, which was bad for morale.

But the English made a series of tactical blunders and lost an entire army in upstate New York. Then they turned their attentions to the South, made more blunders, and lost another entire army in Virginia. Having apparently run out of mistakes, they quit, and America won. Here are the highlights of 10 key battles or campaigns in the American Revolution (see Figure 6-1):

Fort Ticonderoga

Less than a month after the first shots at Lexington and Concord, American troops under Vermont frontiersman Ethan Allen surprised and captured a British fort on the shores of Lake Champlain in New York. The fort wasn't all that big a deal, but the Yanks also captured 60 cannon and mortars, which they eventually used to drive the British out of Boston. The victory was also a big confidence booster for the fledgling American fighters.

Bunker Hill

This battle (see Figure 6-2), on June 17, 1775, was actually fought on Breed's Hill, which is next to Bunker Hill, just outside Boston. About 1,400 Americans held the hill. About 2,500 British troops attacked them in a frontal assault rather than go around and surround them. "Don't fire until you see the whites of their eyes," instructed American leader Israel Putnam. "Then, shoot low." The Brits won, after two charges, but they paid a heavy toll. About 1,000, or 40 percent, of their troops were killed or wounded, while the Americans suffered about 400 killed or wounded. The carnage shook British commander William Howe so much he became overly cautious and conservative in future battles.

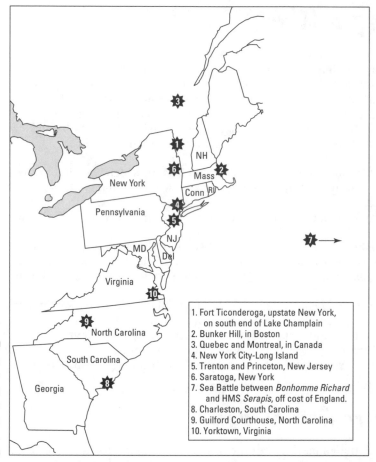

1. Fort Ticonderoga, upstate New York, on south end of Lake Champlain
2. Bunker Hill, in Boston
3. Quebec and Montreal, in Canada
4. New York City-Long Island
5. Trenton and Princeton, New Jersey
6. Saratoga, New York
7. Sea Battle between *Bonhomme Richard* and HMS *Serapis*, off cost of England.
8. Charleston, South Carolina
9. Guilford Courthouse, North Carolina
10. Yorktown, Virginia

Figure 6-1:
Ten key battles of the American Revolution.

Figure 6-2:
The Battle of Bunker Hill.

BATTLE OF BUNKER HILL.

The Canada Campaign

In late December of 1775, American leaders Richard Montgomery and Benedict Arnold launched an invasion of Canada. The Yanks thought the Canadians wouldn't put up much of a fight and after being defeated would join the American cause. Bad thought. Americans lost battles at Quebec and Montreal and were forced to retreat. The loss left Canada firmly in British hands, and gave the Brits a good base from which to launch attacks on New York and New England.

New York

In mid-1776, Washington and his entire army of about 18,000 men moved to the area around New York City, hoping to hem in and defeat a British army of about 25,000. But many of the American troops were raw recruits and panicked and ran in a series of battles in the area. By the fall, it was Washington who was nearly trapped. Under protection of a heavy fog that materialized at just the right time, the American army slipped away into New Jersey, and then to Pennsylvania. It was a major defeat for the American army, but it could have been a lot worse.

Trenton and Princeton

Most eighteenth-century war manuals called for sort of a timeout during the winter months, but Washington apparently skipped that chapter. Smarting from about six months of running away, he moved his army across the ice-choked Delaware River on Christmas Eve, 1776, and surprised a Hessian brigade in Trenton, New Jersey. Actually, it shouldn't have been a surprise at all, since a spy had seen the American troops and sent a note to warn the German commander, Colonel Johann Rall. But Rall was playing cards at the time and slipped the note in his pocket without reading it. The result was that Washington captured more than 900 Hessian troops and 1,200 weapons without losing a single man. He then followed it up with a victory over the British a few days later at Princeton, New Jersey. The victories were smashing morale boosters for the Yanks. "The [local] inhabitants manifested very different feelings towards us from those manifested before," an American soldier wrote after the battles, "and were now ready to take up arms against the British."

Saratoga

In 1777, British General "Gentleman Johnny" Burgoyne proposed to lead a British army into New York and New England from Canada, while the British army already in New York City sailed down to capture Philadelphia. It turned out to be a disaster for the Brits. Burgoyne had no concept of a march through enemy-infested wilderness and took along officers' wives and children. Continually harassed by American troops and running low on food and supplies, Burgoyne's army lost two battles near Saratoga. On October 17, 1777, the British Army of nearly 6,000 men surrendered. News of the American victory helped convince France to enter the war on the American side.

Bonhomme Richard versus Serapis

On September 23, 1779, a U.S. Navy ship named the *Bonhomme Richard* took on the British warship *Serapis* off the coast of England. The American captain, John Paul Jones, saw two of his major guns explode on the first discharge. Undismayed, he pulled alongside the *Serapis* and the two ships pounded each other for more than two hours. At one point, when asked if he would surrender, Jones replied, "I have not yet begun to fight!" Finally, faced with the arrival of another American ship, the *Serapis* surrendered. Jones's own ship was so badly damaged it had to be abandoned, and he transferred his flag to the British ship. But the victory was the greatest single naval feat of the war and shook British confidence in its navy.

Charleston

This was the worst American defeat of the war, which is saying something. In the spring of 1780, about 8,500 British and Loyalist troops and 14 ships surrounded the city, trapping an American army under the command of General Benjamin Lincoln. On May 12, Lincoln surrendered his entire army of 5,500 men, along with huge amounts of weapons.

Guilford Courthouse

Most of the war in the South consisted of British troops beating American troops, and then chasing them, and then beating them again. In December 1780, Congress finally put a competent general in charge of the American forces in the South while Washington was fighting in the North. He was 38-year-old Nathanael Greene, who was probably the only American general to consistently out-strategize his opposition. After a couple of victories at the battles of Cowpens and Eutaw Springs, Greene faced British General Charles Cornwallis at Guilford Courthouse, North Carolina. The British won what was one of the most bitter and bloody battles of the war, but suffered almost 30 percent casualties, while Greene's losses were light. Cornwallis was forced to withdraw out of the Carolinas and back to Virginia. He took his troops to Yorktown.

Yorktown

Washington had been trying for months to coordinate his own troops with the French troops and ships that were supposedly ready to aid the American cause. On top of that, Congress had failed to supply him with desperately needed reinforcements and supplies.

Finally, in May 1781, things began to fall into place with his French allies. Together with two French fleets, French and American armies converged on Yorktown and hemmed in the British army under Cornwallis. The British, meanwhile, mishandled two fleets of their own, and were unable to come to Cornwallis' rescue. On October 19, 1781, Cornwallis surrendered his entire army of 8,000 men. The British band played a tune called "The World Turned Upside Down," and a band hired by the French played "Yankee Doodle." In London, when Lord North, the British prime minister, heard the news, he cried out "O God! It is all over!"

Actually, it wasn't over for more than a year. The British army still held New York, and there were occasional small battles until the formal peace treaty was signed on February 3, 1783.

The British were gracious losers, mainly because they wanted to drive a wedge between America and France. They gave up rights to all the land from the Atlantic Coast to the Mississippi River, and from Canada to Florida, which was far more than the Americans actually controlled. In return, the Americans promised to treat the Loyalists in their midst fairly and set up fair rules so that English creditors could collect pre-war debts. (Neither of those promises was kept.)

American independence had been won. The question now was what to do with it.

Gee, Grandpa, What Else Happened?

September 22, 1776: A 21-year-old Connecticut schoolteacher named Nathan Hale is hanged as a spy for monitoring British troop movements in New York. His last words are a rallying cry for Americans, even though there is no real evidence he ever said them: "I only regret that I have but one life to lose for my country."

October 9, 1776: Spanish missionaries establish a mission on a large bay in Northern California and call it the Mission San Francisco de Asis. The nearby settlement is called Yerba Buena until 1847, when the name is changed to San Francisco.

January 1777: George Washington is granted permission by Congress to inoculate his troops against smallpox. In some cases, inoculation only spreads the disease further.

May 20, 1777: The Cherokee Indians sign a treaty giving up all of their territory in South Carolina.

June 14, 1777: Congress enacts a bill that creates a "United States flag," displaying 13 stars and 13 alternating red and white stripes. At first, a star and stripe is added for each new state, but it's pretty clear after two more states are added that the flag is going to be too big. So they drop the two extra stripes and just add stars.

May 4, 1780: The American Academy of Arts and Sciences is founded in Boston.

1781: Spanish settlers establish a village in California called El Pueblo de Nuestra Señora la Reina de los Angeles de Pociuncula. It's later shortened to "L.A."

1781: A Virginia planter named Charles Lynch starts his own court to deal with lawbreakers. Punishments usually consist of floggings, but some of those convicted are hanged, or "lynched."

May 30, 1783: In Philadelphia, the *Pennsylvania Evening Post* becomes the first daily newspaper in America.

July 8, 1783: The Massachusetts Supreme Court declares the abolition of slavery within the state. By December, all northern states have banned the importation of slaves.

Chapter 7

Blueprints and Birth Pains: 1783–1800

In This Chapter

▶ Bringing order to the colonies

▶ Electing the first president

▶ Establishing an economy

▶ Increasing troubles at home and overseas

▶ Timeline

After winning its independence from Britain, the United States felt a little like a kid who just moved out of his parents' house and wasn't sure what step comes next in growing up. The country had no real government, no sound financing system, and no true foreign friends.

Fortunately, it did have a group of extraordinary individuals — some of whom had helped lead it through the Revolution — who were willing to try and find a form of government that would fit. Putting aside most of their personal differences and aspirations (at least at first), they came up with a system of governing the new country that has become a true wonder of the world.

Making the Rules

America limped through the Revolutionary War guided by the Continental Congress, a group of men selected by colonial legislatures. The Congress, in turn, came up with something called the Articles of Confederation.

Drafted in 1777 but not ratified by all the states until 1781, the Articles were based on the idea that the individual states would be friendly with each other and cooperate when it was in their mutual interest. Each state had one vote in Congress, and it took nine of the 13 states to ratify any decision.

Hoisting a few

They may have been learning some things about government, but most of the Founding Fathers already knew how to bend their elbows. In 1795, it was estimated the average American male over the age of 15 drank 34 gallons of beer and cider, five gallons of distilled spirits, and a gallon of wine every year. Sixty distilleries sprang up during the Revolutionary War in Massachusetts alone. And in a Kentucky county in 1789, residents came up with a corn whiskey that used water flavored by the limestone rocks it flowed over and the charred oak barrels it was aged in. They named it after their county — Bourbon.

Congress ran matters of war and peace, operated the post office, coined money, and dealt with American Indians when the states didn't want to. It had no power to tax or to establish a federal judicial system, and no real power to make the individual states pay attention to its legal authority to make postal, coin, or war-and-peace decisions.

It wasn't an awful system, but it almost guaranteed a continual stream of squabbles among the states. Making things worse were schemes by agents of Spain, France, and England. They tried to get Americans who lived in the western parts of the new country to break away and start their own empires. War hero Ethan Allen, for example, met with British agents to discuss making his beloved Vermont a British province, and narrowly escaped being tried for treason.

Still, at least two good bits of legislation came out of the loose-knit confederation. The first was the Land Ordinance of 1785. It set up the way land owned by the federal government — which basically was territory won from Britain that wasn't claimed by one of the states — would be divided and sold. It called for "townships" to be divided into one square mile, or 640 acres, and sold at public auction. Part of the revenue went to the establishment of public schools.

The second was called the Northwest Ordinance, in 1787. It stated that as new states were admitted to the country, they would be equal in every way to the original 13. It also banned slavery in the new territories, although this was later changed. Both laws were good starts to stabilizing the new country. But ongoing troubles in trying to regulate commerce between the states and in trying to raise money for the federal government still plagued the nation, especially since every state had its own currency and assigned it its own value.

Going back to Philly

James Madison was the first to show up. He was a 36-year-old scholar and politician from Virginia, so frail he could not serve in the army during the Revolution. But he had come to Philadelphia in May of 1787 to help draft a new constitution for the country, and he had so many ideas on the subject he couldn't wait to get started.

Not everyone else was in such a hurry. Although the constitutional convention was supposed to begin May 15, it wasn't until May 25 that enough of the delegates chosen by the state legislatures showed up to have a quorum. Rhode Island never did send anyone.

Eventually, 55 delegates took part. Notable by their absence were some of the leading figures of the recent rebellion against England: Thomas Jefferson was in France, Tom Paine in England, Sam Adams and John Hancock weren't selected to go, and Patrick Henry refused.

But those who did show up were hardly second-stringers. George Washington was there and was unanimously selected the convention's president. Benjamin Franklin, at 81 the oldest delegate, was there. Madison and a handsome 32-year-old self-made success story from New York named Alexander Hamilton were the true stars of the group.

Half of the group were lawyers and 29 were college-educated. Many were wealthy and thus had a bigger-than-most stake in straightening out the country's financial mess. Their average age was 42.

They met in long and highly secret sessions, with armed guards at the doors. Their reasoning was that their task was so difficult, any leaks about what they were doing would only increase outside pressures. They studied other forms of government; they debated. And after 17 weeks, on September 17, 1787, they voted 39 to 3, with 13 absent, their approval of a 10-page document that became the United States Constitution (see Appendix A for a reprint of the Preamble to the Constitution). Then most of them adjourned to a local tavern and hoisted a few.

IN THEIR WORDS
"Four score and seven..."

Stand up and be heard. . . .

"A standing army is like an erect penis — an excellent assurance of domestic tranquility, but a dangerous temptation to foreign adventure."

— Elbridge Gerry, a convention delegate from Massachusetts, arguing against a provision that would allow for a full-time military organization.

The document the delegates created was a masterpiece of compromises. Big states gained more clout when it was decided representation in the House of Representatives would be based on population, while small states got protection from being bullied when it was decided each state would have the same number of members (two) in the Senate. The South won the right to count slaves as three-fifths of a person when determining population for representation in the House; the North got a promise that the slave trade would end for good in 1807. Actually, the South didn't mind this all that much, since it didn't mean slavery itself would end, just the practice of importing more slaves from overseas. In fact, it ensured that the value of slaves already here would increase, thus making their owners richer.

The Constitution gave Congress the power to regulate commerce between states as well as with foreign nations and to pass laws with a simple majority of its members. It gave the presidency a powerful role. It created a federal judicial system, with the Supreme Court at the top. And it left the individual states with a fair amount of independence to make their own laws on most things. No one thought it was perfect, but most of the delegates thought it was a pretty good blueprint from which to build.

While the last members of the convention were signing the document, Franklin pointed to a sun painted on the chair in which Washington was sitting. "I have often . . . looked at that behind the president, without being able to tell whether it was rising or setting," he said. "But now, at length, I have the happiness to know that it is a rising, and not a setting sun."

But they still had to sell the blueprint to the rest of the country.

Selling it

The convention submitted its work to the Congress that was still laboring under the old Articles of Confederation, and Congress accepted it after three days of sometimes-intense debate. But because of the enormity of the issue, Congress also didn't want to be totally responsible if things went wrong (proving that some things never change).

So Congress sent the proposal to the states for ratification. Each state was to elect delegates who would consider the proposed Constitution, and when nine states had approved it, it would become the law of the land.

It was a gamble, because if any of the big states — Virginia, New York, Massachusetts, or Pennsylvania — rejected it and went its own way, the whole deal might fall apart. In addition, a lot of people who hadn't thought much about the need for a central government (which was probably the majority of Americans) weren't sold on the idea at all. But the idea of letting "ordinary" people have a say (actually, only about one-fourth of the population was eligible to vote) did allow a great deal of spirited debate on it. And that allowed pro-Constitution forces a chance to make their case.

The Bill of Rights

The first 10 amendments to the Constitution were added mainly because a lot of Americans believed in the saying "get it in writing." The drafters of the original Constitution didn't spell out specific rights mainly because they didn't think it was necessary. The document defined the powers of Congress, and it was assumed everything left over belonged to individuals and the states.

But some states insisted the specific rights be spelled out as soon as possible after the Constitution was ratified. So James Madison, at the urging of Thomas Jefferson, came up with a list of 19 amendments, 10 of which were ratified by 11 of the states in 1791. The two amendments left out had to do with the number of members of the House of Representatives and prohibiting Congress from setting its own salaries. And for some reason, Connecticut and Georgia didn't get around to ratifying the remaining 10 until 1941. See Appendix B for the list of the 10 amendments that made it.

They did. In a brilliant series of 85 newspaper essays that became known as the Federalist Papers, Hamilton, Madison, and John Jay argued eloquently for adoption of the Constitution. Much more important was the public support of the two most popular men in America, Franklin and Washington. Anti-Constitution forces also made powerful public arguments, but their efforts were not as well organized and lacked star appeal.

The first five states to ratify did so by January 1788. The following month, Massachusetts agreed — but only on the condition that a list of specific individual rights be added to the Constitution as soon as possible (see sidebar "The Bill of Rights"). By July, all but North Carolina and Rhode Island had ratified it, and they fell in line by May 1790.

"Our constitution is in actual operation," Franklin wrote, "and everything appears to promise that it will last. But in this world, nothing can be certain but death and taxes."

Dishing Up Politics, American Style

Now that it had rules, America needed a president, and the choice was a no-brainer. George Washington was unanimously elected in April 1789 by the Electoral College, which had been established by the Constitution and was composed of men elected either by popular vote or by state legislatures. Washington set out from his home in Virginia for the temporary capital at New York (which soon moved to Philadelphia, where it stayed until the federal district that is now Washington D.C. was completed in 1800). Every-where he went, Washington was greeted by parades and cheering crowds.

Washington was not a great politician, although he did know enough to buy 47 gallons of beer, 35 gallons of wine, and three barrels of rum for potential voters in his first campaign for the Virginia legislature. He wasn't a good public speaker and he wasn't a great innovator.

But he was perfect for the new country. He was enormously popular with the public, even those who didn't like his policies. Because of that, other political leaders were wise to defer to him. (At least publicly: Behind his back, John Adams referred to Washington as "Old Muttonhead," and Alexander Hamilton called him "the Great Booby.")

Washington was also good at assembling competent people around him and playing to their strengths while ignoring their faults. And he assembled a heck of a group: Adams was his vice president, Hamilton his treasurer, Thomas Jefferson his secretary of state, old Revolutionary War buddy Henry Knox his secretary of war, and sharp-tongued Edmund Randolph of Virginia his attorney general.

But it wasn't exactly one big happy family. Hamilton and Adams disliked each other even though they shared many of the same political views — Adams once referred to Hamilton as "the bastard brat of a Scotch peddler." And Jefferson and Hamilton were different in a host of ways. Hamilton was short, but impeccable in his dress and manners. Jefferson was tall, and often looked like an unmade bed. Hamilton grew up poor in New York and was illegitimate; Jefferson grew up wealthy in a leading family in Virginia. Hamilton had a deeply abiding distrust of the common man and a deep affection for wealth. Jefferson disliked the upper classes and professed that the farmer was Nature's greatest creation. And while Jefferson was a relatively pleasant guy to be around, Hamilton could be arrogant and snotty.

Given their differences, it shouldn't be surprising the two men were at opposite ends of the political spectrum. And given their abilities and stature, it shouldn't be surprising that people who thought the same way began to form political parties around them. At the time, most politicians at least publicly repudiated the idea of political parties. "If I could not go to heaven but with a [political] party," Jefferson said, "I would not go at all." But people being people, and politicians being politicians, the formation of parties revolving around a certain philosophy of governing was probably inevitable.

The Hamiltonians were called Federalists. In essence, they supported a strong central government, a powerful central bank, government support of business, a loose interpretation of the Constitution, and restrictions on public speech and the press. They opposed the expansion of democratic elections and were generally pro-British when it came to foreign affairs. "Those who own the country," said Federalist John Jay, "ought to govern it."

The Jeffersonians were first called Democratic Republicans, then just Republicans. They favored more power to individual states and state-chartered banks, no special favors for business, a strict reading of the Constitution, giving more people the vote and relatively free speech and a free press. They were generally pro-French. It's too simplistic to say today's Republicans are yesterday's Federalists and today's Democrats are descended from Jefferson's party. Hamilton, for example, supported big federal government programs, which today would make him more of a Democrat, while Jefferson wanted to minimize government, which sounds like the modern Republican. But the Federalists and Republicans were the forerunners of the two-party system that America has pretty much stuck with throughout its history.

By 1796, Washington had had enough of fathering a country. He declined a third term and went home to his plantation in Mt. Vernon, Virginia. Hamilton, who was born in St. Croix and therefore under the Constitution could not be president, hoped to elect someone he could control, and backed a guy named Thomas Pinckney of South Carolina, who was Washington's minister to England. But his plans were thwarted and Vice President John Adams won.

Jefferson was the Republican candidate, and since he came in second, he became vice president, as per the Constitution. (It soon became clear that this wasn't a real good idea. So in 1804, the Constitution was amended to allow candidates to run for either president or vice president, but not both.)

AMERICAN FACES

Noah Webster

While others were creating governments and political parties, Noah Webster was helping to create something just as vital: the American language. Born in 1758 in Connecticut and descended from Puritan governors, Webster graduated from Yale and took up the study of law. But his interests lay in other directions. As a schoolteacher, Webster saw the need for a commonality of language for the new country. He put together a grammar book, a reader, and a spelling primer. The speller became a best seller for decades and helped standardize spelling and pronunciation in the United States. Webster was also a successful lecturer and writer on subjects from politics to meteorology and published a pro-Federalist party magazine. But his name has become synonymous with a different kind of reading material. Webster published his first dictionary in 1806, containing new words such as "caucus," "belittle," and "sot." It was followed by a massive two-volume version in 1828 and a third in 1840 — with 12,000 words and 30,000 definitions that had never appeared in an English-language dictionary before.

"America must be as independent in literature as she is in politics," Webster wrote, "as famous for arts as for arms." He did his part to make it so.

Raising the Dough

Every country needs a sound financial plan (at least every successful country does) and it fell to Hamilton to devise one for America.

The first thing he had to do was establish the new nation's credit. To do that, he had to clean up its existing debts, such as the $54 million the federal government owed foreign and domestic creditors. Hamilton proposed the debt be paid off in full, rather than at a discount as creditors had feared. Hamilton argued that if America didn't make good on what it already owed, no one would want to lend it money in the future.

In addition, he proposed that the federal government also pay off about $21 million in debts the individual states had run up. The old debts would be paid off by issuing bonds. But states like Virginia, which had paid off much of its Revolutionary War debts, were peeved at the thought of the federal government picking up other states' tabs and then sticking all U.S. residents with the bill. So they engaged in a little horse-trading. Virginia withdrew its objections to the plan, and in return Hamilton and the Washington Administration agreed to locate the new federal district next door to Virginia on the Potomac. Whatever advantage Virginia thought that would give it has certainly evaporated by now.

Many members of Congress supported Hamilton's plan to pay off the debts dollar for dollar, especially because many of them either held the old bonds or had snapped them up for next to nothing and stood to make enormous profits. Hamilton himself was accused of using his office to make money off the bonds, but if he was guilty, he didn't do a very good job, since he died broke.

To raise money to help pay off the bonds, the federal government established taxes, called tariffs, on goods imported into the United States. It also slapped a tax of seven cents a gallon on whiskey, which was pretty steep since whiskey in many of the Southern and Western states sold for only 25 cents a gallon.

Finally, Hamilton proposed a nationally chartered bank that would print paper money backed by the federal government, and in which the government would be the minority stockholder and deposit its revenues. To be located in Philadelphia, the bank would be chartered for 21 years. Jefferson howled that the whole idea would cripple state banks and was unconstitutional, but Hamilton, with the backing of Washington, prevailed. The bank's stock sold out within four hours after going on sale.

Hamilton's plan worked, in large part because the American economy kicked into high gear in the 1790s. Another war between France and England helped increase America's share of the world market; trade in the West Indies that had been stunted by the Revolutionary War was revived, and industry, particularly in the North, began to develop.

America, the new kid on the block, now had some change in its pockets.

Earning Respect

A government is only as good as the respect it commands for its citizens, and respect for the new U.S. government wasn't universal. Whiskey makers and people who thought some politicians were jerks — and said so publicly — were among the groups whose respect the new government had to earn.

The Whiskey Rebellion

This is how important whiskey was on the American Frontier: They often used it in place of cash for commercial transactions. It was also the cheapest way to market some of the surplus corn crop. So it's easy to understand why they got a little upset when the fledgling federal government announced it was slapping what amounted to a 25 percent tax on the drink.

Distillers in Western Pennsylvania organized a revolt in 1794, roughing up tax collectors and threatening distilleries that tried to pay the tax. When the state's governor refused to intervene for fear of losing votes, President Washington himself led a massive force of about 13,000 men — a larger army than he had during most of the Revolutionary War — and the rebels scattered.

The short-lived rebellion didn't amount to much, but it provided an early test of the federal government's willingness to enforce federal laws.

Speak no evil

American newspapers had been used as a political weapon almost as long as there had been American newspapers. But the rise of the two-party system in the 1790s greatly increased their use and their sting. Pro-Jefferson editors such as Phillip Freneau and Benjamin Bache squared off against pro-Hamilton scribes such as John Fenno and William Cobbett.

These were nasty fellows with a quill in their hands. Bache once wrote "if ever a nation was debauched by a man, the American nation has been debauched by Washington," and Cobbett opined that America would only be truly free "when Jefferson's head will be rotting cheek-to-jowl with that of some toil-killed Negro slave."

By 1798, the Federalist-controlled Congress had had enough. It narrowly approved the Alien and Sedition Acts. The acts extended the naturalization period from 5 to 14 years, to keep out the foreign riff-raff. And they also made it a crime to publish "any false, scandalous and malicious writing" about the president, Congress, or the government in general.

Hundreds of individuals were indicted under the Sedition Act, but only 10 — all of them Republicans — were convicted. Among them was Congressman Matthew Lyon of Vermont, who had already gained a reputation of sorts by spitting in the face of Federalist Congressman Roger Griswold on the floor of Congress (see Figure 7-1). Lyon was sentenced to four months in jail for writing of President Adams's "unbounded thirst for ridiculous pomp, foolish adulation and selfish avarice." Lyon was re-elected to Congress while in jail.

Partly because its application was so one-sided, the Sedition Act's popularity quickly waned and in the end probably hurt the Federalist cause much more than it helped. The act expired on March 3, 1801, a day before Republican Jefferson assumed the presidency. It was not renewed, and American politicians generally learned it was better to develop a thick hide when it came to the press than to try and slap a muzzle on the First Amendment.

Figure 7-1:
Satirical cartoon of Matthew Lyon fighting Roger Griswold in Congress.

Finding Foreign Friction

Most Americans applauded when the French Revolution began in 1789 and even continued to support it when the revolution turned into the Reign of Terror and thousands of French heads were removed by the guillotine. After all, weren't the French merely doing what America had just done?

But when the revolt spread to once again engulf Europe in war, more sober Americans started to worry. The Federalists, led by Hamilton, didn't want to take the French side against the English. For one thing, they detested the excesses of the French "mobocracy." For another, they realized that England was America's best customer and most of the revenues from tariffs paid on imports came from English ships.

The Jefferson-led Republicans, on the other hand, didn't want to side with the English. The French had backed us in our revolution, they reasoned, and we should do the same.

But America's first two presidents, Washington and Adams, didn't want to side with anyone. Both men saw that the longer America could stay out of the European mess, the stronger the country would become, and thus be able to control its own destiny rather that rely on the fortunes of an alliance.

It wasn't easy staying neutral. British naval ships routinely stopped American merchant ships and forced American sailors into service aboard British ships, a practice called "impressments." French ships also attacked American merchants with England-bound cargoes.

But luck and skillful negotiating kept America out of the Anglo-Franco fracas for a generation. In 1794, Washington sent diplomat John Jay to England. Jay eventually negotiated a treaty with the British in which they agreed to give up their forts in the American Northwest and pay for damages caused by seizures of American ships. But the British did not agree to stop "impressing" American sailors, and Jay agreed the U.S. would repay pre-Revolutionary War debts it still owed. The Jay treaty was greeted with widespread howls of rage in America, but it cooled things down with the British for more than a decade.

The Jay treaty also angered the French, who stepped up their attacks on U.S. ships. In 1797, President Adams sent U.S. envoys to Paris to meet with the French foreign minister, Charles Talleyrand. But before they could, three go-betweens known publicly only as "X, Y, and Z" tried to get a $250,000 bribe from the Americans just for the chance to meet with Talleyrand. The U.S. envoys told X, Y, and Z to stick it and returned home.

So for about two years, the two countries waged an undeclared war on the seas. The newly created U.S. Navy captured about 80 French ships, and the French continued to prey on American vessels. Then Adams did a remarkable thing. Ignoring the fact that war fever was raging and declaring war on France could help him win a second term as president, Adams sent another peace team back to Paris in 1800. This time, the two countries made a deal. Adams kept the U.S. out of war. He also lost reelection to the presidency and sealed the doom of the Federalist Party in doing so.

Gee, Grandpa, What Else Happened?

1783: Father Junipero Serra produces the first wine made in America, at the mission at San Juan Capistrano in California, from grape cuttings brought over from Spain.

Jan. 26, 1784: Benjamin Franklin announces his opposition to the bald eagle as the national symbol, asserting that "the turkey is a much more respectable bird, and withal a true native of America."

John Jay

He was not your average revolutionary. Jay was born into a wealthy New York family in 1745. He became a lawyer and developed a lucrative law practice, hobnobbing with New York's very pro-British aristocracy.

But when the Revolution began, Jay became one of the busiest of American statesmen. Over the course of his career, he: served in both Continental Congresses, was chief justice of the New York Supreme Court, helped negotiate the peace treaty with the British in 1783, negotiated the 1794 treaty with England that avoided war, was the first chief justice of the U.S. Supreme Court, served as the new country's first foreign secretary before cabinet posts were created, was governor of New York for two terms, and helped abolish slavery in that state.

Although an ardent Federalist, Jay was valued by leaders of both parties for his intelligence, diplomatic skills, and willingness to take the heat on unpopular decisions. And his most remarkable accomplishment might have been his ability to do all that and still fit in 28 years of retirement before he died in 1829.

1785: A passenger coach trip between Boston and New York takes an average of 6 days, with 18 hours a day spent in the coach.

1786: The first American performance of "Hamlet" takes place in New York City.

Sept. 24, 1789: Congress establishes a framework for the Federal judiciary, consisting of the Supreme Court, three circuit courts, and 13 district courts.

April 21, 1790: Benjamin Franklin's funeral attracts a staggering 20,000 mourners. Bald eagles gloat; turkeys weep.

May 17, 1792: A group of 24 merchants and bankers start a stock exchange in New York City. They do most of their business under a tree outside the building at 68 Wall Street.

March 8, 1796: The U.S. Supreme Court hands down its first ruling on the constitutionality of a congressional act, in *Hylton v. United States,* a case involving a tax on carriages.

June 26, 1797: A New Jersey inventor named Charles Newbold receives a patent for a cast-iron plow. But farmers fear the iron will poison the soil and don't buy it.

Dec. 14, 1799: George Washington dies. He tells his physician: "I die hard, but I am not afraid to go."

Part II
Growing Pains

The 5th Wave   By Rich Tennant

"Mr. President, the Confederate Army is massing in Virginia, several more of our officers have defected to the South, oh, and bad news — Mrs. Lincoln's redesigned tea service won't be here until Friday."

In this part . . .

As the nineteenth century began, America had cut its umbilical cord with Mother England and was standing — somewhat shakily — on its own two feet. As the nineteenth century ended, the country was ready to enter adulthood.

But it didn't have an easy adolescence. It took several wars with foreign countries, one war with itself, some leaders who were truly great, and some who were truly awful.

In this part, America stretches itself from one ocean to another, tests its commitment to the ideals on which it established its government, and begins to find its place in the world.

Call it *Manifest Destiny*.

Chapter 8

"Long Tom" Becomes President: 1800–1809

In This Chapter

▶ Electing Thomas Jefferson

▶ Creating the courts

▶ Getting the deal of the century — the Louisiana Purchase

▶ Slowing down piracy and dealing with an embargo

▶ Timeline

The turn of the century brought with it what has been called "the Revolution of 1800." The term, first used by Thomas Jefferson, refers to the fact that for the first time in the young country's history, America saw one political party give up power to another.

In this chapter, we see how well it worked, look at the development of the U.S. Supreme Court in the scheme of things, sit in on a land sale and a duel, fight some pirates, and watch a major president make a major blunder.

Jefferson Gets a Job

President John F. Kennedy once hosted a dinner party at the White House and invited a guest list so impressive he joked it was the finest group of genius and talent to sit at the table "since Thomas Jefferson dined alone."

There was as much truth as humor in Kennedy's quip. A tall, loose-limbed man who was said to amble more than walk and who was thus nicknamed "Long Tom," Jefferson was a statesman, a writer, an inventor, a farmer, an architect, a musician, a scientist, and a philosopher.

Thus it may not be surprising that he was also a bundle of contradictions: Jefferson was an idealist who could also bend the rules when he needed to accomplish something; a slave owner who hated slavery; a man who believed Africans were naturally inferior, yet for years had one of his slaves as his mistress; a believer in sticking to the letter of the Constitution, who ignored it on at least one major issue during his presidency; a guy who preached frugality for the country and who died $100,000 in debt.

But his contradictory nature also made Jefferson flexible, and flexibility in a president can be a very valuable asset. In addition, Jefferson, much more than his predecessors George Washington and John Adams, was a true man of the people. He did away with the imperial trappings that had built up around the office, sometimes greeting visitors to the White House in his robe and slippers. That kind of informality added to the popularity he already enjoyed as author of the Declaration of Independence.

But public popularity almost didn't mean doodly squat in the election of 1800, because of the screwy way the drafters of the Constitution had set up the presidential election process. Republican Jefferson received the votes of 73 members of the Electoral College to the 65 votes received by Federalist incumbent John Adams. But the electors were required by the Constitution to list two names (with the second-highest vote-getter becoming vice president). So the 73 electors who voted for Jefferson also listed a New York politician named Aaron Burr. That meant it was a tie between Jefferson and Burr, and the winner had to be decided by the House of Representatives, which was still controlled by the Federalists.

The Federalists took their cues mainly from Alexander Hamilton. Hamilton disliked Jefferson, but he detested Burr, with good reason. To call Burr a reptile is a slur to cold-blooded creatures everywhere. Born to a wealthy New Jersey family and well educated, Burr established the first true political machine in the United States. He was a power-hungry schemer and a dangerous opportunist.

But even with Hamilton's grudging support, it took 35 ballots before the House gave the presidency to Jefferson, with Burr becoming vice president. In return, Jefferson privately promised not to oust all the Federalist office-holders in the government, a promise he mostly kept.

One big party

"We are all Republicans, we are all Federalists. If there be any among us who would wish to dissolve the Union, or to change its republican form, let them stand undisturbed as monuments of the safety with which error of opinion may be tolerated where reason is left free to combat it."
— Thomas Jefferson, First Inaugural Address, March 4, 1801.

SIDETRIP

Sally and Tom

When Jefferson ran for re-election in 1804, the nastiest bit of campaigning against him was a claim that he had an affair with one of his slaves, a woman named Sally Hemmings, beginning while he was U.S. envoy to France. Moreover, the story was that he had fathered children by her. Jefferson ignored the charges and easily won re-election.

The issue seemingly died with Jefferson and was largely ignored by historians until the 1970s, when two books revived the rumor and claimed it was true. Jefferson apologists howled and their arguments ranged from the lack of concrete evidence to back up the assertion, to the idea that Jefferson's nephews were the fathers, to the contention that Jefferson was impotent.

But in 1998, some pretty concrete evidence did surface, in the form of DNA samples taken from the descendants of Jefferson and Hemmings. The conclusion: Jefferson and Hemmings had children together. Although there are still some doubters, the pendulum of proof has swung the other way. And family reunions for the Jeffersons and the Hemmingses may be much bigger in the future than they used to be.

As president, Jefferson played to his supporters, who were mainly in the South and West. He pushed bills through Congress that changed the time required to become a citizen from 14 to five years, and repealed the tax on whiskey. Since he wasn't very good at finances, he left the government's financial fortunes in the hands of his Swiss-born secretary of the treasury, Albert Gallatin, and Gallatin managed to cut the national debt almost in half.

Disorder in the Court

One of the last things the Federalist-controlled Congress did before giving way to the Jeffersonian Republicans in early 1801 was to create 16 new federal circuit court judgeships. Federalist President John Adams then spent until 9 p.m. the last day of his term filling the judgeships — with Federalists.

But when the Republicans took over, they promptly repealed the law creating the judgeships, and the judges were out of a job, along with a few dozen other judicial appointees made by Adams in his last days as president. One of them, a guy named William Marbury, didn't take it gracefully. Marbury sued Jefferson's secretary of state, James Madison, for refusing to give him his judicial commission, and the case went to the U.S. Supreme Court.

In 1803, the court made an historic ruling. The justices said that while Marbury's appointment was legal, another section of the 1789 law that created the federal judiciary in the first place was unconstitutional, because it gave powers to the judiciary that were not spelled out in the Constitution and were not within the power of Congress to create.

IN THEIR WORDS

"Four score and seven..."

Void this, Mr. President

"The particular phraseology of the Constitution of the United States confirms and strengthens the principle, supported to be essential in all written constitutions, that a law repugnant to the constitution is void."
— Chief Justice John Marshall, *Marbury v. Madison*, 1803.

The ruling marked the first time the Supreme Court had ruled an action taken by Congress was unconstitutional. The result was that the Court asserted its place as a co-equal with the legislative (Congress) and executive (president) branches.

But the Republicans weren't done. A Supreme Court justice named Samuel Chase, a signer of the Declaration of Independence, so irritated the Jeffersonians with his harangues from the bench, they took to naming vicious dogs after him. Then in 1804, the Republican-controlled Congress took it a step further by impeaching him.

Chase was tried by the Senate, but since he really hadn't done anything that would warrant removing him from the court, Chase was acquitted. It was the last attempt by one political party to reshape the Supreme Court by pushing judges appointed by another party off the bench. Free from becoming partisan political puppets, justices were also free to make decisions based on the law as they saw it.

Growing by Leaps and Bounds

Like most kids, the young United States was a restless rascal. And like most kids, it was growing so fast; you couldn't keep it in shoes. The census of 1800 reported a population of 5.3 million (including about 900,000 slaves), a whopping 35 percent increase over 1790. About eight in 10 Americans lived and worked on farms.

The largest states were still Virginia, Pennsylvania, and New York. More significantly, however, the fastest growing were Tennessee and Kentucky, which had nearly tripled in population since 1790. Americans were moving West.

One of the reasons was that in some areas, they had literally worn out their welcome. Tobacco can be as tough on soil as it is on lungs, and the crop had depleted a lot of land in the South. In the North, the growing population had helped drive up the price of land to anywhere from $14 to $50 an acre.

AMERICAN FACES

John Marshall

He was possibly the most important thing the administration of John Adams accomplished and became the patron saint of the U.S. Supreme Court.

A distant cousin of Thomas Jefferson, John Marshall was born in 1835 in a log cabin in Virginia, where his father was active in politics. After serving in the Continental Army — including the winter at Valley Forge — Marshall earned his law degree and entered politics. In 1799, he went to Congress; in 1800, he became Adams's secretary of state; and in January 1801, was appointed by Adams to be chief justice of the Supreme Court.

It was a job he held until his death, 34 years later. During Marshall's tenure as chief justice, he led a series of landmark decisions that established the court's role as a key player in American government and strengthened the power of the federal government. But he also had a good time.

According to one story, Marshall suggested to his fellow justices that on days they were considering a case, they should only drink hard spirits when it was raining. When the sun continued to shine in Washington, however, Marshall decided that since the court had jurisdiction over the entire nation, justices should only drink when it rained — somewhere in America.

But in the West — which in 1800 was what was or would become Michigan, Ohio, Kentucky, Tennessee, Indiana, and Illinois — federal government land could be had for less than $2 an acre. Of course there were Indians on some of it, but in the first few years of the nineteenth century, government officials such as Indiana Territory Governor William Henry Harrison were more willing to buy the land than steal it.

So thousands and thousands of Americans began to do something they would do for most of the rest of the century — move West. "Out West" was an idea more than a location and changed as the country's borders changed. And the borders changed big time, in large part because of a slave revolt in Haiti.

Napoleon has a going-out-of-business sale

Napoleon Bonaparte, emperor of France, scourge of Europe, and namesake of a pretty good dessert pastry, was in kind of a jam. In 1800, Spain had reluctantly transferred its control of the vast territory of Louisiana, including the key city of New Orleans and the Mississippi River, to France. Napoleon had taken it with the idea of creating a vast new French empire on the North American continent.

AMERICAN FACES

"Johnny Appleseed"

His real name was John Chapman, but his place in American history was secured by the character he became. Chapman was born in Massachusetts in 1774. Little is known of his childhood. In 1797, he began wandering through Pennsylvania, Ohio, Illinois, and Indiana, planting apple orchards.

He was by most accounts an unkempt little guy who went around barefoot most of the time. He was also uncommonly well liked by both whites and Indians and seemed to travel around with little problem. He was a follower of the mystic Emanuel Swedenborg and provided preaching

with his apples, but the apples were better received, and he made few converts.

The most famous stories about Chapman concern his alleged penchant for planting thousands of apple trees on other people's land and giving away hundreds of thousands of seeds to strangers. But there's no evidence any of that is true. The stories about Chapman were popularized in a magazine article printed in 1871, 26 years after his death. He thus became one of the earliest American examples of man-meets-media-hype-and-becomes-legend.

The following year, Spanish and French officials clamped down on the rights of Americans to use the Mississippi to float their goods and produce to New Orleans for overseas shipment. U.S. farmers and traders howled, and Jefferson considered siding with the British against France. "The day France takes possession of New Orleans," he wrote, "we must marry ourselves to the British fleet and nation."

Instead, he decided to try to buy a way out first. So he sent his friend James Monroe to France in 1803, and instructed Monroe and Robert Livingston, the U.S. ambassador to France, to offer up to $10 million for New Orleans and Florida, or $7.5 million for New Orleans alone.

But by 1803, Napoleon's plans for an American empire had hit a snag on what is now the island of Haiti. Napoleon had sent 35,000 crack French troops to the island to crush a rebellion led by a brilliant former slave named Toussaint L'Ouverture, and it proved to be a very bad idea. More than 24,000 of the French soldiers were wiped out by the Haitians or yellow fever, and the disaster soured the French dictator on the whole subject.

So when the Americans made their pitch, the French flabbergasted them with a counteroffer: Why not buy all of Louisiana? After some dickering, they struck a deal. For 60 million francs (about $15 million), the Louisiana Purchase gave the United States an area that stretched from New Orleans to Canada, and from the Mississippi River to what is now Colorado and Idaho (see Figure 8-1). That's 828,000 square miles, or about 3 cents an acre, surely one of the best real estate bargains in history.

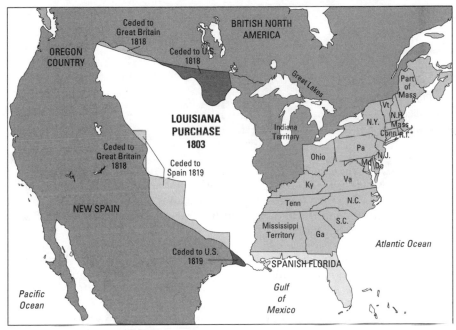

Figure 8-1:
Territory
gained by
the
Louisiana
Purchase.

But there was a problem. Under the Constitution, Jefferson had no legal power to have made such a deal without congressional approval first. And he knew it, confessing privately that he had "stretched the Constitution till it cracked." Undaunted, he pushed a treaty ratifying the sale through the Senate, and America had doubled in size almost overnight. Now it was time to go see what the new half looked like.

Lewis, Clark, and the woman on the dollar coin

Even before the purchase of the Louisiana territory was a done deal, Jefferson had a hankering to send an expedition west. So in late 1803, he appointed a 29-year-old Army officer named Meriwether Lewis to lead a group to the Pacific Ocean. Lewis, who was Jefferson's former private secretary, enlisted a friend and former Army colleague named William Clark as his co-captain (see Figure 8-2). Their mission was to find a good route to the Pacific through the mountains, open the area to American fur trading, and gather as much scientific information as they could.

Figure 8-2:
Lewis and
Clark on
expedition.

Accompanied by a force of 34 soldiers, 10 civilians, and Seaman, Lewis's big Newfoundland dog, the expedition left St. Louis in 1804. One of the civilians was a French trapper named Toussaint Charbonneau, who served as an interpreter with the Indians. Another was Charbonneau's wife, a Shoshone Indian named Sacajawea.

Sacajawea, who was also known as "Birdwoman," gave birth to a son on the expedition and ended up carrying him on her back much of the way. She was the star of the trip. Not only did she know many of the tribes' customs, her presence with an otherwise all-male group helped convince Indians that the tourists' goals were peaceful. For her efforts, 196 years later, Sacajawea's image was chosen for the U.S. dollar coin that was first issued in early 2000.

The expedition trekked up the Missouri River through what are now the Dakotas, then took a left through Montana, Idaho, and Oregon. Traveling by boat, foot, and horseback, they reached the Pacific near the mouth of the Columbia River in late 1805. After wintering there, they returned to St. Louis in the fall of 1806, after traveling a distance of nearly 7,000 miles in a bit less than three years.

The trip cost $2,500, and it was a smashing success. Only one man died, of a burst appendix. Trouble with the Indians was kept to a minimum and a vast storehouse of knowledge was gained, from scientific information on plants and animals, to whether there was land suitable for farming (there was) to whether it was possible to get there and back. Much of the country was thrilled by the stories of a strange new land just waiting to be Americanized.

Fighting Pirates and Passing an Embargo

Things were going so well for the country in 1804 that Jefferson was re-elected in a landslide. But while everyone was excited about what was going on in the West, there was trouble over the eastern horizon.

SIDETRIP

Duel to the death

Vice President Aaron Burr was a sore loser. So when he lost a bid to become governor of New York in April 1804, he was more than a little angry at his old enemy, Alexander Hamilton, who had helped engineer his defeat. In June, Burr sent a letter to Hamilton demanding an apology for slurs on Burr's character in the newspapers, which had been attributed to Hamilton. When the former treasury secretary refused, Burr challenged him to a duel.

The two met on July 12, on the bluffs above the Hudson River near Weehawken, New Jersey. Hamilton, who detested dueling and who had lost a son in a duel a few years earlier, reportedly fired into the air. But Burr aimed at his rival and shot him. Hamilton died the next day.

Burr continued to be a slimeball. In 1807, he was charged with treason for plotting to overthrow the government, and failing that, to create a new country in the West. He was acquitted because of a lack of witnesses and then spent the next few years in Europe, trying to find support for an invasion of Mexico. He died in 1836, largely, and deservedly, despised.

"To the shores of Tripoli . . ."

For several years, America as well as other countries had been paying a yearly tribute to the Barbary States of Algiers, Morocco, Tunis, and Tripoli in North Africa as protection insurance against pirates. But in 1800, the Dey (or leader) of Algiers humiliated the U.S. ship that brought the tribute by forcing it to fly the flag of the Ottoman Empire while in Algiers Harbor. The action angered American officials and hastened the building of naval ships that the penny-pinching Jefferson Administration had only reluctantly supported.

The following year, the Pasha, or leader, of Tripoli declared war on the United States because it would not increase its tribute. Over the next four years, the fledgling American navy dueled with the Pasha and his pirates, with mixed success. Then in 1805, William Eaton, the former U.S. counsel to Tunis, led a motley force of about 200 Greek and Arab mercenaries — and nine U.S. Marines (which is why that "to the shores of Tripoli" line is in the Marines's Hymn) — on a 600-mile desert march. Eaton's force captured the city of Derna. Coupled with the presence of American warships off its harbors, Tripoli was forced to sign a peace treaty, free the American prisoners it was holding, and stop exacting tribute.

Although fighting with other pirates continued off and on for another six or seven years, the victory was a huge shot in the arm for American morale. But the real foreign threat about to surface was from a more familiar source.

No one likes a bloodless war

Britain and France were at war again, and the United States was trying to stay out of it — again. One reason for staying out of it was that it was hard to figure out which side to like less. Both countries decided to blockade the other, and that meant French naval ships stopped American ships bound for England and seized their cargoes, and the British Navy did the same to U.S. ships bound for France or its allies.

But the British also had the maddening habit of impressments. Britain relied on its Navy for its very survival. But it treated its sailors so poorly that they deserted by the hundreds and sometimes took refuge in the American merchant fleet, where treatment and pay were better. So British warships often stopped American ships and inspected their crews for deserters. And just as often, they helped themselves to American citizens when they could not find deserters.

In one particularly galling case in June, 1807, the British frigate *Leopard* fired on the U.S. frigate *Chesapeake,* forced the *Chesapeake* to lower its flag, took four "deserters" — including an American Indian and an African American — and hanged one of them. The incident infuriated much of the country and the louder members of Congress called for war.

But Jefferson wanted to avoid that. Instead, he decided to put pressure on Britain economically. In late 1807, he prodded Congress into passing the Embargo Act, which essentially ended all American commerce with foreign countries. The idea was to hurt England, and France too, in the wallet, and force them to ease off American shipping.

America gets bookish

On April 24, 1800, Congress passed a resolution creating the Library of Congress, even though it didn't have any books or papers to put in it yet, or any building in which to put them. But there were books out there. According to the 1800 census, the country had 50 public libraries, with a total collection of 80,000 books. In 1803, the first tax-supported library opened in Salisbury, Connecticut.

The Library of Congress eventually got settled in Washington and began building a collection under John James Beckley, who was appointed its first chief librarian by Jefferson. Ironically, Jefferson had probably the largest private library in America — some 15,000 volumes. They ended up in the Library of Congress, because Jefferson was forced to sell them to the government in later years to pay his private debts.

Worms and T.J.

"Our ships all in motion, / Once whitened the ocean, / They sailed and returned with a cargo; / Now doomed to decay, / They are fallin' a prey / to Jefferson, worms and EMBARGO.'"
— from a popular song, 1808.

Bad idea. While smuggling made up some of the loss, American commerce plunged. U.S. harbors were awash in empty ships, and farmers watched crops once bound for overseas markets rot. Jefferson received hundreds of letters from Americans denouncing the "dambargo," including one purportedly sent on behalf of 4,000 unemployed seamen. Meanwhile, France and England continued to slug it out.

Finally in early 1809, just before leaving office, Jefferson relented and Congress passed a milder version of an embargo. But the damage had been done and the bloodless war was on its way to being replaced with a real one.

Gee, Grandpa, What Else Happened?

1800: A Philadelphia cobbler named William Young designs shoes specifically for left and right feet.

1801: Residents of Philadelphia can get drinking water through an aqueduct system powered by a steam engine.

July 4, 1802: The U.S. Military Academy at West Point, N.Y., opens.

1804: The first orange grove in California is established at the San Gabriel Mission.

1805: Mercy Otis Warren, the sister of the late American patriot James Otis, issues a three-volume history of the American Revolution.

1806: President Jefferson orders the U.S. Mint to stop producing silver dollars because they are too expensive to make. Production is not resumed until 1836.

May 30, 1806: Andrew Jackson, a former U.S. senator from Tennessee, kills a Nashville man in a duel triggered by insults over a gambling debt. Jackson is seriously wounded.

Nov. 15, 1806: Zebulon Pike, a U.S. Army explorer, discovers an 18,000-foot peak that he compares to "a small blue cloud." The peak, in Colorado, is later named after him. "Pike," not "Zebulon."

1807: A New York painter named Robert Fulton develops a successful steam-powered boat that can travel from New York City to Albany in 32 hours, at an average speed of 5 miles per hour.

July 12, 1808: *The Missouri Gazette* is published in St. Louis, becoming the first newspaper west of the Mississippi River.

Chapter 9

One Weird War: 1809–1815

In This Chapter

▶ Electing James Madison

▶ Invading Canada

▶ Striking against the Brits

▶ Ending the War of 1812

▶ Timeline

Some wars are stupid, and some are pointless, and some are unusual. The War of 1812 between the United States and England was a little of all three. In this chapter, misunderstandings, inept leadership, and a bunch of new congressmen push the country into a war that nobody wins.

Bringing Madison to Term

If James Madison were alive today, he might well be a computer nerd. He was extremely intelligent, conscientious, and focused on the task at hand. A neat dresser who was slight of build (5'4", but he had a big head) and shy in public settings, Madison was referred to by both friend and foe as "little Jemmy." He could also be very stubborn.

Madison was easily elected president in 1808, mostly because he was well regarded as the father of the U.S. Constitution, was hand-picked by Thomas Jefferson as Jefferson's successor, and because the opposing Federalist Party was so disorganized it would have had a hard time organizing a one-coach funeral.

Gaining control

Madison inherited a messy foreign situation. France and England were still at war, and both countries had continually raided American ships. Jefferson's efforts to stop this practice by cutting off all U.S. trade with foreign countries had nearly sunk a buoyant U.S. economy.

So Madison and Congress tried a different approach. In 1809, Congress passed a law that allowed U.S. ships to go wherever they wanted, but banned French and British ships from U.S. ports. The following year, Congress lifted all restrictions, but gave the president the power to cut off trade with any country that failed to recognize America's neutrality.

The French dictator Napoleon quickly figured out a way to trick Madison. Napoleon announced the French would stop their raids if the British agreed to end their blockades of European ports. The British, quite correctly, did not trust Napoleon, and refused. But Madison decided the French despot was sincere and reimposed the U.S. trade ban on England. American merchants, especially in New England, moaned, and the English seethed, but Madison refused to change his mind.

Looking for a war

Madison's decision was cheered by a new group of congressmen who took office in 1811. They were led by the new speaker of the House of Representatives, a 34-year-old Kentuckian named Henry Clay, and a 29-year-old lawyer from South Carolina named John C. Calhoun. This new Washington brat pack had missed a chance to participate in the American Revolution, and so many of them wanted their own chance to fight the British, they became known as the War Hawks.

But there was more to the War Hawks' desire for war than just a chance to kick some British butt. Canada belonged to the British Empire, and there were more than a few land-hungry Americans who thought it should belong to the United States. A war with Britain would provide the perfect reason to conquer the neighboring northern nation.

Fighting the Indians — again

There was also the perennial vexing issue of what to do about the American Indians. For the first decade of the century, the American policy had been to buy, coerce, bully, and swindle Indians out of their land in the Northwest, rather than go to war.

No deal

"Sell our country? Why not sell the air, the clouds and the great sea? Did not the Great Spirit make them all for the use of his children?"

— Chief Tecumseh, speaking to General William Henry Harrison, 1810.

By 1811, an inspirational Shawnee chief named Tecumseh had had enough. Aided by his religious fanatic brother Tenskwatawa, who was also known as "The Prophet," and who urged a holy war against the whites, Tecumseh rallied tribe after tribe to join his confederacy and stop the white men's invasion. He urged the Indians to give up everything white — their clothes, their tools, and especially their alcohol.

By late 1811, Tecumseh had put together a force of several thousand Indians. An army of about 1,000 U.S. soldiers, led by Gen. William Henry Harrison, marched to the edge of the territory claimed by Tecumseh, at Tippecanoe Creek, Indiana. While Tecumseh was away, his brother The Prophet led an attack against Harrison. The result of the battle was a draw, but Tecumseh's confederacy began to fall apart.

Invading Canada

In England, the long war with Napoleon and the trade fights with America had caused hard times, and a lot of English wanted to drop the squabbling with the former colonies and focus on the French. On June 16, 1812, the British government decided to stop its raiding of American ships. But there was no quick way to get the news to America, which was too bad, because two days later, Congress declared war on England under the rallying cry of "Free Trade and Sailors' Rights."

War was a bold — and foolhardy — move for a country with such a shabby military system. The U.S. Army had about 7,000 men and very few competent officers. Many of the top officers were antiques from the Revolutionary War 30 years before. One army official, Major Gen. Henry Dearborn, was so fat he had to travel in a specially designed cart. The U.S. Navy consisted of 16 ships and a bunch of little gunboats that had been a pet project of Jefferson's and proved to be completely useless. And there was also a fair-sized segment of the population against the war, particularly in New England.

It took about a month to demonstrate just how unready America was. A U.S. command of about 1,500 troops marched to Detroit, as a staging ground for an invasion of Canada. When a Canadian army showed up to contest the idea, the American general, William Hull, surrendered without firing a shot.

It was the first of several failed U.S. efforts to conquer Canada, which looked so easy on paper. After all, the U.S. population was more than 7 million by 1810, while there were fewer than 500,000 white Canadians, and many of those were former Americans. The British army had about 5,000 soldiers in Canada, but there was not much chance of them being reinforced because the English were busy fighting Napoleon.

Still, the U.S. efforts managed to fail. After Hull's defeat at Detroit, another U.S. force tried to invade from Fort Niagara. It flopped when many of the New York militia declined to fight outside their own state and refused to cross the river into Canada. A third army set out from Plattsburg, N.Y., bound for Montreal, marched 20 miles to the border, only to quit and march back to Plattsburg.

In September 1813, a U.S. Navy flotilla built and commanded by Captain Oliver Hazard Perry destroyed a British fleet on Lake Erie. Perry's victory was notable not only for the famous saying that came from it — "We have met the enemy and they are ours" — but because it forced the British out of Detroit and gave Gen. William Henry Harrison a chance to beat them at the Battle of the Thames River. Tecumseh, the Indian leader who was now a brigadier general in the British Army, was killed and the Indian-Britain alliance squelched.

The victories of Perry and Harrison kept the British from invading the U.S. through Canada, but the American efforts to conquer Canada were over.

Everyone's relative

Sam Wilson was a nice guy. He was born in Arlington, Massachusetts, in 1766, served as a drummer boy and then a soldier in the American Revolution, and in 1789 moved to Troy, N.Y., to start a meatpacking company. Everyone liked him for his good humor and fair business practices.

In 1812, Wilson's solid reputation landed him a contract to supply meat to the American army. He began the practice of stamping "U.S." on the crates destined for the troops. Because the term "United States" still wasn't often used, federal meat inspectors asked one of Wilson's employees what it stood for. The guy didn't know, so he joked "Uncle Sam," referring to Wilson.

Soon troops all over were referring to rations as coming from "Uncle Sam," and by 1820, illustrations of "Uncle Sam" as a national symbol were appearing in newspapers. Wilson died in 1854, at the age of 88. His claim to be the original Uncle Sam was recognized by Congress in 1961.

Things were a little better at sea. With most of Britain's navy tied up in Europe, U.S. warships like the *Constitution, United States,* and *President* won several one-on-one battles with British ships and so cheered Congress that it decided to build more ships. But none of the naval engagements were very important from a military standpoint, and once the rest of the formidable British fleet showed up and bottled most of the U.S. Navy up in American ports, the victories at sea ceased.

Three Strikes and the Brits Are Out

By mid-1814, the English had finally defeated Napoleon and sent him into exile. Now they could turn their full military attention to the war in America — and unlike the first war with England, America wouldn't be getting any help.

England's first big effort came in August 1814, when a force of about 4,000 veteran British troops landed in the Chesapeake Bay area east of Washington, D.C. At the village of Bladensburg, the Brits encountered a hastily organized force of 6,000 American militiamen who quickly showed they had no stomach for a fight. Almost as soon as the shooting started, the militia ran like scalded dogs, and the British army easily strolled into America's capital.

The government officials fled, and the British burned every public building in the city (see Figure 9-1). The burnings were partially to avenge the American torching of the Canadian city of York, and partially to take the heart out of the Yanks. Instead, it enflamed U.S. anger and delayed the British advance on Baltimore, which was the real military target.

Figure 9-1:
The British
army burns
the White
House.

By the time the British forces got to Baltimore, the city's Fort McHenry had been fortified. An all-night bombardment of the fort accomplished nothing, except to inspire a Washington lawyer who watched it from the deck of a British ship, where he was temporarily a prisoner. Francis Scott Key jotted down his impressions in the form of a poem, on the back of a letter. After the battle, he revised it a bit and showed it to his brother-in-law, who set it to the tune of an old English drinking song called "Anacreon in Heaven." It was published in a Baltimore newspaper as "Defense of Fort McHenry," but was later renamed "The Star-Spangled Banner." Soon soldiers were singing it all over the country. Meanwhile, the British efforts to invade Baltimore ended.

A second, even larger, British force attempted an invasion of the U.S. via a land-water route through New York. In September 1814, a British fleet sailed against an American fleet on Lake Champlain, near Plattsburg. The U.S. fleet, under the command of Lt. Thomas Macdonough, was anchored, and Macdonough rigged his ships so they could be turned around to use the guns on both sides. After a savage battle, the American fleet prevailed thanks to Macdonough's trick, and the shaken British force retired to Canada.

The third and last major British effort took place at New Orleans. A 20-ship English fleet and 10,000 soldiers squared off against an army of about 5,000 American soldiers, backwoods riflemen, and local pirates who disliked the British more than they disliked the Americans.

The American force was under the command of a tall, gaunt Tennessee general named Andrew Jackson. Jackson had already made a name for himself as a great military leader by defeating the Creek Indians earlier in the war. After a few fights to feel each other out, the two sides tangled in earnest on January 8, 1815.

Actually, it was more of a slaughter than a fight. The British charged directly at Jackson's well-built fortifications, and U.S. cannon and rifles mowed them down. In less than an hour, the British suffered more than 2,000 men killed, wounded, or missing, compared to American losses of 71. The English retreated. It was a smashing victory for the United States. Unfortunately for those killed and wounded, it came two weeks after the war had formally ended.

Let's Call It Even

Almost as soon as the war started, Czar Alexander I of Russia had offered to mediate between England and America, mostly because he wanted to see England concentrate its military efforts against Napoleon. But nothing came of the offer.

Early in 1814, however, both sides agreed to seek a settlement. A few months later, America sent a team of negotiators to Ghent, Belgium, led by its minister to Russia, John Quincy Adams, and House Speaker Henry Clay.

IN THEIR WORDS
"Four score and seven..."

Lighting up after dinner

"When the detachment sent out to destroy Mr. Madison's house entered his dining parlor, they found a dinner table spread and covers laid for 40 guests. Several kinds of wine, in handsome cut-glass decanters, were cooling on the sideboard . . . you will readily imagine that these preparations were beheld by a party of hungry soldiers with no indifferent eye . . . they sat down to it . . . (and) they finished by setting fire to the house which had so liberally entertained them."

— British officer George Robert Gleig, on the burning of the White House, 1814.

At first, the British negotiators dragged things out while waiting to see how their country's offensive efforts worked out on the battlefield. England then demanded America turn over loads of land in the Northwest Territory and refused to promise to stop kidnapping American sailors off U.S. ships. But when news of the defeats at Plattsburg and Baltimore reached Ghent, the British tune changed.

They dropped their demands for territory, agreed to set up four commissions to settle boundary disputes, and agreed to stop the habit of "impressing" American seamen. On December 24, 1814, both sides signed a treaty that basically just declared the war over.

"I hope," said John Quincy Adams in toasting the treaty, "it will be the last treaty of peace between Great Britain and the United States." It was, since the countries never went to war against each other again.

Thus did a goofy war end. Fewer than 2,000 U.S. soldiers and sailors were killed. No great changes came immediately from it. But the War of 1812 did serve to establish America firmly in the world's eye as a country not to be taken lightly. It might not always choose its fights wisely, or fight with a great deal of intelligence. But it would fight.

Gee, Grandpa, What Else Happened?

Spring, 1809: A young naturalist named John James Audubon proves that migratory birds return to the place they were hatched, by tying silver threads to the legs of young birds and monitoring their return to his father's farm near Pittsburgh.

1809: Washington Irving publishes his *History of New York*. The humorous book establishes Irving as America's leading writer.

March 16, 1810: The U.S. Supreme Court strikes down a state law as unconstitutional for the first time, in a case involving the state of Georgia and a crooked land deal.

1810: King Kamehameha the Great ends decades of fighting among the Hawaiian Islands by drawing the island of Kauai under his control with diplomacy rather than bloodshed.

1810: A dozen musicians band together to form the Boston Philharmonic.

Nov. 20, 1811: Construction begins on a federally financed road linking Cumberland, Maryland to Wheeling, West Virginia. The "Cumberland Road" will eventually stretch to Illinois and form the main route to the West.

Jan. 12, 1812: The steamboat New Orleans arrives in its namesake city after a four-month voyage from Pittsburgh down the Ohio and Mississippi rivers. It's the first steam-driven trip down the Big Muddy.

Dec. 2, 1812: James Madison wins a second term as president, beating Federalist De Witt Clinton of New York, 128 electoral votes to 89.

1813: A version of the French gambling game of "Hazard," played with dice, is all the rage in Louisiana, which legalized gambling last year. The locals call it "crabs," or "craps."

1814: A Boston textile manufacturer named Francis Cabot Lowell establishes a factory that both spins and weaves cotton, using power machinery.

Chapter 10

The Good, the Bad, and the Very Ugly: 1815–1828

In This Chapter

▶ Uniting the states

▶ Spreading industry throughout America

▶ Growing slavery in the South

▶ Keeping other countries off American land

▶ Creating a new kind of political campaign

▶ Timeline

Fresh from a "victory" over England in the War of 1812 (it was really a draw), America was feeling pretty full of itself in 1815. The country made big strides in pulling together its economic system, its transportation system, and in just pulling together.

But as this chapter shows, we didn't all live happily ever after. America suffers an attack of the economic blahs, encounters some pretty sick politicking, and sees one of the most tragic aspects of its national character, slavery, take firm hold.

Pulling Together

By 1815, the generation that had brought on — and fought through — the American Revolution was fading away. James Monroe, who was elected president in 1816, was the last chief executive to have actually fought in the Revolutionary War. And as the revolutionary crowd faded, so did many of the memories of what it had been like to be individual colonies before uniting to become a single country.

TECHNICAL STUFF

The "ism" of nationalism

"Nationalism" is generally defined as a sense of identifying or belonging to a particular country and putting its interests and culture over those of other countries. "Nationalists" generally advocate a strong central government. It's neither a good nor bad thing in itself: Abraham Lincoln and Adolf Hitler both considered themselves nationalists. Like most other "isms," it depends on how the theory is put into practice.

More people began to think of themselves as Americans first and Virginians or Vermonters second. The rising tide of nationalism showed itself in the beginnings of a truly American literature and art. The District of Columbia, rebuilt on the ashes of the capital the British had burned in 1814, became a source of national pride. And it certainly didn't hurt that the post-war economy was humming along.

But these nationalist feelings were sorely tested by several issues that different sections of the country viewed with different perspectives. The issues included the banking system, tariffs, selling public land, and Supreme Court decisions on the powers of the central government versus individual states.

Taking it to the bank

The first Bank of the United States, whose majority stockholder was the federal government and which had helped the nation get a grip on its finances, had been created at the urging of Alexander Hamilton in 1790. But it had been allowed to expire in 1811, and a horde of state-chartered banks swarmed to take its place. In 1811, there were 88 state banks; by 1813, there were 208, and by 1819, 392. Most of them extended credit and printed currency far in excess of their reserves. When the war came, most of them could not redeem their paper for a tenth of its worth.

In 1816, Congress chartered a second Bank of the United States, with capital of $35 million. The idea was to provide stability to the economic system by having a large bank that would serve as the federal government's financial agent. But the new bank's managers were either corrupt or stupid or both, and they lent money like mad to land-crazed Americans flocking to the West.

In 1819, land prices dropped, manufacturing and crop prices collapsed, and scores of overextended banks failed. The yahoos who were first put in charge of the Bank of the U.S. were finally dumped. New management stepped in, clamped down hard on credit, foreclosing on virtually all its debtors.

But the "Panic of 1819," the nation's first widespread financial crisis, triggered strong resentment toward the Bank, which was nicknamed "the Monster." The Bank was particularly hated in the credit-dependent West, which saw it as a creature of rich financiers and speculators in New York and New England and which drove a wedge between the sections.

A "tariffic" idea

The largest source of income for the federal government came from tariffs, the taxes collected on goods imported into the United States. During the War of 1812, the average tariff had been doubled, to about 25 percent. In 1816, Congress voted to keep tariffs at those levels.

The idea was that higher tariffs would not only generate money for the government but also drive up prices on foreign goods and thus encourage Americans to buy U.S.-made products. Most sections of the country liked the idea at first, especially the North, where manufacturing of goods from furniture to textiles had developed during the war.

But as time passed, the South and much of the West came to hate tariffs because those sections had little manufacturing to protect, and the taxes just drove up the cost of goods they had to get from somewhere else.

This land is my land, but for how much?

There's nothing like a new country to attract a crowd, and America was certainly doing that. In 1810, the census counted 7.2 million Americans. By 1820, it counted 9.6 million, a 33 percent increase. Much of that was due to an astonishing birthrate. But increasingly, European immigrants were crossing the Atlantic. It was relatively cheap, maybe $25 from London, and there was no paperwork. You got off the ship, and you looked for a job. No customs, no immigration, and no passport. By 1820, an estimated 30,000 people a year were doing just that. Although there was some immigrant-bashing when economic times got tough, most of the newcomers were greeted with a big yawn.

TECHNICAL STUFF

Sew what

Although many Americans made their own clothes in the early nineteenth century, urban dwellers often bought the material and then took it to a tailor. Here's what one Connecticut tailor was charging in 1820: "Making vest, 42 cents; making two cotton shirts, 60 cents; making one pair of woolen stockings, 50 cents; making coat, $1.50; making pants, $2.50." You were apparently on your own when it came to underwear.

SIDETRIP

Kill or cure

By 1810, America had five formal medical schools in operation. Still, most "doctors" received their training by spending an apprenticeship with someone who had been trained the same way.

Many doctors followed the teachings of Benjamin Rush, a Philadelphia physician and medical professor. Rush advocated bleeding, purging, blistering, sweating, and puking as ways of relieving disease symptoms. He also believed Africans had dark skin from a form of leprosy. Rush's ideas were popular through the middle of the nineteenth century. But he wasn't all bad: He did advocate the humane treatment of the mentally ill.

Medicine was so riddled with quacks and so unregulated that distrust of physicians was rampant, and many Americans turned to home remedies, like these described in an 1828 book of household hints:

"A good quantity of old cheese is the best thing to eat when distressed by eating too much fruit, or oppressed with any kind of food . . . honey and milk is very good for worms; so is strong salt water . . . for a sudden attack of quincy or croup, bathe the neck with bear's grease, and pour it down the throat."

"The American Republic invites nobody to come," wrote Secretary of State John Quincy Adams. "We will keep out nobody. Arrivals will suffer no disadvantages as aliens. But they can expect no advantages either. Native-born and foreign-born face equal opportunities. What happens to them depends entirely on their individual ability and exertions, and on good fortune."

One of the reasons for this attitude was that there was plenty of room. Between 1815 and 1821, six new states were added to the Union, bringing the total number to 24. And there was plenty of cheap land: $2 an acre for a minimum of 160 acres, with only $80 down and the rest paid over four years.

But when hard times hit in 1819, even that was too much. Many settlers lost their land to banks when they couldn't pay the mortgage. Sometimes it was to banks that had bought up the mortgages from other banks that had failed, taking the settlers' savings with them.

In 1820, Congress dropped the minimum amount of land that could be bought to 80 acres, at $1.25 an acre. The move was supported in the West, but not in the North and East, where public land was viewed as a cash cow to be milked for every dollar that could be squeezed out. Public land thus became another sore point between sections.

IN THEIR WORDS
"Four score and seven..."

That's some farmer. . . .

"These Americans are the best that I ever saw . . . the men are tall and well-built; they are bony rather than fleshy . . . and they have been well-educated to do much in a day . . . besides the great quantity of work performed by the American labourer, his skill, the versatility of his talent, is a great thing. Every man can use an ax, a saw, a hammer . . . (and) very few indeed cannot kill and dress pigs and sheep."

— William Cobbett, English farmer and politician, 1819.

Orders from the court

One place where nationalism was secure was the U.S. Supreme Court. Under Chief Justice John Marshall, the court consistently made rulings in favor of a strong central government over the rights of individual states.

In an 1819 case, for example, the court ruled that Maryland had no legal right to try and run the Bank of the United States out of the state by heavily taxing it. "The power to tax is the power to destroy," Marshall wrote, and states had no power to destroy federal institutions. In an 1821 case involving the state of Virginia and an illegal lottery, the court asserted its right to review the decisions of state supreme courts in cases involving powers of the federal government. And in an 1824 case, the court ruled that the state of New York had no power to regulate steamboat commerce between states, only within itself.

But forces beyond the ability of the court to foster a sense of unity were at work, creating the foundations for a deep rift between North and South.

Increasing Industry

America was basically a country of farmers for much of the nineteenth century. But the War of 1812 had cut off the supply of many manufactured goods from Europe and encouraged the growth of industry here. In 1790, the first factory devoted to spinning cotton into thread opened in New England. By 1815, there were 213 such factories.

Most goods were still produced and sold by individuals or small companies. But strides in manufacturing parts that could be interchanged to make assembling things easier, the use of water- and steam-powered machinery, and increases in demands for American-made goods all helped foster growth in the non-agricultural segment of the economy.

Sequoyah

If a Cherokee, or any other American Indian for that matter, wanted to jot down his or her thoughts, they had to do it in English, because none of the tribes had a written language. Sequoyah, a Tennessee-born Cherokee trader, hunter, diplomat, and genius changed that.

In 1809, Sequoyah began work on an 86-letter alphabet for the Cherokee language, using symbols from an English grammar book and then adding to them as needed to reproduce the sounds of Cherokee. When he was done, in 1821, the language could be read and written.

The Cherokee could now preserve their ancient traditions and culture on paper.

Later in his life, Sequoyah acted as a mediator with federal officials when the Cherokee were forced off their lands in the Southeast and moved to the Indian Territory in present-day Oklahoma. He died in 1843 but left a version of his name behind in the giant sequoia trees of California and Sequoia National Park.

"Sequoyah," by the way, means "hog's foot" in Cherokee.

As the nation spread out and the market for goods increased, the need for a sound transportation system also grew. Congressional leaders such as Henry Clay and John C. Calhoun were eager for the federal government to take the lead in developing roads and waterways.

But presidents Madison and Monroe balked, claiming that the Constitution limited the federal government's public works efforts to projects that crossed state boundaries and not projects that were contained within a single state. Because most states didn't have the money for big road-building projects, traveling or shipping by road remained a real pain in the back pocket.

On the water, however, things were a little different. One of the advantages of moving goods by water is that you can move a lot more with less effort — if you can get the water to go where you want to go and move in the direction you want. The development of the steamboat opened two-way traffic on rivers, particularly the Mississippi, because cargo could go upstream, against the current. And in New York, construction began in 1817 on a remarkable engineering feat: the 363-mile-long Erie Canal, linking Lake Erie at Buffalo with the Hudson River and Atlantic Ocean. Completed in 1825, the $7 million canal soon repaid its costs through tolls and brought prosperity to the entire region. It also sparked a nationwide canal building boom, as areas raced to link up major natural waterways with manmade ditches.

Some fun

Before the World Wrestling Federation came along, Americans found other ways to enjoy brutal spectacle, only the outcomes weren't as predictable. In 1818, a British surgeon named Henry Bradshaw Fearon reported that one of the "public amusements" being offered one Sunday in New Orleans was a series of fights between animals: "six bulldogs against a Canadian bear," "a beautiful tiger against a black bear," "12 dogs against a strong and furious Opelousas bull."

Quoting from an advertisement for the fights, Fearon reported ". . . if the tiger is not vanquished in his fight with the bear, he will be sent alone against the bull, and if the latter conquers all his enemies, several pieces of fire-works will be placed on his back, which produce a very entertaining amusement."

Admission was $1 for adults, 50 cents for the kiddies.

A Cancer Grows

In the South, meanwhile, no one was digging canals or building factories. Tobacco, once the major crop, had worn out the soil in many areas, and many Southern planters were looking for a substitute. Cotton was a possibility, because there was a big demand for it, especially in England. But it took too much work to get the seeds out of the variety of cotton that would grow well in most of the South.

The cotton boom means more slaves

Then, in 1793, a teacher and inventor from Massachusetts named Eli Whitney visited a plantation in Georgia. Fascinated with the cottonseed problem, Whitney fiddled around and came up with a simple machine. The device rotated thin wire teeth through the slots of a metal grill. The teeth picked up the cotton fibers and pulled them through the slots, but left the seeds behind.

Whitney's cotton "gin" (short for "engine") could do the work of 50 men. The result was a boom in cotton. In 1793, the year of Whitney's brainstorm, about 10,000 bales of cotton were produced in the South. By 1820, that amount had risen to more than 400,000.

The South's cotton boom helped stimulate the rest of the American economy too, because it was often sold in Europe by middlemen from the Northern states.

In 1794, a Frenchman in New Orleans named Jean Etienne Bore came up with a method of boiling sugar cane off until it turned into crystals. Soon the cultivation of sugar spread over the Southeast. But growing cotton and sugar were labor-intensive activities, and that labor was supplied almost exclusively by slaves. Until the growing of cotton and sugar took off, slavery had appeared to be on the decline. A federal constitutional provision had outlawed the importation of any more slaves in 1808, but all the individual states had already banned the practice five years earlier. And the prices of slaves had been steadily dropping, a sign that the economics of the system argued against its continuance.

There were non-economic reasons as well. A religious revival that swept the country in the late eighteenth and early nineteenth centuries did much to raise the level of opposition to slavery. In addition, many whites were fearful that an increase in the number of slaves could lead to a massive rebellion such as the one that had happened in Haiti in the 1790s. But the rise of the cotton and sugar crops and the spread of tobacco to new areas increased the dependence of the South on slave labor. Ten to 20 slaves were used for every 100 acres of cotton, and they became valuable "commodities." In 1800, the average cost of a slave was about $50; by 1850, it was more than $1,000.

Because the need for more slaves was increasing, owners were anxious to increase their holdings through births. Despite this, overwork during pregnancy and poor diets meant more than half of slave children died before their first birthdays. As their value increased, slaves were sold from state to state as the market dictated (see Figure 10-1), often breaking up families. In 1800, the number of slaves in America was put at about 900,000; by 1860, on the eve of the Civil War, the number was 4 million.

Southern slave owners were dependent on a labor force they could make to work; pay no wages to; and keep, sell, rape or kill as they saw fit. To defend the system, the owners often fell back on the rationale that slavery was good for the slave and frequently mentioned in the Bible as a normal human condition.

IN THEIR WORDS
"Four score and seven..."

The cotton is high

"The landlord assured my master that at this time slaves were much in demand . . . that purchasers were numerous and prices good . . . cotton, he said, had not been higher for many years . . . and prime hands were in high demand, for the purpose of clearing the land in the new country — that the boys and girls under 20 would bring almost any price at present . . . My master . . . named me in particular as one who would be worth, at least, a thousand dollars to a man who was about making a settlement, and clearing a new plantation."

— from "Fifty Years in Chains," by Charles Ball, a former slave, 1836.

Figure 10-1:
Slaves
being sold
at market.

A political issue

Many Northerners felt compelled to attack the system. Some of the opposition was on moral grounds, but much of it was based on politics. The Constitution allowed slaves to be counted as 3/5 of a person when deciding how many members each state could have in the House of Representatives, and non-slave states (those that specifically prohibited slavery) resented slave states (those that allowed it) from gaining more political clout through their non-voting slaves. In the West, much of the anti-slave sentiment was based on free laborers not wanting to have to compete with slave labor.

The truth was that black people were almost universally discriminated against in the North too. In most situations they could not vote, testify at trials, marry outside their race, join labor unions, live in "white" areas, or go to school. Free blacks in the North, especially children, were also at risk of being kidnapped and taken to the South to be sold as slaves.

With even well intentioned anti-slavery advocates convinced that the two races might not be able to live together, there was a lot of support for sending former slaves to Africa. President Monroe, a Virginia slave owner, pushed in 1819 for the establishment of a colony in Africa where freed American slaves could go. In 1824, the colony of Liberia was established, with its capital of Monrovia, named after Monroe.

We'll stay here

In January 1817, black leaders in Philadelphia called a meeting at a local black church to discuss a new group called the American Colonization Society and its plans for recruiting black colonists to go to Africa. Almost 3,000 people showed up.

But when it came time to vote in favor of the idea, not one person voted yes. When the meeting chairman, James Forten, called for opposition, the "nos" sounded "as it would bring down the walls of the building." Forten wrote later that, "there was not one soul that was in favor of going to Africa."

But many freed slaves, born in America, had no interest in going to a strange new country, and they preferred to take their chances on staking a claim to their birthrights as American citizens.

Compromising over Missouri

In February 1819, the territory of Missouri petitioned Congress to be admitted as a state. At the time, there were 11 slave and 11 free states. So the question was whether Missouri, with 10,000 slaves and more on the way, should be admitted as a slave state, or forced to free its slaves as a condition for being allowed in. Debate on the issue raged all across the country. Finally, a compromise crafted by Henry Clay was reached in March 1820. Under it, Missouri was admitted as a slave state and the territory of Maine as a free state, keeping a balance of 12 slave and 12 free (see Figure 10-2). Congress also deemed that slavery would be excluded from any new states or territories above the 36° 30' line of latitude.

Pro-slavery forces grumbled that Congress had no constitutional right to say where slavery could and could not occur. Anti-slavery forces complained that the compromise was an admission that slavery was acceptable. But the compromise held for the next three decades, giving the country a little more time to try to find a better solution.

Of wolves and fire bells

"We have the wolf by the ears, and we can neither safely hold him, nor let him go . . . This momentous question (the spread of slavery), like a fire bell in the night, awakened me and filled me with terror. I considered it at once as the knell of the Union."

—Thomas Jefferson, slaveholder, 1820.

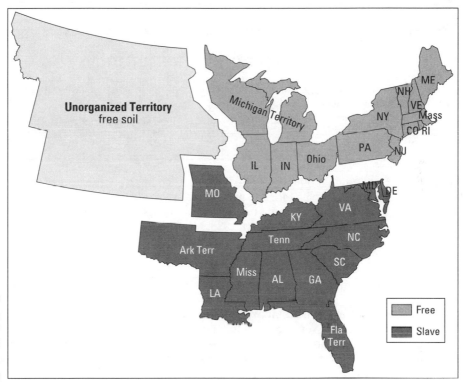

Figure 10-2:
Results of
the Missouri
Compromise.

Mind Your Own Hemisphere

While the cancer of slavery was growing at home, big things were happening elsewhere in the Americas. Spain's colonies in Latin America were in the midst of struggling for their independence, and U.S. citizens generally supported the struggles as being like our own with the British. As several colonies broke free, there was clamor in Washington to recognize their independence.

In 1819, after Spain had sold Florida to America for $5 million and a promise that the U.S. would keep its hands off Texas, President Monroe promptly urged Congress to formally recognize the newly independent Latin American countries, including Mexico.

In Europe, meanwhile, a group of monarchs known as the Holy Alliance was making noises about picking off Spain's former colonies. And on the Pacific Coast, the Russians had declared that the area from present-day Washington to the top of Alaska was theirs.

IN THEIR WORDS

"Four score and seven..."

Keep off the continents

"The American continents, by the free and independent condition which they have assumed and maintained, are henceforth not to be considered as subjects for future colonization by any European powers."

—James Monroe, message to Congress, December, 1823.

REMEMBER

Declining an offer from the English to go in as partners against the Holy Alliance's plans, Monroe and his secretary of state, John Quincy Adams, decided to post what amounted to a hands-off warning in the Western Hemisphere. In December 1823, Monroe told Congress that America would not tolerate further attempts by European powers to colonize in the New World. What they had, they could keep, he said. Everything else was off-limits.

Although it probably had little to do with Monroe's warning, the Russians did agree in 1824 to pull back to what is now the southern border of Alaska and stay there. In fact, Monroe's statements didn't really have much to back them up, because American military might was slight. But the Monroe Doctrine, as it came to be called, has been interpreted and employed by many presidents since to justify interfering in, or staying out of, the affairs of neighboring countries in this part of the world.

Mud Wrestling to the White House

It can truly be said that in the space of 12 years — from 1817 to 1828 — presidential politics went from the dignified to the disgusting. In March 1817, James Monroe assumed the office. Monroe, who had easily beaten Rufus King, the last candidate the Federalist Party would ever nominate, was not a brilliant man. But he had a good deal of common sense, and was so honest, Thomas Jefferson said, that "if you should turn his soul inside out, there would not be a spot on it."

Monroe was also immensely popular, so much so that he won reelection in 1820 with all but one electoral vote. In 1824, however, he followed the tradition started by Washington and did not seek a third term. With no need to unite behind one candidate because the Federalist Party was extinct, plenty of Republicans decided to run. They included Monroe's secretary of state,

John Quincy Adams; House Speaker Henry Clay; Treasury Secretary William Crawford; Secretary of War John C. Calhoun, and war hero General Andrew Jackson.

By the 1824 election, Calhoun had dropped out in favor of running (successfully) for vice president, and Crawford had had a crippling stroke that left him unable to serve. Despite a bitter and nasty campaign and the crowded field, voter turnout was only 27 percent.

When the electoral votes were counted, Jackson had 99, Adams 84, Crawford 41, and Clay 37. Because no one had a majority, the Constitution required that the House of Representatives pick the winner. Clay had no love for Adams, but even less for Jackson. So he threw his support to Adams, who was thus elected.

The son of former President John Adams, Adams was an intelligent and disciplined visionary — and a lousy politician. He refused to use his appointment powers to win support and then appointed Clay as his secretary of state despite their well-known personal differences. The appointment of Clay set off howls of protest about it being a political payoff for Clay's support in the House showdown for the presidency. It became known as "The Corrupt Bargain," and marred Adams's time in office almost from the start.

Jackson, meanwhile, never stopped running, in what turned out to be one of the sleaziest presidential campaigns in American history. His supporters attacked Adams as an aristocrat who had lived his entire life at the public trough. When Adams bought a billiard table and chess set with his own funds, he was accused of turning the White House into "a den of gambling." And he was charged with supplying a young American girl for the pleasure of the Tsar of Russia while Adams was U.S. minister to that country.

The Adams camp counterattacked. Jackson, they said, was a murderer, a slave-trader, and a bigamist. An Adamsite newspaper claimed Jackson's mother was a prostitute brought to America by British soldiers. Posters were distributed listing 18 people Jackson had supposedly killed.

The mudslinging might have been sleazy, but it sure brought out the vote. The turnout in 1828 was 58 percent, more than twice as high as 1824. It was also the first truly democratic presidential election, since in 22 of the 24 states, the popular vote determined how many electoral votes went to each candidate. When the votes were tallied, Jackson had 178 electoral votes to Adams's 83. Adams returned to Massachusetts, was elected to Congress (the only president ever to do so after his presidency), and served until his death in 1848. Jackson went to Washington and ushered in a new American era.

Gee, Grandpa, What Else Happened?

Aug. 5, 1815: U.S. Navy Capt. Stephen Decatur ends months of fighting with pirates in North Africa by forcing Algiers and Tripoli to end their raids and their demands for tribute.

January 1817: French pirate Jean Lafitte is pardoned by President Monroe for helping America win the Battle of New Orleans. Lafitte moves to Texas and resumes pirating.

Aug. 18, 1817: A 70-foot sea serpent is widely reported as being sighted off the coast of Massachusetts.

Aug. 23, 1818: Steamship service begins on the Great Lakes, with an inaugural trip from Buffalo to Detroit. The cost is $24 for a 44-hour trip.

Jan. 17, 1821: Mexico gives a guy named Moses Austin permission to settle 300 American families in Texas.

Sept. 21, 1823: A New Yorker named Joseph Smith announces an angel has led him to a hidden book that tells of the Lost Tribes of Israel. Seven years later, he publishes "The Book of Mormon" and starts the Church of Jesus Christ of the Latter-Day Saints.

Feb. 4, 1826: James Fenimore Cooper publishes his fourth novel, *The Last of the Mohicans.*

July 4, 1826: Thomas Jefferson and John Adams both die on the 50th anniversary of what America has come to celebrate as Independence Day. Jefferson's last words: "Is it the fourth? . . . It is well."

1827: A Massachusetts inventor named Joseph Dixon opens the first lead pencil factory in America. The pencils lack erasers.

May 19, 1828: President Adams signs a bill that steeply raises tariffs on a number of items. Supporters of Andrew Jackson had introduced the bill (which they called the "Tariff of Abominations") in an effort to embarrass Adams. They figured the bill had no chance of passing. They figured wrong.

Chapter 11

The Influences of Andrew Jackson: 1829–1844

- -

In This Chapter

▶ Starting a Democratic dynasty — Jackson takes office

▶ Debating states' rights

▶ Bringing inventions to life

▶ Driving the Indians out West and freeing Texas

▶ Finding new presidents

▶ Timeline

- -

*T*he election of Andrew Jackson in 1828 began a Democratic dynasty (by then the Democratic Republicans of Jefferson's time were calling themselves just Democrats). For 24 of the next 32 years, Democrats would occupy the White House, and Jackson's policies and philosophy would set the tone for many of them.

In this chapter, Jackson's democracy holds sway, a speech helps get the North ready to fight the Civil War, railroad trains come on the scene, shameful treatment of the American Indians becomes formal government policy, and we remember the Alamo.

Old Hickory

Andrew Jackson was not in a good mood when he arrived in Washington in early 1829 to become president. His beloved wife, Rachel, had died two months before, shortly after discovering that she had been the target of vicious personal attacks during the 1828 election. Jackson was sure the discovery contributed to her death, and he was bitterly angry.

Hero worshipping

"I never saw such a crowd here before. Persons have come 500 miles to see General J ackson, and they seem to think the country has been rescued from some general disaster."

— Sen. Daniel Webster, at Jackson's inauguration, 1829.

But if Jackson was angry, the thousands of his supporters who came to see him take the oath of office were jubilant. Jackson was the first Westerner to win the office and the first to come from humble beginnings. While some came just to cheer their hero, many had also come hoping for a cushy government job.

More than 20,000 people surrounded the Capitol for the inauguration. Jackson gave a speech that hardly anyone heard and then fought his way through the crowd and went off to a reception at the White House. So did almost everyone else. Hordes of people crowded into the place, drinking, eating, and stealing souvenirs. Jackson escaped through a back window and spent the first night of his presidency in a nearby hotel.

Jackson's supporters were referred to as "the mob" by Washington onlookers used to more refinement and less tobacco spitting, but "the mob" also reflected a growing sense of democracy in America.

More people had the vote and were using it. The turnout for the presidential election of 1824 had been 27 percent of the eligible voters. In 1828, it was 58 percent, and in 1840 it was 78 percent. Cheap newspapers and magazines were flourishing, giving the common man access to ideas and information. And a fight for providing free public schools had begun, eventually spreading to every state in the West and North. The average guy was finding his voice, and in Jackson, a focus for his admiration.

Jackson was the first president since Washington who hadn't been to college. He was tall and thin (6'1", 145 pounds) with a full mane of silver-gray hair and hawklike features. His father had died before he was born, and the family was so poor they could not afford a headstone for his grave. Jackson's mother became a housekeeper, and the family went to live with a brother-in-law.

As a boy, Jackson received a sword cut on his head from a British officer who thought the boy hadn't been humble enough, and Jackson learned a lesson, which was never to let a slight or insult go unanswered. He had a violent temper, although he often pretended to be angry just to get his way. Like many military men, he was often inflexible when he made up his mind. His friends called him "Old Hickory" or "Gineral"; his foes called him "King Andrew" (see Figure 11-1).

Figure 11-1:
Political cartoon of President Jackson as king.

As a Western lawyer and politician, Jackson had seen first-hand how the West was often at the mercy of financial interests in the East, and he had a Westerner's distrust of banks. But as a wealthy man by the time he became president, he was not a champion of the idea that all men are equal. Instead, he believed that every man should have an equal chance to succeed, and that no one's rights were more important than another's — unless you were a woman, an Indian, or an African American.

Jackson was also a believer in the statement offered by a New York politician at the time: "To the victors belong the spoils of the enemy." That meant replacing federal officeholders who had been appointed by previous administrations with his own appointees — what became known as the "spoils system." Jackson's theory was that there was nothing very tough about doing most government jobs and they should be rotated to bring new ideas and approaches to them.

Actually, Jackson didn't invent the idea; all the presidents since Washington had done it to some degree. In fact, in his eight years in office, Jackson only turned out about 20 percent of the 1,100-member federal bureaucracy. And many of them needed turning out, because they were inept or corrupt.

The great moon hoax

In 1833, a four-page newspaper appeared on the streets of New York City, called the *Sun*. It was different from other American newspapers in that it favored sensational crime over ponderous politics, was hawked on the streets by newsboys, cost only a penny — and it sometimes made up wild stories that were printed as fact.

In August 1835, the *Sun* published a series of stories it said were reprinted from the *Edinburgh Journal of Science*. They "revealed" the discovery by British astronomer Sir John Herschel

of life on the moon. The life included bison, trees, and four-foot-tall furry winged bat men.

The stories electrified the city. The *Sun's* circulation grew to 19,360, the largest of any newspaper in the world. Rival editors frantically tried to match the stories, and when they couldn't, stole them.

In September, *Sun* publisher Benjamin Day admitted it was all a hoax. But rather than be angry, most readers were amused, and the *Sun's* popularity shone on.

One tough bark

They called Andy Jackson "Old Hickory" because he was tough, and it was a good thing he was. During his life, he was shot in the shoulder and chest, and the bullet in his chest was never removed; he fell down a flight of stairs and almost bled to death; he suffered from recurring bouts of malaria and dysentery; he suffered two pulmonary hemorrhages; and he had a kidney disease. Also the medicine he took for his various ailments rotted his teeth. He lived to be 78. Perhaps if they had nicknamed him "Old Diamond," he might still be alive.

But the spoils system did much harm, too. It changed the qualifications of holding a federal post from being able or experienced to being a campaign worker or contributor. It helped political machines by giving them something with which to reward supporters and it reduced the efficiency of government. It would be decades before civil service reforms would fix some of the problems created by Jackson's efforts to democratize the government.

Nullify This

John C. Calhoun had waited a long time to be president. Intelligent but humorless, the South Carolinian had served as vice president under John Quincy Adams and was now vice president under Jackson. Then, as now, the best thing about being vice president was that it made becoming president easier, and Calhoun figured to follow Jackson into the White House. But two relatively trivial things happened to throw him off-course and, in a way, helped push the country toward civil war. The first involved the wife of Jackson's old friend and secretary of war, John Eaton. Peggy Eaton had a reputation as being something of a slut, which she may or may not have deserved. But Washington society's leading females — led by Calhoun's wife — snubbed her, refusing to invite her to their parties or to attend parties where she was invited.

Jackson, whose own wife had been the target of scandalous gossip, was enraged at the snubs. At one point he called an evening Cabinet meeting to defend Mrs. Eaton. The issue, dubbed "Eaton Malaria" by Washington wags, dominated the first months of Jackson's presidency and drove a wedge between Jackson and Calhoun. The second incident involved a letter Jackson received from Calhoun's enemies, which suggested that Calhoun, while a member of James Monroe's cabinet, had called for Jackson to be court-martialed for invading Florida when it was still owned by Spain. When confronted, Calhoun could only provide vague half-answers. The rift between the two men grew wide, and Jackson turned his successor-favor to Martin Van Buren, a wily New Yorker who had helped get him elected and was his secretary of state.

Calhoun eventually resigned as vice president and was immediately elected a senator from South Carolina. When it was clear he would not become president, Calhoun abandoned his support of a strong central government and became a champion of the rights of states to pick and choose what federal laws it would obey, a theory of government called "nullification."

The speech that helped win a war

Calhoun's embrace of states' rights and nullification further pushed him away from Jackson. Even though he was a Westerner and a slave owner, Jackson was an ardent nationalist. At a White House dinner, when nullification proponents tried to test his loyalties by offering a series of toasts about states' rights, Jackson responded "Our Federal Union — It must be preserved!" (To which Calhoun replied "The Union — next to our liberty, the most dear!")

But despite Jackson's support, nationalism was having a tough time. In the Senate, a debate on January 26, 1830, on whether to stop selling public land in the West gradually turned into a debate on nullification. Sen. Robert Hayne of South Carolina gave a long, impassioned, eloquent speech in favor of the idea, pointing out that it was the only way a state could safeguard its interests and not be dominated by other areas.

Then Daniel Webster of Massachusetts took the floor. Webster was one of the greatest orators in American history. Dark and imposing, with eyes that glowed like coals and a deep but pleasing voice, Webster spoke for hours. The people, not the states, had ratified the Constitution, he said, and if the states were allowed to decide which sections they would or would not subscribe to, then the country would be held together by nothing but "a rope of sand."

Webster's speech had a spectacular effect. Within three months, 40,000 copies had been published, and within a few years, parts of it were standard reading in textbooks throughout the North and West. Hundreds of thousands of young Northerners and Westerners were exposed to its sentiments — including a 21-year-old man on his way to Illinois named Abraham Lincoln. For many of them, they became words worth fighting for.

All together now

"While the Union lasts we have high, exciting, gratifying prospects spread out before us, for us and our children . . . when my eyes shall be turned to behold for the last time the sun in heaven . . . let their last feeble and lingering glance rather behold the gorgeous ensign of the republic . . . and in every wind under the whole heavens, that other sentiment dear to every true American heart — Liberty *and* Union, now and forever, one and inseparable!"

— Daniel Webster, Jan. 26, 1830.

A "tarrible" idea

In 1828, Congress had passed a bill that set high *tariffs,* or taxes, on a bunch of imported goods. The tariffs were favored in the North, because they drove up prices of imported goods and thus made goods produced in Northern factories more attractive. The West was okay with it, because revenues from the tariffs were supposed to pay for public works projects the region needed. But the South, without factories and with less need for roads and canals, hated them.

In 1832, Congress passed a new tariff schedule that was lower than the 1828 rates. But it wasn't enough for the South Carolina legislature. Legislators called for a special convention, and the convention decided that not only was the tariff null and void in South Carolina, the state would militarily defend its right to nullify the law.

The move infuriated Jackson and he sent some Army and Navy units to the state while he prepared a larger force "to crush the rebellion." Fortunately, cooler heads prevailed. Henry Clay, the great negotiator, came up with a compromise tariff that reduced the rates over a decade. The South decided it could live with that without losing face. Both sides claimed victory and a bloody civil clash was once again delayed.

Creating Inventions to Improve American Life

With South Carolina back in the fold, Jackson was easily re-elected in 1832, despite his ill health and his earlier statements that he would only serve one term. Part of the reason he sought a second term was to thrash his old foe, Henry Clay, who was the first nominee of the new National Republican Party. (It would soon take the name of the opposition party to the king in England and become the Whigs.) Another part of the reason for Jackson running was because he had some unfinished business with a bank.

While he was working on that, other people were finding better ways to get around, get something to eat, and express themselves, with a bunch of inventions and innovations.

Making a withdrawal

The charter of the country's only nationwide bank, the Bank of the United States, was due to expire in 1836, and Clay pushed a bill through Congress in 1832 to extend it. But Jackson vetoed the bill, contending the Bank was a private monopoly that fed off the little guys and little banks and benefited only a handful of rich American and foreign investors.

SIDETRIP

Nat Turner's rebellion

Despite all the rhetoric about how well they treated their slaves and how happy the slaves were, Southern slave owners' deepest fear was that the humans they so degraded would some day rise up to seek freedom — and revenge. Slave rebellions, in fact, had occurred in both Northern and Southern states and had been responded to with harsh brutality.

In 1822, for example, just the rumor of a possible uprising resulted in the execution of 37 slaves in South Carolina. In August 1831, however, a preacher/slave named Nat Turner led 70 followers on a murderous rampage around Southampton, Virginia. Before it was over,

Turner's group had murdered 57 white men, women, and children. The rebellion was broken up quickly, and after two months in hiding, Turner was captured and hanged, along with 19 others.

But the rebellion sent shock waves through the South. In retaliation, about 100 slaves were slain at random. New laws were passed to make it harder for owners to free slaves, to restrict the ability of slaves to travel without supervision, and to censor anti-slavery material. Any serious talk of the South voluntarily freeing its slaves ceased.

It was true that the Bank's stock was controlled by relatively few men. There was also truth to the charge of corruption. The Bank's president, Nicholas Biddle, was a brilliant but arrogant aristocrat who often loaned money at no or low interest to the "right people" — including dozens of members of Congress — while clamping down hard on banks in the West. But since 1819 the Bank had provided stability to the economy by requiring local banks to keep adequate gold and silver reserves to back up the currency they issued and to be careful on making loans.

After his veto, Jackson decided to try and kill the Bank off rather than wait until 1836. So he ordered that all federal funds be withdrawn from it and deposited in smaller banks. When his treasury secretary balked, he got a new one, and when that one balked, he got a third who agreed to go along.

At first, everything was all right, mostly because the economy was sailing along. The federal government's budget deficit dropped to zero for the first time in history, and there was even a surplus, which was shared with the states for things like road building and education. But then the boom busted.

Jackson ordered that all public land could only be sold for silver or gold, not paper currency. Land sales sagged from 22 million acres to 6 million in one year. Local banks held mortgages that weren't being paid, and they couldn't foreclose because the land was worth little and no one could buy it anyway.

In 1837, after a bank panic, the country sank into a four-year recession. But by that time Jackson was out of office, and it was someone else's problem.

Riding the train

On Sept. 18, 1830, a nine-mile race was held on the outskirts of Baltimore. The entries were a horse pulling a carriage and a noisy contraption on wooden wheels called a steam locomotive engine. The horse won, after the engine broke down. But it was a relatively short-lived victory for Old Paint, because the railroad had arrived in America.

Although trains had been operating in England for some years, the Baltimore & Ohio line's "Tom Thumb" was the first in the United States. By the end of that first year, the B&O had carried 80,000 passengers along a 13-mile track. In South Carolina, a 136-mile line between Charleston and Hamburg was opened in 1833. By 1840, 409 chartered railroads had laid 3,300 miles of track, and by 1860, America had close to 30,000 miles.

Early trains had their flaws. Sparks caused fires along the tracks and in the rail cars and the rails had a nasty habit of coming up through the bottoms of the cars. There was also the occasional explosion, which hardly ever happened with horses.

But trains had an enormous impact. The demands for labor to build tracks encouraged immigration, and the demand for capital to finance the lines attracted foreign investment. The ability to transport large amounts of goods and agricultural products opened new markets and linked old ones. Communications were vastly improved, and it got a whole lot easier to go from here to there.

"When I hear the iron horse make the hills echo with his snort, like thunder, shaking the earth with his feet and breathing fire and smoke," conceded the author and philosopher Henry David Thoreau, "it seems the earth had got a race now worthy to inhabit it."

Reaping what you sow

As the nation grew, so did the need to feed it. Steel plows, most notably the kind developed by an Illinois blacksmith named John Deere, had made it easier to plant crops. But harvesting, especially grain, was a laborious process that involved men swinging heavy scythes all day long and then going back and picking up all the threshed grain.

In 1831, a Pennsylvania man named Cyrus McCormick came up with a rolling machine that both cut down the grain and threw it onto a platform. McCormick's machine could do the work of 15 men, and faster. By 1860, he was making 4,000 harvesters a year and selling them on the installment plan so farmers could afford them. America's breadbasket got much bigger because of it.

AMERICAN FACES

Horace Mann

Of all the reform movements in the 1830s and 1840s — temperance, the abolition of slavery, women's suffrage — the most effective was the "common school" movement, an effort to provide compulsory free education to children.

Its leader, Horace Mann, was anything but common. Born in 1793, Mann became a Massachusetts legislator. In 1837, he drafted a bill that created the state's school board, and then he became its secretary. Mann advocated tax-supported schools that would bring together kids from all economic, cultural, and ethnic backgrounds. He fought for higher salaries for teachers and better schoolhouses, established the first American teacher training school, and encouraged women to become teachers.

Mann's exuberance and persistence spread, and by the 1850s, every state outside the South had free elementary schools and teacher-training institutions. Mann died in 1859, having lived up to his own advice: "Be ashamed to die until you have won some victory for humanity."

Communicating across America and the Atlantic

In New York, meanwhile, a painter named Samuel F.B. Morse was tinkering with a device that could send messages using electricity. Called the telegraph, Morse's device was patented in 1841. He then got Congress to put up $30,000 so he could string electric wire between Washington and Baltimore. On March 24, 1844, the first message — "What hath God wrought?" — was sent. In 1856, the Western Union Company was formed, and by 1866, a trans-Atlantic telegraph cable had been laid between America and Europe.

The telegraph was the first true mass communications medium. By the end of the century, there were few places in the world that could not send and receive messages. Not everyone, however, was impressed. When someone remarked that with the telegraph, Maine could now talk to Florida, the writer Ralph Waldo Emerson reportedly observed, "Yes, but has Maine anything to *say* to Florida?"

Removing the Indians

An Indian name for Andrew Jackson was "Long Knife," and not because they considered him a swell guy. For his part, Jackson contended he did not hate Indians despite the fact that as a soldier he had killed them and burned their villages. He just didn't want them where they would be in the way.

SIDETRIP

On tonight's menu. . . .

One thing you can say about nineteenth-century Americans, they didn't waste much when it came to chow. Some samples from an 1836 book called "The Frugal Housewife": "A bullock's heart is very profitable to use as a steak, broiled just like beef. There are usually five pounds in a heart, and it can be bought for 25 cents . . . Calf's head should be cleansed with very great care . . . The brains, after being thoroughly washed, should be put in a little bag, with one pounded cracker, or as much crumbled bread, seasoned with sifted sage and tied up and boiled one hour. After the brains are boiled, they should be well broken up with a knife, and peppered, salted and buttered."

So Jackson wholeheartedly supported a policy that was actually started by President James Monroe. The policy was to systematically move all the Indians east of the Mississippi River to west of the Mississippi, or off the fertile acreage of the river valley and onto the dusty prairies of what is now Oklahoma.

In 1830, Congress passed the Indian Removal Act and set aside $500,000 for the job. By the time the odious job was done in the 1840s, more than 100,000 Indians had been moved off more than 200 million acres of real estate. Jackson and others contended that the forced exodus was actually a humane gesture, because the only practical alternative was to exterminate them. This attitude conveniently ignored the fact that thousands of Indians died of disease, hunger, and exposure on the forced marches — giving rise to the term "Trail of Tears." Of all the nation's leaders, only Henry Clay spoke out against the policy.

Two tribes did not go easily. The Sauk and Fox tribe, led by Chief Black Hawk, originally crossed the Mississippi, and then came back. Met by a large U.S. military force, which included an Illinois militia volunteer named Abe Lincoln, the tribe surrendered after bloody fights in which women and children were slaughtered along with the Indian braves. In Florida, the Seminoles under Chief Osceola used the swamps and Everglades to fight for a decade before ultimately surrendering. The Seminole war cost the U.S. military $20 million and 1,500 lives.

In the Southeast, the "civilized tribes" of the Cherokee, Creek, Choctaw, and Chickasaw had actually been pretty adaptable to the encroaching white man's ways. They built roads and houses, raised cattle, and farmed. Some even owned slaves. When the state of Georgia tried to force the Cherokee off their land, they appealed to the U.S. Supreme Court, which ruled in the Indians' favor. It didn't help. What the state couldn't do, the federal government could. By the end of the 1840s most of the Indians in the Eastern United States were gone, pushed West to await being pushed some more.

A shameful march of progress

"The Indians had their families with them, and they brought in their train the wounded and sick . . . three or four thousand soldiers drive before them the wandering race of aborigines. These are followed by the pioneers who pierce the woods, scare off the beasts of prey . . . and make ready the triumphal march of civilization."

— Alexis de Tocqueville, after watching a band of Choctaw Indians forced across the Mississippi, 1831.

Claiming Independence for Texas

Everyone wanted Texas. President John Quincy Adams offered $1 million for it; Andrew Jackson upped the offer to $5 million. But the newly independent country of Mexico wasn't interested in selling, even though it was sparsely settled and Mexico had no firm plans for the area. But for some unexplained reason, it did allow Americans to settle there. In 1821, a Connecticut man named Moses Austin contracted with Mexico to bring 300 American families to an area near San Antonio. Austin died shortly afterwards, but his son Stephen took over and led the settlers to the area in 1823.

By 1834, Austin's colony had 20,000 white colonists and 2,000 black slaves. That was four times the number of Mexicans in Texas. Slavery was abolished in Mexico in 1831, but Austin ignored the law, as well as the one requiring the settlers to convert to Roman Catholicism. More and more, the settlers began thinking of themselves less as Mexican subjects and more as a cross between Mexicans and Texans — or "Texians," as they called themselves.

The area began to attract restless and sometimes lawless Americans who were not as peaceful as the Austin bunch. These included Sam Houston, a soldier and good friend of Jackson's; the Bowie brothers, Louisiana slave smugglers who had designed an impressive long knife that bore their name; and Davy Crockett, a Tennessee ex-congressman and daredevil backwoodsman with a flair for self-promotion.

Remembering the Alamo

In 1835, Mexican President Antonio Lopez de Santa Anna proclaimed a new constitution that eliminated any special privileges for Texas, and the Texians declared their independence. They kicked the Mexican soldiers out of the garrison at San Antonio, and a motley force of 187 Texians and American volunteers set up a fort in an old mission called the Alamo.

On March 6, 1836, after a 13-day siege and a brief pre-dawn battle, Santa Anna's army of about 5,000 overran the Alamo, despite heavy Mexican losses, and killed all its defenders (see Figure 11-2). The victory accomplished little for Santa Anna, but "Remember the Alamo" became a rallying cry for Texians. The slaughter of another Texas garrison at Goliad, after it had surrendered, further enflamed the cause. Six weeks after the Alamo fell, an army led by Sam Houston surprised and defeated Santa Anna at the San Jacinto River, and Santa Anna was captured.

Figure 11-2: Battle of the Alamo.

Becoming a state

Texas ratified a constitution, which included slavery, and waited to be annexed to the United States. But Jackson was in no hurry. He did not want a war with Mexico over Texas and risk the election of his handpicked successor, Martin Van Buren. And the fact that Texas was pro-slavery would upset the delicate balance between free and slave states.

Jackson did formally recognize Texas on his last day in office in March 1841, after Van Buren had been elected. But it wasn't until December 1845 that the Lone Star Republic became the Lone Star State.

Fighting for the Presidency

In the 16 years between 1820 and 1836, America had three presidents. In the eight years between 1836 and 1844, it also had three.

The first was Martin Van Buren, who was the first president born under the U.S. flag. Van Buren was a New York lawyer and governor whose political machine helped elect Jackson. Dubbed "the Little Magician" for his political skills, Van Buren snuggled up to Jackson and became his favorite, serving as secretary of state and vice president and winning Jackson's considerable support in beating Whig candidate William Henry Harrison.

A waste of blood

"In our opinion, the blood of our soldiers as well as that of the enemy was shed in vain . . . the massacres of the Alamo, of Goliad . . . convinced the rebels that no peaceable settlement could be expected, and that they must conquer, or die."

— Vicente Filisola, a Mexican soldier who fought at the Alamo, 1836.

Unfortunately for him, Van Buren took office just as the Panic of 1837 and its subsequent economic recession was hitting the country. It lasted most of his term, and he was blamed for it. But he did manage to strike a blow for labor while in office, agreeing to lower the working day for federal employees to 10 hours.

Despite his vast political skills, Van Buren was out-foxed by the Whigs when he ran for re-election. It began when a Democratic newspaper reporter sneered at Harrison, who was again Van Buren's opponent: "Give him (Harrison) a barrel of hard cider and settle a pension of two thousand a year on him, and . . . he will sit the remainder of his days in a log cabin."

It turned out that didn't sound like a bad idea to a lot of voters. Harrison, an old Indian fighter who had defeated Tecumseh at the Battle of Tippecanoe Creek in 1811, was actually a moderately wealthy Virginia farmer. But the Whigs seized on the chance to present him as a tough frontiersman. Rallies were held featuring log cabins and plenty of hard cider, and "Old Tippecanoe" squashed Van Buren in the election.

At his inauguration on March 4, 1841, the 68-year-old Harrison gave a long and pointless speech in a pouring rainstorm, without a hat. He fell ill with pneumonia and died a month later, the first president to die in office.

His successor was the newly elected vice-president, John Tyler, a stubborn slave owner from Virginia who had only become a Whig because he had a falling out with the Democrats and Jackson over the issue of nullification and states' rights.

Tyler enjoyed the distinction of being the only sitting president thrown out of his own political party, when he refused to go along with Whig policies in Congress and vetoed a bunch of Whig bills. In 1844, Tyler started his own party, the Democratic-Republicans, for awhile so he could run again. But he gave up the idea after Jackson asked him to step aside.

The Whigs put up Henry Clay in 1844, who had been running unsuccessfully for president for 20 years. The Democrats, after a long and heated convention, nominated a *dark horse,* or surprise, candidate in James K. Polk, of

Tennessee. Polk was an ardent follower of Jackson, so much so that he was called "Young Hickory."

It was a very close election, but Polk squeaked through. He made few promises during his campaign, among them: To acquire California from Mexico, to settle a dispute with England over the Oregon border, to lower the tariff, and not to seek a second term. He kept all of them.

Gee Grandpa, What Else Happened?

Oct. 16, 1829: The Tremont Hotel opens in Boston, featuring 170 rooms, European-style forks with four tines instead of the U.S. two-tined version, and indoor toilets.

Jan. 1, 1831: Abolitionist editor William Lloyd Garrison opens a newspaper called *The Liberator* in Boston. He editorializes "I am in earnest — I will not equivocate — I will not excuse — I will not retreat a single inch — AND I WILL BE HEARD."

Oct. 14, 1834: Henry Blair becomes the first African American to receive a U.S. patent, for a corn harvester.

Jan. 30, 1835: Andrew Jackson survives the first assassination attempt on a U.S. president, when a lunatic claiming to be an heir to the British throne points two pistols at him in the Capitol. The would-be assassin pulls the triggers at point-blank range but, miraculously, they both misfire.

Sept. 1, 1836: Narcissa Whitman and Eliza Spalding, the wives of two Protestant missionaries, become the first white women to travel overland to the Pacific Coast, arriving at a mission in Oregon.

Oct. 30, 1838: Oberlin College in Ohio becomes the nation's first institution of higher learning to admit women.

May 10, 1839: Mormon leader Joseph Smith moves the religion's headquarters to Illinois after attacks and persecutions in Missouri.

March 30, 1842: A Georgia doctor, Crawford Long, becomes the first physician to use an anesthetic (ether) during an operation.

Feb. 25, 1843: The British flag is raised over the Hawaiian Islands. It comes down five months later, the Brits apologize, and the islands return to Hawaiian rule.

April 1844: A German brewer, Jacob Best Sr., introduces a lighter kind of beer, called "lager," to Milwaukee. It catches on.

Chapter 12

War, Gold, and a Gathering Storm: 1845–1860

● ●

In This Chapter

▶ Getting gold fever

▶ Watching America diversify

▶ Dividing a country

▶ Timeline

● ●

*I*n the 1840s, it seemed America had an unscratchable itch for elbowroom. It annexed Texas, quarreled with England over Oregon, and took half a million square miles of real estate away from Mexico. A good part of the nation — and the world, for that matter — came down with Gold Fever too.

In the 1850s, however, much of the country's attention was on trying to cure the seemingly incurable disease of slavery, without amputating the Union.

Heading South of the Border

President James K. Polk was a hard worker with a thick hide, which are pretty good traits in a president. He worked 18-hour days, and he didn't miss many days at work. He was also a very goal-oriented guy, and one of his goals was to get California. That would give America a base on two oceans and fulfill its "manifest destiny" to stretch from sea to sea.

But Mexico was not in a selling mood. Mexican leaders were furious at the admission of Texas as a state in December 1845, even though it had been independent from Mexico for almost 10 years. So when Polk sent diplomat James Slidell to Mexico City in late 1845 with an offer to buy California for around $25 million, Mexican leaders refused to even meet with Slidell.

It's just supposed to be ours

The term "Manifest Destiny" became popular in the 1840s as a way of explaining how it was geographically natural for America to expand its borders to conform with the continent. A New York journalist named John L. O'Sullivan first used the term in 1845, when he wrote the country must fulfill "our manifest destiny to overspread the continent allotted by Providence for the free development of our yearly multiplying millions." It was a convenient way of saying God wanted us to beat up Mexico and take a big chunk of its land.

Starting a war

Polk then decided to take it by force, pushing the United States into its first war with another country just to gain territory. A young Army lieutenant named Ulysses S. Grant called it "one of the most unjust [wars] ever waged by a stronger against a weaker nation."

It took a little prompting to get it started without firing the first shot. Polk sent an "army of observation," under the command of Gen. Zachary Taylor to the banks of the Rio Grande River, an area that Mexico considered its territory. The army was gradually built up until there were about 4,000 U.S. troops there in April 1846. Taylor's soldiers managed to provoke a small attack by Mexican troops, and the war was on.

It wasn't much of a war. The United States lost 13,000 men, 11,000 of them to disease, and lost not a single major battle. The Mexican army was badly led, badly equipped, and badly trained. The American army, while sometimes short on supplies because Polk was a penny pincher, was very well led, chiefly by Taylor and Gen. Winfield Scott.

Taylor, whose men called him "Old Rough and Ready" because he was tough and because he was something of a slob in his personal appearance, was a career soldier. So was Scott, whose nickname was "Old Fuss and Feathers" because he had a taste for pomp and showy uniforms. Scott and Taylor were ably supported by West Point-trained officers such as Grant and Capt. Robert E. Lee, as well as other men to whom the Mexican War would prove a training ground for the Civil War 15 years later.

The first major battle, at Palo Alto, gave a taste of what was to come. Taylor led 2,300 soldiers against a Mexican army of 4,500, and routed them. In a follow-up fight, a U.S. force of 1,700 scattered a Mexican force of 7,500. American losses totaled less than 50 men for the two fights; the Mexicans lost more than 1,000.

In fact, the biggest American worry was that it might have to fight Britain at the same time, over a dispute in the Northwest. American officials insisted that a boundary line between America and Canada be drawn at 54°, 40 minutes of latitude (which would have given us Vancouver, British Columbia). A slogan from Polk's campaign, "54-40 or fight" became popular with some of the more pugnacious members of Congress. But in July 1846, the two sides agreed to compromise at 49°.

Capturing California and the West

The U.S. then turned its full attention to acquiring California, which was rather easily captured, despite the occasional bumbling and bickering of the American commanders. Many of the Mexicans in California considered themselves "Californios" first, and weren't overly concerned about a U.S. takeover.

In Mexico, meanwhile, U.S. forces kept their undefeated streak going. Mexican forces were now commanded by General Antonio Lopez de Santa Anna, of Alamo infamy. Santa Anna, who had been in exile in Cuba, talked U.S. officials into helping him sneak back into Mexico, where he promised he would sell his country out. Once there, he promptly took over command of the army and vowed to crush the hated Yankees. But he lied about that, too.

In September 1846, Taylor's troops took the city of Monterrey, Mexico. In March 1847, Scott captured the fortified seaport of Vera Cruz after a three-week siege. And in September 1847, his forces captured Mexico City, all but ending the war.

The formalities were taken care of in the Treaty of Guadalupe Hidalgo. It gave America more than 500,000 square miles of Mexican territory (see Figure 12-1), including California, Nevada, Utah, Arizona, most of New Mexico and parts of Wyoming and Colorado. Mexico dropped claims to Texas. And, perhaps to soothe a guilty conscience, Polk agreed to pay Mexico $18.25 million, about 80 percent of what he offered before the war.

Lonesome cow

Samuel A. Maverick was a Texas pioneer with a stubborn streak. Starting in about 1846, the San Antonio cattleman began refusing to brand his cattle. Why isn't clear. Maybe he was just lazy or contrary, or maybe he figured it was a good way to be able to claim all the unbranded cattle in the area. Whatever the reason, his surname became synonymous with someone who goes his or her own way.

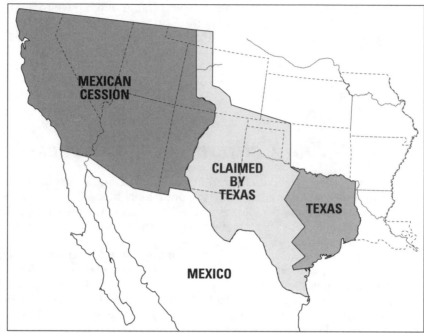

Figure 12-1:
Territory
won from
Mexico.

Not everyone was thrilled. In Congress, a gangly representative from Illinois named Lincoln attacked the war as unjust aggression. In Massachusetts, the contrary writer Henry David Thoreau refused to pay his poll tax because the money might be used to support the war. His aunt paid it for him after he spent only one night in jail, but the essay that came out of it, "Civil Disobedience," became a handbook for non-violent protestors and passive resistance demonstrators around the world well into the next century.

Much of the dissent about the war stemmed not just from being uncomfortable about picking on Mexico, but because of fears it was designed to acquire more territory for the spread of slavery. "They just want Californy / So's to lug new slave states in / To abuse ye and to scorn ye / And to plunder ye like sin," wrote poet James Russell Lowell in 1848. But even as Lowell wrote, another, richer, reason was lying on the bottom of a California river.

Rushing for Gold

On the chilly morning of Jan. 24, 1848, a man looked down into a sawmill ditch off the American River, about 40 miles east of Sacramento, California, (or 120 miles east of Yerba Buena, which soon became better known as San Francisco). The man, a dour carpenter from New Jersey named James Marshall, saw a pea-shaped dollop of yellow metal glinting in the gravel.

"Boys," Marshall told the group of laborers who were helping build the sawmill, "By God, I believe I have found a gold mine."

What he had really found was the ignition switch for one of the most massive migrations in human history: the California Gold Rush. It was quite literally a rush, once the news got out. That took awhile. Although rumors of the find surfaced in the East not long after Marshall's discovery, no one paid much attention. Then President Polk announced in December 1848, that there looked to be enough gold in California to pay for the costs of the Mexican War many times over. That made people sit up and take notice.

Going West

More than 90,000 people made their way to California in the two years following the first discovery and more than 300,000 by 1854 — or one of about every 90 people then living in the United States. The stampede ripped families apart and stripped towns of a large percentage of their young men. Not all of the prospectors were American. An 1850 census showed that 25 percent of those counted were from countries as far away as Australia and China.

It wasn't easy getting there. From the East Coast, one could take a 15,000-mile, five-month voyage around the tip of South America. More than 500 ships made the voyage in 1849 alone. You could also cut across the Isthmus of Panama and take two months off the trip, if you were willing to risk cholera and malaria. By land, the 2,200-mile journey from trailheads in Missouri or Iowa might take three or four months — with a lot of luck (see Figure 12-2).

OFF FOR CALIFORNIA.

Figure 12-2:
Cartoon of people flocking to California.

Free, not flea

"Jane, I left you and the boys for no other reason than this: To come here and procure a little property by the sweat of my brow so that we could have a place of our own, that I might not be a dog for other people any longer."

— 49er Melvin Paden, in a letter to his wife, 1850.

Some of those who came were already famous, like explorer and soldier John C. Fremont, who got rich when a land agent bought him property in the foothills rather than along the ocean — which is where Fremont wanted to buy — and the foothills land proved to be drenched in gold. Some became famous later, like the New York butcher who made enough money from a meat shop in the Gold Rush metropolis of Hangtown to open a meatpacking plant in Milwaukee. His name was Phillip Armour.

History recalls them as the 49ers, since the first big year of the Gold Rush was 1849. They called themselves Argonauts, after the mythical Greek heroes who sailed in the Argo with Jason to search for the Golden Fleece. Most of them found nothing but disappointment, and many found death.

With few women to add a touch of civilization and balance, and no government, it was a pretty rough place. In just one July week in 1850 in a town called Sonora, two Massachusetts men had their throats slit, a Chilean was shot to death in a gunfight, and a Frenchman stabbed a Mexican to death. The town of Marysville had 17 murders in one week, and at the height of the Gold Rush, San Francisco averaged 30 new houses and two murders a day.

A miner making $8 a day (about $165 in 1999 dollars) was doing eight times better than his coal-mining counterpart in the East. But prices were outrageous too. A loaf of bread that cost 4 cents in New York cost 75 cents in the goldfields. All in all, most gold seekers were not any better off than laborers in the rest of the country.

What was worse, many of the diggers had always believed in the American adage that working hard would bring success. Finding gold, America learned, depended a lot more on luck than good intentions. Of course there were other ways to find gold than digging for it. Men like Collis Huntington, Charles Crocker, Leland Stanford, and Mark Hopkins — who became known as California's "Big Four" — made fortunes selling miners supplies and then branching into other pursuits such as banks and eventually railroads.

But there was gold, and plenty of it. During the Civil War alone, California produced more than $170 million worth of bullion, which helped prop up wartime Union currency.

The Gold Rush had other impacts as well. Although many of the 49ers came and left after a relatively short stay, many of them also stuck around. From a non-Indian population of about 18,000 in January 1848, California grew to a resident population of 165,000 within three years. San Francisco became a booming U.S. port and doorway to the Pacific. The growth and importance of the state also helped spur long-delayed congressional approval of the proposal for a transcontinental railroad.

Eventually the state was to become a magnet for different kinds of gold rushes. The beginning of the aerospace industry, Hollywood, the beginnings of the computer age in Silicon Valley, and the birth of the biotechnology industry all had California roots. But before all that could happen, it had to become a state.

The Compromise of 1850

Zachary Taylor was probably the least political of all American presidents. He served 40 years in the Army, but never held any other office before being elected president. In fact, he had never even voted in a presidential election. But the popularity of "Old Rough and Ready" carried him to the White House in the 1848 election after Polk lived up to his promise not to seek a second term.

Taylor had expressed no opinions during the campaign about the hottest issue of the time, slavery, and had no plans for what to do about all that land he had just helped take from Mexico. At the time, the country was equally, if uneasily, divided into 15 free and 15 slave states. So when California asked to be admitted as a state, the debate raged on which side it should fall. Its own constitution banned slavery, mostly on the practical grounds that gold miners didn't want to compete with slaves digging for their masters. The president agreed.

Grave stakes

In the Calaveras County mining camp of Carson Creek, in 1851, a miner named Israel Norman died. Norman was very well liked, so his colleagues decided to have a formal funeral for him. Another miner, who had been a preacher in the East, officiated, and they dug the grave about 100 yards from the camp.

As the minister began the eulogy, one of those in attendance began to play absently with a handful of dirt from the grave — and noticed it was loaded with gold. "The congregation is dismissed," the preacher cried. Norman was hastily buried elsewhere.

The little lady and the big book

Harriet Beecher Stowe was a diminutive Connecticut woman whose father, husband, and brothers were all Protestant ministers, and who dabbled in writing from time to time to bring in a little extra money. But when the Fugitive Slave Law was passed, it ticked her off enough to write a novel about slavery. She called it *Uncle Tom's Cabin.*

The book, a soap-opera story with stereotypical characters, was published in Boston in 1852 — and it was a sensation. It sold 10,000 copies in one week, 300,000 copies in its first year and more than 1.5 million copies worldwide. Its chief effect was to put human faces on an issue that many Northerners had thought about only in political terms. It outraged Southerners, who felt it was grossly unfair.

Stowe was hailed as a saint; she was also mailed the ear of a "disobedient slave." Stung by accusations that her book exaggerated the plight of slaves, Stowe wrote a second book called *A Key to Uncle Tom's Cabin,* in which she documented all of the abuses in the first book.

Uncle Tom's Cabin became one of the most powerful propaganda pieces ever written. In 1862, Stowe was introduced to Abraham Lincoln. "So," Lincoln reportedly said to her, "you're the little woman that wrote the book that made this great war."

Those aging giants of Congress, Henry Clay of Kentucky and Daniel Webster of Massachusetts, urged yet another compromise approach. But Taylor was adamant that California be admitted without delay as a free state. Southerners, led by their own aging giant, John C. Calhoun of South Carolina, were just as adamantly opposed. Representatives from nine southern states met in Nashville in June 1850, to consider leaving the Union if California were made a free state.

Fortunately for everyone but himself, Taylor helped solve the problem by suddenly dying of typhoid fever. His successor, a pliable fellow from New York named Millard Fillmore, was much more acceptable to a deal. Pushed by the last great speeches given by Clay and Webster, and with the help of a U.S. Senate newcomer from Illinois named Stephen Douglas, a deal was reached.

The Compromise consisted of a series of five bills. California was admitted as a free state; New Mexico and Utah were admitted as territories, with the slavery question to be settled later; Texas received $10 million for land it gave the new territory of New Mexico; the slave trade was abolished in Washington, D.C.; and a fugitive slave law was approved that made it much easier for slave owners to recapture escaped slaves by getting federal help.

The Fugitive Slave Law put all black people at risk, since all a slave owner had to do was sign a paper saying the person was an escaped slave, show it to a federal magistrate, and slap the chains on. Although only a few hundred African Americans were victims of the law, it outraged many Northerners, and anti-slavery resentment grew. But talk of dissolving the Union died down. For the last time, a compromise worked. Clay, Calhoun, and Webster would all be dead before it fell apart.

Coming Over and Spreading Out

One thing you could say with certainty in the middle of the nineteenth century was that there sure were a lot more Americans than there were at the start of the nineteenth century. The country's population in 1860 was 31.4 million, nearly four times more than it had been a half-century before. Of the world's predominantly white nations, only France, Russia, and Austria had larger populations.

Many of the new Americans had been born elsewhere. The number of immigrants to America in 1830 was about 25,000. By 1855, the number was closer to 450,000. They came from as close as Mexico and Canada and as far away as China and Japan. When they got here, they tended to stay with their fellow expatriates, where the language, food, and culture were more familiar, creating mini-nations.

They also increasingly stayed in cities, even if they had come from a farm background. In 1840, there were 10 Americans living on farms to every 1 that lived in a town. By 1850, that ratio was 5 to 1, and many of the new city dwellers were from foreign shores.

Living dangerously

The parts of the cities they dwelled in were usually like something from a horror movie: dark, smelly, filthy, and violent. Many of the immigrants were so appalled that reality didn't match their glittering visions of America that they went back home.

Because of the glut of people wanting any kind of a job when they got here, wages in the largest cities were pitifully low. In 1851, New York newspaperman Horace Greeley estimated it took a minimum of $10.37 a week to support a family of five, and that didn't include money for medical needs or recreation. The average factory worker, laboring six days a week for 10 or 11 hours a day might make $5, which meant everyone in the family had to do something to make ends meet.

Because they were newcomers, and because most native-born Americans still lived in smaller towns or on farms, there was little appetite for reforms or cleaning up the cities. That wouldn't come until the numbers of immigrants got even larger, and middle-class Americans began being more affected by it.

Train lubricant

"In eighteen hundred and forty eight, / I learned to drink my whisky straight. / 'Tis an elegant drink and can't be bate / For working on the railway."

— From a popular 1848 song. "Paddy Working on the (Erie) Railway."

And still they came, from 600,00 immigrants in the 1830s to 1.7 million in the 1840s to 2.6 million in the 1850s. Most of them were from just two areas in Europe: Ireland and the German states. More than 70 percent of the immigrants between 1840 and 1860 were German or Irish.

For the Irish, it was come or starve. A fungus all but wiped out Ireland's potato crop in 1845, and there was a widespread famine. So more than 1.5 million Irish scraped up the $10 or $12 one-way fare and piled into America-bound ships for an often hellish two-week trip in a cargo hold. Many of the ships had brought Southern cotton to Britain, and in a way they were bring back the North's cash crop — cheap labor to work in factories and build railroads.

Many of the Irish settled in New York City or Boston. Politically savvy, they served first as soldiers for the big-city political machines and then as bosses. Even so, they were harshly discriminated against in many places, and "N.I.N.A." signs hung in many employers' windows. It stood for "No Irish Need Apply."

Almost as many Germans came as Irish during this period, although they were more likely to spread out. The Germans also came because of food shortages or other tough economic times. But many decided to come after efforts failed to throw off despotic rule in the various German states in the late 1840s. Generally better off financially and better educated than other immigrant groups (they brought the idea of "kindergarten," or "children's garden," with them), many Germans pushed away from the Eastern cities to the Midwest, especially Wisconsin.

The rise in immigration also increased anti-immigrant feeling, especially in areas where the newcomers were competing with people born in America for jobs. In 1849, an organization surfaced called the Nativists. They were better known as the "Know Nothing Party," because members supposedly replied, "I know nothing" when asked by outsiders what was going on at their meetings. The Know Nothings demanded an end to immigration, a prohibition on non-natives voting or holding office, and restrictions on Roman Catholics.

The Know Nothings made a lot of noise for awhile. Renamed the American Party, they attracted more than one million members by 1855 and managed to elect several governors and scores of congressmen. Their 1856 presidential candidate, Millard Fillmore, even managed to carry Maryland. But the Know Nothings faded away as the Civil War approached, torn apart by differences between Northern and Southern members over the dividing issue of slavery.

Trailing the Mormons

Although one of the Know Nothings' chief targets had been Roman Catholics, Americans in the mid-nineteenth century were generally a pretty tolerant bunch when it came to religion. About three-fourths of them were regular churchgoers, and there were so many denominations that no one church dominated. By 1860, almost every state had repealed laws against Jews or Catholics holding public office, and the question "what can you do?" was more prevalent than "how do you worship?"

Of course try telling that to a Mormon in 1846. The Church of Jesus Christ of Latter Day Saints began in 1830 with the publication of the Book of Mormon by a New York man named Joseph Smith. To escape persecutions, Smith moved his headquarters to Ohio, and then Missouri and then on to Nauvoo, Illinois, on the banks of the Mississippi. Nauvoo became one of the most thriving cities in the state.

But the Mormons' habits of working hard, sticking to themselves, and having more than one wife at a time seemed to irk outsiders, and the persecutions began again. This time Smith and his brother were killed by a mob, and Mormon leaders decided they needed some distance between themselves and the rest of America.

Led by a strong and capable lieutenant of Smith's, Brigham Young, the Mormons moved west, many of them pushing two-wheeled carts for hundreds of miles. Finally, they settled in the Great Salt Lake Basin, a forbidding region in Utah that most other people thought of as uninhabitable. Establishing a rather rigidly run society and economic system, the Mormons thrived. By 1848, there were 5,000 living in the area, many of them Europeans who had been converted by Mormon missionaries.

Many of the Mormons fought in the Mexican War as a way of "earning" what had been Mexican territory. In 1850, Utah became a territory. But its statehood was delayed for almost 50 years, in part because of the Mormons' refusal until then to drop their practice of multiple wives, or polygamy.

Wagons ho!

Although it's often attributed to Horace Greeley, it was actually Indiana journalist John B. Soule who advised in 1850, "Go West, young man, Go West!"

America's game

Just who baseball's parents were isn't clear. Versions of the game had been played in England since well before the Mayflower got here, and more were devised as America grew: cricket, one old cat, bittle-battle, stick ball, rounders, and town ball.

But the game could be said to have been born on the Elysian Fields, in Hoboken, New Jersey, on June 19, 1846. It was there the New York Knickerbockers club squared off against a team called the New York Nine. They played under rules — nine-member teams, a diamond-shaped infield — devised by a New York bank teller and member of the Knicks' team, Alexander Cartwright.

Cartwright's rules caught on, and eventually they evolved as the basis for the National Pastime. But it didn't help his team that day. Some of the Knicks' best players had refused to go all the way to Hoboken to play, and the team lost 23-1.

He was a little late. Even before the Gold Rush, Americans in ever-increasing numbers were moving west. Despite the awesome dangers and hardships, settlers piled their belongings into a fortified farm wagon and started out, mostly from St. Joseph or Independence in Missouri.

Some of them stopped on the Great Plains of Kansas and Nebraska, while others pushed on to the West Coast. By 1846, 5,000 Americans had settled in the Willamette Valley in the Oregon Territory, and by 1859, the territory had become a state. America's "manifest destiny" was being achieved.

The women's movement

As more and more women got involved in the fight over slavery, many of them came to resent how in many ways they were also second-class Americans. Like slaves, women could not vote, they could not retain their property when they got married, and they could legally be beaten by their husbands.

A woman's view

"I have heard much about the sexes being equal; I can carry as much as any man, and can eat as much too, if I can get it. I am as strong as any man I know . . . I can't read, but I can hear. I have heard the Bible and have learned that Eve caused man to sin. Well if woman upset the world, do give her a chance to set it right side up again."

— Sojourner Truth, a freed slave who became one of America's most outstanding orators, at a women's rights convention, 1851.

Leaders such as Lucretia Mott, Elizabeth Cady Stanton, and Susan B. Anthony began to publicly demand more rights. In 1848, feminists met at Seneca Falls, N.Y., at a women's rights convention. Stanton read a "declaration of sentiments" that paraphrased the declaration Thomas Jefferson had written 72 years before: "All men *and women* are created equal."

Although some states began allowing women to keep their own property after marriage, and some colleges began admitting women in the 1840s, the feminist crusade was overshadowed by the fight over slavery. For many of their rights, women would have to wait.

The Beginning of the End

The issue of slavery not only overshadowed the women's movement, it overshadowed virtually every part of American life. The Methodist and Baptist churches split into North-South factions because of it. Families with branches in the North and South stopped speaking to each other. It even strained business relations, in a country where hardly anything got in the way of making a dollar.

And it was showing no signs of going away by itself. Despite a federal ban on importing slaves, the slave population grew from 3.2 million in 1850 to almost 4 million in 1860, almost all of it through childbirths. So expensive had slaves become that some Southerners had begun calling for an end to the ban on new slaves from Africa.

Factoring a slave's life

Actually, about 75 percent of Southern families didn't even own any slaves. But even non-slave owners defended it. Slaves received the benefits of being exposed to the Christian religion, of having cradle-to-grave shelter and food, and of being a contributing part of Southern society. That was more, they said, than many Northern factory workers could say. (Of course that ignored the fact that even the most miserable factory worker could still make his own choices as to where he worked, did not have to submit to beatings from his employer, and was not very likely to see his wife and children taken from him and sold off to some other state.)

Pro-slavery forces also pointed out that slaves were actually well treated if they behaved. "Negroes are too high [priced] in proportion to the price of cotton," explained a slave owner in 1849, "and it behooves those who own them to make them last as long as possible." And, slavery's defenders said, what would the nation do with them if all the slaves were freed?

SIDETRIP

Canes and congressmen

This is how emotional the issue of slavery was: In the Spring of 1856, Massachusetts Sen. Charles Sumner, an acid-tongued abolitionist, launched a long and personal attack on South Carolina Senator Andrew P. Butler, an elderly man who had the unfortunate habit of drooling. So nasty was Sumner's attack on Butler, who was not there at the time, that Sen. Stephen Douglas warned "That damn fool will get himself killed by some other damn fool."

The "other damn fool" turned out to be Butler's nephew, a congressman named Preston Brooks. Two days after Sumner's speech, Brooks approached him as he sat at his desk on the Senate floor and began beating Sumner with a cane until he fell bloody and unconscious to the floor. "I gave him about 30 first-rate stripes," Brooks later bragged. Sumner was so badly shaken he could not return to Congress for three years. Brooks resigned his House seat, and then was reelected. The North got a martyr out of the deal, the South a hero.

That was a question that stopped many Northerners who opposed slavery but did not agree with the abolitionists' demand for an immediate end to it. "If all earthly power were given me, I should not know what to do as to the existing situation," admitted Abraham Lincoln in 1854, who was then in private practice as a lawyer.

But Lincoln and others balked at the idea of slavery being allowed to spread, and that's what the fighting was about.

Shedding blood in Kansas

The South wanted a railroad, and Kansas and Nebraska wanted to be states, and the combination of wants caused even more troubles. Spurred by the California Gold Rush and westward expansion, Congress was getting ready to decide on a route for a transcontinental railroad.

The route that made the most sense, and the route the South wanted, started in New Orleans and moved across Texas before ending up in San Diego. It was the shortest route, and went most of the way through already organized states or territories. But Sen. Stephen A. Douglas of Illinois was pressing hard for a central route, starting in Chicago. Douglas owned a lot of real estate in the area and stood to make a sizeable chunk of cash if the trains ran through his property. Trouble was, his route went through land that had been given to the Indians. (There's more on the spread of the railroads in Chapter 15.)

So Douglas pushed a bill through Congress that "organized" the area into the Kansas and Nebraska territories. To win Southern support, his bill also repealed the Missouri Compromise of 1820, which would have prevented slavery in the new territories. Instead, it said the people of Kansas and Nebraska should decide for themselves, a process he called "popular sovereignty."

The North seethed with anger. Douglas was burned in effigy all around the North and ripped in the press. Nebraska proved to be too far north to attract much pro-slavery interest. But Kansas became a warm-up for the Civil War. Anti-slavery forces clashed with pro-slavery forces, and both sides were guilty of terrorism and guerilla warfare.

One of the effects of Douglas's bill was to kill off the Whig Party, whose leaders were wishy-washy on the whole subject. In its place came the Republican Party, which was strongly against the spread of slavery. In 1856, the Republicans ran John C. Fremont, a famous explorer and military man, against the Democrats' James Buchanan, a former Pennsylvania congressman and secretary of state, who had Southern sympathies. Buchanan, a heavy man with tiny feet and almost no backbone, won. He proved to be just about worthless as president.

Making a "dredful" decision

Dred Scott was a slave who was temporarily taken by his master to Illinois, which was a free state. When they returned to Missouri, Scott sued for his freedom, claiming that his time in Illinois, on free soil, made him an ex-slave.

But the seven Southern members of the U.S. Supreme Court, led by Chief Justice Roger Taney, found against Scott in 1857. The court decided that as a black man, Scott was not a U.S. citizen and thus had no right to sue; that as a Missouri resident, Illinois laws didn't apply to him; and that as a slave, he was property, just like a mule, and the government had no right to deprive his master of property without a good reason. The decision absolutely infuriated people in the North. The court's contention that Scott had no more rights than a mule caused many moderate Northerners to take a harder look at the true injustice of slavery.

The decision, along with the Fugitive Slave Law of 1850, also added greatly to business on the "Underground Railroad." That was the name given to a network of abolitionists in the North and South who worked together to get escaped slaves to freedom, often in Canada. It's estimated that the system, which involved "conductors" and "stations," or hiding places, helped from 50,000 to 100,000 people with their escape.

Squaring Off for a Showdown: The Lincoln–Douglas Debate

In 1858, Lincoln challenged Douglas to a series of seven debates, as part of their race for a U.S. Senate seat in Illinois. It was a classic confrontation. Douglas, the incumbent, was barely five feet tall, with a big head made larger because of his pompadour hairstyle. He was resplendent in finely tailored suits and arrived for the debates in a private railroad car. Lincoln was 6'4", with a homely face topped by a shock of unruly hair. He wore ill-fitting suits that stopped well short of his wrists and ankles and arrived for the debates on whatever passenger train was available.

Their debate strategies were simple. Douglas tried to make Lincoln look an abolitionist, which he wasn't, and Lincoln tried to make Douglas look like he was pro-slavery, which he wasn't. But they did have a fundamental disagreement on what the eventual outcome of slavery would be.

Douglas won the election. But Lincoln won a national reputation. In the meantime, the country edged closer to a final showdown, needing only a spark to set off the firestorm. It got two.

Spark No. 1: John Brown

John Brown was an Ohio abolitionist who was crazier than an outhouse rat. He believed he had been commanded by God to free the slaves, and he went about it by killing people in the Kansas fighting. On Oct. 16, 1859, Brown led a group of 18 white and black men on a raid on the federal arsenal at Harpers Ferry, Virginia. After killing the mayor and taking some hostages, Brown's gang was surrounded by militia and U.S. troops under the command of Capt. Robert E. Lee. Brown and five others were captured, and the rest killed. After a trial, Brown was hanged. Many Southerners were convinced Brown had done what a lot of Northerners wanted to do; many Northerners considered him a martyr to a noble cause.

Spark No. 2: Lincoln's election

Lincoln, now a national figure, was nominated by the young Republican Party as its 1860 presidential candidate, mostly because they thought he would appeal to the North and the West. The Democrats were split, however, by the slavery issue. Douglas was the official nominee, but a splinter group supported Buchanan's vice president, John Breckenridge of Tennessee. Still a fourth group of moderates, called the Union Party, supported John Bell of Kentucky.

IN THEIR WORDS
"Four score and seven..."

Oh yeah? Sez you

"If each state will only agree to mind its own business and let its neighbors alone . . . this republic can exist forever divided into free and slave states, as our fathers made it and the people of each state have decided."

— Stephen A. Douglas, 1848.

"A house divided against itself cannot stand. I believe this government cannot endure, permanently half slave and half free. I do not expect the Union to dissolve — I do not expect the house to fall — but I do expect it will cease to be divided. It will become all one thing or all the other."

— Abraham Lincoln, 1848.

When the votes were in, Lincoln had won less than a majority of the popular vote, but easily won the electoral vote, and was the new president. But even before he could take office, seven Southern states had already pulled out of the Union. Buchanan did nothing to try and stop them, and once the fighting started, they were followed by four more.

As the sun rose on the morning of April 12, 1861, secessionist guns fired on Fort Sumter, in Charleston Harbor, South Carolina. America's Civil War had begun.

Gee, Grandpa, What Else Happened?

Sept. 10, 1846: Inventor Elias Howe is granted a patent for a sewing machine with an eye-pointed needle.

April 19, 1847: A Poughkeepsie, N.Y., restaurant operator, James Smith, comes up with a hard candy drop that he says soothes sore throats. He has two flavors, black licorice and wild cherry. His sons William and Andrew eventually grow beards and take over Dad's cough drop business.

Jan. 11, 1848: A cooperative venture among six New York newspapers is launched to distribute news via the telegraph to member newspapers around the country. It's called the Associated Press.

May 10, 1849: A riot outside a New York theater leaves 20 people dead. The trouble stems from a feud between American actor Edwin Forrest and British actor William Macready and is fueled by Irish gangs who stir up anti-British feelings.

August 1851: Songwriter Stephen Foster publishes the song "Old Folks at Home," having changed the line "way down upon the Yazoo River" to "way down upon the Swanee River." It's a huge hit.

July 4, 1853: Publisher and women's rights advocate Amelia Bloomer appears in public in baggy pantaloons under a short skirt. They become known as "bloomers."

July 1853: U.S. Navy Commodore Matthew Perry meets with representatives of the emperor of Japan. Perry is in Japan with a fleet of American warships to see about opening trade with that country.

March 3, 1855: Congress agrees to spend $30,000 to import some Egyptian camels and see if they can be substituted for horses in the arid wastes of West Texas. The camels are eventually shipped to California.

Oct. 7, 1858: A stagecoach owned by the Overland Mail Company arrives in Los Angeles, 20 days and 2,600 miles after leaving St. Louis, a new record.

Aug. 27, 1859: Oil begins flowing from a Pennsylvania well drilled by Edwin L. Drake, a former railroad conductor. At 69 feet deep, it's a lot shallower than most oil wells will be in the future.

Chapter 13

A Most Uncivil War: 1861–1865

In This Chapter
▶ Welcoming Lincoln to the White House
▶ Assessing the North's and South's strengths and weaknesses
▶ Ending slavery
▶ Discovering how the North won
▶ Timeline

1t pitted brother against brother. It killed more American soldiers than any other war in the nation's history. But from the terrible struggle emerged a country that had fought its toughest enemy — itself — and won.

In this chapter, the Civil War unfolds. It also takes a look at the beginning of the end of slavery, and at one of the most extraordinary men in American — and world — history. (For a concentrated look at the Civil War, check out *The Civil War For Dummies* by Keith Dickson, IDG Books Worldwide, Inc.)

A Man Called Lincoln

Abraham Lincoln began his presidency by sneaking into Washington. Because of a suspected assassination plot in Baltimore, Lincoln's railroad car was re-routed so he arrived at a different time than publicly announced. His family took the announced route and was taunted by jeering pro-Southern crowds along the way.

It was an inauspicious beginning to a tough job. Within a few months of taking office, 11 states — Texas, Alabama, Arkansas, Virginia, Louisiana, Georgia, Tennessee, South Carolina, North Carolina, Mississippi, and Florida — had left the Union and four more — Kentucky, Missouri, Maryland, and Delaware — called the Border States, were thinking about it. The man in charge of sorting the whole thing out had actually received only about 40 percent of the popular vote in being elected. He was more of a puzzle than a leader to most Americans.

AMERICAN FACES

Jefferson Davis

As president of the Confederate States of America, Jeff Davis may have been Lincoln's counterpart, but he was in very few ways his equal. He was stiff, unyielding, narrow-minded, and humorless. In fact, he may have been the anti-Lincoln.

Born in 1808, Davis was a West Point graduate who was wounded and decorated for bravery in the Mexican War. He was also a U.S. senator and served as secretary of war under President Franklin Pierce. With his brother, Davis owned a Mississippi plantation and believed in good treatment of slaves. But he also firmly believed in slavery. "You cannot transform the Negro into anything one-tenth as useful or as good as what slavery enables them to be," he said.

After Lincoln's election, Davis resigned his Senate seat. Although he first opposed secession, he accepted the presidency of the Confederate states as a compromise candidate.

His presidency was plagued by mediocre cabinet members, quarreling among the rebel states who didn't want to be told what to do by a central government, and Davis's own inability to think anyone could possibly be right if they didn't agree with him.

When the South's major armies surrendered at the end of the Civil War, Davis fled with what was left of the government's treasury and vowed to fight on. He was soon captured, however, and thrown in a prison cell for almost two years without a trial. On his release, he went to Canada for awhile and then returned to Mississippi, where he spent his remaining years writing about how the war's outcome was everyone else's fault. He died in 1889. More than 250,000 people attended his funeral, many of them nostalgic for the "Old South" he represented.

What makes a president

Lincoln was an enormously complex person. He had a great sense of humor, but also had an air of deep sorrow and melancholy about him. Two of his four sons died before he did, and his wife suffered from various mental and emotional illnesses. He was fiercely ambitious and firm of purpose. He was modest and cheerfully ready to poke fun at himself, but sometimes sank into deep despair and doubt about his own abilities. He did not drink at a time when many men routinely drank to excess, was skeptical when it came to organized religion (although he professed a belief in God), and was not shy about telling racy stories.

He was tall and ungainly-looking (6 feet, 4 inches tall and 180 pounds), with large hands and feet, and his enemies often referred to him as a gorilla or ape. He often dressed all in black and wore a stovepipe hat in which he sometimes stored his correspondence, and he spoke with a high squeak, which may have been why he kept his speeches short. He was strong, having been a champion wrestler in his youth. He was also homely, but seemingly at ease with it. One popular and perhaps apocryphal story about Lincoln is that when a young girl suggested he grow a beard to improve his appearance, he whimsically did so between the election and his inauguration.

Lincoln's greatest gift may have been his ability to use people, in the best sense of the term. He could overlook someone's faults and even their dislike of him, if he thought they had something to offer, and he did it with humor and grace. When a troublemaker reported to him that his secretary of war, Edwin Stanton, had called the president a "damned fool," Lincoln replied: "Then I must be one, for Stanton is generally right, and he always says what he means."

He had plenty of need and opportunity to use his gift of getting the most out of people. Throughout his presidency, Lincoln had few close friends or advisers. His cabinet (notably William Seward, secretary of state; Salmon P. Chase, secretary of the treasury; and Stanton, the secretary of war) represented a wide range of political philosophies. The biggest thing they had in common was their low opinion of their boss.

Fortunately, Lincoln had a talent for making his point without being confrontational. He was often exasperated at the reluctance of his leading generals to fight, particularly Gen. George B. McClellan. But Lincoln did not want to be seen as micro-managing the war. So he once drolly observed, "If General McClellan does not want to use the army, I would like to borrow it." And he was able to rally people in the North to keep fighting, first for the cause of preserving the Union, and later for the cause of ending slavery.

Views on slavery states and the state of the Union

Lincoln was born in Kentucky in 1809. His mother died when he was nine. His father was an unsuccessful farmer who moved the family to Indiana, and then to Illinois. Lincoln had almost no formal schooling. After leaving home, Lincoln took a flatboat trip down the Mississippi, worked in a store, studied law, and was elected to the state legislature at the age of 25. In 1846, he was elected to Congress, but by 1850 he had given up on politics. As the slavery debate grew hotter, however, Lincoln decided to reenter the political arena in 1854 and fight the spread of slavery.

IN THEIR WORDS

"Four score and seven..."

Good guess

"I will make a prophecy that will perhaps sound strange at the moment. In 50 years, perhaps sooner, Lincoln's name will stand written at the honor roll of the American Republic next to that of Washington, and there it will remain."
—Major Carl Schurz, Oct. 12, 1864.

That he opposed slavery is clear. "If slavery is not wrong, then nothing is wrong," he wrote. "I cannot remember when I did not so think and feel." But like most white Americans, he thought black Americans were inferior, and he was not in favor of immediate freedom for slaves. He also did not think blacks and whites could live together.

"My first impulse would be to free all the slaves and send them to Liberia, to their own native land," he once said. "But a moment's reflection would convince me, that whatever high hope (as I think there is) there may be in this, in the long run, its sudden execution would be impossible."

He put a higher value on preserving the Union than on ending slavery. "If I could save the Union without freeing any slaves," he wrote, "I would do it; and if I could save it by freeing all the slaves, I would do it; and if I could save it by freeing some and leaving others alone, I would also do that."

He was also adamant that no states would be allowed to leave the Union without a fight. "A husband and wife may be divorced," he said, "but the different parts of our country cannot . . . Intercourse, either amicable or hostile, must continue between them."

Uh, thanks for coming Abe

One of the most famous speeches in American history is Lincoln's "Gettysburg Address" (see Appendix D). Its simple eloquence not only summed up the cause of the Union, but the cause of any people seeking a better world.

But the speech was not exactly a big hit when it was delivered on Nov. 19, 1863. The occasion was the dedication of the national cemetery at the site of the Battle of Gettysburg in Pennsylvania. The cemetery had been ordered because many of the 8,000 bodies after the battle had been so hastily buried that they had become exposed again.

Lincoln was not even the featured speaker. That honor fell to Edward Everett, a famous orator who had been a U.S. senator and president of Harvard University. Everett spoke for nearly two hours and delivered some 1,500 long and windy sentences before he finally sat down.

Lincoln, who contrary to myth did not write his 268-word speech on the back of an envelope during the train trip to Gettysburg, spoke for about three minutes, in his high, reedy voice. He was interrupted several times by applause. When he was done, a Philadelphia newspaper reporter on the stage leaned over and whispered to Lincoln, "Is that all?" Lincoln replied "Yes, for the present."

Although some newspapers commended the speech, others said it stunk. "Anything more dull and commonplace would not be easy to produce," humphed the *Times of London*. Lincoln shared his critics' opinion of the speech. "I failed, I failed, and that is all that can be said about it," he said. Seldom was he more wrong.

Not everyone in the North felt the same way. As the war progressed, opposition to it formed around "Peace Democrats" who called for negotiating a way to let the "wayward sisters go in peace." The more radical of these, who actually called for disloyalty to the federal government, were called "Copperheads," after the poisonous snake that strikes without warning.

The generally patient Lincoln had no patience with The Copperheads. He suspended in some areas the rights to a speedy trial and to be charged with a specific crime when arrested. More than 13,000 people were arrested and held without trial during the war. His administration also suspended the publication of some newspapers, suspended voting in some areas of the Border States, and arranged for soldiers to get leave so they could go home and vote, presumably for him. In doing so, Lincoln disregarded the Constitution in his drive to preserve the Union, and several of his actions were declared unconstitutional by the Supreme Court — but only after the war.

Even so, Lincoln feared he would not be re-elected in 1864. To help ensure it, the Republican Party formed a temporary alliance with Democrats who favored the war to create the Union Party. The Democrats put up George McClellan, a Union general whom Lincoln had twice removed from command. Despite his misgivings, Lincoln won 55 percent of the popular vote and a comfortable 212-21 margin in the Electoral College.

Fortunately for the country, the war remained Lincoln's responsibility to the end. "With malice to none, with charity to all, with firmness in the right, as God gives us to see the right, let us strive on to finish the work we are in," he said in his Second Inaugural Address, "to bind up the nation's wounds."

North versus South: The Tale of the Tape

If London bookies had been taking bets on the outcome of the American Civil War, they might have set the odds a little in favor of the South. It's true the North had some big pluses, including:

- A population of about 22 million, compared to about 9 million in the South, of which 3.5 million were slaves.
- Seven times as much manufacturing, which meant the Union Army was always better supplied.
- A far better railroad system, with 75 percent of all the track in America in the North, which greatly aided the transport of troops and supplies.
- Control of the Navy and the merchant fleet.
- A central government already in place.

> ✔ Immigration during the war that added thousands of new recruits to the army.
>
> ✔ A more diverse economy.
>
> ✔ Lincoln.

But the South had a number of advantages as well. The Confederacy didn't have to conquer the North or even win a lot of big battles, it only had to fight long enough for the North to give up its quest to bring the Southern states back in the Union. A defensive war is much cheaper to fight in terms of both men and materials. While its population was smaller overall, it still had about 200,000 men available to fight within a short time of the war's start.

Since much of the fighting would be on its territory because the North had to conquer it to get it back in the Union, the South had home-field advantage, not only in knowing the terrain, but in having the incentive to defend their homes and farms. While the idea of letting slaves fight was out of the question for most Southerners (and most slaves), their presence at home meant the South's farms and plantations could be kept running. Of course as the war progressed, the South found that fighting on the home field wasn't all it cracked up to be at the beginning.

The South also had much better luck in finding able military leaders to start with, particularly a courtly and brilliant Virginian named Robert E. Lee, and his right-hand man, a former military school instructor who liked to suck on lemons, named Thomas J. Jackson. And the South also had history on its side. Secession by determined regions had succeeded in Latin America, with the original 13 American colonies, in the Netherlands, and in Greece, to name a few.

To win the war, reasoned Gen. Winfield Scott, the ranking Northern general who was 75 years old and so fat he couldn't get on a horse, the first thing to do was suffocate the South by blockading its coast. Next, cut the South in half by seizing the Mississippi River. Then chop it up by cutting across Georgia and then up through the Carolinas. Finally, capture its capital, Richmond.

Scott's plan was sneered at by many Northern newspapers as being too timid. Forget Scott's "anaconda plan," they argued, march directly to Richmond and get the whole thing over with. But Lincoln recognized the worth of the approach advocated by Scott, who soon retired. He also recognized that the way to win was not to try and conquer and hold Southern territory, but beat the South's armies over and over again.

Confederate President Davis favored a much simpler plan. Make the Northern armies press the fight, whip them, and push them back North, and break the morale of the Northern people to support the war. General Lee concurred at first and then realized that the South's limited resources might be better used in a quick and decisive strike to take the heart out of the North. Twice he tried to take the fight to the Union. Twice his limited resources forced him to go home.

The most-shouldered arm

Although close to 100 different long guns were used during the Civil War, the most common was the Springfield Rifle. It was 4 feet, 8 inches long; weighed 9 pounds; and cost the Union $14.93 apiece. A veteran could load and fire it two to three times a minute, and kill at up to 300 yards. It fired a .58-caliber bullet designed by a Frenchman named Minie. The Minie ball spun down a grooved barrel, which gave it a straight path.

But it was no cinch to operate: 1. Infantryman tears open paper cartridge that contains powder and ball. 2. Pours powder down barrel. 3. Pushes bullet into muzzle. 4. Rams bullet down barrel with ramrod. 5. Pulls back hammer 6. Puts percussion cap beneath hammer. 7. Aims and shoots. 8. Ducks.

Freeing the Slaves

One of Lincoln's most pressing problems was what to do about slaves. As soon as the Northern troops first moved into Southern territory, escaped slaves began to pour into Union Army camps. One general declared the slaves as "seized" property and put them to work in labor battalions to earn their keep. But other generals who favored abolition immediately declared them freed, and Lincoln was forced to rescind the orders. One reason was that he felt that as president, freeing slaves was his responsibility alone. But a more practical political reason was that he had to be careful not to antagonize the slave-holding states that had stayed loyal to the Union: Kentucky, Missouri, Delaware, Maryland, and later West Virginia, which broke away from Virginia during the war. What he really hoped for was that each state would abolish slavery on its own, compensate slave owners, and that federal funds could be used to send freed slaves to Africa.

An alright guy

"I took the [Emancipation] proclamation for a little more than it purported, and saw in its spirit a life and power far beyond its letter . . . Lincoln was not . . . either our man or our model. In his interests, in his associations, in his habits of thought, and in his prejudices, he was a white man. [But] he was one whom I could love, honor, and trust without reserve or doubt." —abolition leader and former slave Frederick Douglass.

Announcing the Emancipation Proclamation

In June 1862, "radical" Republicans in Congress who were impatient with Lincoln's caution mustered enough votes to abolish slavery in the District of Columbia and the U.S. territories. Congress also authorized Lincoln to allow the Union Army to enlist African Americans who wanted to fight. Prodded by the congressional actions, Lincoln then told his cabinet in July that he intended to proclaim freedom for slaves as of January 1, 1863. But he wanted to wait until the Union Army had won a big battle.

On September 22, five days after the Union gained what was really more of a tie than a win at Antietam Creek, he made his proclamation public. Lincoln announced that as of January 1, all slaves in any state still in rebellion "shall be, then, thenceforth and forever free."

Lincoln's Emancipation Proclamation actually didn't free a single slave. It did not apply to slaves in the Border States, and slave owners in the Confederacy certainly didn't obey it. But it did have a number of other effects. In the South, it reinforced the will of the pro-slavery forces to fight on, since it was clear that if they lost, slavery would end. In the North, it angered many people who were comfortable with fighting to preserve the Union, but not to free a bunch of people who might then come North and compete with them for jobs. Union Army desertions increased and enlistments decreased after the announcement.

Fighting a just fight

At first, Lincoln's proclamation angered just about everyone. Abolitionists thought it didn't go far enough, and other people thought the government had no right to take away the Southern slave owner's "property." But gradually many Northerners came to embrace the idea of abolishing slavery as a moral cause, and Lincoln's move added another reason for the North to continue to fight. Just as important, it was cheered by working people in England and France. At one point, a letter of support was sent to Lincoln that claimed to be from 20,000 laborers in England. That kind of support helped ensure European leaders would not risk the wrath of public opinion and come to the aid of the South.

Who Won What Where

The Civil War was mostly a young man's fight. Although no records were kept, it's a safe bet the vast majority of the enlisted men were under 21 years of age and more than a few were in their early teens. It was also truly "a brothers' war," with families and friends divided by their allegiances. Mary Lincoln, the president's wife, had three brothers killed fighting for the South. The South's leading general, Robert E. Lee, had a nephew who was an officer in the Union Navy. U.S. Senator John Crittenden of Kentucky had a son who was a major general in the Confederate Army and another son who was a major general in the Union Army.

Because of the fraternal flavor of the two armies, it wasn't unusual for them to engage in friendly banter between battles, sometimes even getting together for a game of baseball, or to trade tobacco for coffee during truces.

The friendliness didn't stop the carnage (see Figure 13-1), however. More than 600,000 American soldiers died during the Civil War. That's more than the number who died in World War I, World War II, and the Korean War combined. About two-thirds of that number died from diseases rather than battle wounds, and it's estimated that the average soldier ended up in the hospital at least once or twice a year. If they left the hospital, they were lucky. Sanitary conditions were awful, and 75 percent of the operations consisted of amputations, many of them needless.

The Northern forces almost always outnumbered their Southern opponents. At the end of the war, the Union Army had about 960,000 men in uniform, the Confederates about 445,000. In addition to having a larger population to draw from, the North's forces also included thousands of European immigrants who took up a rifle almost as soon as they got off the boat.

Figure 13-1:
Carnage from a Civil War battlefield. Photo taken by Matthew Brady, the most famous of the war's photographers.

And thousands of black Americans fought for the North, after they were allowed to join the army in 1863. They were paid $7 a month, about a third of what white soldiers got and fought under white officers. But they fought well, suffering a higher percentage of casualties than white soldiers and earning the grudging respect of those they fought against and alongside.

Meet the generals

What each side did have, at least by the close of the war, was a great general at the head of its army. In the South, it was Robert E. Lee, the son of a Revolutionary War general who went broke, did two years in prison, and eventually left the family to die in the West Indies. A West Point graduate, Lee was actually asked by Lincoln to take over the Union Army before the war began. But Lee's loyalties were to his native state of Virginia. He was honorable, courteous, fearless, skillful, and not afraid to take a chance.

His Northern counterpart was Ulysses S. Grant, the shy and sloppy son of a storekeeper. Grant was also a West Point grad but who had resigned his commission to avoid a court martial for drunkenness. He rejoined the Army and rose through the ranks to command mainly because unlike some of his contemporaries, he was not afraid to get into a fight with the enemy. "He is the gentlest little man you ever saw," Lincoln remarked. "He makes the least fuss of any man I ever knew." Grant was highly intelligent, determined, compassionate — and a cold-eyed killer, if that's what it took to win.

On the seas

The North's first objective was to blockade the Southern coast and cut off the South's ability to trade its cotton in Europe for arms and supplies. After a slow start, the blockade was ultimately highly effective. The Union Navy was far superior in numbers of ships and guns. But the South did manage to scrounge up a navy of its own from refitted private ships or ships built for the South in England during the war, and sank or captured scores of Union merchant ships.

One of the Confederacy's ships was a Union vessel called the *Merrimac,* which had been sunk. Southern ship fitters raised it, covered it with iron plates, and renamed it the *Virginia.* For a few days, it terrorized the Union fleet off Hampton Roads, Virginia, sinking two Union ships and threatening to decimate the entire group. But the North's own hastily constructed ironclad ship, the *Monitor,* showed up in the nick of time. On March 9, 1862, the two met in a four-hour battle that basically ended in a tie. The *Virginia* was eventually burned and the *Monitor* sunk, but their battle was significant in that it was the first battle between two ironclad ships — and spelled the doom of wooden war ships.

The land war

Part of the North's blockade included capturing the city of New Orleans and gaining control of the mouth of the Mississippi River. Starting in 1862, largely under the leadership of Grant, the Union Army began taking Tennessee and slowly moving up and down the Mississippi, cutting the South in half.

Hairstyles, hookers, and uniforms

Like most major conflicts, the Civil War gave birth to a number of new terms that are still part of the American language. One of them came from the hairstyle of a Union general who wore his whiskers down the front of his ears along his jaw line, but not a full beard. His name was Ambrose Burnside, and his whiskers became known as "sideburns." Another Union general, Joseph "Fighting Joe" Hooker, became known for the large numbers of prostitutes that hung around his army while it was in the Washington area. They were jokingly called "Hooker's Division." Although "hookers" was already a term for ladies of the night, the general helped nationalize it and ensure its lasting place in the language. And "Shoddy" was originally the name given to the recycled wool material Union Army uniforms were made from. But the material was so inferior and came apart so easily, the word "shoddy" took on its current meaning.

In the East, Lee twice took the war to the North. But each time he was forced to return to Southern territory when he was opposed by larger armies and faced uncertain supply lines. Starting in late 1863, the North began grinding down Lee's army in Virginia while another Union army under General William T. Sherman marched diagonally across Georgia and then up into the Carolinas, destroying everything in its path that could be used by the enemy. "We have devoured the land," Sherman wrote his wife. "All the people retreat before us, and desolation is behind."

Here are 10 of the key battles or campaigns of the war (see Figure 13-2):

John Singleton Mosby

He was known as "the Gray Ghost," a Confederate raider who General Grant threatened to hang without trial if he was captured — and who received a job from Grant after the war.

Mosby was born in Virginia in 1833 and was a lawyer when the war broke out. He became the leader of a cavalry unit that specialized in operating behind Union lines, raiding, stealing supplies, and cutting communications. Mosby became a legendary figure, carrying two pistols instead of the customary cavalry sword. On one famous raid, Mosby burst into a room where a prostitute was entertaining a Union general. When the indignant, and naked, general, who didn't recognize his visitor, asked him if he had captured Mosby, Mosby replied, "No, but he has got you!"

After the war, Mosby returned to his law practice. He became friends with now-President Grant, who appointed him U.S. counsel to Hong Kong. After working for the railroad in California, he held a number of other federal jobs. He died in Washington D.C. in 1916, at the age of 83.

Figure 13-2:
Key Civil
War battles.

1. Fort Sumter, April 12-14, 1861
2. Bull Run, 1st battle, July 21, 1861
   2nd battle, Aug. 29-30, 1862
3. Shiloh, April 6-7, 1862
4. Antietam Creek, Sept. 17, 1862
5. Chancellorsville, May 1-4, 1863
6. Gettysburg, July 1-3, 1863
7. Vicksburg, May 5-6, 1864
8. Chickamauga, Sept. 19-20, 1863
9. The Wilderness, May 5-6, 1864
10. Appomattox Courthouse,
    April 9, 1865

✔ **Fort Sumter.** After the first Southern states had seceded, they began seizing federal forts and shipyards inside their borders. Major Robert Anderson, commander of the fort in Charleston Harbor, South Carolina, agreed to surrender the fort as soon as the food ran out, which was the honorable thing to do. But Southern forces wouldn't wait, and at dawn on April 12, 1861, they fired the first shots of the war. Anderson surrendered when he ran out of ammunition, and the only casualties were two Union soldiers killed when a cannon exploded. But the war had begun, and the fact the South fired first was a big help to recruiting efforts in the North.

✔ **Bull Run.** The first large fight of the war took place near Manassas Junction, Virginia, on July 20, 1861. Despite the fact that it was a brutally hot day, hundreds of residents from nearby Washington, D.C. came out to picnic and watch the fight, thinking it might be the highlight of what many expected to be a 90-day war. Neither army was trained or prepared, and for most of the day it was utter confusion. Then Confederate forces got the upper hand, and Union forces panicked and ran. The Rebel army was too tired to chase them. But all thoughts of a 90-day war evaporated.

✔ **Shiloh.** Grant's army was caught napping on April 6, 1862, near this little town in Tennessee and was on the brink of being routed when he launched a counterattack that managed to push the Confederate army back. The victory helped solidify the Union army's dominance in the West.

✔ **Antietam.** Lee's first push into Northern territory took place near this creek in Maryland on Sept. 17, 1862. The battle was fought in a narrow field between Antietam and the Potomac River. Lee was outnumbered and could not maneuver. This was one of the bloodiest battles of the war, with 22,000 killed or wounded. Lee was forced to return across the Potomac and gave Lincoln the "victory" he wanted to announce the Emancipation Proclamation.

✔ **Chancellorsville.** The Union army, under Gen. Joseph Hooker, tried to surround Lee's Army in Virginia on May 1, 1863. But Lee took a brilliant gamble, divided his smaller army, and attacked first. It was a complete Confederate victory, but a costly one. Lee's top general, Thomas Jackson, who was nicknamed "Stonewall" for his courage during battles, was mistakenly shot and killed during the fight by his own troops.

✔ **Gettysburg.** Lee again pushed into Northern territory in early July 1863, this time into Pennsylvania. In a massive battle from July 2 to July 4, Lee's army hurled itself at Union forces led by Gen. George Meade. But the South's effort failed, and Lee was once again forced to withdraw.

✔ **Vicksburg.** This Mississippi town was the last Confederate stronghold on the Mississippi River. Coordinating with Union naval forces moving up from New Orleans, Grant masterfully moved his outnumbered army around the city and laid siege to it. It surrendered July 4, 1863, giving the North complete control of the river.

✔ **Chickamauga and Chattanooga.** These were the first of the big battles in Tennessee from September to November 1863, which led to Sherman's march across Georgia. At Chickamauga, Union Gen. George H. Thomas withstood a furious attack and saved the Union army from a rout. After the Union army was surrounded at Chattanooga, Grant led a rescue effort and drove off the Confederate forces.

✔ **The Wilderness.** This was a series of battles in Virginia in late 1864 in which Grant used his superior numbers to wear down Lee's army. The carnage was terrible, and Grant's critics accused him of being a butcher. But the strategy worked. Lee's army could not break off to try and stop Sherman's march through the heart of the South. And by March 1865, the Union forces outnumbered the Confederacy's by 2 to 1.

> ✔ **Appomattox Courthouse.** This wasn't a battle, but the site in Virginia where on April 12, 1865, Lee formally surrendered to Grant. The Southern army was exhausted, outnumbered, and half-starved. Grant generously fed the defeated Southerners, allowed them to go home, and take their horses and mules with them. Although some units fought on for a few more weeks, the Civil War was for all intents and purposes, over.

Two More Reasons Why the North Won

Generally, it's hard to win a war without money or friends, and the South had neither. Its economy, you should pardon the expression, went south, and it failed to convince any major European powers to join the fight on its side.

The Southern economy was based solely on agriculture. When the Civil War started, there was only one iron foundry in the entire South, in Richmond, which had very little in gold and silver reserves. Still, it was sure its cotton would be enough.

"You dare not make war upon our cotton," a Southern politician boasted before the war. "No power on earth dares make war on it. Cotton is King."

The idea was that European nations, particularly England, depended on Southern cotton to keep their textile industries going, and it's true that England got 80 percent of its cotton from America before the war. The South figured that if the Union's blockade cut off Southern cotton to England, England would intervene on behalf of the South.

But the idea had some holes in it. The first was that when the war started, there was a glut of cotton in England, partly because it had stocked up when war clouds loomed on the horizon, and partly because it started getting more from Egypt and India. Secondly, British laborers backed the Union and hated slavery, and would not support the South even if it meant costing them jobs, which it did. British leaders, even those who favored the South and also favored the idea of two smaller Americas than one big one, did not want to buck popular sentiment.

Actually, England and the Union came close to war a couple of times, most closely when a Union ship stopped an English ship at sea and arrested two Confederate diplomats on their way to London. This was clearly against international law and might have given the Brits an excuse to come in with the South. But Lincoln wisely released the two diplomats and shrugged the whole thing off as a misunderstanding.

With no European allies and with the Union blockade working, the South's economy went completely in the toilet. In 1861, there were about $1 million in Confederate paper currency circulating. But by 1863, there were $900 million, and a Confederate dollar was worth about two cents in gold.

In the North, the economy actually grew during the war. Advances in agriculture and manufacturing, and the discoveries of vast gold and silver reserves in the Far West kept things moving pretty well despite the manpower drain caused by the war.

Losing a Hero

But the worst manpower drain of all came on April 14, five days after Lee surrendered to Grant at Appomattox. It was Good Friday, 1865, and President Lincoln decided to go to Ford's Theatre in Washington to see the comedy "Our American Cousin."

At about 10:30 p.m., during the second act, an actor and Southern sympathizer named John Wilkes Booth snuck into the presidential box and shot Lincoln in the back of the head. Lincoln was taken to a lodging house across the street from the theater, where he lingered until the next morning and then died, surrounded by several members of his cabinet. "Now he belongs to the ages," said Secretary of War Edwin Stanton.

Booth was from a prominent American acting family. He was born in Maryland and was a white supremacist who had plotted to kidnap Lincoln and use him as a bargaining chip to end the war on better terms for the South. But Lee's surrender changed the plot to assassination. Booth made his escape from the theater after stabbing a Union officer who was in Lincoln's box, and jumping to the stage, breaking his leg in the attempt. He was cornered in a barn in Virginia a week later and was shot to death or killed himself, it was never clear which. Four other conspirators were hanged, and four people were convicted of helping the conspirators after the fact, and were sentenced to prison.

America's four-year Civil War was over. The healing from it would take more than a century.

Gee, Grandpa, What Else Happened?

April 20, 1861: A man named Thaddeus Lowe lands in South Carolina after flying a hot air balloon 900 miles from Cincinnati, the longest flight to date.

Aug. 5, 1861: President Lincoln signs into law the nation's first income tax, meaning that everyone who makes more than $800 a year has to fork over 3 percent to the federal government.

Oct. 24, 1861: The first transcontinental telegram is sent from Sacramento by California Supreme Court Chief Justice Stephen Johnson to President Lincoln at the White House. The cost of subsequent transcontinental telegrams is $6 for every 10 words.

Nov. 4, 1862: A gun that fires hundreds of bullets per minute by rotating a cluster of barrels with a crank is patented by its inventor, Richard Gatling. The gun's production is held up because the first batch is destroyed in a fire, delaying its appearance on Civil War battlefields.

June 2, 1863: Harriet Tubman, a former slave who is known as the "Moses" of the Underground Railroad for her working in helping escaping slaves, leads black Union Soldiers into South Carolina to help free 800 slaves.

Feb. 17, 1864: A Confederate submarine named the *H.L. Hunley* sinks a Union ship, off Charleston. It's believed to be the first successful sub attack in military history. But the success is relative, since the *Hunley* gets stuck in the hole it makes in the enemy ship, and is also lost.

Nov. 25, 1864: An attempt fails by Confederate agents to burn down New York City. The agents set 19 fires, including blazes at most of the city's major hotels, but they fail to ignite properly. The only serious damage is done to P.T. Barnum's museum.

April 7, 1865: About 1,600 people, including 1,450 Union soldiers just released from Confederate prison camps, are killed when a boiler on the steamboat they are taking up the Mississippi River explodes.

Nov. 18, 1865: *The New York Saturday Press* publishes a short story by a young Missouri writer named Sam Clemens. The story, "The Celebrated Jumping Frog of Calaveras County," is published using Clemens's pen name, "Mark Twain."

Dec. 25, 1865: The Chicago Union Stockyard accepts its first shipment of 761 pigs.

Chapter 14

Putting It Back Together: 1865–1876

In This Chapter

▶ Reconstructing the South

▶ Electing Presidents Johnson, Grant, and Hayes

▶ Living with political corruption

▶ Timeline

*T*he bullet that killed Abraham Lincoln at the end of the Civil War may also have killed any chance of coming up with a practical solution toward putting the country back together — and figuring out what to do with 3.5 million former slaves who had won their freedom, and not much else.

In this chapter, a defiant South, a wrathful and power-mad Congress, and a stubborn and nasty-tempered president combine to make a mess of what has come to be known as the "Reconstruction" period. We also see a very good military leader become a very bad political leader and wrap the whole thing up with a stolen presidential election.

A Southern-fried Mess

The 11 Southern states that had decided to leave the Union in 1860 and 1861 were basket cases by 1865. Only Texas, where there hadn't been that much fighting, was in relatively decent shape. Southern cities such as Atlanta, Charleston, and Richmond were in ruins.

Whipped

"A city of ruins, of desolation, of vacant houses, of widowed women, of rotting wharves, of deserted warehouses, of weed-wild gardens, of miles of grass-grown streets, of acres of pitiful and voiceful barrenness — that is Charleston, wherein rebellion loftily reared its head five years ago . . . I fell into some talk with [a local resident] . . . when I asked him what should be done, he said 'you Northern people are making a great mistake in your treatment of the South. We are thoroughly whipped; we give up slavery forever; and now we want you to quit reproaching us. Let us back into the Union, and then come down here and help us build up the country.'"

— Massachusetts journalist Sidney Andrews, 1865.

There were few businesses of any kind still operating, little capital to start new businesses, and few outsiders willing to risk investing in the area. For example, 7,000 miles of railroad track were laid in the South between 1865 and 1879. In the rest of the country, 45,000 miles were laid. Before the war, the South's economy had been based almost strictly on agriculture, mainly cotton, tobacco, and sugar, and all of them suffered: Southern cotton production in 1870 was half what it had been in 1860. The education system had virtually disappeared. The old plantation system was gone. So were more than 250,000 of the South's young men. "Pretty much the whole of life has been merely not dying," wrote the Southern poet Sidney Lanier.

Starting life anew

For millions of African Americans, the whole of life had become pretty darned confusing. They had their freedom, but it wasn't clear what to do with it. Few had any education or training. Some thought freedom meant freedom from work. Many more were fearful that to continue working for white people would put them in danger of being enslaved again. And many believed a widespread rumor that the Federal government would be giving each slave "40 acres and a mule" to start their own farms.

There never was such a plan. The government did organize the Freedman's Bureau in 1865, designed to help the freed slaves during their transition from slavery to freedom by providing food, education, and other support. From 1865 to 1868, before it was allowed to go out of business, as many as 200,000 ex-slaves were taught to read. About 10,000 black families were settled by the bureau on land that been confiscated by Union troops, although most of them were eventually forced off the land by whites who swindled them out of it or used dubious legal means. The bureau also provided aid to poor Southern whites.

Blanche Kelso Bruce

Next time you have a $2 bill that was printed in say, 1880, in your pocket, take a look at the signatures on it. One of them belongs to a Virginia man who started life as a slave and became a prosperous landowner and United States senator.

Blanche Kelso Bruce was born in 1841 and worked as a field hand. When the Civil War began, Bruce escaped. He eventually settled in Missouri, where he organized the state's first school for African Americans. In 1869, Bruce moved to Mississippi, where he held a series of

political offices. In 1874, he became the first African American to be elected to a full term in the U.S. Senate. As a senator, Bruce investigated banking scandals, advocated economic aid for freed slaves, and helped obtain levee system and railroad projects for Mississippi.

In 1880, Bruce was appointed registrar of the U.S. Treasury, where his duties required a facsimile of his signature on U.S. currency. He was also a lecturer, a writer, and an educator. Bruce died in 1898, having left his name in American history as well as on a lot of money.

Becoming sharecroppers

Most blacks and many whites could not afford to buy land of their own, so a new form of farming became the basis for the Southern agricultural economy: sharecropping. Under sharecropping, the farmer farmed land owned by someone else, and they shared the profits.

But what happened in most cases was the sharecropper had to borrow money to make ends meet until the next crop was harvested. This left him with so little when the crop was harvested that he had to borrow on the next crop. Thus many sharecroppers, black and white, became virtual slaves to debt.

The sharecropping system became dominant in many parts of the South, replacing the plantation system. In 1868, perhaps one-third of the area's farms were tended by renters. By 1900, that percentage grew to about 70 percent. The system, coupled with low cotton prices and the ravages of the boll weevil, virtually guaranteed that few farmers could become successful, no matter how hard they worked.

Finding Bitter Solutions

One of the topics American historians like to speculate on is what might have happened if Lincoln had not been shot. Would he have been able to come up with a plan to reunite the states and give the former slaves their rightful place in society? Would that have led to better race relations sooner in America?

Probably not. Lincoln, like most mid-nineteenth century white Americans, felt it was impossible to just free the slaves and make them socially equal. "There is an unwillingness on the part of our [white] people, harsh as it may be, for you free colored people to remain with us," he told a group of African Americans during the war. His hope was to resettle the freed slaves somewhere else, either in Africa or the Caribbean. But most black Americans had no firsthand experience with Africa or any other country except the country where they were born, and they had no desire to leave.

Piecing the Union back together

Lincoln did insist, however, that the former slaves be treated as equals when it came to the law. He pushed Congress into passing the Thirteenth Amendment to the Constitution, barring slavery. And during the war he set out a general plan that discussed how to reunite the country when the war was over, assuming the North won. Under this plan, most Southerners could become U.S. citizens again simply by taking a loyalty oath. Those who couldn't, mostly high-ranking Confederate officials, could apply for reinstatement on a case-by-case basis.

When 10 percent of a state's population had taken the oath, the state could set up a new government, and apply for readmission to the Union, as long as it agreed to give up slavery and provide an education system for blacks. After Lincoln was killed in April 1865, his vice president, Andrew Johnson, adopted practically the same plan. By the time Congress convened in December, all the Southern states had organized new governments, ratified the Thirteenth Amendment, and elected new representatives and Senators for Congress.

But Congress, dominated by "Radical" Republicans, did not like the deal. For one thing, many of the men the South had elected to represent them in Washington were the same guys who had run the Confederacy — including Alexander Stephens, the ex-Confederate vice president who was in federal prison awaiting trial on treason charges. That kind of in-your-face attitude irritated the Radicals, who felt Southerners weren't sorry enough for causing the war.

IN THEIR WORDS

"Four score and seven..."

Sorry — not!

"Oh I'm a good old rebel / Now that's just what I am; / For the 'fair land of freedom,' / I do not care a damn. / I'm glad I fought agin it - / I only wish we'd won / And I don't want a pardon / For anything I've done."

— from a popular Southern song, 1865–66.

AMERICAN FACES

Thaddeus Stevens

He had a clubfoot, a razor tongue, and was one of the most sincere white men in America when it came to rights for African Americans. Stevens was born in 1792 in New England. He moved to Pennsylvania, where he practiced law, got into politics, and was elected to the House of Representatives and then the U.S. Senate.

Stevens was that rarity of rarities, an honest politician. He was unmoved by either flattery or criticism. But he was also fanatical in his hatred for the South, a hatred fueled in part by the destruction of his Pennsylvania factory by Southern troops on their way to Gettysburg. Stevens never married, but for years had a black housekeeper and it was rumored they were lovers. He never confirmed or denied it.

As the most radical of the Radical Republicans, he virtually led the country for more than a year because of his power in Congress. Stevens advocated taking the land from the South's wealthiest plantation owners and dividing it among former slaves. But that was too radical even for his colleagues. He did successfully push for other laws designed to protect the basic rights of African Americans.

When he died in 1868, he was buried in a black cemetery. "I have chosen this," read his epitaph, "that I might illustrate in my death the principles which I advocated through a long life: Equality of Man before His Creator."

REMEMBER

But what was even more infuriating to the North were the "Black Codes." These codes were established by state legislatures to keep the former slaves "under control." They varied from state to state and did give blacks some rights they had not had before: the power to sue in court, own certain kinds of property, and legally marry. But they also prohibited them from bearing arms, working in most occupations other than farming or manual labor, or leaving their jobs without permission. They restricted African Americans' right to travel and fined them if they broke any of the codes. To the Radicals, and even many moderate Northerners, the Black Codes were simply a substitute form of slavery.

So Congress passed a series of bills designed to strengthen the rights of blacks — and President Johnson vetoed them as unconstitutional interference in states' rights, or as infringing on the powers of the presidency. One thing he could not veto, though, was the Fourteenth Amendment, since the Constitution required that proposed amendments go directly to the states for approval. The amendment, ratified in 1868, entitled all people born or naturalized in the United States — including slaves — to U.S. citizenship and equal protection under the law.

Using violence to keep blacks down

Many whites in the South were outraged, particularly poorer whites who already felt they were competing with ex-slaves for jobs. Groups such as the Ku Klux Klan (KKK), Knights of the White Camellia, and Pale Faces sprung up. They used weird costumes and goofy rituals to intimidate blacks from exercising their rights. When intimidation failed, they and other white mobs and paramilitary groups resorted to violence. Hundreds of African Americans were beaten, driven from their homes, or brutally murdered.

Blacks weren't the only targets. The KKK and similar groups also terrorized carpetbaggers and scalawags. *Carpetbaggers* were Northerners who came to the South to participate in rebuilding it — and make a lot of money at it. *Scalawags* were Southerners who helped in the process. While it's true some of these people were basically just vultures feeding off the defeated Southern corpse, many actually did a lot of good, reviving the school system, helping to rebuild the railroads, and so on.

But the terrorist activities of the white supremacist groups were very effective in "keeping blacks in their place." And the groups had unwitting allies in the president of the United States and Northerners who were losing interest in reforming the South.

The Tailor-made President

Andrew Johnson may have been the poorest president ever, at least in terms of his humble beginnings. He was born in North Carolina to impoverished parents, and his father died when Johnson was 3 years old. He never went to school and became a tailor's apprentice at the age of 14.

Johnson taught himself to read and became involved in politics at the age of 17. When the Civil War broke out, he became military governor of Tennessee. In 1864, the Republican Lincoln picked the Democrat Johnson to be his vice presidential running mate. The thought was that a pro-Union Democrat would balance the ticket and attract more votes.

But when Lincoln was killed, the country was left with a stubborn and ill-tempered president who had none of Lincoln's gift of leadership. Johnson didn't like blacks, didn't like rich Southerners, and didn't like the Republican-controlled Congress. In 1866, Johnson took what was called a "Swing Around the Circle," traveling around the Northern states to campaign for Democrats running for Congress and against the Fourteenth Amendment, which would give blacks full citizenship.

Taking control of Congress

The trip was a disaster. Johnson was booed and jeered by Northern crowds who viewed him as a pro-South bozo. The Republicans dominated the election and had such overwhelming majorities in Congress that they easily passed any bill they wanted and then easily overrode Johnson's vetoes. Pushed by Radical Republicans like Thaddeus Stevens of Pennsylvania and Charles Sumner of Massachusetts, Congress passed a series of Reconstruction acts designed to force the South into line. See Figure 14-1 for an example of the South's feelings toward Reconstruction.

One Reconstruction act, passed in 1867, divided the South into five military districts, each governed by a general and policed by the army. To be allowed to re-enter the Union and get rid of military rule, Southern states had to agree to ratify the Fourteenth Amendment. They also had to guarantee in their state constitutions the right to vote for African Americans. That was particularly galling to Southerners because many Northern states did not allow blacks to vote.

Adding salt to the wound, Congress also approved and sent to the states the Fifteenth Amendment, which guaranteed all adult males everywhere the right to vote. This was done to ensure the Southern states did not renege on their promise to give blacks the ballot — and also because it was embarrassing for the Radical Republicans to be from Northern states that did not let African Americans vote.

The amendment greatly angered many American women, who found that they were now second-class citizens to black males as well as white ones when it came to voting. And Southern states gradually got around the law anyway by requiring blacks to pass difficult "literacy" and "citizenship" tests before they could vote.

One result of giving newly freed slaves the vote was that they elected some of their own to state legislatures. The resulting black-white governments in some states created sound and fair tax and education systems, built roads and levees, and gave property rights to women. In others they were dominated by leeches and thieves of both races, although white politicians were by far the worst offenders. One "carpetbagger" governor managed to "save" more than $4 million on an annual salary of $8,000 a year.

Figure 14-1:
Political
cartoon of
the time
about
Recon-
struction.

RE·CONSTRUCTION,

Elizabeth Blackwell

She wanted to be a doctor, and she got to be one because of a joke. Blackwell was born in England in 1821, the daughter of a sugar broker. She moved with her family to America when she was 11.

Blackwell was rejected by 17 medical schools before she applied in 1847 to Geneva Medical College in New York. The faculty, opposed to letting her in, decided to leave it up to a vote of the students. And as a joke, the all-male student body approved her admission. But the joke was on them. Two years later, she graduated at the head of her class, the first woman to earn a medical degree in America or Europe. "Sir," she told the dean on accepting her diploma, "by the help of the most high, it shall be the effort of my life to shed honor on this diploma."

Which she did. After U.S. hospitals refused to hire her, Blackwell opened her own clinic in New York City, where she was eventually joined by her sister and a third female physician. In 1868, she opened the Women's Medical College of New York, which remained open until 1899, when Cornell University Medical School began admitting women. Throughout the last half of the nineteenth century, Blackwell was a champion of women's roles in medicine. She died in 1910.

Attempting impeachment

Meanwhile, in Washington, the Radicals weren't satisfied with being able to run over Johnson's vetoes. They wanted him out of the White House, which, under the Constitution, would then fall to the leader of the Senate, Benjamin Wade of Ohio.

So the Radicals laid a trap. Congress passed a bill that required the president to have Senate approval before he could fire any of his appointees. Johnson, who believed the act was unconstitutional, promptly took the bait and fired his Secretary of War, Edwin Stanton, who was a Radical stooge anyway.

Congress then impeached Johnson for violating the law, and he was put on trial by the Senate in April 1868. The country regarded it as a great melodrama, and tickets to the Senate gallery were the toughest buy in town. On May 10, 1868, the vote was taken to remove Johnson from office. It was 35 to 19 — one short of the two-thirds needed. Seven Republican senators voted against removing Johnson. All of them sacrificed their political careers as a result.

But they may have preserved the U.S. government. Removing Johnson solely on political grounds could have created the basis for a congressional dictatorship, where Congress could dominate the presidency by threatening to dump any president who didn't go along with its wishes.

SIDETRIP

A lamp, a cow, and a hot town

It had been a long dry year in Chicago. A drought had made the bustling city tinder-dry, and not a place to be careless with fire. But on the morning of October 8, 1871, someone was. Legend has it it was a Mrs. O'Leary, on De Koven Street. She went to her barn to milk the cow, the cow kicked over the kerosene lamp, and one of the most disastrous fires in U.S. history began. (Mrs. O'Leary later denied the story.)

However it started, by the time it was out, more than a day later, it had killed 250 people, left nearly 100,000 homeless, destroyed more than 17,000 buildings, and done close to $200 million worth of damage.

Contributions poured in from around the world, as did government help. The fire missed the city's vital railroad yards and stockyards, and within a few years Chicago had risen from the ashes, like a phoenix. Only not in Arizona.

The trial also may have marked the beginning of the end of Northern interest in Reconstruction. Many Northerners were as prejudiced against blacks as many Southerners. They were sick of the issue. They wanted to put the war, and its aftermath, behind them. "The whole public are tired out with these autumnal outbreaks in the South," wrote a federal official to a Southern governor, in refusing to provide military aid when the KKK interfered in local elections. "Preserve the peace by the forces of your own state."

Growing Corruption in Politics

When Americans elected Ulysses S. Grant president in 1868, they expected him to be the same kind of chief executive as he was a general — brave, tenacious, and an inspiring leader. But Grant had no political experience and little political philosophy. Neither did many of the people he appointed to be his cabinet and top aides. His one asset was his personal honesty, and unfortunately it was an asset not shared by the people around him.

Almost from the time Grant took office, his administration was awash in corruption. Scandal after scandal broke over the White House like waves: Cornering the gold market, efforts to annex the Caribbean island of Santo Domingo, speculating on railroads, ripping off the Indians, and stealing liquor tax revenues were all grist for the corruption mill. Grant's administration became known as the "Great Barbecue," because everyone helped themselves.

Taking a cue from the White House

Political corruption was by no means limited to the federal government or the Grant Administration. State and local governments were scandal-tainted as well, and the country became caught up in what Mark Twain labeled "The Gilded Age." Everyone, it seemed was in a fever to make money, and the most hungry became known, not always with disdain, as "robber barons."

In California, Colis P. Huntington bribed legislators and congressmen to get concessions for his railroad. In Pennsylvania, John D. Rockefeller bought and bullied lawmakers to aid his Standard Oil Company. Worst of all may have been in New York City, where a political boss named William M. Tweed created a web of elected officeholders, bureaucrats, and contractors and looted more than $100 million from the city treasury.

Trying to change the tides

Despite the stench, Grant was re-elected in 1872, easily defeating Democratic candidate Horace Greeley, the longtime editor of the *New York Tribune*. But by 1874, the scandals and the mess of Reconstruction — which ruined Republicans' chances of winning anything in the South — combined to let the Democrats take control of the House of Representatives.

With all the corruption — and the public's growing disgust — it wasn't surprising that both political parties nominated presidential candidates known for their integrity in 1876. The Republicans put up Rutherford B. Hayes, a former Union general who had been governor of Ohio for three terms. The Democrats countered with New York Governor Samuel B. Tilden, who had gained admiration for helping to bring down the Boss Tweed Ring in New York City.

IN THEIR WORDS

"Four score and seven..."

A generous crook

"The Great Fisk died this morning. No loss to the community — quite the reverse — but it's a pity he should have escaped the state prison in this way . . . By talent and audacity he raised himself to the first rank among business scoundrels . . . illiterate, vulgar, unprincipled . . . [but] he was liberal to distressed ballet dancers and munificent to unfortunate females under difficulties."

— Lawyer George Templeton Strong, describing the death of "robber baron" James "Jubilee Jim" Fisk in 1872.

Indigestion on wheels

One day in 1872, a Providence, Rhode Island, man named Walter Scott loaded a wagon with sandwiches, boiled eggs, and other food and parked it outside a downtown newspaper office in the evening. Since all the restaurants in town had closed at 8 p.m., Scott had plenty of customers. Soon other "lunch wagons" began rolling down streets all over American cities. In 1884, a guy in Worcester, Massachusetts, named Sam Jones got the idea to put stools in his lunch wagon so customers could sit down.

But the wagons drew complaints from residents and competing restaurant owners and were banned or restricted in many towns. So the wagon owners simply rolled their wagons on to vacant lots, took off the wheels, and called themselves restaurants. By the 1920s, people were eating as many breakfasts and dinners at the wagons as lunches, and instead of lunch wagons, we started calling them "diners."

Fixing a presidency

What was surprising was that the presidential election between these two men turned out to be perhaps the most tainted in U.S. history. When the returns came in, Tilden seemed to have 203 electoral votes and Hayes 166. But the Republican Party leaders, who controlled the people who oversaw the elections, arranged to invalidate thousands of Democratic votes in Florida, South Carolina, and Louisiana, which changed the electoral vote count to 185–184 for Hayes.

The Democrats naturally challenged the new results, and a special commission was created to look into it. The commission consisted of ten members of Congress, five from each party, and five members of the Supreme Court (three Republicans and two Democrats). The commission voted 8–7, along party lines, to give the election to Hayes.

Northern Democrats were outraged, but Southern Democrats saw an opportunity and offered a deal: They would drop any challenge to the commission's vote if Hayes would remove the last of the federal troops from Southern states and let the states run their own affairs. The Republicans eventually agreed, and Hayes became president.

It was a disgustingly fitting end to Reconstruction. African Americans were largely abandoned by the federal government, and white Americans outside the South turned their attentions elsewhere, mostly to the West.

Gee, Grandpa, What Else Happened?

1866: The first oil pipeline in the nation is completed, connecting the Pitthole, Pennsylvania oil fields to a railroad five miles away.

Jan. 1, 1867: The 340-foot steamship *Colorado* begins carrying mail from San Francisco to China.

Nov. 6, 1868: U.S. Army Gen. William T. Sherman and Chief Red Cloud of the Ogallala Sioux sign a peace treaty, ending two years of fighting and promising part of Wyoming and the Dakota Territory to the Indians.

Nov. 27, 1868: The Seventh Cavalry, under Lt. Col. George A. Custer, launches a surprise attack on Arapaho and Cheyenne Indians under Chief Black Kettle and kills more than 100 Indians, including dozens of women and children, and more than 900 Indian horses.

Jan. 12, 1869: An organization called the National Convention of Colored Men is established, with noted black journalist and orator Frederick Douglass as its president.

May 10, 1869: The nation's first transcontinental railroad is completed with a ceremony at Promontory Point, Utah. The new railway cuts a trip from New York to San Francisco from three months to eight days.

Sept. 6, 1870: A woman named Louisa Swain becomes the first American female to cast a legal ballot. She votes in Laramie, Wyoming. The Wyoming Territory is the first area in the country to give women the vote.

Aug. 1, 1873: San Francisco's first cable car begins operating up Clay Street on Nob Hill. It carries 60 passengers on its first day.

Dec. 14, 1873: Congress passes an act prohibiting the sending of "obscene" materials through the mails, including birth control instructions and abortion information.

May 17, 1875: A horse race billing itself as the "Kentucky Derby" is run at the new Churchill Downs track in Louisville. Owners of the winner, Aristides, claim a purse of $2,850.

Part III
Coming of Age

The 5th Wave   By Rich Tennant

1924 - GEORGE GERSHWIN COMPOSES AN AMERICAN CLASSIC

Rhapsody in Brown
Rhapsody in Plaid
Rhapsody in Puce
Rhaps im

By George Gershwin

"Hey George, give it a rest. Let's have lunch. I picked up some bluefish. Man, I love bluefish. Do you love bluefish, George?"

In this part . . .

America was 100 years old in 1876 and still in its ado-lescence. It had gone through a childhood that was marked by some rough times, particularly when it was torn apart by the Civil War.

But it had also had some remarkable luck. It was a coun-try blessed with tremendous resources, and it had great leaders when it needed them most.

In this part, the country begins to put its resources, both natural and human, to work. It takes its place as a world leader, endures both very good and very bad eco-nomic times, and emerges from a world war as a very grown-up nation.

Chapter 15

Growing Up: 1876–1898

In This Chapter

▶ Moving west

▶ Forcing Indians off their land — again

▶ Welcoming immigrants

▶ Creating big business

▶ Remembering some forgettable presidents

▶ Battling with Spain for some islands

▶ Timeline

Americans have always been restless, and in 1876 they were hungry, too — for success. There seemed to be so many ways and places to be successful, and it seemed so important to so many people.

In this chapter, the country starts its final push toward filling in the gaps between the coasts — and its final pushing aside of the original Americans. Railroads help do both, as well as usher in the birth of truly huge businesses. A string of mediocre presidents don't do much of anything, and a war with Spain launches America on the road to empire.

Spreading to the West

When settlers in America first started moving west (about ten minutes after they got here), they generally did so because of the lure of free land and the chance to put down roots. After the Civil War, however, Americans moved west as much to make a buck as to settle into a new life. The West was seen as a bottomless treasure chest of resources to exploit.

Mining for money

Some of those resources were mineral. Starting with the California Gold Rush of 1849, the West saw a steady stream of gold, silver, and copper discoveries touch off "rushes," as hordes of miners careened like pinballs from strike to strike. In 1859, thousands descended on Pike's Peak in Colorado, looking for gold. Later that year, it was the Comstock silver lode in Nevada. In 1861, it was Idaho; in 1863, Montana; in 1874, the Black Hills of Dakota; and in 1876, it was back to Colorado.

Towns with 5,000 inhabitants sprang up virtually overnight, composed of would-be millionaires and the gamblers, thieves, swindlers, prostitutes, and liquor sellers that accompanied them. They formed a violent society. Justice, if it existed at all, was often in the form of "vigilance committees" or "vigilantes," who set themselves up as the law and sometimes didn't bother with a trial before stretching a defendant's neck.

Those who made most of the money from mining were symbolic of what was happening in the rest of the country. Big corporations, financed by stockholders from the East and Europe, had the capital to buy the equipment needed to mine on a large scale, and they reaped most of the profits. The average miner made little, and many of them ended up going to work as laborers for the large companies.

But mining had some positive impact on the West besides the wealth it created. The miners were the first to open much of the West and helped encourage the railroads to come. Some of those who came for the booms stayed on after the inevitable busts that followed. Because miners had to set up governments in a hurry to deal with the instant towns, political organization took root. Coupled with the mineral wealth, these organizations gave the mining areas clout in Congress. This helped speed the admission of new states, such as Nevada.

By the dawn of the new century, the big fever-producing mineral strikes were over in the West. But they were replaced by the rush to extract oil — "Black Gold" — beneath Western lands, particularly in Texas and Oklahoma.

Ranching cattle

After the Civil War, Texas soldiers returned to find as many as five million cattle roaming around the state. They were descendants of animals brought to the area hundreds of years before by Spanish explorers and conquerors. There was plenty of grazing land, and enough water, and the cattle were a hardy breed.

Now, Texans were as fond of beef as the next state's inhabitants, but they really wanted to find a way to share their wealth on the hoof with the rest of the nation. Cattle that were worth $3 to $4 a head in Texas could be sold for 10 times that much in Eastern states, if you could get them there. Cattle drives to the East and even California had been tried before. But many of the cattle died before the drives were over, and the survivors were worn thin by the effort.

AMERICAN FACES

Bat Masterson

Unlike many of his contemporaries — Billy the Kid, Jesse James, John Wesley Hardin — William Barclay Masterson made a successful, and peaceful, transition from the Wild West to the twentieth century.

Born in Canada in 1853, Masterson left home at the age of 17 to become a buffalo hunter and Indian fighter. At the age of 23, he killed his first man in a saloon gunfight, over a woman. Masterson was shot in the leg and for the rest of his life walked with a limp. In 1877, he became sheriff of Ford County, Kansas, and with his brothers Jim and Ed held a variety of law enforcement jobs in Dodge City, Kansas and Tombstone, Arizona, where he worked with his pal Wyatt Earp.

Well-dressed and well-groomed, the derby-wearing Masterson carried two pearl-handled revolvers and knew how to use them. He was a true quick-draw artist, and his reputation stopped many fights before they started. After careers as a gambler and saloonkeeper, Masterson was appointed a U.S. marshal by President Theodore Roosevelt. In 1905, he hung up his guns for good and became a sportswriter and editor for the *New York Morning Telegraph*. He died in 1921 at his desk, at the age of 68.

The last words he typed were reportedly these: "I have observed . . . that in life we all get about the same amount of Ice. The rich get it in the summer and the poor get it in winter."

After the war, however, some bright guys got the idea to shorten the distances by driving cattle to the railroads that were moving West, and then shipping them East by rail. Rail met cow at "trailheads" in Abilene and Dodge City in Kansas, Ogalalla in Nebraska, and Cheyenne in Wyoming. By 1871, 750,000 head of cattle were moved through Abilene alone. By 1875, the refrigerated car allowed the cattle to be slaughtered and butchered in Midwest cities like Kansas City and Chicago before being shipped east.

The rise of the cattle industry also gave rise to an American icon: the cowboy. Hollywood has turned the cowboy into a romantic figure who was quick on the draw with a six-shooter and spent most of his time drinking whiskey and playing poker in town, with a beautiful blonde dancehall girl perched at his shoulder.

In truth, the cowboy was most likely an ex-Confederate soldier or former slave who spent most of his life on the back of a short-legged cow pony, hundreds of miles from the nearest bar or woman. He was brave and tough, but he was far less likely to use his pistol on his fellow man than he was on rattlesnakes or as a noisemaker. He was likely in his late teens or early 20s, and about one in five were African Americans. He worked for $25 a month and ate beans, bacon, and black coffee day after day.

By the early 1890s, the day of the cowboy and the cattle drive was coming to an end. Like other aspects of American life, inventions (such as barbed wire) and investments (by Easterners and Europeans) turned ranching into big business, and cowboys became caretakers on large fenced ranches rather than riders of the range. A far less glamorous, but much more numerous, type of Westerner was now dominant: the sodbuster.

Farming the land

In the wake of the miner and the cowboy came the farmer. The railroads were eager to colonize the areas they controlled with potential customers and offered land near their tracks through giant advertising efforts in the East and Europe. The federal government tried various ways to sell public lands, most of them badly managed.

Regardless, the settlers rushed in. The populations of Minnesota, Kansas, and Nebraska doubled or tripled. The Dakotas went from 14,000 residents after the Civil War to 500,000 in 20 years. In 1889, the "Cherokee Strip" in Northern Oklahoma was purchased from Indians and thrown open to settlement, and by 1900 the Oklahoma Territory had a population of about 800,000.

Most of the farmers faced a blizzard of hardships: drought, grasshopper invasions, prairie fires, and, well, blizzards. There was even foreign competition. In the 1870s, crop failures in Europe helped drive up prices and open markets for American farmers. But in the 1880s, crop prices fell and new producers in Australia and India came on the scene.

More and more farmers in the West found themselves in the same plight as those in the war-torn South. The number of farms with a mortgage, or that were farmed by tenant farmers, steadily increased as the last 20 years of the century passed.

Still, between 1870 and 1900, the number of American acres under cultivation more than doubled, from 407 million to 841 million acres. The frontier had been mined, ranched, and farmed into submission.

IN THEIR WORDS

"Four score and seven..."

Forget farming

"My husband I pity, he is wasting his life / To obtain a scant living for his children and wife. / The Sabbath which once was a day of sweet rest / Is now spent toiling for bread in the West. / After five years hard toiling with hopes that were in vain / I have such despair on this desolate plain."

— from a song by a Colorado farmer's wife, 1887.

SIDETRIP

Happy 100th, America

In 1871, Congress decided to put on a big to-do to celebrate America's 100th birthday. It took awhile to raise the dough, but on May 10, 1876, 13 giant bells chimed, 100 cannons fired a salute, and an 800-voice choir sang the "Hallelujah Chorus" to open the U.S. Centennial Exhibition in Philadelphia.

The fair, spread over a 248-acre park, featured exhibits from all over the world, but the highlights were the proud displays of Yankee know-how. Crowds, which included President U.S. Grant and Emperor Don Pedro II of Brazil, gasped and gaped at the largest steam engine ever built up to that time; an ice box that used ammonia as its refrigerant; and a printing process that printed, cut, and sorted pages for up to an hour at a time.

The first prize for new inventions went to a device its inventor, Alexander Graham Bell, called the telephone. The Brazilian emperor put the thing to his ear and quickly dropped it, exclaiming, "My God, it talks!" But Bell's invention drew smaller crowds than an exotic exhibit from Central America. It featured a strange fruit, called the banana.

Ousting "Undesirables"

General Philip Sheridan never said: "The only good Indian is a dead Indian." What he did say, however, was just as bad: "The only good Indians I ever saw were dead."

There were plenty of dead American Indians by 1876. When Columbus arrived, there were probably 1 million to 1.5 million Indians living in what is now the United States. By the time of the Civil War, the number had dropped to about 300,000, with two-thirds of them living on the Great Plains.

The Plains Indians generally tolerated the white man crossing their territory on the way to California and Oregon. But when the newcomers began to settle in, tensions grew and both sides resorted to violence.

In 1862, a tribe of Sioux went on the offensive in Minnesota against encroaching settlers, killing more than 700 whites before the militia defeated them and hanged 38 of the tribe's leaders. In 1864, a Colorado militia colonel named John Chivington attacked a peaceful band of Cheyenne at Sand Creek, Colorado, and killed 133 people, most of them women and children. Many white Americans were appalled at Chivington's brutality.

Once the Civil War was over, a debate began in earnest on what to do about "the Indian Problem." Ideas ranged from extermination to reservations to ending tribal customs and forcing Indians to adopt white culture. All of them were tried to varying degrees. Between 1859 and 1876, soldiers and Indians fought at least 200 pitched battles (see Figure 15-1) and signed 370 treaties. "They made us promises more than I can remember," noted one Sioux leader, "but they never kept but one. They promised to take our land, and they did."

Figure 15-1:
Typical scene in the West: Indians and white men fighting.

They also all but wiped out the American bison, or buffalo, which to the Plains Indians was a walking supermarket. The tribes not only ate the buffalo, but also wore clothes and blankets from it, and used its bones for tools and its dried dung for fire fuel. In 1840, there were an estimated 40 million buffalo on the Plains.

But buffalo were dumber than rocks when it came to being hunted, placidly grazing while hunters with long-range rifles blazed away and picked off the herds one by one for their hides, or meat, or just for the hell of it. By 1875, only a million buffalo were left, and by 1893, less than 1,000. The Plains Indian was starved into submission far more than he was outfought.

In 1868, after a series of Indian victories on the Plains, both sides agreed to a grand scheme in which two large reservations would be created, one in Oklahoma and one that took in all of western South Dakota. That included the Black Hills, which were sacred to the Sioux (more properly known as Lakota).

Putting up a fight

Six years later, an expedition led by Col. George Armstrong Custer discovered gold in the Black Hills. White prospectors poured into the area. The government, powerless to stop them, then offered to buy the land from the Indians, and was refused. The last great Indian war began, and for the first time, the Plains tribes united into a formidable fighting force.

On June 25, 1876, a force of 212 soldiers led by Custer — including two of his brothers — foolishly attacked an Indian encampment at the Little Big Horn River in South Dakota. It proved to be populated by 2,500 warriors. Custer and his men were wiped out to the last man.

I quit

"I am tired of fighting. The old men are all dead ... it is cold and we have no blankets. The little children are freezing to death ... Hear me my chiefs. I am tired; my heart is sick and sad. From where the sun now stands, I will fight no more forever."

—Nez Percé Chief Joseph, before surrendering to Army troops, 1877.

"Custer's Last Stand" horrified people in the East as well as the West, and the army greatly increased its efforts to end the Indians' ability to fight back. The battle proved to be the beginning of the end for the Plains Indians. Over the next decade, tribe after tribe was gradually worn down by hunger and continual pursuit by the army. What happened to the Plains tribes was repeated throughout the West: the Apache in Arizona, the Crow and Blackfoot in Montana, the Ute in Colorado, the Nez Percé in Idaho, all were decimated by hunger, disease, and harassment by the whites.

In 1887, Congress passed a law that divided land into individual allotments for Indians, as part of an effort to turn them into small farmers. It also provided for an education system, and eventual U.S. citizenship. However well intentioned the law was, it didn't work. Most Indians didn't want to be farmers, or U.S. citizens. The education system never amounted to much, and white Americans were too hungry to share what had belonged to the Indians in the first place. Many Indians eventually signed away their land for a few cents an acre to speculators, who promptly resold it to settlers for a few dollars an acre.

In 1890, a misunderstanding led to a cavalry attack on a group of Cheyenne who were under military escort, near a creek called Wounded Knee, in South Dakota. The soldiers killed more than 200 men, women, and children, then left their bodies in the snow for three days before burying them in a mass grave. It was the last major violence between the Indians and whites, and a tragic and horrifyingly typical response to America's "Indian Problem."

Legalizing discrimination

While White America was pushing the Indians to adopt white ways and become part of white culture, it was pushing to keep African Americans out. Reconstruction had failed to give blacks equal rights, and a conservative U.S. Supreme Court ensured the failure would last another 50 or 60 years.

Crazy Horse

He was named after his father after proving himself in battle, which was probably a good thing, because in his early years, Crazy Horse was called "Curly." Born probably around 1842 near the Belle Fourche River in South Dakota, the Lakota (Sioux) warrior began his fight against the white invaders of his homelands in 1865. He became known as a daring fighter who used tricks and guerilla tactics well. In 1866, he helped lure 80 soldiers into an ambush in which all of them were killed.

Eleven months after leading the combined tribes against Custer at the Little Big Horn, Crazy Horse surrendered to troops that had been relentlessly harassing his band. He was taken to Fort Robinson, Wyoming, where he was held for several months.

"They say we massacred him [Custer]," he said during his captivity, "but he would have done the same thing to us had we not defended ourselves and fought to the last. Our first impulse was to escape . . . but we were so hemmed in that we had to fight."

In September 1877, while still in custody, he was stabbed to death by a soldier, under questionable circumstances. Crazy Horse became a mythic figure among Indians of all tribes.

In 1883, the Court ruled the federal government had no right to interfere with discrimination by private enterprises or individuals. In 1896, in a case called *Plessy vs. Ferguson,* it decided states had the right to legally segregate public facilities, from schools to trains. And in 1899, the Court ruled that states could erect schools for white kids only, even if there were no schools for blacks.

Encouraged by the decisions, Southern states passed what were called "Jim Crow" laws (named after a popular song that depicted African Americans as shiftless children), which tried to completely separate the races. Blacks could not cut white hair, nurse white sick people, or even drink from the same drinking fountain. They also established elaborate tests that black would-be voters had to take in order to get a ballot. The result was that the level of black voting dropped like a boulder off a bridge.

But the Jim Crow laws weren't enough. During the 1890s, the South averaged 130 lynchings a year. They were so commonplace, they were sometimes advertised in advance in newspapers. The North generally shrugged at the Jim Crow laws and ignored the lynchings. "The Negro's day is over," shrugged Yale Professor William Graham Sumner. "He is out of fashion."

Even the best-known African American leader of the day was not ready to challenge the injustices. Born into slavery, Booker T. Washington had become a schoolteacher, the founder of a major vocational school in Alabama called the Tuskegee Institute, and an eloquent advocate of African Americans improving themselves economically.

To do it, Washington urged blacks to "accommodate" whites when it came to demands for segregation, in return for white help in obtaining black schools and economic opportunity. "The wisest among my race understand that the agitation of questions of social equality is the extremest of folly," he argued. While it's easy to criticize Washington's approach today, it might have been a matter of accepting reality in 1896, especially when the reality included a rope.

White America didn't care much for Chinese immigrants either. "The Yellow Peril," many of whom were brought to America to work on the railroads at half the wages paid to white workers, were viewed as a competitive labor threat to American-born workers. Anti-Chinese riots broke out in San Francisco in 1877. In 1882, Congress passed a law prohibiting all Chinese immigration for 10 years. The ban, called the Chinese Exclusion Act, was later extended to last indefinitely, and was not repealed until 1943.

Populating the East

The law that excluded immigration by Chinese also banned criminals, the mentally ill or retarded, and those likely to end up as public charity cases. Otherwise, America's front door was wide open, and people poured in. Between 1866 and 1915, 25 million immigrants came to the United States (see Figure 15-2). Most of them came from Italy and Southeastern Europe, but they also came from Scandinavia, Russia, Poland, Germany, Ireland, England, and France. By 1910, 15 percent of the country's total population was foreign-born. Most of them came to escape hard economic times at home, despotic governments, or both. Many times their expectations were unrealistically high. "America is all puddings and pies!" enthused one young man as he stepped off the ship in New York.

Figure 15-2:
Immigrants arriving in America.

Nickel-and-diming it

The growth of the cities helped spark the development of retail stores designed to do a high volume of business by selling low-cost goods. In February, 1879, a self-described "boob from the country" of upstate New York, named Frank W. Woolworth, opened the "Great Five-Cent Store" in Utica, New York During its first months, it took in a grand total of $2.50 a day.

Undismayed, Woolworth figured his store was just in a bad location and opened another in Lancaster, Pennsylvania. It featured a "5-cent counter" in the front of the store that was supposed to lure customers in the door, where they might buy some higher-priced items.

The idea worked. By 1900, Woolworth had 59 stores, and by 1913, he was wealthy enough to pay $13.5 million cash to construct what was then the tallest building in the world, the Woolworth Building in Manhattan. By the way, that's 270 million nickels.

Despite the warning of a popular immigrant guidebook to "forget your past, your customs, and your ideals," many of the new Americans clung to their own languages, customs, and cuisines, and gravitated to communities populated by others from their country. The presence of so many immigrants in so short a time caused alarm in some "natives," who feared the newcomers would weaken their chances in the job market and pollute American culture. But it wasn't until 1921, after World War I had created millions of refugees in Europe, that Congress tightened immigration policies.

In the meantime, as much as 80 percent of the immigrant wave settled in Northern cities. By the turn of the century, more than a third of Chicago's populace was foreign-born, and there were more Irish in New York City than there were in Ireland. The immigrants weren't the only newcomers in town. By 1900, 30 million Americans lived in cities, about a third of all U.S. residents. The number of cities larger than 100,000 increased from nine to 50 between 1860 and 1910.

Slum Life

"All the fresh air that enters these stairs comes from the hall-door that is forever slamming . . . The sinks are in the hallway, that all tenants may have access — and all be poisoned alike by the summer stenches . . . Here is a door. Listen! That slow, hacking cough, that tiny helpless wail — what do they mean? The child is dying of measles. With half a chance, it might have lived; but it had none. That dark bedroom killed it."

— Reporter Jacob Riis, in "How the Other Half Lives," 1890.

IT STARTED HERE

And dribble before you shoot. . . .

James Naismith had an unruly class on his hands. The Canadian-born YMCA teacher was training would-be YMCA instructors in Springfield, Massachusetts, in the winter of 1891. His boss had ordered him to come up with a new indoor game that would get the class re-enthused about exercise in the winter.

Naismith tried variations of soccer and lacrosse. They proved too rough. After two weeks, he was still stumped. Then it began to fall in place. First, use a big round ball that didn't require a stick to hit it. Second, eliminate running with the ball, so no tackling was required. Third, set up goals through which to chuck the ball.

"I met Mr. Stebbins, the superintendent of buildings," Naismith later recalled, "and I asked him if he had two boxes about 18 inches square. Stebbins thought a minute, and then said: 'No, but I have two old peach baskets down in the store room.'" By noon, Naismith had nailed up the peach baskets, and two nine-man teams were playing "basket ball" — as opposed to what presumably would have been "box ball."

But many parts of the big cities were festering sores. Fire protection, street cleaning, sewage systems, garbage collection, and water treatment barely existed. The Chicago River was an open sewer. Baltimore's sewers emptied into the tidal basin and in the summer heat, journalist H.L. Mencken wrote, it "smelled like a billion polecats."

Housing was often designed to cram the most people into the least space. It wasn't uncommon for 24 four-room apartments to be built on a 2,500 square-foot lot. Tenement slums took on fitting names, such as "Hell's Kitchen," "Bone Alley," or "Poverty Gap."

Gradually, things improved in the major urban areas. No one, rich or poor, wanted to live in filth, and once the link between disease and poor sanitation was firmly established, city leaders began to develop adequate sewage and water systems. Public transit systems, based on streetcars or trolleys, were put in place. But none of it happened overnight, and more than a few farmer-turned-city-dwellers must have yearned more than once to be home on the range.

Inventing Big Business

As America reached its young adulthood in the last part of the nineteenth century, it began to shake off its rural roots and become an industrial city slicker. From 1859 to 1899, the value of the country's manufactured products rose 622 percent, from $1.8 billion to $13 billion, and America became the world's leading manufacturer. It rode its way to the top on the train.

Building the railroads

The railroad system was America's first truly big business and its growth and impact were enormous. In the 41 years from 1830 to 1870, about 40,000 miles of track were laid in the country. But in the 20 years from 1871 to 1890, more than 110,000 miles were laid. In 1869, the first transcontinental line, linking the East and West coasts, was opened, and by 1900, there were four more.

By 1890, annual railroad freight revenues totaled $1 billion — which was more than twice what the federal government gathered yearly in revenue. The railroads not only transported goods and people, they dictated where towns would grow and businesses would locate. They employed more than one million people by 1900. They helped push Congress to create four standard time zones across the country, so train schedules could be worked out.

The railroads created or greatly expanded other industries, because of its demand for things like steel for rails and passenger and freight cars. And it helped speed development of America's telegraph system, because where the rails went, the wires went. With telegraph stations at most train stations, the Western Union Company was sending 40 million messages a year by 1883, over 400,000 miles of wire.

Despite all those grand and glorious numbers, the railroad boom wasn't exactly a shining example of American free enterprise at its best. The rails were laid mostly on public land given to the railroads by the federal government (and the state of Texas) — more than 240,000 square miles, or an area the size of Germany — along with more than $60 million in taxpayer-financed grants or loans.

The real thing

John Pemberton was an Atlanta pharmacist, but he was also a man with a vision: He wanted to make the perfect drink. So he came up with a syrup that combined the coca leaf and the kola nut. Mixing it in a big kettle, he lugged it down to a local pharmacy, where it sold for 5 cents a glass — and averaged nine sales a day.

Pemberton died in 1888, and the formula for "Coca-Cola" (a name created by Pemberton's bookkeeper from the two main ingredients) was sold to a clever marketing man named Asa B.

Candler. Candler realized that advertising was the key to making the product a national brand and devoted an unheard-of $50,000 a year to marketing the drink. Other executives who followed him perfected distribution and bottling techniques, and today billions of bottles and cans are sold in more than 150 countries.

P.S.: Among other things, Pemberton claimed his drink could cure headaches and dyspepsia. He made no rash claims about diet dyspepsia.

Because the federal government did not want to get directly in the railroad building business, the land was thought of as an incentive to attract private investment. The railroad companies would sell most of the land near its tracks, and that's where they would make their money, since it was thought that it would take years to turn a profit from rail operations.

The system was ripe for corruption, and scandals were plenty. The Union Pacific line, for example, was built by the Credit Mobilier Construction Company, which was owned by the same people who owned the railroad. They took fat federal grants and awarded themselves exorbitant contracts — and bought off inquisitive congressmen with bribes of heavily discounted railroad stock.

The business attracted titans of industry (or robber barons, depending on how you viewed them). There was Cornelius Vanderbilt in the East, Thomas A. Scott in the Midwest, James J. Hill in the Northwest, and Jay Gould in the Southwest. Each had their railroad fiefdoms and battled with the others for government favors. But not all of the country's big wheels concentrated on trains, because there were fortunes to be made in other fields too.

Manufacturing steel

Before the Civil War, steel was a rare and expensive building material, mainly because the process to make it from iron ore was a lengthy one. But a process that became widely used in the early 1870s greatly shortened the process, and greatly increased the amount you could make at one time.

In America, steel making became synonymous with one man: Andrew Carnegie. Born in Scotland, Carnegie came to America at the age of 13 and got a job working in a Pennsylvania factory for $1.50 a week. He moved to a job with Western Union, saved his money, made smart investments, and by the time he was 28, was making $50,000 a year.

Carnegie eventually focused on steel. He hired chemists to perfect the production process, developed markets for steel, reinvested his profits, and expanded. He bought up vast holdings of iron ore and coal so he could corner the supply of raw materials. By 1890, America was producing 4 million tons of steel per year, mostly for the railroads, and 70 percent of it was made by Carnegie's steel plants near Pittsburgh.

In 1901, Carnegie sold out to financier J. P. Morgan, for the staggering sum of $447 million. In his later years, he gave away more than $300 million of his fortune through philanthropies that included building 2,811 public libraries and donating 8,000 organs to churches.

SIDETRIP

> # By-product to buy product
>
> Robert A. Chesebrough was looking for a way to keep from going broke. He had a kerosene company in Brooklyn, but the big oil finds in Pennsylvania undercut his prices and threatened to drive him out of business.
>
> So Chesebrough went to Pennsylvania with the idea of getting into the oil business. When he came back to Brooklyn, he brought with him some pasty gunk that stuck to the oil drills and was considered a nuisance. The young chemist fooled around with the stuff, purified it, and called it "petroleum jelly." He also found that it
>
> seemed to help cuts and burns heal faster. So Chesebrough hit the road, offering free samples of his "Vaseline" (it's unclear where the name came from) if people would try it.
>
> The salve was a smash success, and by the 1870s, Chesebrough had made a fortune. Vaseline was used for everything from preventing rust on tractors to getting stains out of furniture. And its inventor had one more use for it. Every day, Chesebrough ate a spoonful of the stuff as a health aid. He lived to be 96.

Drilling and refining oil

In the 1850s, whale oil — the primary fuel for providing light — had become very expensive, and people began to look for an alternative. Gradually, drilling for oil became practical enough that kerosene made from refined petroleum began replacing whale oil.

The Carnegie of oil was John D. Rockefeller, a Cleveland businessman who had made some money during the Civil War selling meat and grain. In 1870, Rockefeller combined five companies he owned into the Standard Oil Company. A ruthless and brilliant businessman, Rockefeller bought up competition or drove it out of business by undercutting prices. Political bribery was also a standard tool of Standard Oil: One critic noted that Rockefeller "had done everything to the Pennsylvania legislature except refine it." By 1879, Standard Oil controlled 90 percent of the nation's refining capacity, a huge network of pipelines and large oil reserves, and by 1892, Rockefeller had a fortune of $800 million.

IN THEIR WORDS
"Four score and seven..."

> # Caveat emptor, chump
>
> "Let the buyer beware; that covers the whole business. You cannot wet-nurse men from the time they are born until the time they die. They have to wade, and get stuck, and that is the way men are educated."
>
> —Sugar baron Henry O. Havemeyer, to a congressional committee investigating the sugar industry, 1895.

Producing the telephone and light bulb

New industries were also springing up around new inventions. In 1876, a teacher of the deaf, Alexander Graham Bell, invented the telephone. By 1880, 85 cities and towns had phone networks, and by 1900, there were more than 800,000 telephones throughout the country.

In 1879, inventor Thomas A. Edison came up with a practical electric light bulb, and over the next 20 years, America began to be wired up. At first, direct current (DC) was used, but DC didn't work over distances of more than a few miles. Then a fellow named George Westinghouse began using alternating current, which allowed high voltage to be sent long distances through transformers and then reduced to safer levels as it entered buildings. The switch from steam engines to electric power made factories safer and more efficient too.

Creating trusts

In 1882, Standard Oil organized the first of the nation's "trusts." A trust oversaw virtually all of an industry's operations, from production to price-setting to distribution and sales. It was supposedly run not by a single company, but by "trustees." The trusts issued certificates to stockholders in the industry's companies and paid dividends. Virtual monopolies like Standard Oil could then argue that they did not control an industry, the trust did.

Monopolies weren't all bad. Because of the economies of doing business on a large scale, costs could be kept down, and prices lowered. The price of kerosene, for example, dropped a fair amount once Standard Oil dominated the market. Of course with no competition, prices were at the mercy of the monopolies, and could — and often did — swing up again. In addition, the sheer size and power of the monopolies was worrisome to some Americans.

Carnegie and other giants of capitalism immodestly preached the "Gospel of Wealth," arguing that it was natural for a few people to have most of the wealth, a sort of economic "survival of the fittest." As long as they used their fortunes to benefit society, they contended there was nothing wrong with it.

But opening libraries and donating church organs didn't put bread on the table of the average working guy. Labor unions began to try to do that after the Civil War by organizing on a large scale. Most notable were groups called the Knights of Labor and the American Federation of Labor (AFL). In 1877, America faced its first national labor strike when railroad workers walked off the job after wages were cut. State and federal troops were called in, hundreds of strikers were killed or wounded, and service was restored at the point of a gun.

Elizabeth Jane Cochrane

A lot of people can claim to give a little extra to their jobs, but Elizabeth Cochrane became a thief, went insane, and traveled around the world for hers. She was a pioneer investigative journalist who later became a successful businesswoman. The world knew her better by her pen name: Nellie Bly.

Cochrane was born in Pennsylvania in 1864. She became a journalist at the age of 18 after writing a letter to a Pittsburgh newspaper in support of women's rights. The editor liked her writing and offered her a job.

She eventually went to work for Joseph Pulitzer at the *New York World,* and became famous for going undercover to get the story. She posed as a thief and was arrested to see how police treated woman prisoners. She pretended to be insane and spent 10 days in an asylum for a story on the sad plight of the mentally ill. In 1889, she traveled around the world in a little more than 72 days as a stunt to see if she could break the fictional record set in the Jules Verne novel "Around the World in 80 Days."

Cochrane left newspapers in 1895 after marrying. When her husband died, she assumed control of his businesses. She returned to journalism in World War I and reported from the battlefields. Cochrane died in 1922 at the age of 58, a newswoman to the end.

In May 1886, an AFL strike for an eight-hour day for workers led to a clash at Chicago's Haymarket Square between police and strikers. A bomb killed seven cops and injured 67 others. The police, who had killed four strikers the day before, fired into the crowd and killed four more, and seven strike leaders were eventually convicted and four were hanged. The incident was condemned by anti-union forces as an example of how the labor movement was controlled by "anarchists" and "radicals."

In 1894, a strike against the Pullman railroad car company spread over 27 states and paralyzed the country's railroads. Federal troops were called out, and a court order ended the strike. The Haymarket Square riot and Pullman strike dealt severe blows to the chances of things getting better for the average working stiff through labor unions. America was progressing, but not all of its citizens were.

Electing a String of Forgettable Presidents

America has had good presidents and bad presidents, but it's doubtful it has ever had as many mediocre presidents in a row as it did between 1876 and 1900. It wasn't a case of boring elections. Party splits and factions, and the fact that winners got to milk the government for jobs, made for intense and nasty campaigns. There were plenty of big issues too, from tariffs to bank panics to civil service reform. The men elected to deal with them, however, were a forgettable bunch. Here they are, before we forget them:

- ✔ **Rutherford B. Hayes** (Republican, 1877–1881). Hayes was a Civil War hero who was very politically cautious. He hated making tough decisions, so he avoided them. The Democrats controlled Congress most of the time he was president, so he accomplished little. He chose not to run for a second term and might not have been nominated anyway.

- ✔ **James A. Garfield** (Republican, 1881–1881). He was assassinated four months after taking office by a disgruntled office seeker. He was also the last president to be born in a log cabin.

- ✔ **Chester A. Arthur** (Republican, 1881–1885). Arthur was a lifelong politician who never won an election, except as Garfield's running mate. He was a fairly dignified and businesslike president, but he accomplished little.

- ✔ **Grover Cleveland** (Democrat, 1885–1889, 1893–1897). Cleveland was the only president to serve two non-consecutive terms and the only one to have personally hanged a man. He accomplished the latter feat while sheriff in Buffalo, New York. He managed the former by losing his re-election bid in 1888 to Benjamin Harrison, and then defeating Harrison in 1892. Cleveland was elected the first time despite the revelation that he fathered a son by a woman he never married. His second term was marked by an economic depression. He did not win nomination for a chance at a third term.

- ✔ **Benjamin Harrison** (Republican, 1889–1893). He was the grandson of President William Henry Harrison. Six new states — Washington, Idaho, Montana, Wyoming, North Dakota, and South Dakota — were admitted during his administration. That was pretty much it.

- ✔ **William McKinley** (Republican, 1897–1901). By most accounts, Bill McKinley was a nice guy. He was an Ohio congressman and governor and very devoted to his invalid wife. He also had friends in high places, especially political boss Mark Hanna. Hanna and others helped elect McKinley president. He defeated Democrat-Populist William Jennings Bryan in 1896, and again in 1900. He was assassinated by a crazy anarchist in 1901. As he lay wounded, McKinley urged his killer not be harmed. But they executed him in the electric chair anyway.

The Rise of Populism

Times were tough on the farm in the 1890s. Crop prices fell as production rose. Credit was hard to get and interest rates were high. Many of the rural areas' best and brightest had taken off to seek their fortunes in the cities.

The hard times triggered a political movement called Populism. Populists sought higher crop prices and lower interest rates. They wanted a system where farmers could deposit crops in storage facilities and use them as collateral for low-interest government loans.

They also wanted more money put into circulation and more silver coins made. The idea was that more money in circulation would raise prices, while their mortgage payments would stay the same. But it was also risky. Money based on the amount of gold reserves the country had was more stable than money based on silver, since the amount of silver reserves was increasing and therefore could "cheapen" the value of money as the price of silver dropped.

Republicans generally opposed the Populist ideas, while Democrats generally lined up with the Populists. The Democrats nominated 36-year-old Nebraska Congressman William Jennings Bryan as their 1896 presidential candidate. Bryan, an outstanding orator, gave a rousing speech at the Democratic convention in favor of "free silver," by exclaiming "you shall not crucify mankind upon a cross of gold." But Bryan lost to Republican William McKinley anyway, mostly because McKinley's supporters raised and spent $3 million on his campaign.

Declaring War with Spain

When Cuba revolted against Spain in 1868, most Americans weren't much interested. But in 1898, when the Caribbean island rebelled again, America took notice. The difference was that by 1898, the United States was Cuba's best customer for its sugar and tobacco crops, and its biggest investor.

How are ya, Hawaii?

The islands of Hawaii had always been a great place to visit for Americans. Yankee traders visited there in the 1790s. In the 1840s, the islands were home to American whaling ships. And by 1860, many U.S. citizens owned land there.

In 1875, America dropped a ban on Hawaiian sugar that had been urged by U.S. sugar growers, and became the islands' best customer; and in 1887, Hawaii granted America exclusive rights to use Pearl Harbor as a coaling station and repair base for U.S. ships.

But Hawaii's becoming a U.S. territory took some doing. In 1893, white businessmen led a successful rebellion against Queen Liliuokalani. The rebels promptly petitioned to be annexed to the United States. But President Grover Cleveland rejected the offer. The new Hawaiian government asked again in 1897, but this time the Senate rejected it. Finally, in 1898, Hawaii became a U.S. territory. In 1959, it became the fiftieth state.

So when the fighting destroyed American property in Cuba, the country's interest was aroused. Some Americans wanted to free Cuba from Spanish oppression. Some wanted to protect U.S. economic interests, and others saw it as a chance to pick off some of Spain's colonies for America.

The anti-Spain flames were fanned by New York newspapers that tried to outdo each other in reporting about Spain's "atrocities." "You furnish the pictures," New York publisher William Randolph Hearst told an illustrator for his *New York Journal,* "and I'll furnish the war."

In January 1898, the U.S. battleship *Maine* was sent to Havana when it was reported American lives were in danger. On February 15, the *Maine* mysteriously exploded, killing 260 U.S. sailors and officers. By April, America and Spain were at war.

It was, in the words of one American official, "a splendid little war." In the Philippines, a U.S. fleet commanded by Commodore George Dewey blasted a Spanish fleet and U.S. soldiers easily took the islands. Cuba took a little longer, but it also fell. The four-month war cost 5,642 American lives, all but 379 to disease. And a grown-up America now had the makings of an empire on its hands.

Gee, Grandpa, What Else Happened?

Aug. 2, 1876: Legendary Western gunfighter, scout, and law enforcement officer James Butler "Wild Bill" Hickok is shot in the back and killed while playing poker in Deadwood, South Dakota. Hickok is holding a pair of aces and a pair of eights when he is shot, which comes to be known as a "dead man's hand."

Dec. 15, 1877: Thomas Edison files a patent application for a new invention he calls the phonograph.

May 30, 1880: An Irish-American named Paddy Ryan wins the heavyweight boxing championship of the world by knocking out the reigning champ, England's Joe Goss. It is Ryan's first recorded fight and ends in the eighty-seventh round.

Oct. 26, 1881: Deputy Marshall Wyatt Earp, his brothers Virgil and Morgan, and friend Doc Holliday, square off against four men in a gunfight at the O.K. Corral in Tombstone, Arizona. The Earps and Holliday win.

May 25, 1883: The world's longest bridge, linking Brooklyn to Manhattan over the East River, opens. The Brooklyn Bridge costs $16 million and 26 lives and takes 14 years to finish.

Oct. 28, 1886: The 305-foot-tall Statue of Liberty is dedicated in New York Harbor. The statue is a gift from the people of France; the pedestal it stands on was paid for by American donations.

Aug. 6, 1890: Electrocution is introduced as a "humane" alternative to hanging in the execution of a convicted ax murderer named William Kemmler in New York. It takes several jolts to kill him, and his body is a bloody, charred mess.

Aug. 29, 1893: A Chicago mechanical engineer named Whitcomb Judson is granted a patent for a device he calls a "clasp locker." We call it a zipper.

Jan. 29, 1896: A Chicago medical researcher named Eric H. Grubbe uses X-rays to try to destroy the tumors of a breast cancer patient. Grubbe discovers that heavy doses of X-rays can kill living cells. He makes the discovery by accidentally burning his hand with the X-ray machine.

June 12, 1899: Proving the Wild West isn't entirely tamed, the "Wild Bunch," led by Butch Cassidy and Harry Longbaugh, better known as the Sundance Kid, rob a train in Wyoming of $60,000.

Chapter 16

Growing Out: 1899–1918

· ·

In This Chapter

▶ Winning colonies from Spain

▶ Bringing in Teddy Roosevelt

▶ Improving conditions across America

▶ Getting America in the air and on the road

▶ Fighting for women's right to vote

▶ Migrating north

▶ Joining the First World War

▶ Timeline

· ·

*A*s the 1800s turned into the 1900s, America was entering young adulthood. It had just won a short and sloppily fought, but easily won, war with Spain. As a result, the country found itself, for the first time in its history, with an overseas empire formed by the colonies it won from Spain.

This chapter covers how Uncle Sam reacted to his new role as a force to be reckoned with in the world — and how Americans handled changes in how they worked, how they got around, and how they governed themselves.

Here Today, Guam Tomorrow

Suddenly, there was a lot more than the country to take care of. There was Hawaii, formally annexed in 1898, Guam, Puerto Rico, and the Philippines, all won from Spain. Cuba was technically free, but because of restrictive treaties was in reality an American fiefdom.

On February 6, 1899, the Senate ratified the treaty with Spain that gave the U.S. Guam and Puerto Rico. The Spanish threw in the Philippines too, after American negotiators offered $20 million for the islands. The Senate vote was 57 to 27, only two more than the two-thirds needed, and the close vote mirrored a sharp division of opinion about whether it was a good idea for America to have colonies.

TECHNICAL STUFF

Imperialism

Imperialism is basically the political idea that we can run your country better than you can because we have a better system of government. In practical terms, the imperialist also viewed the occupied territory as sort of an automatic teller machine for withdrawals of natural resources, or as a great place for strategically located military bases.

Opponents to the idea of American colonies formed the Anti-Imperialist League, a strange bedfellows group that included author Mark Twain, steel tycoon Andrew Carnegie, and labor leader Samuel Gompers. Those who opposed imperialism (see the sidebar "Imperialism" for a definition of the term) had different reasons. Some believed it was un-American to impose American culture or government on other people. Some were afraid of "mingling" with "inferior" races. Laborers feared competition from poorly paid workers in other countries, and conservative business leaders feared foreign entanglements would divert capital.

Proponents, led by Theodore Roosevelt, then governor of New York, argued that annexation would open the Orient for U.S. business, prevent other nations from seizing the former Spanish colonies, and better position the United States as a world military power. President William McKinley opined it was America's duty to "educate the Filipinos and uplift and civilize and Christianize them," conveniently ignoring the fact that most Filipinos were already Roman Catholic, a fairly substantial Christian religion. Such attitudes sparked a war with the newly liberated Filipinos that took several years and thousands of casualties on both sides before the United States prevailed.

To a large extent, the nasty fight in the Philippines soured the American appetite for imperialism. But protecting U.S. business interests overseas remained a priority, and a strong feeling still existed that the country needed to maintain a high profile in international affairs. No one felt that way more strongly than McKinley's vice president, Theodore Roosevelt. Republican Party leaders added the headstrong Roosevelt to McKinley's ticket in 1900 mainly as a way to shut him up in the obscurity of the vice presidency.

But on September 6, 1901, while visiting the Pan-American Exposition in Buffalo, New York, McKinley was shot by a self-proclaimed anarchist. McKinley died a week later.

"Now look!" cried GOP political boss Mark Hanna of McKinley's death and Roosevelt's succession to the presidency. "That damned cowboy is President of the United States!"

Making a Lot of Noise and Carrying a Big Stick

Depending on whether you liked him or not, Theodore Roosevelt was either the energetic embodiment of the nation he led, or a macho blowhard who really should have taken more cold showers.

A puny, asthmatic child, Roosevelt literally built himself into a human dynamo with strenuous exercise and a non-stop personal regimen. His walrus mustache, thick round spectacles, and outsized teeth made him a political cartoonist's dream (see Figure 16-1); his relative youth, — at 43, he was the youngest president the country had ever had — his energy, and his unpredictability made him the bane of GOP political bosses.

Figure 16-1:
Political cartoon of Theodore Roosevelt.

Roosevelt was fond of repeating an old African proverb that suggested "Speak softly, and carry a big stick; you will go far." In practice, however, he was much fonder of the stick than of speaking softly. A leading imperialist under McKinley, Roosevelt relished the role of America as policeman to the world. In 1903, Roosevelt encouraged Panama to revolt against Colombia so the U.S.

TECHNICAL STUFF

The Panama Canal

Roosevelt considered the Panama Canal his greatest accomplishment as president, and so did a lot of sea-goers, because it cut 7,800 miles off the voyage from New York to San Francisco by eliminating the necessity to sail around the tip of South America. The canal took about 10 years to build and cost $380 million, or about $7.5 million for each of its 50.72 miles. At the height of construction in 1913, more than 43,400 people were working on it, 75 percent of them laborers from the British West Indies. Hundreds of workers died from disease or accidents. About 240 million cubic yards of earth were moved. And because of the canal's angle, ships entering from the Atlantic actually enter the Pacific 23 miles *east* of where they enter. Go figure.

could secure rights from the Panamanians to build the Panama Canal. In 1905, he brokered the treaty that settled a war between Russia and Japan, for which he won a Nobel peace prize.

Roosevelt set the tone for presidents who followed him. Both Taft and Woodrow Wilson had their own versions of "gunboat diplomacy," particularly in Latin America. In 1912, U.S. Marines landed in Nicaragua after a revolution there threatened American financial interests. In 1915, U.S. troops went to Haiti when revolution began to bubble and stayed until 1934. Also in 1915, Wilson sent U.S. Army troops into Mexico under General John J. "Black Jack" Pershing to chase Mexican revolutionary Francisco "Pancho" Villa, who had raided into American territory. The "punitive expedition" almost triggered a war with Mexico and added to a widely held notion in the rest of the hemisphere that Uncle Sam was something of a bully.

The "expedition" was also an example of a U.S. tendency to get involved in other countries' affairs. The tendency, which sprang sometimes from idealism and sometimes from pure self-interest, would last the rest of the twentieth century.

Progressing Toward Reform

While America was busy reforming things in other countries, there was also a burgeoning movement for reforms at home, in virtually every business and social institution. At the core of the effort was a loose and diverse coalition of journalists, politicians, and single-cause crusaders, who because they sought progress were called "Progressives." They helped turn the first two decades of the century into what's known as the "Progressive Era."

The first step in many of the causes undertaken by the Progressives was in exposing particular evils. This was often done by reporters and writers who looked into everything from machine politics to child labor to the preparation of food. While journalists had written exposes for years, the muckrakers' impact was magnified by the fact they were often published in a fairly new medium: the popular (and cheap) magazine.

The magazines included *McClure's, The Saturday Evening Post,* and the *Ladies' Home Journal.* The muckrakers included Ida Tarbell, who exposed the inner workings of the Standard Oil monopoly; Lincoln Steffens, who wrote about the corruption of many big-city governments; and Upton Sinclair, whose novel on meatpacking practices in Chicago, called *The Jungle,* made the entire country queasy.

The muckrakers were joined in their quest for reforms by political figures at the local, state, and national levels, such as California Governor and then-U.S. Senator Hiram Johnson, Mayor Tom Johnson of Cleveland, and Governor Robert LaFollette of Wisconsin.

When the Progressives couldn't prevail over entrenched corrupt political machines, they sought to change the rules, pushing for reforms such as

- **Direct primary elections:** Voters and not bosses picked party nominees

- **The referendum:** Voters could repeal unpopular laws

- **The recall:** A means of getting rid of officials before their terms expired

- **The initiative:** Allowed voters to circumvent balky legislatures and propose laws directly

Other Progressives, meanwhile, fought to improve working conditions for women and children, secure welfare assistance for widows, and get insurance for workers hurt in industrial accidents. Spurred mainly by fundamentalist religious groups in the South and Midwest, and women's temperance groups, a decade-long effort to abolish the production and sale of alcoholic beverages gained momentum, culminating in the Eighteenth Amendment — "Prohibition" — which went into effect on January 16, 1920.

The result of all this progress was impressive, and included:

- The Meat Inspection Act and Pure Food and Drug Act in 1906, creating new rules and regulations for the preparation and handling of food and medicine.

- The breaking up of the bank and beef monopolies in 1907 and the Standard Oil trust in 1911.

- The Federal Reserve Act of 1913, which divided the country into 12 districts, each with their own bank and board of directors to oversee banking practices and policies and prevent panics and bank failures.

- The Seventeenth Amendment in 1913, which provided for the direct election of U.S. Senators rather than having them selected by state legislatures.

But even with the reforms, not everyone was completely happy.

Contracting Labor Pains

While the nation generally prospered, it was by no means a uniform prosperity. For every Rockefeller or Carnegie in 1900, there were hundreds of thousands of people making the average annual wage of $400 to $500 — about $100 less than was needed to maintain what was deemed a "decent" standard of living.

"The Muckrakers"

Like most presidents before and after him, Teddy Roosevelt had little use for the press. So it's probably not surprising that it was Roosevelt who hung the term "muckrakers" on a group of young journalists who specialized in exposing the seamier side of American life, even though Roosevelt was something of a reformer himself. The term referred to a character in the seventeenth-century allegorical novel *Pilgrim's Progress,* who used a rake to constantly clean up the moral filth around him, while ignoring a celestial crown offered him.

A change was occurring in the U.S. work force. As manufacturing expanded, jobs moved from the farm to the factory. In 1900, there were about 10 million farm-related jobs, versus about 18 million non-farm jobs. By 1920, there were still about 10 million farm-related jobs, but there were more than 30 million jobs not related to agriculture. Women held 20 percent of all manufacturing jobs, and 1.7 million children under the age of 16 had full-time jobs.

"Full-time" meant just that. In the Pittsburgh steel mills, for example, 10-year-old boys were paid 14 cents an hour to work 12 hours a day, six days a week. Factory conditions were often horrendous. Between July 1906 and June 1907, 195 people died in the steel mills of Pittsburgh, about one every other day. In 1911, 146 workers, most of them women, were killed when a fire roared through the Triangle Shirtwaist Factory in New York. Fire exits had been locked to keep workers from sneaking out for breaks.

Anxious to improve conditions, American workers increasingly tried to follow the example of the industrialists and combine into large groups to have strength through numbers. In 1904, the American Federation of Labor, which focused mainly on skilled workers, had 1.7 million members. The number grew to more than 4 million by 1920.

But unions often faced brutal reprisals. In Ludlow, Colorado, a 1914 strike against the Colorado Fuel & Iron Company resulted in state militia and private police firing on strikers. Fourteen people were killed. Eleven of them were children.

Sometimes, the government intervened. In 1902, a strike of more than 800,000 coal miners dragged on for months when mine operators refused to negotiate. Fed up, President Roosevelt summoned both sides to Washington and threatened to send federal troops into the mines and appropriate the coal for the national good. Finally, a presidential commission granted the miners a raise and a shorter workday.

But more typical was a 1912 textile mill strike in Lawrence, Massachusetts. After a state law required mill owners to limit the weekly hours of women and children to 54, the owners responded by speeding up production paces and cutting wages by 32 cents a week — or about the price of eight loaves of bread. The International Workers of the World organized a strike of more than 10,000 men and women.

After 63 days that included beatings by police, the killing of a woman striker, the sending of strikers' children to other cities because strikers couldn't feed them, and a failed attempt to bomb one of the mills and frame the strike leaders, the owners gave in and granted the strikers all of their demands. Within a year, however, most of the concessions had been rescinded, and the pre-strike conditions returned.

It would be at least another generation before unions became a national force.

Transporting America

Unions weren't alone in their aspirations for improving the life of working-class Americans. In Detroit, a generally unlikable, self-taught engineer named Henry Ford decided that just about everyone should have an automobile, and thus the right to go where they wanted, when they wanted.

So Ford's company made one model — the Model T. You could have it in any color you wanted, Ford said, as long as it was black. And because of his assembly-line approach to putting them together, you could have it relatively cheaply.

It was a good plan. The price of a Model T dropped from $850 in 1908 to $290 by 1924. As prices dropped, sales went up, from 10,000 in 1909 to just under a million in 1921. Within two decades, Ford and other carmakers had indelibly changed American life. The average family could now literally get away from it all, creating a new sense of independence and self-esteem. New industries, from tire production to roadside cafes, sprang up. And by the end of the 1920s, it could be persuasively argued that the automobile had become the single most dominant element in the U.S. economy.

Federal income tax

One of the Progressives' ideas was that people who made more money could afford to pay more taxes. A federal income tax had been tried before, during the Civil War and in the hard economic times of 1894. But the U.S. Supreme Court, on a 5–4 vote, struck down the 1894 effort as unconstitutional. The Sixteenth Amendment, pushed by Progressives, proposed in 1909 and ratified in 1913, gave Congress the power to slap a federal tax on income, and it promptly did so: one percent on annual income above $4,000, and two percent on income above $20,000. Of course the rates have gone up since then.

"The Wobblies"

Formed in 1905 by socialists and militant unionists, the Industrial Workers of the World was a radical labor force that favored action rather than negotiations and often resorted to violence. For reasons somewhat unclear, the IWW was disparaged as "The Wobblies." Foes of the union also said IWW stood for "I Won't Work."

The group favored one all-encompassing union rather than unions divided by craft or industry, and it targeted unskilled laborers, minorities, and women. Although it probably never had more than 150,000 members in any one year, the IWW had great influence on labor relations, because of its zeal, and the threat it posed to business owners. By the end of World War I, however, the union had become hugely unpopular because of its association with socialism, and it was all but defunct by 1920.

When it came to getting from here to there, others were looking up. In December 1903, two brothers who owned a bicycle shop in Dayton, Ohio, went to Kitty Hawk, North Carolina. There they pulled off the world's first powered, sustained, and controlled flights with a machine they had built. Fearful of losing their patent rights, Orville and Wilbur Wright did not go public with their airplane until 1908, by which time other inventors and innovators were also making planes.

Unlike the automobile, however, the airplane's popularity didn't really take off until after its usefulness was proved in World War I.

Suffering for Suffrage

By the time the twentieth century arrived, American feminists had been seeking the vote for more than 50 years. Their desire was fanned even hotter in 1869, when African-American males were given the right to vote through the Sixteenth Amendment while women of all races were still excluded.

One place where women were increasingly included was in the workplace. As the country shifted away from a rural, agrarian society to an industrial, urban one, more and more women had jobs — eight million by 1910. Moreover, they were getting better jobs. In 1870, 60 percent of working women were in domestic service. By 1920, it was only 20 percent, and women made up 13 percent of the professional ranks.

They were getting out of the house for more than just jobs, too. In 1892, membership in women's clubs was about 100,000. By 1917, it was more than one million. And the divorce rate rose from one for every 21 marriages in 1880 to one in nine by 1916.

Because women had always had non-traditional roles in the West, it wasn't surprising that Western states and territories were the first to give females the vote: Wyoming in 1869, Utah in 1870, Washington in 1883, Colorado in 1893, and Idaho in 1896. By 1914, all of the Western states except New Mexico had extended the voting franchise to women.

By 1917, the movement was building momentum (see Figure 16-2). In July of that year, a score of suffragists tried to storm the White House, were arrested, and were taken to the county workhouse. President Woodrow Wilson was unamused, but sympathetic, and pardoned them. The next year, a constitutional amendment — the Nineteenth — was submitted to the states. Ratified in 1920, it gave women the vote in every state.

Figure 16-2:
Women marching for the right to vote.

But many leaders of the women's movement recognized the vote alone would not give women equal standing with men when it came to educational, economic, or legal rights.

"Men are saying, perhaps, 'thank God this everlasting women's fight is over,'" said feminist leader Crystal Eastman after the Nineteenth Amendment was ratified. "But women, if I know them, are saying 'now at last we can begin.'"

Migrating to Cities as the Promised Land

Women weren't the only Americans on the move. Between 1914 and 1918, more than 500,000 African Americans left the farms of the South for jobs in Northern cities.

The movement was part of the "Great Migration," which stretched from the 1890s to the 1960s, and eventually resulted in more than six million black people leaving the South. This migration was spurred first by the Jim Crow laws, the lynchings, and the poverty of the post-Civil War South. Then, as the war in Europe simultaneously sparked U.S. industrial expansion and cut off the flow of immigrant workers, jobs opened up by the thousands. Henry Ford, for example, offered to pay the astronomical sum of $5 a day in his plants, and despite his racist views, he hired blacks.

The black populations of Northern cities swelled. In Chicago, for example, the African-American community grew from 44,000 in 1910 to 110,000 by 1920.

But moving North didn't mean leaving racism behind. Many Northern whites resented their new neighbors. The resentment was fueled in 1915 when the wildly popular new movie, "The Birth of a Nation," portrayed blacks as deranged and dangerous creatures who lorded their emancipation over white Southerners.

Nor was there much interest in black issues among Progressive leaders. When a delegation of black leaders met with President Woodrow Wilson in 1914 to protest segregation in federal offices, he angrily all but pushed them out the door.

The unrest led to race riots. In 1917 in East St. Louis, Illinois, white rioters went on a rampage in the black community. When it was over, 39 blacks and nine whites were dead. In the summer of 1919, more than 25 race riots broke out in cities across the country. The worst was in Chicago, where an incident at a segregated swimming beach sparked a six-day riot that resulted in 38 people dead and more than a thousand left homeless by riot-sparked fires, and didn't stop until federal troops were called in.

AMERICAN FACES

Jeanette Pickering Rankin

She was the first woman to serve in Congress and the only member of Congress who voted against both world wars. Born on a ranch near Missoula, Montana, in 1880, Rankin graduated from the University of Montana in 1902 and was a social worker before becoming a field secretary for the National American Woman Suffrage Association. After Montana approved the vote for women in 1914, Rankin decided in 1916 to run for one of the state's two seats in the House of Representatives, as a Republican, and won. As a congresswoman, she was one of 56 members of Congress who voted against President Wilson's call for a war resolution in 1917.

As a result, she lost a race for a U.S. Senate seat in 1918, moved to Georgia, and devoted her energies to pacifist organizations. In 1940, Rankin returned to Montana, where she ran again for Congress and won — in time to be the lone member of either house to vote against war with Japan in 1941. She did not run for re-election and died in California at the age of 92.

Of Rankin's vote against two world wars, John F. Kennedy said: "Few members of Congress have ever stood more alone while being true to a higher honor and loyalty."

Hands off!

"A woman's body belongs to herself alone. It does not belong to the United States of America or any other government on the face of the earth." — Margaret Sanger, who first coined the term "birth control" and founded the first birth control clinic in the United States in 1916. In 1921, she organized the American Birth Control League, the forerunner of Planned Parenthood.

Still, when President Wilson called on Americans to "help make the world safe for democracy" in 1917, more than 375,000 African Americans entered the military.

"If this is our country," explained black leader W.E.B. DuBois, "then this is our war."

The War to End All Chapters

Theodore Roosevelt had been president nearly eight years by the time of the 1908 election, having filled most of the assassinated McKinley's second term and winning his own term in 1904. Even though there were no term limits to stop him, Roosevelt decided not to run in 1908. Instead, he gave his blessing to William Howard Taft, a fellow Republican. But in 1912, Roosevelt became restless and decided to run against Taft, as the candidate of the Progressive, or "Bull Moose" Party. The result was that Americans chose the Democrat in the race, a scholarly former president of Princeton University and son of the South named Thomas Woodrow Wilson.

Progressive in his domestic policies, Wilson was something of a cautious imperialist abroad. He subscribed to the idea that America had a leading role to play in world affairs; he just didn't want to fight about it.

The country did get embroiled in a few Latin American fights, and Wilson did send troops into Mexico in 1916 after Mexican revolutionaries led by Pancho Villa raided into American soil. But as the European powers squared off in 1914 in what was to be four years of mind-numbingly horrific war, America managed to somewhat nervously mind its own business. Wilson, in fact, won re-election in 1916 using the phrase "he kept us out of war."

As time passed, however, the country began to increasingly side with Britain, France, and other countries fighting Germany. The sinking by a German submarine of the British passenger ship *Lusitania* in 1915, which resulted in the deaths of 128 Americans, inflamed U.S. passions against "the Huns."

Propagandistic portrayals of German atrocities in the relatively new medium of motion pictures added to the heat. And finally, when it was revealed German diplomats had approached Mexico about an alliance against the United States, Wilson felt compelled to ask Congress for a resolution of war against Germany. He got it on April 6, 1917.

The U.S. military was ill prepared for war on a massive scale. There were only about 370,000 men in the Army and National Guard combined. Through a draft and enlistments, that number would swell to 4.8 million in all the military branches by the end of World War I.

At home, about half of the war's eventual $33 billion price tag was met through taxes, the rest through the issuance of war bonds. Organized labor, in return for concessions such as the right to collective bargaining, agreed to reduce the number of strikes. Labor shortages drove wages up, which in turn drove prices up. But demand for goods and services because of the war soared, and the economy hummed along, despite government efforts to "organize" it.

Over there, however, no one was humming. American troops, like their European counterparts before them, found that modern warfare was anything but inspiring. The first U.S. troops were fed into the lines as much to shore up the morale of the Allies as anything else. But by the time the Germans launched their last desperate offensive, in the spring of 1918, more than 300,000 American troops had landed in France. By war's end in November, the number of Yanks had swelled to 1.4 million.

Led by Major General John "Black Jack" Pershing, a celebrated veteran of the Spanish-American and Philippines wars, the American Expeditionary Force (AEF) fought off efforts by Allied commanders to push the AEF into a subordinate role as replacement troops.

Starting with the battles of Cantigny, Chateau-Thierry, and Belleau Wood in France, the AEF proved itself an able force. In September 1918, the Americans launched an attack on a German bulge in the lines near Verdun, France. U.S. and French troops captured more than 25,000 prisoners, and the German military back was all but broken. At the 11th hour of the 11th day of the 11th month of 1918, Germany called it quits, and the fighting stopped.

American losses — 48,000 killed in battle, 56,000 lost to disease — seemed trifling compared to the staggering costs paid by other countries: Germany, 1.8 million dead; Russia, 1.7 million; France, 1.4 million; Austria-Hungary, 1.2 million; Britain, 950,000.

"The War to end All Wars," as it was called, turned out to be just another test of humans' aptitude for killing other humans in large quantities.

AMERICAN FACES

W.E.B. DuBois

William Edward Burghart DuBois was decidedly not what most white Americans thought of when they thought about black Americans. He was born to a poor but respected family in a Massachusetts town with a population that was less than one percent black, had degrees from Harvard and the University of Berlin, became one of the country's leading sociologists, and was an eloquent orator and stylish writer.

DuBois was best known for his forceful disagreements with another African American leader, Booker T. Washington, most famously expressed in DuBois's 1903 book, *The Souls of Black Folk*. While Washington stressed self-help

and material gain over seeking equal legal and social rights with whites, DuBois believed Washington's approach would only continue black oppression. In 1905, DuBois took a leading role in the Niagara Movement, the forerunner of the National Association for the Advancement of Colored People (NAACP), which he helped found in 1909. Disillusioned with the direction of the NAACP, he resigned in 1934. From 1932 to 1944 he was head of the Department of Sociology at Atlanta University and has been called the Father of American Sociology. He died in Ghana in 1963, at the age of 95.

Gee, Grandpa, What Else Happened?

Sept. 8, 1900: A devastating hurricane and tidal wave slam into Galveston, Texas, destroying much of the city and killing 8,000 people.

April 1904: Innovators at the World's Fair in St. Louis give the world iced tea, and ice cream in edible containers called "cones."

Jan. 12, 1906: The Intercollegiate Athletic Association changes the rules of college football to allow the forward pass, in the hopes that fewer players will be killed or seriously injured.

April 18, 1906: An earthquake and subsequent fire ravage San Francisco, killing more than 1,000 people and leaving 250,000 — half the city's population — homeless.

July 4, 1910: Heavyweight boxing champion Jack Johnson, an African American, defeats former champ and "great white hope" Jim Jeffries in a fight in Reno, Nevada. Johnson's win sets off race riots across the country, and at least eight black people are killed.

April 15, 1912: The passenger liner Titanic, the largest moving thing ever built by man up until its time, hits an iceberg in the North Atlantic. The "unsinkable" ship sinks, triggering shock around the world, and, over the next 85 years, several movies.

Oct. 14, 1912: After being shot in the chest by an insane man in Milwaukee, Bull Moose Party presidential candidate Theodore Roosevelt gives an 80-minute speech. Roosevelt recovers from the wound, but loses the election.

April 24, 1913: The Woolworth Building in New York City is formally opened. At 55 stories, it is the tallest building in the world.

Oct. 16, 1916: Margaret Sanger opens a birth control clinic in Brooklyn, New York. More than 100 women seeking advice are in line when it opens.

May 15, 1918: The federal government's airmail system is launched. On the initial flight from Washington D.C., the pilot misses Philadelphia and crashes near Waldorf, Maryland.

Chapter 17

Bathtub Gin, Jazz, and Lucky Lindy: 1919–1929

. . . .

In This Chapter

▶ Pushing for the League of Nations

▶ Terrorizing minorities and turning immigrants away

▶ Electing Harding, Coolidge, and Hoover

▶ Making the rich richer and the poor poorer

▶ Creating a thriving popular culture

▶ Enforcing Prohibition

▶ Finding heroes

▶ Timeline

. . . .

*W*ith World War I over, America turned its attention back toward itself — and was kind of uneasy about what it saw. Things seemed to be happening at too fast a pace. Young people were challenging old ways, an attempt to make the country more moral through a prohibition on liquor had the opposite effect, and the economy was making some Americans rich — and causing a lot more to spend like they were.

In this chapter, the heroes and villains of the 1920s are visited, along with the rise of mass media, and their impact on the country. It was only a decade-long trip, but it was a helluva ride.

Trying to Keep the Peace

Nearly a year before World War I was over, President Woodrow Wilson had already come up with a plan of "14 Points," in which he outlined his version of a peace treaty. It was viewed by leaders of America's allies as both simplistic and overly optimistic. The French prime minister even sneered that since mankind couldn't keep God's 10 Commandments, it was unlikely to keep Wilson's 14 Points.

IN THEIR WORDS

"Four score and seven..."

Peace plan now, or war later

"I can predict with absolute certainty that within another generation there will be another world war if the nations of the world do not concert the method by which to prevent it."

— Woodrow Wilson, during his tour to drum up support for the League of Nations, September, 1917.

But so eager was Wilson to play a major role in making the peace, he did something no other American president had ever done: He left the country while in office. In December 1918, a month after the fighting ended, Wilson went to Paris to meet with the leaders of France, England, and Italy. The "Big Four" (which soon became the Big Three after the minister from Italy left in a snit) soon drafted a peace treaty that included almost nothing Wilson wanted. Instead, the Treaty of Versailles required Germany to accept the blame for the war, pay $15 billion to the winning countries, give up most of its colonies, and limit the future size of its military forces. But it did include something Wilson *really* wanted: The formation of a League of Nations, whose members would promise to respect each others' rights and settle their differences through the League.

REMEMBER

Wilson brought the treaty and the idea of the League back to America and presented them to the U.S. Senate for its constitutionally required approval. But the Democratic president was facing a Senate dominated by Republicans, led by Massachusetts Senator Henry Cabot Lodge, chairman of the Foreign Relations Committee.

Some senators — dubbed "the Irreconcilables" — were adamantly against the idea of "foreign entanglements" like the League. Others wanted what amounted to relatively minor tweaking of the proposal. If Wilson had agreed to go along with a few changes, he could have gained the two-thirds approval he needed.

But Wilson stubbornly refused to negotiate. Each side dug in and launched thunderous attacks on the other. Wilson made more than 40 speeches in three weeks on an 8,000-mile journey around the country.

Wilson's valiant effort proved politically futile and personally tragic. In early October, he had a stroke. The next month, the Senate resoundingly rejected the League and the peace treaty, and then rejected it again in March 1920, when it was brought back for reconsideration. America would go it alone for another generation, or until the next world war.

Restricting Immigration and Challenging the Natives

One of the reasons many Americans opposed joining a league of nations was they just didn't like foreigners. A 1919 economic mini-boom created high inflation, which meant higher prices, which meant labor strife, as millions of workers struck for higher wages. In 1919 alone, more than 3,500 strikes involving more than 4 million workers took place. Then the economy dropped sharply, unemployment soared, and Americans looked for someone to blame.

They found plenty of targets. One group was the communists. The Russian Revolution scared many Americans by demonstrating how an uprising by a small group of radicals could overthrow the government of a mighty nation. Actually, there were relatively few communists in America, and they wielded relatively little clout. But nearly every labor strike was denounced as communist-inspired. A series of bombs mailed to leading American capitalists like J.P. Morgan and John Rockefeller also alarmed the country, even though none of the explosives reached their targets. It all added to what became known as "the Red Scare."

The chief Red-hunter was U.S. Attorney General A. Mitchell Palmer, who had hopes of becoming president. Palmer created the General Intelligence Division within the Justice Department and put an ardent young anti-communist named J. Edgar Hoover in charge of it. On January 2, 1920, Palmer's agents arrested about 6,000 people — many of them U.S. citizens — in 33 cities. Some were held for weeks without bail. Many were beaten and some were forced to sign confessions. But only 556 were eventually deported. When a gigantic communist uprising predicted by Palmer failed to materialize, the Red Scare, and his presidential hopes, deflated.

Closing the gate

The bad taste left by World War I also showed itself in anti-immigration feelings. A fear that war-torn Europe would flood America (immigration increased from 110,000 in 1919 to 430,000 in 1920 and 805,000 in 1921) led to the Emergency Quota Act of 1921. The act limited immigration from any one country to three percent of the number from that country already in the U.S. In 1924, the quotas were cut to two percent, and all Japanese immigration was banned, an action that deeply humiliated and angered Japan. In 1929, Congress limited total immigration to no more than 150,000 per year. The fire under America's "melting pot" had cooled off considerably.

Return of the Klan

Xenophobia — the fear or hatred of strangers or foreigners — also showed itself in the resurgence of the Ku Klux Klan in the early 1920s. The Klan had all but died out by 1880, but was revived in 1915 in Georgia and spread around the country. By 1924, it probably had 4.5 million members, many of them in the Midwest, and 40,000 Klansmen marched in Washington D.C. in August 1925. Both major political parties felt the organization's influence in local, state, and even national elections.

The new Klan targeted not only African Americans, but also Latinos, Jews, Roman Catholics, socialists, and anyone else who did not embrace the Klan's views of what was moral and patriotic.

In 1925, an Indiana Klan leader was convicted of abducting and assaulting a young girl, who subsequently killed herself. The widely publicized scandal, coupled with exposes of how some Klan leaders had siphoned off funds from the group, led to a demise in its popularity. The klowns of the KKK never again approached their earlier influence.

Darwin versus God

The Klan's greatest influence developed in small and mid-sized cities and in rural areas, and the repressive attitudes it catered to were also quick to embrace "fundamentalism," or the idea that everything in the Bible was literally true. In 1925, fundamentalists succeeded in passing a law in Tennessee that prohibited the teaching of Darwin's theory of evolution in public schools.

When a young Dayton, Tennessee high school teacher named John Scopes decided to challenge the law, America had its great show trial of the decade (and the basis for the play and movie "Inherit the Wind.") Scopes was defended by Clarence Darrow, one of the greatest trial lawyers of the century and a leader of the American Civil Liberties Union. William Jennings Bryan, the aging thrice-defeated Democratic presidential candidate and famous orator, joined the prosecution.

"And we look stupid too"

"We are a movement of plain people, very weak in the matter of culture, intellectual support, and trained leadership . . . It lays us open to the charge of being 'hicks' and 'rubes' and 'drivers of second-hand Fords.' We admit it."

— Hiram Evans, "Grand Wizard" of the Ku Klux Klan, 1926

Aimee Semple McPherson

She preached glory-and-salvation instead of fire-and-brimstone, thought heaven would look like a cross between Washington D.C. and Pasadena, and was adored by millions as "Sister."

McPherson was born in 1890 in Canada. With her first husband, she became a missionary and toured the world, but when her husband died in China, she returned to America and married an accountant. That marriage fell apart, however, when McPherson refused to give up her evangelical career.

In 1921, she showed up in Los Angeles and started the Foursquare Gospel Mission. She opened the Angelus Temple in Los Angeles's Echo Park in 1923 and used brass bands, massive choirs, and fancy sets to draw nightly crowds in the thousands. She became a national figure, and people came from all over the country to hear her preach and be "healed" by her touch.

In 1926, McPherson went swimming at a local beach and disappeared. Thirty-seven days later, she reappeared with a story about being kidnapped and held in the Arizona desert before she escaped. The story was a sensation, at first for its own sake and then when skeptical reporters suggested she had really been on a month-long tryst with a married man.

McPherson's popularity waned in the 1930s, but she continued to preach until 1944, when she died at the age of 53 from a possible accidental overdose of sleeping pills. The church she founded still uses Angelus Temple as its headquarters and claims a worldwide membership of more than two million.

Bryan repeatedly ridiculed the idea that man could be descended from apes. But he made a big mistake when he took the stand himself to defend the Bible. Under shrewd questioning by Darrow, Bryan admitted that parts of the Bible could not logically be interpreted literally.

Scopes was found guilty anyway, and fined $100, although the conviction was later overturned on a technicality. The trial took the wind out of the fundamentalist sails for awhile, but debate on the issue has never fully left the American scene since.

Keeping Republicans in the White House: Harding, Coolidge, and Hoover

Three Republicans succeeded Wilson as president in the 1920s — Warren G. Harding, Calvin Coolidge, and Herbert Hoover — and all three were firmly in favor of the status quo, even though the status quo was rapidly changing.

AMERICAN FACES

Marcus Garvey

He was born in Jamaica, lived in New York and England, and wanted to go to Africa and take all of black America with him. The youngest of 11 children, Garvey moved to New York in 1916, started a newspaper, and began organizing a back-to-Africa movement he had begun in Jamaica, called the Universal Negro Improvement Association.

Garvey believed there was no way African Americans would ever get a fair chance in America and should go to Africa — a philosophy that, ironically, was enthusiastically supported by the Ku Klux Klan. He was openly contemptuous of whites, opposed interracial marriages, and denounced efforts by some African Americans to "look white" by using skin lighteners and hair straighteners.

While some other black leaders thought Garvey — who liked to wear outlandish military-style uniforms in public — was a demagogue, his appeal to black pride earned his efforts a large following. By the early 1920s, Garvey had more than two million followers. He used their financial support to start more than 30 black-owned businesses, including a steamship company that he hoped would help take African Americans to Liberia. But those plans fell apart when Liberia's government, fearful of a possible Garvey-led revolution, refused to deal with him.

In 1925, Garvey was convicted on what quite possibly were trumped up federal mail fraud charges. He served two years of his prison sentence, and then was deported to Jamaica on orders of President Coolidge. When Garvey died in 1940 in England, he was largely forgotten. But his efforts helped form the roots of black pride and black nationalism that flourished later in the twentieth century.

Harding was a handsome, affable newspaper publisher and politician from Ohio. His record as a state legislator and U.S. senator was almost entirely without distinction, but he was a popular guy anyway — especially with newly enfranchised women voters — and was easily elected in 1920.

Harding's administration was ripe with scandal, much of it involving buddies he appointed to various offices. The worst was called "Teapot Dome," and involved the secret leasing of public oil reserves to private companies by Harding's secretary of interior, Albert B. Fall, in return for $400,000 in interest-free "loans."

Harding himself was never implicated in any of the scandals, but he suffered nevertheless. "I have no trouble with my enemies," he told a reporter, "but my damned friends, my God-damned friends . . . they're the ones that keep me walking the floor nights."

REMEMBER

Harding died of a heart attack while visiting San Francisco in August 1923. He was succeeded by Coolidge, his vice president. "Silent Cal," as he was called, was actually a witty guy from Vermont who liked to have his picture taken wearing silly headgear. Coolidge was easily elected to his own term in 1924, on the platform that government should do what it could to promote private enterprise, and then get out of the way. "The man who builds a factory builds a temple," he pronounced. "The man who works there worships there."

Coolidge didn't much care for being president, and chose not to run again in 1928. Instead, the country elected Hoover, an Iowa farm boy turned civil engineer who had won international kudos for organizing massive food programs for Europe after World War I. He easily defeated New York Governor Al Smith, extending Republican control of the White House. Like Harding and Coolidge, Hoover was a firm believer that America was on the right track economically.

"We in America are nearer to the final triumph over poverty than ever before in the history of the land," Hoover said. "We shall with the help of God be in sight of the day when poverty will be banished from the nation." As it turned out, he was wrong.

Spending Money Made for Good Times: Or Did It?

One of the overriding themes sung by Harding and echoed by Coolidge and Hoover was "a return to normalcy," and there was nothing more normal, as far as they were concerned, than the pursuit of financial wealth. So their administrations established policies that were designed to help that pursuit.

Helping the rich

These three presidents reduced the national debt by cutting spending on government programs. They increased tariffs to protect U.S. manufacturing from foreign competition. They cut taxes for the wealthy, arguing it would help create incentives for the rich to invest more, which would create more jobs, more products, and more wealth for everyone. And the Federal Reserve Board kept interest rates low so those who weren't wealthy could borrow money to invest.

It seemed to work. Businesses became more productive by using new techniques that made workers and machinery more efficient. Chemical processes, for example, tripled the amount of gasoline that could be extracted from crude oil. Advances in electricity transmission sped development of larger manufacturing plants. U.S. manufacturing output rose 60 percent in the 1920s.

Rich, or feeling like it

"You can't lick this prosperity thing. Even the fellow
that hasn't got any is all excited over the idea."

— Will Rogers, American humorist, 1928.

Increasing American spending habits

The 1920s also saw the rise of two elements that are still both banes and
blessings to the American consumer: advertising and installment buying.
Spurred by the development of national media such as radio and popular
magazines, which made it possible to reach audiences from coast to coast,
advertising became a $1.25 billion-a-year industry by 1925. In addition, the
idea of buying "on time," or paying a little each week or month, plus interest,
became more and more popular. Between 1920 and 1929, installment buying
increased 500 percent. By 1929, more than 60 percent of American cars, large
appliances, and pianos were being purchased "on time."

The drive to sell government bonds during World War I made the average
American more confident in buying securities like stocks and more willing to
invest money rather than save it. The increased availability of capital enabled
industries and retailers to expand, which in some cases meant lower prices.
The Piggly Wiggly grocery store chain grew from 515 stores in 1920 to 2,500 in
1929; A&P from 4,621 to more than 15,000.

Making it difficult on the poor

But below the surface, there were indications of trouble. More and more
wealth was being concentrated in fewer and fewer hands, and government
did far more for the rich than the poor. It was estimated, for example, that
federal tax cuts saved the hugely wealthy steel tycoon Andrew Mellon more
money than was saved by all the taxpayers in the entire state of Nebraska.

Supreme Court decisions struck down minimum wage laws for women and
children and made it easier for big businesses to swallow up smaller ones
and become de facto monopolies. And union membership declined as organized labor was unable to compete with the aura of good times.

Probably worst off were American farmers. They had overexpanded production during World War I to feed the troops, and when demand and prices
faded after the war, they were hit hard. Farm income dropped by 50 percent
during the 1920s, and more than 3 million left farms for towns and cities.

SIDETRIP

Let's eat

"Bell's Sunday Dinner, 12 noon to 9 p.m.: Radishes, olives, green onions, sliced tomatoes and mayonnaise, vegetable salad, rice and cocoanut fritters with vanilla sauce, roast young turkey with dressing and jelly, chicken fricassee with egg dumplings, fried Belgian hare and country gravy, prime ribs of beef, mashed potatoes, fresh string beans, fresh peach pudding, layer cake, assorted pies, coffee, tea, milk or buttermilk: 75 cents."

— from a newspaper ad for a Sacramento, California restaurant, 1925.

REMEMBER

The affection Republican administrations felt for business did not extend to agriculture. Coolidge twice vetoed bills that would have created government-guaranteed minimum prices for some farm goods; an idea called "parity." "Farmers have never made money," he explained. "I don't believe we can do much about it."

Ain't We Got Fun?

A lot of people think the "roaring twenties" was a decade in which everyone spent a huge amount of time dancing the "Charleston" and drinking. That, of course, was not true. They also went to the movies, listened to the radio, read, and played games. The decade, in fact, was marked by an explosion of popular culture, pushed by the development of mass media, which was pushed by post-war advances in technology.

Going to the movies

By the mid-1920s, movie making was one of the top five industries in the country, in terms of capital investment, and a former farm community in California called Hollywood had become the film capital of the world. By 1928, America had 20,000 movie theaters, and movie houses that looked like ornate palaces and seated thousands of patrons were built in every major city.

Millions of Americans flocked each week to see stars like Charlie Chaplain and Rudolph Valentino on the silent screen. In 1927, with the release of *The Jazz Singer*, the screen was no longer silent, and "talkies" made the movies even more popular.

Movies, and their stars, had a huge impact. They influenced fashion, hairstyles, speech patterns, and sexual mores — and reinforced cultural and racial stereotypes and prejudices.

Clara Bow

One producer said she "danced even while she is standing still," and the writer F. Scott Fitzgerald called her "someone to stir every pulse in the nation." She was the movies' first true female sex symbol.

Bow was born in 1905 in Brooklyn, to an alcoholic father and a mother so unbalanced she tried to cut Bow's throat when she learned her daughter was going into movies. By the time she was 25, Bow had already starred in almost 50 films and was making as much as $7,500 a week. Moreover, she was the ultimate 1920s flapper: the "It Girl" ("it" referring to sex appeal) who did

what she wanted when she wanted with whom she wanted.

Personal scandals and the coming of sound to movies (she had a thick Brooklyn accent) marked the end of Bow's career by 1933. She married a cowboy star named Rex Bell (who later became lieutenant governor of Nevada) and was in and out of mental institutions until her death in 1965. Like many of her successors, it's questionable how much Bow really liked the role of femme fatale. "The more I see of men," she once observed, "the more I like dogs."

Listening to the radio

At the beginning of the 1920s, radio was entirely for amateurs. "Ham" operators listened mostly to messages from ships at sea over homemade sets. But in 1920, the Westinghouse Company in Pittsburgh established the first commercial radio station, KDKA. Almost overnight, stations sprang up all over the country. By 1924, there were more than 500, and by 1927 the Radio Corporation of America (RCA) had organized a 19-station National Broadcast Company (NBC).

Radio brought major sporting events and election returns "live" into American homes — and also the makers of soap, the sellers of life insurance, and the purveyors of corn flakes. U.S. business had its first true national medium for advertising, and Americans accepted that the price of "free" radio was commercials. By 1929, more than 12 million American families had radio sets.

Radio stinks

"What have you done with my child? You have sent him out on the street in rags of ragtime to collect money from all and sundry. You have made of him a laughingstock of intelligence,

surely a stench in the nostrils of the gods of the ionosphere." — Dr. Lee De Forest, inventor and guiding force behind long distance radio transmissions, 1928.

Listening to music and writing literature

Radio, along with the increasing popularity of the phonograph, made popular music even more, well, popular. The hottest sound was called "jazz," which stressed improvisation and rhythm as well as melody and had its roots deep in the musical traditions of African Americans. Its stars included Bessie Smith, Ferdinand "Jelly Roll" Morton, and Louis Armstrong, and it was a key part of what became known as the "Harlem Renaissance," a confluence of African American genius in the arts that flourished in the 1920s in New York City. Jazz became wildly popular in other parts of the world as well and was recognized as the first truly unique form of American music.

Literature, on the other hand, was most heavily influenced by writers who were either disillusioned with post-war America or who chose to satirize Americans' seeming penchant for conformity. Among them: novelists F. Scott Fitzgerald (*The Great Gatsby*, 1925), Sinclair Lewis (*Babbitt*, 1922), and Ernest Hemingway (*A Farewell to Arms*, 1929); playwright Eugene O'Neill ("Strange Interlude," 1928); and poets e.e. cummings, Carl Sandburg, and Langston Hughes.

Playing games

When it wasn't being entertained, America was seemingly entertaining itself in the 1920s, so much so that one contemporary observer called it "the age of play." Shorter workdays and weeks and more disposable income (or at least what seemed like more disposable income) gave Americans more time and money to enjoy themselves. Sports like golf and tennis boomed. Public playgrounds for kids became popular. Crossword puzzles and a game called Mah Jong became rages. And of course, all that play made Americans thirsty.

SIDETRIP

Tiled out

Parlor games have come and gone in American culture since there's been an American culture, but the Mah Jong craze of the 1920s may have been the only one to require costumes. An ancient Chinese game played with a set of 144 colored tiles, Mah Jong hit the West Coast in 1922 and soon became immensely fashionable across the nation. Many women refused to play, however, unless they were suitably attired in elaborate oriental robes.

So many sets were being produced at the height of the Mah Jong craze that Chinese manufacturers ran out of the traditional calf shins they made the tiles from, and had to send to Chicago slaughterhouses for cow bones. The fad faded after about five years of wild popularity. One possible reason was ennui created by confusion: By mid-decade, more than 20 different sets of rules for the game had been published.

Drying Out America: Prohibition

Even before the country's inception, Americans had been a hard-drinking bunch, and the social and private costs they paid for it had been high. But on June 16, 1920, the nation undertook a "noble experiment" to rid itself of the effects of Demon Rum. It was called Prohibition, and it was a spectacular failure.

Actually, there is some statistical evidence that Americans drank less after Prohibition began than they did before. But overall, the ban on booze was a bad idea. For one thing, it encouraged otherwise law-abiding citizens to visit illegal "speakeasies." The number of "speaks" in New York City at the end of the decade, for example, was probably double the number of legal saloons at the beginning.

Gangsters like "Scarface" Al Capone and George "Bugs" Moran made fortunes selling bootleg booze and became celebrities doing it, despite the violence that was their normal business tool. Figure 17-1 shows the violence of that time. Capone's Chicago mob took in $60 million a year at its peak — and murdered more than 300 people while doing it. But bullets weren't the gangsters' only tools. They bought off or bullied scores of federal, state, and local officials to look the other way, which only added to public disrespect for law and government.

Figure 17-1:
St. Valentine's Day Massacre in Chicago.

Part of the disrespect was well deserved. Although Congress and a string of presidents paid lip service to the idea of Prohibition to make the anti-liquor lobby happy, many of the politicians were regular customers for the bootleggers. Congress provided only 1,550 federal agents to enforce the ban throughout the entire country, and criminal penalties for bootlegging were relatively light.

AMERICAN FACES

George Remus

He was known as "King of the Bootleggers," an attorney whose most famous client turned out to be himself.

Remus was born in Germany in 1876 and came to America when he was five years old. He trained as a pharmacist, but became a lawyer in 1900 and specialized in criminal defense. When Prohibition began, his clients were often bootleggers, and Remus saw a profession that paid a lot more than lawyering.

Moving to Cincinnati, which was near most of the major distilleries that could still legally make alcohol for medicinal purposes, Remus used his pharmacist's license to buy huge amounts of the legal alcohol. Then he had an army of employees "steal" it on the way to his warehouses and turn it into illegal hooch. Despite five arrests, Remus lived a lavish life, complete with a $125,000 swimming pool at his mansion. He once threw a party where each of the 200 guests received diamond jewelry or new cars.

During one of his jail stints, Remus's wife took up with a federal Prohibition agent. On his release from prison, Remus promptly shot and killed his errant spouse. Acting as his own attorney, he pled temporary insanity and was acquitted after the jury deliberated all of 19 minutes. Remus eventually retired from bootlegging when the business got too violent for him. He died in 1952 at the age of 75.

One more thing: The "King of Bootleggers" never touched the stuff himself.

Changing Morals

Many observers saw Americans' unenthusiastic support of Prohibition, at the time, as an example of the country's slipping morals. So was the behavior of young people. Perhaps more than any generation before them, the youth of the 1920s embraced their own music, fashion, and speech. The automobile gave them a way to get away from home, at least temporarily, and also a place to be sexually intimate.

Other things contributed to the shifting moral patterns of the times: the sexy images from Hollywood "flappers," the growing availability of birth control devices, the use of sex by advertisers to sell everything from cars to toothpaste, and the growing emancipation of women.

REMEMBER

There was no question that the inequities between the sexes continued. Women made less than men in the same jobs and were still subject to a double standard that their place was in the home with the kids. But women now had the vote. More and more were entering the workplace, from 8.4 million in 1920 to 10.6 million in 1930. The more relaxed state of things allowed women to dress more comfortably. They could smoke and drink and go out with men alone without the certainty they would be called "loose." And perhaps most important, fewer of them cared if they were.

"Four score and seven..."

No men necessarily needed

"The outstanding characteristic of the flapper is not her uniform, but her independence and will to be prosperous . . . Girls will no longer marry men who merely support them — they can support themselves better than can many of the men of their own age. They have awakened to the fact that the 'Superior Sex' stuff is all bunk."
— Journalist Samuel Crowther, 1926.

Ushering in an Age of Heroes

If there was one thing the 1920s had a lot of, it was heroes. The advent of radio and the increasing popularity of national magazines and tabloid news-papers provided an arena for stars to shine, and armies of public relations agents pushed and shoved their clients into the spotlight.

There were movie stars. Clara Bow reportedly got 45,000 fan letters a week. When screen heartthrob Rudolph Valentino died of a perforated ulcer in 1926, several women reportedly committed suicide. More than 30,000 mourners filed past his $10,000 casket, which had a glass plate above his face so they could have one last look. There were vaudeville stars like magician Harry Houdini and humorist Will Rogers.

Every sport had its own gods or goddesses. In swimming there were Gertrude Ederle and Johnny Weismuller; in football, Red Grange and Knute Rockne; in boxing, Jack Dempsey and Gene Tunney; in golf, Bobby Jones; and in tennis, Bill Tilden.

And in baseball, there was the moon-faced son of a Baltimore saloonkeeper. His name was George Herman Ruth, but everyone called him "Babe." For most of the decade, Ruth was perhaps the most photographed man in the world. A fine pitcher, he became the greatest slugger in history and almost single-handedly restored baseball as the national pastime after a fixed World Series in 1919 had threatened to ruin it. So popular was Ruth that his team, the Yankees, moved into a new stadium in New York, it was dubbed "the house that Ruth built."

REMEMBER

But as big as Ruth was, he may have been second to a tall, thin, and modest airmail pilot from Detroit named Charles A. Lindbergh. On May 20, 1927, Lindbergh lifted off alone from a New York airfield in a $6,000 plane laden with gasoline and sandwiches. Lindbergh headed over the Atlantic, and 33½ hours later landed in Paris, the first man to fly nonstop between the two continents.

The world went nuts. Lindbergh was mobbed everywhere he went (see Figure 17-2). He stayed an American hero the rest of his life, despite his pre-World War II enthusiasm for Hitler's Germany. And his flight was a giant shot in the arm for aviation.

Figure 17-2:
A ticker tape parade is held for Charles Lindbergh following his famous flight.

Lindbergh's "Spirit of St. Louis" wasn't the only thing in the air as the 1920s came to a close. The economy continued to hum along at a frenetic pace. "Stock prices have reached what looks like a permanently high plateau," said Yale economics professor Irving Fisher on October 16, 1929.

Eight days later, the plateau collapsed. An overinflated stock market crashed, costing investors $15 billion in a week. America was plunged into an economic mess the likes of which it had never seen before.

Gee, Grandpa, What Else Happened?

December 1919: A three-month strike by the nation's steelworkers ends in failure for labor as demands for an eight-hour day are refused. Twenty people are killed in strike-sparked clashes. (They do get their eight-hour day four years later.)

1920: News from the census: More than half of America's 105.7 million people live in urban areas, literacy rates are up to 94 percent, and the average life expectancy is up to 54 years.

September 1921: A Dallas candy and tobacco wholesaler named J.G. Kirby opens a roadside stand where patrons drive up to get barbecued pork sandwiches without leaving their cars. "People are so lazy, they don't want to get out of their cars to eat," Kirby explains.

Nov. 6, 1923: A former U.S. Army officer named Jacob Schick patents a new grooming device called the electric razor. But he lacks the money to market it until 1931 — just as the Depression hits full-force.

Feb. 12, 1924: A young composer named George Gershwin debuts a jazz-based piece called "Rhapsody in Blue." It's hailed as a whole new kind of "serious music."

Aug. 5, 1925: The comic strip "Little Orphan Annie" makes its first appearance in the *New York Daily News.*

March 16, 1926: A Massachusetts physicist named Robert Goddard launches a liquid-fuel rocket that goes high in the sky over his Aunt Effie's farm, for 2.5 seconds. *The New York Times* makes fun of Goddard's prediction that someday such rockets will fly in space. *The Times* apologizes 43 years later, just before Apollo 11 lands on the moon.

May 9, 1926: Explorers Richard Byrd and Floyd Bennett circle the North Pole in a plane. The flight lasts almost 16 hours.

April 7, 1927: A new invention called television is unveiled, as potential investors in New York watch Commerce Secretary Herbert Hoover give a speech in Washington. They can't change the channel, as much as they might want to.

Feb. 14, 1929: Seven members of George "Bugs" Moran's gang, and a dog, are gunned down in a Chicago garage by killers wearing police uniforms. The murders are believed to have been ordered by rival gangster Al Capone.

Chapter 18

Uncle Sam's Depressed: 1930–1940

In This Chapter

▶ Enduring the Great Depression

▶ Failing minorities

▶ Incorporating FDR's New Deal programs

▶ Working for and against the system

▶ Timeline

During one of his last speeches as president, in December 1928, Calvin Coolidge noted that America could "regard the present with satisfaction and anticipate the future with optimism." And much of the country did both. But as the 1930s dawned, it became painfully apparent that Americans had been prematurely satisfied and overly optimistic.

This chapter takes a look at what triggered the Great Depression, and what it meant. We also meet Franklin Roosevelt, another of those great men who seem to come along every now and then in American history, just when the country needs one.

Analyzing the Causes and Consequences of the Great Depression

America had gone through hard times before: a bank panic and depression in the early 1820s, and other economic hard times in the late 1830s, the mid-1870s, and the early and mid-1890s. But never did it suffer an economic illness so deep and so long as the Great Depression of the 1930s.

Economists have argued ever since as to just what caused it. But it's safe to say there were a bunch of intertwined things that contributed. Among them:

✔ **The stock market crash.** The stock market soared throughout most of the 1920s, and the more it grew, the more people were eager to pour money into it. Many people bought "on margin," which meant they paid only part of a stock's worth when they bought it, and the rest when they sold it. That worked fine as long as stock prices kept going up. But when the market crashed in late October 1929, they were forced to pay up on stocks that were no longer worth anything. Many more had borrowed money from banks to buy stock, and when the stock market went belly-up, they couldn't repay their loans and the banks were left holding the empty bag.

✓ **Bank failures.** Many small banks, particularly in rural areas, had overextended credit to farmers who, for the most part, had not shared in the prosperity of the 1920s and often could not repay the loans. Big banks, meanwhile, had foolishly made huge loans to foreign countries. Why? So the foreign countries could repay their earlier debts from World War I. When times got tough and the U.S. banks stopped lending, European nations simply defaulted on their outstanding loans. The result of all this was that many banks went bankrupt. Others were forced out of business when depositors panicked and withdrew their money. The closings and panics almost completely shut down the country's banking system.

✓ **Too many poor people.** That may sound sort of goofy, but it's a real reason. While the overall economy had soared in the 1920s, most of the wealth was enjoyed by relatively few Americans. In 1929, half of the families in the country were still living at or below the poverty level. That made them too poor to buy goods and services and too poor to pay their debts. With no markets for their goods, manufacturers had to lay off tens of thousands of workers, which of course just created more poor people.

✓ **Farm failures.** Many American farmers were already having a hard time before the Depression, mostly because they were producing too much and farm product prices were too low. Things were so bad in some areas that farmers burned corn for fuel rather than sell it. Then one of the worst droughts in recorded history hit the Great Plains. The Midwest became known as the "Dust Bowl." Dry winds picked up tons of topsoil and blew it across the prairies, creating huge, suffocating clouds of dirt that buried towns and turned farms into abandoned deserts.

Going from plus to minus

Anyone who doubts the Great Depression deserves the adjective "great" probably hasn't studied numbers like these: More than 5,000 banks closed between 1930 and 1933, 9 million savings accounts were wiped out, and depositors lost $2.5 billion. Unemployment rose from less than 1 million in 1929 to more than 12 million by 1933 — equal to about 25 percent of the total U.S. workforce. Capital investment dropped from $10 billion in 1929 to $1 billion in 1932. The stock market's industrial index dropped from 452 in September 1929 to 58 in July 1932. The Gross National Product went from $1.04 billion in 1929 to $76.4 billion in 1932. And farm income dropped 60 percent in the three years after 1929. In 1932, per capita income from farming was only $80 a year for farmers.

SIDETRIP

The Lindbergh kidnapping

Almost everybody loved Charles Lindbergh. The lanky aviator had remained a true American hero after his historic solo flight across the Atlantic in 1927. So it made national headlines when someone climbed in a second-story window of Lindbergh's Hopewell, New Jersey, home and snatched his 20-month-old son, Charles Jr.

The nation held its breath for six weeks, during which time Lindbergh responded to a ransom demand by paying $50,000. But on May 12, the body of the missing baby was found in the woods about five miles from the Lindbergh home. An illegal immigrant and escaped convict from Germany named Bruno Richard Hauptmann was arrested for the crime after most of the ransom money was found in his garage. Hauptmann was convicted and executed in the electric chair in 1936, still declaring his innocence.

As a result of the crime, Congress passed what became known as the "Lindbergh Law," which basically made kidnapping a federal crime, and thus allowed the FBI to enter the hunt for kidnappers.

REMEMBER

Whatever the causes, the consequences of the Great Depression were staggering. In the cities, thousands of jobless men roamed the streets, looking for work. It wasn't unusual for 2,000 or 3,000 applicants to show up for one or two job openings. If they weren't looking for work, they were looking for food. Bread lines were established to stop people from starving (see Figure 18-1). And more than a million families lost their houses and took up residence in shantytowns made up of tents, packing crates, and the hulks of old cars. They were called "Hoovervilles," a mocking reference to President Hoover, whom many blamed (somewhat unfairly) for the mess the country was in.

Figure 18-1: Many wait hours in line for bread.

Thousands of farmers left their homes in states like Oklahoma and Arkansas and headed for the promise of better days in the West, especially California. What they found there, however, was most often a backbreaking existence as migrant laborers, living in squalid camps, and picking fruit for starvation wages.

Americans weren't sure what to do. In the summer of 1932, about 20,000 desperate World War I veterans marched on Washington D.C. to claim $1,000 bonuses they had been promised they would get, starting in 1946. When Congress refused to move up the payment schedules, several thousand built a camp of tents and shacks on the banks of the Potomac River and refused to leave. Under orders of President Hoover, federal troops commanded by General Douglas MacArthur used bayonets and gas bombs to rout the squatters. The camp was burned. No one was killed, but the episode left a bad taste in the mouths of many Americans.

Even Worse Off. . . .

The majority of America's minorities had never had it good, so it's not surprising that the Depression made their lot even more miserable.

Shoving aside African Americans, Mexicans, and Native American Indians

More than half of African Americans still lived in the South, most as tenant farmers or "sharecroppers," meaning they farmed someone else's land. Almost all of those who worked and weren't farmers held menial jobs that whites hadn't wanted — until the Depression came along. When it did, the African Americans were shoved out of their jobs. As many as 400,000 left the South for cities in the North, which didn't help much. By 1932, it's estimated half of the black U.S. population was on some form of relief.

There also wasn't much of a "We're all-in-this-together" mentality. Segregation continued in nearly every walk of life, more than 60 blacks were murdered by lynching and other mob violence, and federal anti-lynching laws were defeated in Congress. Even many of the bold federal programs that came into being in the 1930s blatantly discriminated against African Americans. Wage-setting programs allowed employers to pay black workers less than whites, farm aid programs often ignored African-American farmers, and job creation programs provided disproportionately fewer jobs to African Americans.

SIDETRIP

Justice, Southern-style

In March 1931, nine young black males were taken from a freight train near Scottsboro, Alabama, and arrested for vagrancy. Then two white women who were traveling in the same freight car accused the boys of gang-raping them.

Despite mountains of evidence that the women were lying, an all-white jury quickly convicted the youths, and eight of them were sentenced to death. A communist-backed group called the International Labor Defense took up their cause,

and the U.S. Supreme Court ordered a new trial. Five of them were retried and found guilty again; and again the verdict was thrown out by the Supreme Court as unconstitutional, since blacks had been excluded from the jury.

None of the defendants were ever executed. One escaped, and the other four were paroled after serving years in prison for the crime of being black in the wrong place at the wrong time.

Some of the programs, however, helped everyone. Segregation in federal jobs did begin to slowly crumble, and some labor unions opened their membership to minorities. Such crumbs were enough to make many black voters leave the party of Lincoln behind, which they felt had done nothing for them, and vote Democratic for decades to come.

REMEMBER

Other minority groups suffered similarly. Mexico had been exempted from the immigration restrictions of the 1920s, and as a result, hundreds of thousands of Mexicans came to the United States, mostly to the Southwest. Prior to the Depression, they were at least tolerated as a ready source of cheap labor. In the 1930s, however, they were pushed out of jobs by desperate whites. Many thousands were deported, even some who were legal U.S. citizens, and as many as 500,000 returned to Mexico. Those of Asian descent, mostly on the West Coast, were likewise pushed out of jobs or relegated to jobs only within their own communities.

American Indians had been largely forgotten by the U.S. government since the 1880s, which was not a good thing. The general idea had been to gradually have Indians disappear into the American mainstream. In 1924, Congress made U.S. citizens of all Indians who weren't already citizens, whether they wanted to be or not.

But preliminary studies done in the 1920s found that "assimilation" had failed. In 1934, Congress changed direction and passed laws that allowed Indians to retain their cultural identity. Although well meaning, it did little for their economic well-being, and they remained perhaps the worst-off of America's minority groups.

Keeping women at home — or work

With jobs scarce, a strong feeling prevailed that women should stay home and let men have the jobs. There was even a federal rule that two people in the same family could not both be on the government payroll. But two things occurred that actually increased the number of women in the workforce during the decade. The first was that many families simply could not survive without an extra income. The second was that many men abandoned their families to look for work, or because they were ashamed they could not find work. Marriage rates dropped for the first time since the early 1800s.

Developing organized labor

If the sun peeked through the Depression's clouds on anyone, it might have been organized labor. The captains of industry and business lost much of their political clout during the 1930s, and new laws made organizing easier.

The decade also saw a telling split in labor. The traditionalists who ran the American Federation of Labor (AFL) wanted to concentrate on organizing workers according to their specific skills or craft. But that left out thousands of workers who had no specific skills, and also sometimes pitted workers for the same company against each other.

In 1936, John L. Lewis, the passionate leader of the United Mine Workers, led a split from the AFL and formed the Congress of Industrial Organizations (CIO). The CIO was more receptive to not only unskilled workers, but also women and minorities. By 1938, it had 4 million members.

The United Auto Workers (UAW) also flexed its muscles in the decade. The UAW used sit-down strikes, where workers would simply stop and sit down at their posts, making it much more difficult to use strikebreakers. In 1937, General Motors, the third-largest company in the country, recognized the UAW after a 44-day strike.

IN THEIR WORDS
"Four score and seven..."

Me first

"I shall order the men to disregard your order. I shall then walk up to the largest window in the plant, open it . . . remove my shirt and bare my bosom. Then when you order your troops to fire, mine will be the first those bullets will strike."

— CIO leader John L. Lewis, in response to Michigan Governor Frank Murphy's question about what Lewis would do if Murphy issued an order to the National Guard to evict striking auto workers in January, 1937. Murphy tore up the order.

AMERICAN FACES

W. Lee "Pappy" O'Daniel

He may have been the only man ever elected governor on the basis of flour and his singing voice. Even in Texas.

O'Daniel was born in Ohio in 1890. In 1925, he moved to Fort Worth as sales manager of a flour milling company and two years later he got the idea to start a radio program as a way to sell more flour. Backed by a group called the "Light Crust Dough Boys" (whose members included future country music legend Bob Wills), O'Daniel sang, gave advice to housewives, advocated following the 10 Commandments and the Golden Rule, and made a household phrase out of "please pass the biscuits, Pappy."

In 1938, on something of a whim, O'Daniel asked listeners if he should run for governor. When the answer was a resounding yes, he entered the race, mostly, he said, to boost flour sales. To the surprise of nearly everyone, he won. More than 50,000 people attended his inauguration, which was held at the University of Texas football stadium. O'Daniel did almost nothing of note as governor, but was re-elected in 1940, and then elected to the U.S. Senate, where he served until 1949. He died 20 years later, after another successful career in life insurance.

P.S.: One of the fellows he beat in the U.S. Senate race was a brash, young congressman named Lyndon B. Johnson.

That same year, steelworkers won recognition of their union by U.S. Steel, the giant of the industry. Other steel companies, however, refused to go along, and confrontations were often violent. On Memorial Day, 1937, police opened fire on marching strikers and their families in South Chicago, killing 10 and wounding 90. The tragedy became known as the "Memorial Day Massacre" and served as a rallying cry for labor.

All told there were more than 4,500 strikes in 1937, and labor won more than three-fourths of them. By 1940, more than eight million Americans were members of organized labor.

FDR: Making Alphabet Soup

In 1932, Herbert Hoover was president of the United States. In 1933, he was toast. Much of the country blamed Hoover for the Depression, although the groundwork for it had been laid long before he was elected in 1928. Hoover's big mistake was he kept saying things would get better if everyone just had a little patience — and things just got worse.

Electing a reformer

By the time the 1932 presidential election came along, it was a foregone conclusion that the Democrats could nominate a dead dog and still beat Hoover. Fortunately for the country, they passed up deceased canines and chose the governor of New York. His name was Franklin Delano Roosevelt.

He was a distant cousin of Theodore Roosevelt, the only son of a wealthy railroad executive who attended the best private schools and graduated from Harvard. After becoming a lawyer, Roosevelt served in the state legislature, became assistant secretary of the Navy, and had a seemingly boundless future.

Then, in 1921, he was struck by polio and crippled. But Roosevelt had an indomitable spirit. He battled back and was elected governor of New York in 1928 and earned a reputation as a reformer. The Democrats nominated him after some behind-the-scenes maneuvering by newspaper publisher William Randolph Hearst and business tycoon Joseph Kennedy, campaigned on the promise of a "New Deal," and easily defeated Hoover.

Despite his aristocratic background, Roosevelt was wildly popular with the average guy, many of whom did not know he could walk only with leg braces and crutches. (News photographers and newsreel cameramen took care not to take shots of him in "awkward" poses.) But he was also hated by many conservatives and business leaders who considered him a traitor to his class.

Eleanor Roosevelt

She began her marriage to her distant cousin in his shadow and became his "legs." She also became one of the most beloved — and hated — first ladies in U.S. history.

Roosevelt was born into a wealthy New York family in 1884. After an unhappy childhood marked by the death of her parents, she married Franklin in 1905. Over the next decade, Eleanor had six children, found out her husband was playing around, and seemed destined to be either divorced or in the background as a politician's wife.

But Eleanor rose to the occasion. As first lady, she broke tradition and held more than 350 press conferences of her own — but for female journalists only. She was a tireless champion for civil rights and women's issues and often represented her husband, whose polio prevented him from traveling easily, around the country. But her activism also earned her vitriolic hatred from people who didn't like her husband, her politics, or the fact she was an independent woman.

After FDR's death, Eleanor served as a U.S. delegate to the United Nations and as a roving ambassador-at-large. She died in 1962, at the age of 78.

Who's afraid of a little depression?

"First of all, let me assert my firm belief that the only thing we have to fear is fear itself — nameless, unreasoning, unjustified terror that paralyzes needed effort to convert retreat into advance. In every dark hour of our national life a leadership of frankness and vigor has met with that understanding and support of the people themselves, which is essential to victory. I am convinced that you will again give that support to leadership in these critical days."

—Franklin Roosevelt, Inaugural Address, March 4, 1933.

He may have been the perfect president for the time. He was friendly and approachable, and exuded sympathy and self-confidence. He knew how to compromise, and like Lincoln and Washington, he knew how to get the best out of people. He was lucky — before taking office he narrowly escaped an assassin's bullets while riding in a car with Chicago Mayor Anton Cermak in Miami (Cermak was killed). He was also not afraid to do something, even if it proved to be wrong: "Take a method," he said, "and try it. If it fails, try another. But above all, do something."

Giving hope for better lives with New Deal programs

He did something. In his first 100 days in office, supported by healthy Democratic majorities in Congress, Roosevelt pushed through a dazzling array of programs designed to jumpstart the country. They included:

- **Emergency Banking Act:** Three days after he took office, FDR closed all banks. Then on March 9, he pushed through Congress a bill that reopened the banks under close supervision. The bill, which took all of eight hours to go through, also authorized the treasury to issue more currency.

- **Civilian Conservation Corps (CCC):** This created 1,300 camps around the country to give young men new jobs (at $30 a month, with $22 sent home to their families) in conserving natural resources. By 1941, the CCC had employed 2.5 million men, who planted more than 17 million trees and made improvements in scores of state and national parks.

- **Federal Emergency Relief Act (FERA):** The FERA eventually provided a total of $500 million in aid to state and local governments.

- **Civic Works Administration (CWA):** The CWA provided about 4 million jobs in building roads, airports, schools, sewer systems, and other civic projects.

✔ **Agricultural Adjustment Act (AAA):** Basically, it paid farmers not to produce so much food. That bailed farmers out, at least a little, and increased farm prices to more profitable levels.

✔ **Homeowners Loan Act:** This provided funds to help keep homeowners from losing their homes to mortgage foreclosures.

✔ **Tennessee Valley Authority Act (TVA):** One of the most innovative of the New Deal programs, the TVA created an independent public agency that oversaw the development of dams and other projects in the Tennessee River Valley. The TVA covered 40,000 square miles in seven states. It built 16 dams, took over five more, and provided electric power to 40,000 families that previously had none. The TVA also supplied fertilizer, provided flood control and better river navigation, and reforested vast areas.

✔ **Truth in Securities Act:** This Act required new stocks and bonds offered for sale to be registered with the new Securities Exchange Commission (SEC) and required brokers to fully disclose all background information.

✔ **Glass-Stegall Banking Act:** This Act mandated that banks get out of the investment business and restricted use of bank money on stock speculation. It also created federal guarantees for personal bank accounts.

✔ **National Industrial Recovery Act (NIRA):** An ambitious program designed to get industries to cooperate in setting maximum hours, minimum wages, and price controls, through an organization called the National Recovery Administration (NRA). The NIRA was declared unconstitutional by the Supreme Court in 1935 for giving too much power to the program's non-government administrators.

✔ **Works Projects Administration (WPA):** This organization created a host of federal projects that ranged from cleaning slums and providing electricity to rural areas, to painting murals on the walls of public buildings and putting on plays for audiences that paid only what they could afford.

In 1935, Roosevelt added to his alphabet soup of programs by getting Congress to pass the Social Security Act, which began a sweeping federal system of unemployment insurance and retirement pensions paid for by both employer and employee through payroll taxes. In 1938, he signed the Fair Labor Standards Act, which created a national minimum wage of 25 cents per hour and a maximum workweek of 44 hours.

By the time the 1936 elections rolled around, things were looking up. Unemployment had dropped from 12 million to about 9 million. Average weekly earnings had increased from $17 to $22. So despite Republican predictions that the Democrats were creating a socialist state, FDR was easily re-elected.

AMERICAN FACES

Harry Hopkins

He was the big dealer in the New Deal, a super social worker who was Franklin Roosevelt's most trusted aide and whose no-b.s. approach to things earned him the nickname "Sir Root of the Matter" from Winston Churchill.

Hopkins was born the son of a harness maker in Iowa in 1890. After graduating from college, he became a social worker and eventually ran relief programs in New York for FDR when Roosevelt was governor. In the White House, Hopkins ran several New Deal programs and agencies and was made secretary of commerce in 1938.

He wasn't shy about spending government money, either: One Hopkins-run program spent $1 billion in less than six months, making even FDR wince. When a New Deal congressional critic suggested there were better ways to deal with the Depression in the long run, Hopkins snapped: "People don't eat in the long run, Senator, they eat every day."

When World War II broke out, Hopkins served as FDR's alter ego and go-between with other world leaders. After FDR's death, Hopkins helped plan the United Nations. Never in good health, he died in 1946, at the age of 55.

Implementing court-packing tactics

One of the things that had stuck in FDR's craw during his first term was the nine-member U.S. Supreme Court, which was dominated by conservatives and had thwarted some of Roosevelt's plans. So in February 1937, he proposed that he be allowed to appoint a new federal judge for every judge that refused to retire within six months of reaching the age of 70. This "court-packing" tactic would have raised the number of Supreme Court justices to 15.

Roosevelt's ploy worked — sort of. Although Congress ultimately rejected it, the high court began making decisions that were more favorable to the New Deal. Within a few years, six justices retired, enabling Roosevelt to appoint liberals to the court. But the fight also weakened FDR politically. During his second term, Roosevelt's programs slowed considerably. The economy dipped again in 1937, and Republicans made gains in Congress in 1938.

How well the New Deal actually worked is debatable. Many of the programs had big price tags. The National Debt, which was about $22.5 billion when FDR took office, was nearly double that by 1940, and so was the size of the federal bureaucracy. Moreover, millions of people were still out of work.

What is undebatable is the fact that the New Deal had greatly increased the role of the federal government in people's lives. And most people felt a lot better in 1940 than they did in 1932. Americans were pleased enough, in fact, with FDR's performance by 1940 to give him what they had given no other president — a third term.

The birth of a hero

You may have read Superman was born on the planet Krypton, but it was really Cleveland, on a hot summer night in 1934. And his parents were a couple of teenagers looking for a career in Depression-ravaged America.

Jerry Siegel was a 19-year-old would-be writer who had dallied in science fiction. His pal, 19-year-old Joe Shuster, was an artist. So when Siegel came up with an idea for a comic character with super powers during a sleepless night, the two decided to put together a comic strip. They dressed their hero in a red, blue, and yellow costume and took him around to every comic strip syndicate in America — and were rejected faster than a speeding bullet.

In 1938, however, D.C. Comics decided to take a chance, and Superman appeared for the first time in Action Comics #1 (a copy of which sold for $75,000 at a 1995 auction). Siegel and Shuster got less than $150 for him, although they were eventually given pensions and medical insurance from D.C. after several lawsuits.

Created as an antidote for Depression blues, the Man of Steel has become an icon perhaps second only to Mickey Mouse as a larger-than-life pen-and-ink character. And who knows? Without him, we might not have super bowls, superstars, or super-sized fast food meals.

Critics, Crooks, and Crimefighters

Of course, not everyone was in love with FDR. Many Republicans refused to even say his name, referring to him as "that man in the White House." The 1930s also spawned a gaggle of colorful critics and crusaders who made themselves heard above the hard times.

Huey Long

He was a traveling salesman, a lawyer, and a world-class demagogue. Long was elected governor of Louisiana in 1928 on a populist platform, and actually did some good things for the state, such as made school textbooks free and improved roads and highways. But he also ran a corrupt administration that was not above roughing up, blackmailing, or slandering those who opposed him. By 1930, the "Kingfish" was as close to an absolute dictator as there was in the country. He controlled the legislature and had himself elected a U.S. Senator, thus controlling both the Senate seat and the governor's office at the same time.

Originally an FDR supporter, Long broke with the White House mostly out of ego. He proposed a "Share Our Wealth" program that called for confiscating family fortunes of more than $5 million and annual incomes over $1 million and guaranteeing every family $2,500 a year, a homestead, and a car. Long had a national following and announced he would run against FDR at the head of a third party in 1936. Private polls showed he might garner four million votes, enough to tip the election to the Republicans. But he never got the chance. In September 1935, Long was shot to death on the steps of the Louisiana capital by a man whose family he had ruined.

Frances E. Townsend

Townsend was an elderly California doctor who was selling real estate in Long Beach in 1935 when he had an idea that he just couldn't help sharing: Providing $200 a month for life to everyone 60 years old or older. It would be financed by sales taxes, and every pensioner would have to spend their entire pension every month, which he said would stimulate the economy. Actually, more experienced economists pointed out the scheme would take half the national income to provide for eight percent of the population.

Despite the crackpot smell of the idea, "Townsend Clubs" sprang up all over the country, with as many as 5 million members. The idea died out only gradually after the Roosevelt Administration proposed the Social Security system.

Charles E. Coughlin

A Roman Catholic priest, Coughlin was, after Roosevelt himself, the best radio orator in America. Broadcasting from the Shrine of the Little Flower in Royal Oak, Michigan, Coughlin was a super-patriot who ripped into Wall Street, Big Business, and Oppressive Bosses. Originally, he supported FDR, but soon became an ardent foe, advocating the nationalization of banks and ripping into Roosevelt as a communist tool of Jewish bankers.

Coughlin created the National Union for Social Justice, which drew more than 5 million members in less than two months. But his increasingly shrill attacks on Jews and Roosevelt created a backlash, and by mid-1940 the bombastic cleric had quieted down considerably.

A "democratic" kingmaker

"I'm for the poor man — all poor men. Black and white, they all gotta have a chance. 'Every man a king,' that's my motto."

— Huey Long to a journalist, 1932.

Despite the fact that their schemes were pretty looney-tunes, FDR's more vocal and visible critics did put some pressure on FDR to continue to press for reform, especially during his first term. "I am fighting communism, Huey Longism, Coughlinism, Townsendism," FDR said with some exasperation. "I want to save our system, the capitalist system (but) I want to equalize the distribution of wealth."

Meanwhile, a guy named Hoover was fighting "outlawism."

Bad guys and G-men

While some were coming up with political proposals to redistribute wealth, others had a more pragmatic approach: They stole it. The 1930s saw the rise of the modern outlaw. Instead of six-guns and horses, they used Tommy guns and Fords. Some of them became folk heroes, robbing banks that many people felt had robbed their customers.

There was Charles "Pretty Boy" Floyd, who reportedly robbed more than 30 banks and killed 10 men before he was gunned down in 1934. There was Arizona "Ma" Barker, whose gang consisted mainly of her four sons, and who died in a shootout with the law. And there was John Dillinger.

An Indiana native, Dillinger robbed a grocery store in 1924 and was caught. He did nine years in prison, and when he got out started a 14-month crime spree that made him one of the most famous, or infamous, men in America. Dillinger killed 10 men, engineered three daring jail breaks, escaped from two gun battles with the law, and stole as much as $265,000.

Shirley Temple

She was less than four feet tall, and she was the biggest thing in Hollywood, dancing, singing, and mugging her way into the hearts of a country that really needed someone to hug.

Born in 1928 in Santa Monica, Temple made her first movie at the age of 3. She went on to make 24 more during the 1930s, and was the number one box-office attraction every year from 1935 to 1938. Movies like "Little Miss Marker" and "Captain January" earned the curly-headed charmer $300,000 a year. And thousands more were added by royalties from the sales of Shirley dolls, dresses, dishes, soap, and books. Little girls all over the country wanted to look, sound, and be adored as much as Shirley.

Temple retired from films in the late 1940s and had a brief career on TV. She married oil executive Charles A. Black in 1950 and gradually became active in politics. She served as a U.S. representative to the United Nations, ambassador to Ghana, and chief of protocol for the State Department in the 1970s.

SIDETRIP

That Orson is a panic. . . .

Mercury Theater players had a dull story on their hands and a deadline looming for their live Halloween-eve performance on CBS radio in 1938. But writer Howard Koch did his best with H.G. Wells's novel "War of the Worlds," bringing the Martian invasion into the 1930s and relocating it from England to New Jersey. And Mercury leader Orson Welles used all of his considerable acting talent to make it as realistic as possible.

In fact, he and the rest of the cast did too good a job. Despite several announcements it was just a radio show, many in the show's audience of six million thought there was a real Martian invasion going on. Panic spread. Thousands of people called police to ask what to do. In New Jersey, families hastily packed and took to the roads, clogging major thruways. One woman tried to drink poison rather than wait until the Martians killed her.

It took two days to calm things down and criminal charges were even considered against Welles. In the end, however, the show got a big new sponsor, Campbell Soup, and Welles was invited to the White House.

"You know, Orson," President Roosevelt told him, "You and I are the two best actors in America."

He also became something of a Robin Hood. He once asked a farmer during a bank robbery if the $50 in his hand was his. When the farmer replied it was, Dillinger told him to keep it. "Dillinger does not rob poor people," a fan wrote the newspapers. "He robs those who became rich robbing poor people. I am for Johnnie." In the end, such popularity did Dillinger little good. Federal agents killed him in 1934 as he left a movie theater in Chicago.

Fighting the bad guys were the "G-men," a nickname given the Federal Bureau of Investigation agents by George "Machine Gun" Kelly. The "G" stood for government, and the head G-man was an owlish-looking, fiercely intense man named J. Edgar Hoover. As head of the FBI, Hoover combined a fanatical sense of duty and a flair for public relations to make his agency a beacon of heroism and integrity.

Serving as director from 1924 to his death in 1972, Hoover was one of the most powerful figures in twentieth century America. His almost pathological hatred of communism, his dictatorial manner, and his unethical and quite probably illegal use of the bureau against political and personal enemies have stained his name. But in the 1930s, millions of American boys wanted to be him.

Gee, Grandpa, What Else Happened?

1930: The U.S. population has reached 122.7 million, a dramatic 30.7 million increase over 1920. Los Angeles is now the fifth largest city in the country, and Arizona is the fastest-growing state.

Dec. 10, 1930: Novelist Sinclair Lewis becomes the first American to win the Nobel Prize for literature.

May 21, 1932: Aviatrix Amelia Earhart becomes the first woman to fly solo across the Atlantic, landing in Ireland 15½ hours after leaving Newfoundland.

Dec. 17, 1933: The Chicago Bears defeat the New York Giants 23–21 in the first championship playoff game in the National Football League.

1934: Animator Walt Disney introduces the world to a new character in the cartoon "Little Wise Hen." The character is neither wise nor a hen, but an ill-tempered duck named Donald.

1936: Two years after the death of founder W.D. Fard, new leader Elijah Muhammad moves the Nation of Islam's (Black Muslims) headquarters from Detroit to Chicago.

May 6, 1937: The German dirigible Hindenburg explodes while nearing its mooring at Lakehurst, New Jersey. Thirty-five of the ninety-seven people on board are killed, along with a member of the ground crew.

Nov. 11, 1938: On her national radio show, singer Kate Smith does a 20-year-old Irving Berlin song that has never been performed in public before. It's called "God Bless America."

July 4, 1939: Baseball great Lou Gehrig tells 62,000 fans at Yankee Stadium goodbye and calls himself "the luckiest man on the face of the earth." Gehrig, who played in 2,130 consecutive games, has amyotrophic lateral sclerosis, a disease that will kill him in two years and become known as "Lou Gehrig's Disease."

Oct. 24, 1940: The 40-hour workweek, approved by Congress two years earlier, goes into effect.

Chapter 19

The World at War: 1941–1945

In This Chapter

▶ Heading toward war

▶ Contributing to the war effort

▶ Fighting overseas and at sea

▶ Using the first atomic bomb

▶ Timeline

*V*ery few Americans had any use for the dictators of Europe and Asia, but even fewer had any interest in fighting them. World War I had left a bad taste in the mouths of many, and the lingering effects of the Depression were still being felt. The U.S. didn't need a foreign headache.

But as this chapter shows, sometimes a fight just can't be avoided, particularly when it seems half the world is being run by monsters. Faced with the most widespread and horrific war in human history, Americans respond magnificently. They also develop and unleash a weapon that will forever change the future of mankind.

Trying to Avoid War — Again

Despite the hangover from World War I and America's refusal to join the League of Nations, the country didn't exactly become a hermit in the 1920s and 1930s. In 1922, U.S. government and private interests helped feed more than ten million starving Russians. The country also provided more than $100 million in aid to Turkey, Greece, and other Mediterranean countries in the 1920s and forgave or reduced World War I debts.

On the diplomatic front, the U.S., Great Britain, Japan, France, and Italy agreed in 1922 to limit their warship building. And in 1928, French foreign minister Aristide Briand and U.S. Secretary of State Frank Kellogg convinced themselves and 15 other countries to formally agree not to go to war with each other. As completely unrealistic as the agreement might have been, so eager for peace was the U.S. Senate that it ratified the "Kellogg-Briand Pact" on an 85-to-1 vote.

Closer to home, the administrations of presidents Harding and Coolidge were not at all shy about interfering in Latin American countries' internal affairs, if it suited the interests of U.S. businesses. Starting with President Hoover, however, and continuing under Roosevelt, America began a "good neighbor" policy toward Central and South America. The policy basically pledged that we would maintain pleasant relations and generally mind our own business.

America tried to keep to that policy elsewhere in the world as well. In Asia, Japan was becoming more and more hostile toward its neighbors, and U.S. diplomats made periodic attempts to convince the Japanese to slow down. But Japan had been insulted in 1924 when the U.S. closed its doors to Japanese immigration and wasn't in much of a mood to listen. And Americans weren't interested in a fight, even after Japan invaded China, nor even after Japanese planes "accidentally" sank a U.S. gunboat in a Chinese river in 1937.

In Europe, Italy, run by a buffoonish thug named Benito Mussolini, invaded Ethiopia in 1936 with not much more than a whimper from the U.S. When Germany, under an evil madman named Adolf Hitler, took Austria and Czechoslovakia in 1938, President Roosevelt did send letters to both Hitler and Mussolini, asking them not to conquer any more countries. They laughed at him.

Roosevelt was not being timid as much as he was being a practical politician. America was still reeling from the effects of the Great Depression, and most Americans were more interested in figuring out how to pay next month's rent than in who ran Austria. A 1937 survey found that 94 percent thought U.S. policy should be directed at keeping out of foreign wars rather than trying to stop them.

The great stone faces

John Robinson had this idea for a sculpture. A BIG sculpture. Robinson was the state historian of South Dakota in the 1920s, and he thought it would be cool to turn a cliff in the state's Black Hills into a tribute to figures from the Old West, such as Buffalo Bill Cody. So he and other supporters of the idea hunted up an Idaho sculptor named John Gutzon de la Mothe Borglum. Borglum liked the concept, but not the subject.

In 1927, with the blessing of South Dakota — and eventually about $1 million from Congress — Borglum began using dynamite to blast away granite from the side of a mountain named (for some reason) after a New York lawyer named Charles Rushmore. Instead of Old West figures, however, Borglum carved the heads of four American presidents: George Washington, Abraham Lincoln, Thomas Jefferson, and Theodore Roosevelt. The job wasn't finished until October 1941, when Mt. Rushmore National Memorial opened to the public. Borglum didn't live to see it. He died in March 1941. But his son (somewhat appropriately named Lincoln) carried on his work, and more than 2.7 million visitors view the mammoth effort every year. Very few ask, "Where's Buffalo Bill?"

An "isolationist" movement, whose most popular leader was aviator hero Charles Lindbergh, gained strength and held rallies around the country, exhorting Roosevelt and Congress to keep the U.S. sheltered from the growing storm clouds in Asia and Europe. Congress and FDR agreed, approving laws in 1935 and again in 1937 that prohibited the sale of American weapons to any warring nation.

But much of the rest of the world continued to rush toward conflict. On September 1, 1939, Germany invaded Poland. Great Britain and France had signed a pact pledging to come to Poland's defense and declared war on Germany. World War II had begun. France was badly prepared for war and collapsed quickly under the German "Blitzkrieg," or "lightning war." By mid-1940, England stood alone against Hitler and his allies, which for the time being included the Soviet Union, led by its own evil madman, Josef Stalin.

Roosevelt, like most Americans, was still not eager for war. But unlike the ardent isolationists, he also figured it was inevitable and began to take steps to get ready for it in 1940 and 1941. They included:

- ✔ Authorizing the doubling of the size of the U.S. Navy.

- ✔ Pledging to come to the aid of any North, Central, or South American country that was attacked.

- ✔ Pushing Congress to approve the first peacetime military draft in U.S. history. The draft required the registration of all men between the ages of 21 and 35 (about 16 million men). About 1.2 million were drafted for a year's service, and 800,000 reservists were called to active duty. (In October 1941, just before the 18-month period expired, Congress fortuitously voted to extend the draft. But it was a very close vote: 203–202.)

- ✔ Trading 50 old U.S. Navy destroyers to England in return for leases on military bases on English possessions in the Caribbean.

- ✔ Pushing the "Lend-Lease Act" through Congress, which authorized FDR to sell, trade, lease, or just plain give military hardware to any country he thought would use it to further the security of the United States.

- ✔ Ordering the Navy to attack on sight German submarines that had been preying on ships off the East Coast.

Despite all the preparations, many Americans still refused to believe war was inevitable. Then on a sleepy Sunday morning less than three weeks before Christmas, 1941, a Japanese naval and air force launched a surprise attack on the U.S. naval base at Pearl Harbor, Hawaii. More than 2,400 U.S. military men were killed, 150 planes destroyed, and eight battleships sunk or were badly damaged.

December 7, in Roosevelt's words, had become "a day that shall live in infamy."

No bloodshed, I promise

"And while I am talking to you mothers and fathers, I give you one more assurance. I have said this before, but I shall say it again and again and again: Your boys are not going to be sent into any foreign wars."

— Franklin Roosevelt, a few days before being elected to a third term as president, November 1940.

Gearing Up For War

Despite all the warning, the U.S. wasn't completely prepared when war broke out. The Depression had rubbed out much of the country's machine and tool industries, the military was woefully under-supplied, and many soldiers found themselves drilling with toy guns and wooden tanks. In a way, however, the Depression was a good preparation for what was to come: Americans had learned to scrimp and persevere. And having been pushed into a fight, they were eager to oblige.

Getting industry and the economy in shape for the World War

Gearing up the industry needed to wage a global war on two fronts was also handicapped by the lack of manpower. More than 15 million Americans eventually served in the military. Training and supplying them was a staggering challenge. It took more than 6,000 people to provide food, equipment, medical services, and transportation to 8,000 soldiers. In addition, supplies of many raw materials such as rubber, manila fiber, and oil were in short supply. And to top it off, President Roosevelt was a great leader, but not a great administrator.

Still, Americans rose to the occasion. When FDR called for the production of 50,000 planes in a year, it was thought to be ridiculous. By 1944, the country was producing 96,000 a year. Technology blossomed. When metals became scarce, plastics were developed to take their place. Copper was taken out of pennies and replaced with steel; nickel was removed from nickels. War-inspired pragmatism even affected fashions: To save material, men's suits lost their pant cuffs and vests, and women painted their legs to take the place of nylons.

There were other sacrifices as well. Gasoline and tires were rationed, as well as coffee, sugar, canned goods, butter, and shoes. But the war proved to be more of an economic inconvenience than a real trial for most people.

TECHNICAL STUFF

The statistics of war supplies

Some facts and figures about production during the war: Aircraft, 296,429; Naval ships, 87,620; Artillery, 372,431; Bullets, 41.59 million; Tanks and self-propelled guns, 102,351; Trucks, 2.46 million.

Of course all that military hardware had a hefty price tag. The federal government spent about $350 billion during World War II — or twice as much as it had spent *in total* for the entire history of the U.S. government up to that point. About 40 percent of that came from taxes; the rest through government borrowing, much of that through the sale of bonds.

All that money had to go someplace. A lot of it went to the West, especially California, where ten percent of all the federal war spending took place. But the American economy rose just about everywhere else too. The civilian workforce grew 20 percent. The Gross National Product (the total of goods and services produced) more than doubled between 1939 and 1945. Wages and corporate profits went up, as did prices.

In October 1942, Congress gave the president the power to freeze agricultural prices, wages, salaries, and rents. The Roosevelt Administration created the Office of Price Administration (OPA) to oversee prices and wages. But the OPA proved generally ineffective, and the economy mostly ran itself.

Working with labor unions during war times

The serious labor shortage created by the war was a big boost to union membership. Early on, FDR got labor to agree to a "no strike" pledge and a 15 percent limit on wage increases.

IN THEIR WORDS

"Four score and seven..."

"Da" for the working Yank

"To American production, without which this war would have been lost." — toast by Soviet dictator Josef Stalin, October 1943.

Henry J. Kaiser

Henry Kaiser had never built a ship before, so he didn't know he was doing it "wrong." All he knew was he was doing it fast — and helping to win the war. Kaiser was born in New York in 1882. He left school at the age of 13 to go to work and eventually ended up on the West Coast as an engineer. During the Depression, he helped to build major dams in the West, such as Boulder and Grand Coulee, and when the war started, he was asked to help provide ships.

He did it by using assembly line methods, building sections and then welding them together. Traditional shipbuilders were skeptical that it would work. But Kaiser's method streamlined the process of building a cargo vessel, called a "liberty ship," from 245 days to 17. By 1943, Kaiser's shipyards were producing an average of two ships a day, helping to keep England fed, providing supplies for overseas troops, lowering enemy morale, and earning Kaiser the nickname "Sir Launch-a-lot."

Kaiser was by no means limited to ships. He also built magnesium and aluminum plants to provide parts for planes and built the first steel producing plant in the West. After the war, he made Jeeps and got into health care. He died in 1967, having proved that you can't stop a Kaiser when he's on a roll.

Even so, there were thousands of work stoppages, especially as the war wore on. The government actually seized the nation's coal mines in 1943 after a major strike and also seized the railroads in late 1943 to avert a strike. Congress eventually passed a law requiring unions to wait 30 days before striking.

Many perceived the strikes as slightly treasonous, and "there are no strikes in fox holes" became a popular response to labor stoppages. Still, as labor leaders pointed out, things were a lot better for a lot of working Americans: Average weekly wages went from $24 in 1939 to $46 in 1944.

Employing women for the war effort

Millions of women entered the workforce to take the place of the men who were off to the military. By 1943, 17 million women filled a third of civilian jobs, five million of them in war factories (see Figure 19-1). "If you've followed recipes exactly in making cakes, you can learn to load shells," proclaimed billboards recruiting women to the workplace.

Some companies offered childcare or provided meals to take home as incentives to lure women into the workplace. But women were still given the short end of the stick when it came to wages: In 1944, women got an average of $31.21 for working in war-related factories, while men doing the same jobs were paid $54.65.

Figure 19-1: Woman working in a war plant.

Making strides — African Americans help out with the work shortage

Many African Americans had hoped their service in World War I would help bring them equality in post-war America. But they were wrong. So when World War II started, some black leaders were wary. "Our war is not against the Hitler in Europe," editorialized one black newspaper, "but against the Hitlers in America." Some black leaders demanded assurances that loyalty this time around would be rewarded with more decent treatment.

In response, Roosevelt established the Fair Employment Practices Commission and charged it with investigating cases where African Americans were discriminated against in war industries. The commission enjoyed some success. But the real economic boost for blacks came from the labor shortage, which fueled the movement of many from the South to industrial cities in the North and West.

Rose Monroe

It was a classic case of life imitates art imitates life. Early on in World War II, the government started propaganda campaigns to help get women involved in the war effort. One such campaign was built around a poster of an attractive (and well-muscled), bandana-wearing woman named "Rosie the Riveter." There was even a popular song to go along with it.

But Rosie was a fictional character — until actor Walter Pidgeon visited an aircraft plant in Ypsilanti, Michigan, to make a short film promoting war bonds. There he met a young widow named Rose Monroe, who was riveting planes to support her family. Pidgeon signed her up to be in the film, and she became an inspiration for millions of women entering the workforce for the first time.

Born in 1920 in Kentucky, Monroe went to work after her husband died in a car accident. After the war, Monroe drove a cab, owned a beauty shop, started a construction company, and earned a pilot's license. She died in 1997, still an inspiration to new generations of working women.

About 700,000 African Americans also served in the military and some strides in equality were made. Blacks were admitted into the Air Force and Marines for the first time. The Airforce enlisted some 600 black pilots and the first African American general in the Army. Some military units were even integrated toward the end of the war, although it was more for practical reasons than to further civil rights.

Even so, race relations remained mired in racism and distrust. Several cities had race riots, the worst of which was in Detroit in 1943, when 34 people died. Angry that the racism of Hitler was being fought against while the racism at home was largely ignored, many African Americans began taking a more active role in asserting their legal rights. The ranks of the National Association for the Advancement of Colored People swelled from 50,000 before the war to more than 400,000 at war's end.

Returning for work after being kicked out — Latinos

In 1942, the U.S. and Mexican government reached an agreement to allow Mexican workers — "braceros" — to enter the United States to help make up the manpower shortage. Thousands of Mexicans, some of whom had been thrown out of America during the Depression, entered the country, mostly to take agricultural jobs in the West.

The sudden influx sometimes caused friction, particularly in California. In Los Angeles, tensions between outlandishly garbed Latino youths and sailors led to the "zoot suit" riots of 1943. City officials actually passed a law prohibiting the wearing of zoot suits in public as a way to avoid further confrontations.

The "Battle of Los Angeles"

On February 2, 1942, less than two months after Pearl Harbor was attacked, U.S. Naval intelligence in Southern California issued a warning that a Japanese attack might occur that night.

Sure enough, in the wee hours of February 25, radar picked up unidentified blips about 120 miles off the coast of Los Angeles. Then planes were reported near Long Beach, and then four anti-aircraft batteries began firing at something off Santa Monica. Within minutes, other guns opened fire. Confusion reigned over the next three hours as contradictory reports poured in.

By the dawn's early light, Los Angeles residents saw the results of the attack: no downed enemy planes, no bomb damage, a few traffic accidents, and one man dead from a heart attack.

Eventually it was decided that it had been a false alarm and the fuss had probably been caused by weather balloons (or UFOs, as some folks now insist). Whatever the cause, for a few hours the fighting had come uncomfortably close to the home front.

Winning cuisine

If an Army travels on its stomach, the U.S. rode to victory in World War II on Spam. Yes, Spam, the ubiquitous canned meat product made from pork shoulder and ham.

Invented in 1937 by the Hormel Foods company, Spam hit its culinary stride when the war began, as a substitute for rationed beef. Because it didn't need refrigeration, it was ideal for feeding troops — and they ate more than 100 million pounds of it.

Spam was also fodder for G.I. humor: "meatloaf without basic training," "the ham that didn't pass its physical," "the reason war is hell." But Spam was a lifesaver for countries whose food supplies had been pinched by the war. Soviet leader Nikita Khrushchev once stated that without Spam, the Russian army would have starved. And it fries up so much better than caviar.

Treating the Japanese Americans poorly

By far the most shameful aspect of World War II on the home front was the treatment of Japanese residents. About 125,000 people of Japanese descent lived in the U.S., 110,000 of them on the West Coast. Seventy thousand, called "Nisei," were born here. The rest, called "Issei," were born in Japan and emigrated.

In the wake of Pearl Harbor, many of their neighbors began to view both groups with suspicion and even hatred. "A Jap's a Jap," said Lieutenant General John DeWitt, who was in command of the West's defense. "It makes no difference whether he is an American or not."

In February 1942, Roosevelt ordered the forced evacuation of all Japanese residents from the West Coast, supposedly to lessen the potential for them to engage in seditious or traitorous acts. They were moved to bleak concentration camps in remote areas. Many lost virtually everything they owned: homes, farms, businesses, and even personal possessions.

Despite their treatment, about 8,000 Nisei volunteered to serve in the military. One group, the "Fightin' 442nd," was one of the most decorated combat units of the war.

It wasn't until the 1980s and 1990s that the Nisei were compensated for some of what they lost. In the meantime, Roosevelt's action was upheld by the U.S. Supreme Court as a justifiable hardship. "Hardships are a part of war," said Justice Hugo Black, "and war is an aggregation of hardships."

Dealing With the War in Europe

Shortly after Pearl Harbor, FDR met with English Prime Minister Winston Churchill to decide what the forces of the "Allies" should do against the "Axis" powers — Germany, Italy, and Japan. The most pressing threat, they decided, was Hitler's Germany. The German army seemed to be on the brink of defeating the Soviet army, its one-time ally. If the Russians fell, Germany could turn its full attention to Britain.

Soviet dictator Josef Stalin wanted the Allies to launch an invasion of German-held Europe as soon as possible, because Russia was being mauled by the Germans. But Churchill wanted to nibble at the edges of the German empire while bombing Germany from the air, and FDR went along with the Brits.

Despite their sharp differences, however, Roosevelt, Churchill, and Stalin managed to put them aside and generally cooperate. That proved to be a key ingredient in the Allies' ultimate success. The trio met several times during the war to plot strategy and negotiate about what the world would be like after the war.

One of the most immediate problems was dealing with the menace posed by German submarines, or "U-boats," in the Atlantic. Traveling in packs, the subs sank three million tons of Allied shipping in the first half of 1942 alone. But the Allies worked out a system of convoys and developed better anti-sub tactics. Most importantly, they built far more cargo ships than the Germans could possibly sink.

In the summer of 1942, Allied planes began bombing targets inside Germany. Eventually, the bombing would take a terrible toll. In 1943, 60,000 people were killed in the city of Hamburg, and the city of Dresden was all but destroyed.

Yalta

The most important of the meetings of FDR, Churchill, and Stalin actually came toward the end of the war, at Yalta, a former palace on the Black Sea in the Soviet Union.

Roosevelt came to Yalta hoping to establish the groundwork for a practical and powerful United Nations, to be formed after the war, and also to convince the Russians to enter the war against Japan and help speed up the end of the war.

Stalin eventually agreed, but at a price. In return, the Soviet dictator got the other two to agree to give the Soviets control over broad areas of Europe and a promise that each of the major nations on the UN Security Council would have veto power over council decisions. As it turned out, the price Roosevelt paid was far too high for what he got in return.

Nazi nitwits

Adolf Hitler had an itch to bring the war to America. So in mid-June, 1942, German subs landed four men on Long Island, New York, and four more on a Florida beach. They also landed cases of explosives. All of the men had lived in America before and spoke fluent English. Their mission was to sabotage U.S. factories, incite terror, and disrupt the economy.

But they turned out to be an octet of oafs. Several of them went on shopping sprees. Several blabbed about their mission to relatives — and two of them blabbed to federal agents.

Within two weeks of their arrival, all of them had been arrested by the FBI. After a military trial, all eight were convicted of espionage. Six of the Germans were executed, while the two who confessed were imprisoned for the rest of the war and then deported.

Hitler's itch was never scratched. Not a single case of enemy-directed sabotage was ever verified during the war.

In the fall of 1942, Allied armies, under a relatively obscure American commander named Dwight D. Eisenhower, launched an attack in North Africa against Hitler's best general, Erwin Rommel. The green American troops were whipped soundly at the Kasserine Pass in Tunisia. But in a return match — while Rommel was in Germany — a combined U.S. and British force defeated the Germans at El Alamein and drove them out of Egypt.

From Africa, the Allies invaded Sicily, and then advanced into the Italian mainland. Mussolini was overthrown and eventually executed by his own people. But the German army poured troops into the country and it took until the end of 1944 for Italy to be completely controlled.

The greatest crime

The greatest crime in Europe did not occur on the battlefield. German leaders had come up with a "final solution" for what they perceived was a problem with Europe's Jews — and that was to murder them. The Holocaust resulted in the deaths of six million Jews and four million other "undesirables" such as gays, Gypsies, and the mentally and physically handicapped.

The Holocaust was not a secret in America. Stopping it, however, was not a priority in the Allies' war strategy. The reasons why probably ranged from anti-Semitism to what was perceived as more pressing needs. Whether more attention to it would have made a big difference is open to debate, but downplaying the horror of the Holocaust was not among America's finest moments.

On the Eastern Front, meanwhile, the Russian army had gradually turned the tables on the invading Germans and began pushing them back, despite staggering civilian and military losses. And in England, the Allies, under the leadership of Eisenhower, were preparing the greatest invasion force the world had ever seen.

On June 6, 1944 — "D-Day" — the Allied forces swept ashore on the beaches of Normandy in France. By August, the U.S. 3rd Army, under the brash, belligerent, and brilliant General George S. Patton, pushed deep into France and to the edge of Germany itself.

A little more than a week before Christmas, 1944, however, the Germans launched a desperate counterattack. Known as the Battle of the Bulge, the surprise attack succeeded at first, costing the U.S. 77,000 casualties. But the Germans were low on men and supplies and could not sustain the attack. By late January 1945, the Allies were again on the offensive.

In April, the U.S. and Russian armies joined up at the Elbe River and advanced on Berlin. Hitler committed suicide, and on May 7 — "V-E," or "Victory in Europe" Day — Germany surrendered.

Roosevelt did not live to see the victory. The president had won a fourth term in 1944, despite rumors about his failing health. But on April 12, 1945, while vacationing at Warm Springs, Georgia, FDR died suddenly of a cerebral hemorrhage. The nation was staggered at the loss of the man who had led them through the Depression and the war. One New York housewife was asked if she heard the radio bulletins of FDR's death and replied "For what do I need a radio? It's on everybody's face."

The new president, a former hat salesman from Missouri named Harry S. Truman, was as stunned as anyone. "Being president is like riding a tiger," Truman later wrote. "I never felt that I could let go for a single moment."

Dealing With the War in the Pacific

Less than 12 hours after the bombing of Pearl Harbor, the Japanese attacked U.S. air bases in the Philippines, destroying scores of U.S. planes. Within a few months, they conquered Guam, Wake Island, Hong Kong, Singapore, the Dutch East Indies, Burma, and the Philippines. Drunk with victories, Japanese forces continued to expand their dominance in the Pacific during the first few months of the war.

About the only good news for the Allies came on April 18, 1942, when a squadron of B-25 bombers launched from an aircraft carrier and led by Colonel James Doolittle managed to bomb Tokyo. The planes did little damage and none of the planes made it back, with most of the crews having to ditch them in China. Still, Doolittle's raid was a huge shot in the arm for sagging American morale.

Visiting France by ship

Some numbers on the D-Day invasion: 175,000 men were landed in the first day, a number that swelled to 325,000 in the first week, and eventually to 2.5 million. They were delivered by 5,300 ships and supported by 50,000 vehicles and 11,000 planes.

U.S. strategists decided to strike back on two fronts. The first, under General Douglas MacArthur, would move north from Australia, through New Guinea, and then back to the Philippines. The second, under Admiral Chester Nimitz, would move west from Hawaii, and then hopscotch from island to island toward Japan itself.

But first the Japanese offense had to be stopped. The initial stopping came in early May 1942, at the Battle of the Coral Sea, northwest of Australia. It was the first naval fight in history where the fighting ships never actually saw each other: All the combat was done by planes from each side's aircraft carriers. The battle was pretty much a draw, but the Japanese fleet carrying invasion troops to New Guinea had to turn back, marking the first time the Japanese had not won outright.

The real turning point, however, came between June 3 and June 6, in a fierce naval battle near the U.S.-held Midway Island. Tipped to Japanese plans by intercepting their messages and breaking their codes, U.S. forces managed to sink four Japanese aircraft carriers, losing only one. The victory returned control of the central Pacific to the Allies.

A few months after the Battle of Midway, the U.S. took the offensive in the Solomon Islands, winning battles at Gavutu, Tulagi, and Guadalcanal. It took six grueling months to take Guadalcanal, but by mid-1943, the Japanese forces were either retreating or on defense nearly everywhere.

Now it was our turn. In February 1944, forces under Nimitz won victories in the Marshall Islands, and in the fall, allied forces reopened supply lines in Southeast Asia into China. In mid-1944, a U.S. armada struck the Marianas Islands of Tinian, Guam, and Saipan, and on October 20, 1944, MacArthur made good an earlier promise and returned to the Philippines.

As the Germans did at the Battle of the Bulge, the Japanese threw everything they had into a counteroffensive. And like the Germans, they lost. The Battle of Leyete Gulf cost Japan four more carriers and all but ended its ability to mount an offensive. Next came the battle for the island of Okinawa, just 370 miles south of Japan itself. The Japanese sent suicide planes called "kamikazes" ("divine wind") on one-way trips into U.S. ships, and while they were horrifyingly effective, they weren't enough. After 50,000 Allied and 100,000 Japanese were killed or wounded, Okinawa fell in late June 1945.

U.S. submarines were taking a huge toll on Japanese supply lines, sinking more than half of all the enemy's cargo ships by the end of the war. American planes, meanwhile, had been softening up the Japanese mainland. In May 1945, they dropped napalm on Tokyo, killing 80,000 people. The bombings were designed to make the eventual invasion of Japan easier. Even so, U.S. strategists figured it would take more than a year of fighting and more than one million American soldiers killed or wounded before the Japanese homeland would fall.

What the strategists did not count on was a terrible new weapon that had been conceived in New York and Tennessee and spawned on the deserts of New Mexico.

Dropping the Bomb

Even before the war began, scientists fleeing from Nazi Germany had warned U.S. officials the Germans were working on developing a huge new bomb that would be triggered through an atomic reaction. The U.S. government then began pouring what would amount to more than $2 billion into what would be called "the Manhattan Project," because it started in New York.

Work continued at top-secret bases in Oak Ridge, Tennessee, and Los Alamos, New Mexico, under the direction of physicist J. Robert Oppenheimer. The project was so hush-hush that Vice President Harry Truman was not told of it until he assumed the presidency after FDR's death. On July 16, 1945, the world's first atomic bomb was detonated at a testing ground in New Mexico.

On July 26, 1945, Allied leaders delivered a surrender ultimatum to Japan, but it was rejected by that country's military leaders. Then on August 6, 1945, a single B-29 bomber nicknamed "Enola Gay" dropped an atomic bomb on the city of Hiroshima. The bomb killed 75,000 people and injured another 100,000 in the city of 340,000. Thousands more eventually died from the radiation.

Debate has raged ever since as to whether Japan would have surrendered if the bomb had not been dropped. But at the time, there was little hesitation about its use on the part of the man who made the decision, President Truman. "I regarded the bomb as a military weapon," he said later, "and never had any doubt that it should be used."

Another "useless" war product

The Japanese conquests in Southeast Asia had cut off much of America's rubber supplies. So the U.S. turned to synthetic rubber and went looking for an alternative that would be even cheaper.

In 1943, a General Electric scientist named James Wright mixed boric acid and silicone oil and formed a gooey substance that bounced, stretched, and even picked up impressions from newsprint and comic books.

Trouble was, no one could find a practical use for it. In 1949, however, a Connecticut man named Paul Hodgson borrowed $147, bought the rights to the stuff from G.E., and began marketing it in little plastic eggs in time for Easter.

"Silly Putty" was a smash hit with kids, and Hodgson left a tidy $140 million estate when he died in 1976, proving that it is possible to make gold from goo.

Japan was stunned by the destruction of the Hiroshima bomb, but its leaders hesitated in surrendering. Three days later, another A-bomb was dropped on Nagasaki. The next day, Japan surrendered. The final ceremony took place on September 2, aboard the USS Missouri in Tokyo Bay.

World War II, the bloodiest and most devastating war in human history, was over.

About 30 million civilians and military personnel around the world had been killed. American losses, compared to the other major combatant countries, had been light: about 300,000 killed and another 750,000 injured or wounded.

But while the war was over, a new age that included the threat of even more horrible wars was just beginning.

Gee, Grandpa, What Else Happened?

Aug. 10, 1941: Dean Dixon becomes conductor of the New York Philharmonic, the first African American to lead a major U.S. orchestra.

July 17, 1941: Two Cleveland Indians pitchers combine to stop New York Yankees star Joe DiMaggio's 56-game hitting streak.

Feb. 23, 1942: A Japanese submarine lobs shells at a Santa Barbara, California oil refinery. The attack does $500 worth of damage to the roof of a pump house.

IN THEIR WORDS

"Four score and seven..."

A witness to doom

"I am become Death, the Shatterer of Worlds."

—J. Robert Oppenheimer, quoting an ancient
Indian epic poem, after witnessing the first
atomic bomb explosion.

Nov. 28, 1942: A fire at the Coconut Grove nightclub in Boston kills 492 people, most of whom had been celebrating after a college football game.

1943: A shortage of tin for cans hurts sales of Campbell's Soup to the point that it has to cancel sponsorship of the "Amos 'n Andy" radio show. The show goes off the air, ending 15 years of broadcasts.

June 9, 1943: A new law requiring the withholding of federal income taxes from paychecks goes into effect.

April 3, 1944: The U.S. Supreme Court rules in a Texas case that a person cannot be denied the right to vote in a political primary on the basis of his race.

Dec. 16, 1944: A plane carrying popular U.S. musician and bandleader Glenn Miller is lost over the English Channel. It was possibly shot down by mistake by an Allied plane.

July 28, 1945: A B-25 bomber crashes into New York City's Empire State Building, killing 13 people and injuring 26.

Oct. 30, 1945: Shoe rationing ends.

Part IV
America in Adulthood

The 5th Wave   By Rich Tennant

In this part . . .

With the end of World War II, America found itself as the richest and most powerful country in the world. But almost as soon as the "hot war" was over, it was replaced by a tense and perilous "cold war." This was not just a struggle among nations, but between the political ideologies of capitalism and communism. It would last for 50 years and at times get very warm.

The half-century after World War II also saw Americans embrace the medium of television, which would allow them to watch history as it unfolded: assassinations, a war in Southeast Asia, a generational revolution, a president's fall — and a television actor become president.

This part ends with the miracle of the silicon chip and the modern plagues of drug addiction and AIDS — and the start of a new millennium.

Chapter 20

The Fast Fifties: 1946–1960

● ●

In This Chapter

▶ Cooling down relations with Russia and heating things up in Korea

▶ Testing Americans' loyalty

▶ Letting the good times roll

▶ Working against segregation

▶ Timeline

● ●

*I*f you asked most Americans in 1945 how they felt about Russia, they would probably have responded with warm and fuzzy statements about our brave ally against the horror of Hitler. Ask them in 1950, or 1955, or 1960, however, and you would likely have received a very different answer.

In this chapter, Americans combat communism at home and abroad, real and imagined. They move to the suburbs, eat in their cars, and discover a new medium/religion called television. They also embrace a form of music with its roots in the African-American culture — but many are much less willing to embrace African Americans themselves.

Starting a Cold War and Hot "Police Action"

Just who was to blame for the Cold War depends on how you look at it. From the Soviet perspective, America hadn't suffered nearly as much during World War II. It was the only country with the atomic bomb (at least until 1949, when the Russians successfully tested their own bomb). Both of those factors made the U.S. too powerful to be trusted. Plus, America was being too nice to the losing countries of Germany and Japan. And the Union of Soviet Socialist Republics (U.S.S.R.) was determined to surround itself with countries that would not be a threat to it in future wars.

IN THEIR WORDS
"Four score and seven..."

Heavy drapes

"From Stettin in the Baltic to Trieste in the Adriatic, an 'iron curtain' has descended across the continent."

—Winston Churchill, referring to the spread of Soviet influence across Europe, in a March 5, 1946, speech in Fulton, Missouri.

From the U.S. point of view, the Soviet Union was uncooperative, pushy, and uncomfortably interested in spreading its influence by working to create communist governments in other countries.

The United Nations

After World War I, the U.S. Senate voted against joining the League of Nations. This time around, however, the Senate voted 89 to 2 in favor of joining the United Nations (UN), which had its first meeting in 1946 in London and then moved to its permanent home in New York City.

The UN consisted of two main bodies. One was the General Assembly, where every member nation had a seat. The other was the Security Council, which had five permanent members — the U.S., the Soviet Union, Great Britain, France, and China — and six seats that rotated among other countries. Each of the permanent members could veto any council action, which meant it was virtually impossible for the UN to do anything the top powers didn't want it to.

So while the United Nations did have some success in international cooperation when it came to subjects like health and education, it could do little to slow down the nuclear arms race or prevent the Super Powers from interfering in other countries.

The world as a chess board

The first big test of will between the U.S. and U.S.S.R. came in the Mediterranean. Communist-backed rebels in Greece and Turkey were trying to overthrow the governments in those two countries. Britain had been assisting the Greek and Turkish governments, but was in deep economic trouble at home and could not continue.

So Harry Truman went to Congress. Truman was a former U.S. senator from Missouri who had been made vice president in 1944 and succeeded Franklin Roosevelt as president when Roosevelt died in 1945. Truman was a blunt, honest, and outspoken guy. (He once suggested that a music critic who had panned his daughter Margaret's professional singing debut might end up with a black eye and sore groin should he ever run into Truman.) He often complained about what a tough job it was to be president. But most of the time he wasn't shy about doing it — and to hell with anyone who didn't like the way he did it.

Speaking before Congress in March 1947, Truman asked for $400 million to help the Greek and Turkish governments. He also asked to send U.S. military advisers to both countries, at their request. In what became known as the "Truman Doctrine," Truman drew a sharp distinction between the communist "way of life" and the Free World. Congress went along, eventually sending more than $600 million to the two countries by 1950.

Truman's "doctrine" was part of an overall strategy of "containment" of communism. The idea was to make other countries prosperous enough they wouldn't be tempted by communism. Other elements of the containment strategy included:

- ✔ **The Marshall Plan.** Named after General George C. Marshall, who became Truman's secretary of state, the plan provided about $12 billion in U.S. aid to 16 countries in Western Europe to help them recover from the ravages of the war. The plan was a rousing success, and by 1952, much of Western Europe was well on its way to economic recovery.

- ✔ **The Point Four Program.** This was sort of a junior Marshall Plan. Proposed by Truman in 1949, it provided about $400 million to underdeveloped countries in Asia, Latin America, and Africa, for developing industry, communications, and technological systems.

- ✔ **NATO.** In 1949, the U.S. and 11 Western nations formed the North Atlantic Treaty Organization (NATO). The countries agreed to come to the aid of any member nation that was attacked and to develop an international security force that would help discourage aggression by non-NATO countries.

The Berlin airlift

The Soviet Union, of course, did not watch all this U.S. activity from a hammock. After the war, temporary governance of Germany had been divided among France, Britain, the U.S., and Russia. The city of Berlin was deep in the Russian sector, but run by all four nations. So when the Soviets became irritated at all the "containment" in 1948, they blockaded Berlin, hoping to force the Western countries out of the city completely.

Instead, the Western countries mounted a huge airlift, shipping food and other supplies over the blockade and into the city. In May 1949, the Soviets lifted the blockade. But the tensions made both sides realize that there would be no easy solution to reestablishing a new Germany. So the Western powers agreed to create one country out of their half and the Soviets one out of the other half. East Germany and West Germany would not be just Germany for more than 40 years.

The "miracle of '48"

Despite some success overseas, Truman was considered a political dead duck as the 1948 elections drew near. The Republicans had gained seats in Congress in 1946. Truman's former secretary of commerce, Henry Wallace, had decided to run as a liberal third-party candidate, sure to take votes from Truman. Segregationist Strom Thurmond, governor of South Carolina, also decided to run as an independent candidate. The Republicans were running Governor Thomas Dewey of New York, a man who was considered solid, if a bit dull (someone suggested he looked like the little plastic guy on wedding cakes).

But true to form, Truman decided to "give 'em hell." He stumped around the country, ragging on the Republican-controlled Congress as a bunch of do-nothings and pledging to change things at home and abroad if given another term. When the votes were counted, Truman had pulled off the biggest upset in presidential political history, and the Democrats had taken back Congress. Their reward was another war.

The Korean War

The Cold War was at its hottest in Korea. After World War II ended, the Russians controlled the northern part of the country and the United States the south. In 1949, the Soviets left a communist government in charge in the north and the U.S. left a pro-Western government in the south. China, meanwhile, finished its civil war and was now firmly in the control of communists.

On June 24, 1950, the North Koreans began a seesaw yo-yo of a war by invading South Korea. (World diplomats called it a "police action," as if that would make the dead less dead.) A few days later, Truman ordered U.S. troops to the aid of South Korea and convinced the UN to send military aid as well.

The UN troops, which were mostly American, were under the command of General Douglas MacArthur, a capable egomaniac. Because the North Korean attack was such a surprise, the U.S. and South Korean forces were pushed into the far southern corner of the Korean peninsula by September. But

MacArthur pulled off a risky but brilliant amphibious landing behind the North Koreans. By November, he had driven the enemy deep into North Korea and was poised to push them into China.

Then, the Chinese army poured troops into the fight and pushed the UN troops back into South Korea before the UN forces reorganized and counter-attacked, forcing the Chinese back behind the 38th parallel of latitude, where the war had started in the first place.

For the next 18 months, an uneasy truce was in place, although it was often interrupted by sporadic fighting. Finally, in July 1953, an agreement to call the whole mess a draw was reached.

The Korean War cost 33,000 U.S. dead, about 110,000 wounded, and more than $50 billion. It also cost Truman politically. When MacArthur publicly disagreed with Truman over Truman's decision not to invade China, the general was fired. MacArthur returned to a hero's welcome in America, and Truman was unfairly pilloried as being soft on communism.

He did not run for re-election in 1952. Instead, the country turned to its most popular military figure in decades, Dwight David Eisenhower. "Ike" had paid little attention to politics for most of his life and didn't even make up his mind which party to join until shortly before accepting the Republican nomination. He was a conservative man who had been a great military leader in World War II. As a president, his greatest attribute may have been he didn't screw things up too much. "Eisenhower," someone once observed, "proved the country could get along pretty well without a president."

Uncle Sam's big stick

One thing Eisenhower's administration wasn't shy about was injecting itself into other countries' internal affairs. In 1953, the U.S. sent operatives from the Central Intelligence Agency to Iran to topple a communist-influenced government and reinstate the dictatorial Shah. The following year, the CIA pulled off a coup in Guatemala, ousting a communist-backed but constitutionally elected leader and replacing him with a U.S.-friendly president.

It wasn't only ideology that motivated America. In Iran, the U.S. made sure Iranian oil was kept flowing toward America and not the Soviet Union. In Guatemala, the interests of American fruit companies were being protected.

In Asia, the U.S. was busy providing aid to France to help it fight a communist rebellion in its colony of Vietnam. By 1954, the French had lost the northern half of the country, and by 1956 the U.S. was steadily increasing the amount of aid it was sending to South Vietnam.

"Doominoes"

"You have a row of dominoes set up, and you knock over the first one, and what will happen to the last one is the certainty that it will go over very quickly."

— President Eisenhower, explaining why the U.S. needed to stop the communists in Vietnam, April 7, 1954.

Finding Commies under the Bed

Not all the world's communists were in other countries. Since the 1920s, there had been a communist party in the U.S. that had taken orders from party leaders in the Soviet Union. Most of the time they had almost no impact on anything, other than to be convenient targets for various conservative political causes.

After World War II, however, "communist" became a much dirtier word. Being a "real" American meant being an ardent anti-communist. U.S. government officials helped fuel the fire by talking almost daily about spies and the dangers of communists and communist sympathizers.

Part of the reason for the anti-communist fears was that America's biggest post-war rivals, the Soviet Union and China, were run by communists. Part was bewilderment over the success the communists were having in Asia and Eastern Europe. And part was the failure to keep the atomic bomb the exclusive property of America.

Whatever the reason, commie hunting became a national pastime. In 1947, the House Un-American Activities Committee (HUAC) — dominated by Republicans who included a freshman member from California named Richard M. Nixon — began searching for communists within and without government. One place they looked was Hollywood. Allegations were made that some moviemakers were producing films with a pro-communist flavor. Actors, directors, and writers were called before the committee. Ten who refused to testify were jailed; others were "blacklisted" and couldn't get jobs in the industry for years afterward. But no great plot to undermine America through the movies was ever uncovered.

Hiss and Chambers

The committee caught a much bigger fish in 1948. Whittaker Chambers, a *Time* magazine editor who said he had been a communist until 1937, told the committee that a former member of Roosevelt's State Department, Alger Hiss, had passed information to Russian spies.

Hiss denied the charges, even after Chambers produced from a hollowed out pumpkin what he said was microfilm passed between the men. Neither could be prosecuted for espionage because too much time had passed. But Hiss was found guilty of perjury and sentenced to five years in prison. The Hiss conviction helped Nixon get elected to the Senate in 1950 and win a place as Eisenhower's running mate in 1952.

The Rosenbergs

Hiss wasn't the only trophy for the commie hunters. In February 1950, it was revealed that a British scientist had given atomic secrets to the Soviets. Among his allies, it was announced, were a New York couple named Julius and Ethel Rosenberg. The Rosenbergs were charged with getting information from Ethel's brother, who worked on the U.S. bomb project in New Mexico. They were convicted of treason, and executed in 1953.

Federal worker loyalty

Despite some reservations that things were getting out of hand, President Truman didn't leave all the ferreting out of communists to Congress. In 1947, Truman ordered a government-wide "loyalty" review. By the time it was done, more than 3 million federal workers had been reviewed. More than 2,000 workers resigned and about 200 were fired.

AMERICAN FACES

Helen Gahagan Douglas

She was an actress, an opera singer, and a congresswoman — and the "pink lady" of American politics. Douglas was born in New Jersey in 1900. She left college to appear in a Broadway play in 1922, and her beauty and talent made her a star. After a few plays, Douglas turned to opera, then returned to the theater and became a leading Broadway actress.

With her husband, actor Melvyn Douglas, Douglas moved to California and became active in Democratic politics. After working to better the plight of migrant farm workers, Douglas won a seat in Congress in 1944, representing a heavily African-American district in Los Angeles.

In 1950, Douglas ran for the U.S. Senate against another member of Congress, Richard Nixon. Nixon had won a national reputation as a communist hunter and wasted little time implying that Douglas was, if not an outright commie, "pink right down to her underwear."

Douglas's liberalism did not play well with voters, especially after the Korean War broke out, and Nixon easily defeated her. She left politics, became an author, and died in 1980. As part of her legacy, she left behind a nickname she gave Nixon that stuck with him all the way to the White House: "Tricky Dick."

A shot at polio

Every summer it showed up, just like picnics and baseball and trips to the swimming hole: a crippling disease that most often struck children and left them paralyzed or dead. In 1952 alone, more than 21,000 U.S. children were infected.

Jonas Salk wanted to do something about the poliomyelitis virus. Salk, a New York-born physician and University of Pittsburgh Medical School researcher, worked for almost eight years to develop a vaccine. Finally, after exhaustive trials, the government licensed the vaccine on April 12, 1955. Salk refused to become rich by patenting the vaccine and

hoped the federal government would take over its distribution. The idea was greeted icily by the Eisenhower Administration. Secretary of Health, Education, and Welfare Oveta Culp Hobby called it "socialized medicine by the back door."

But Salk's vaccine, delivered via injections, eventually was distributed free by the government and saved thousands of children from the disease. In 1961, an oral vaccine developed by Dr. Albert Sabin was licensed and administered around the world. Polio is now virtually unknown in the U.S. and rare in other countries.

Not to be outdone, Congress passed bills in 1950 and 1952 — over Truman's vetoes — that made it illegal to do anything "that would substantially contribute to the establishment . . . of a totalitarian dictatorship." They also required "communist front organizations" to register with the Justice Department and denied admission to the country of aliens who had ever been a member of a "totalitarian" group, even as children.

"Tail-Gunner Joe"

He was a liar, a drunk, and a generally loathsome weasel, and for a few years he was one of the most powerful men in America. In February 1950, Senator Joseph McCarthy of Wisconsin gave a speech in West Virginia. In the speech, McCarthy said he had a list of 205 known communists working in the State Department. It was nonsense, but it made national headlines, and McCarthy repeated it and similar charges over the next four years.

Shut up, Senator

"Let us not assassinate this lad further, Senator. You have done enough. Have you no sense of decency, sir? At long last, have you no sense of decency?"

—Army counsel Joseph Welch, to Senator Joseph McCarthy during hearings on suspected communists in the Army, June 9, 1954.

McCarthy, who claimed to have been a tail gunner who saw lots of action during World War II, actually had never seen any combat. But he was a formidable opponent in the commie-hunting field. Even General George Marshall and President Eisenhower were ripped by him, without retaliation by either man. Every time he made a charge that proved to be untrue, McCarthy simply made a new charge. The tactic became known as "McCarthyism."

By the summer of 1954, however, McCarthy's antics were wearing thin. When he began a series of attacks on the Army for "coddling" communists during congressional hearings, they were televised. Many Americans got their first look at McCarthy in action and were repulsed. In December 1954, he was censured by the Senate. He died in obscurity three years later, of problems related to alcoholism.

Having It All

Despite fears that the country might return to the hard times of the Depression after the war, the American economy hummed along. There were plenty of jobs for returning servicemen (although many of those who had the jobs during the war, particularly women and minorities, didn't want to give them up). For those who didn't have jobs, there was the G.I. Bill of Rights, which passed Congress in 1944 and provided veterans more than $13 billion in the decade after the war for college tuition, vocational training programs, or money to start a business.

A booming economy

Thanks to a $6 billion tax cut and all the savings from buying bonds during the war, Americans had plenty to spend. The high consumer demand for goods triggered high inflation — 14 percent to 15 percent the first two years after the war for goods in general, and a painful 25 percent for food. The high costs of things in turn triggered a lot of labor unrest, with 5,000 strikes in 1946 alone and major troubles in the coal and rail industries. President Truman reinstated wartime price controls to deal with inflation, and the Republican Congress passed a bill called the Taft-Hartley Act in 1947 that restricted labor union power.

By 1949, the economy had adjusted to the ending of the war, and the country entered an almost unprecedented economic boom. From 1945 to 1960, the Gross National Product (the amount of goods and services produced) increased from $200 billion to $500 billion per year. Thousands of smaller companies merged or were gobbled up by large corporations, as were many family farms, by large "company" farms.

The economy wasn't the only thing growing. The birth rate boomed as men and women pushed apart by the war made up for lost time. The population grew 20 percent in the 1950s, from 150 million to 180 million, and the generation born between 1946 and 1960 became known as the baby boomers. Along with the economy and the population, Americans' appetite for the good life (the number of private cars and the number of hot dogs consumed doubled in the 1950s) and the perceived need to "keep up with the Joneses" also grew.

The burbs

Having your own car meant you could live farther away from where you worked — and a lot of people did just that. The suburbs grew 47 percent in the 1950s as more and more Americans staked out their own little territory. New housing starts went from 1 million a year before the war to 100,000 during it, and with the population boom, the need climbed to 1.5 million annually.

To fill the need, home builders turned to assembly line techniques. The leading pioneer was a New York developer named William J. Levitt. A former Navy Seabee who knew how to build things in a hurry, Levitt bought 1,500 acres on Long Island, and on March 7, 1949, opened a sales office — with more than 1,000 customers already waiting. A basic Levitt four-room house on a 6,000-square-foot lot sold for $6,900, about 2½ years' wages. Levitt built them in waves, with each set of specialists following each other. The "cookie cutter" approach in "Island Trees" (later changed to "Levittown") was criticized as stifling individuality. But to the 82,000 people living in 17,000 new houses, it was home. Other builders followed all over the country, and 13 million new homes were sold during the decade.

Getting kinky with Kinsey

It looked pretty boring, for a "dirty book." After all, the author had spent most of his professional career studying the lives of all 93 kinds of gall wasps. But *Sexual Behavior in the Human Male* exploded into U.S. homes in 1948, with its detailed — if somewhat dry and scholarly — account of what was going on in the American bedroom.

Its author was Alfred C. Kinsey, an Indiana University zoologist. Kinsey and his staff interviewed thousands of people about their sexual habits and then compiled the results. The book sold an astonishing 200,000 copies in a few months, at the then-hefty price of $6.50 apiece. A second Kinsey book, *Sexual Behavior in the Human Female,* was published in 1953, and it was even more sensational, selling 250,000 copies in hardback. Kinsey died in 1956 at the age of 62, before he could publish more of his findings.

But those he did publish — on topics such as extramarital affairs, female orgasms, and homosexuality — are credited, or blamed, with loosening U.S. attitudes toward sex and encouraging more tolerance for deviations from the sexual norm. If there is such a thing.

IT STARTED HERE

The Golden Age of grease

Drive-in restaurants were nothing new in 1948 America, and Richard and Maurice McDonald were bored with theirs. The brothers had opened their barbeque joint eight years before in San Bernardino, California, and they were tired of all the teens that hung around the place after they ate, as if it were a clubhouse.

So in 1948, the McDonalds fired their carhops, cut their menu to nine items, dropped the price of their hamburgers from 30 cents to 15 cents, replaced tableware with paper bags and cups, and pre-assembled much of the food. It was true fast food and perfect for the speeded up post-war society.

Among the people who loved the approach was a Chicago milkshake machine salesman named Ray Kroc. Kroc convinced the McDonalds to make him their franchising agent, and then eventually bought them out completely in 1961. By the time he died in 1984, there were 7,500 McDonald's outlets. Today there are more than 25,000 in 116 countries.

And why did Kroc stick with the brothers' name even after he bought them out? Because, he once explained, no one was going to buy a "Kroc burger." Or a "Big Kroc," for that matter.

"No man who owns his own house and a lot can be a communist," Levitt said. "He has too much to do." Of course his sentiments didn't extend to African Americans: They were excluded from buying homes at his developments for fear they would scare away white buyers.

The tube

There was less discrimination when it came to selling consumer products, and one of the most popular products in the 1950s was the television (see Figure 20-1). At the start of the decade there were about 3 million TV owners; by the end of it, there were 55 million, watching shows from 530 stations. The average price of TV sets dropped from about $500 in 1949 to $200 in 1953.

Figure 20-1: A family gathers around a TV to watch their favorite program.

Like radio before it, the spread of television had a huge cultural impact. Beginning with the 1948 campaign, it made itself felt in U.S. politics. One wonderful effect was that it made speeches shorter. Politicians and commentators alike began to think and speak in "sound bites" that fit the medium. By 1960, the televised debates between candidates Richard Nixon and John F. Kennedy were considered a crucial element in Kennedy's narrow victory. It also helped make professional and college sports big businesses and sometimes provided excellent comedy and dramatic shows to vast audiences that might not otherwise have had access to them.

But mostly it was mindless junk, "a vast wasteland" in the words of Federal Communications Commission chairman Newton Minnow. It was designed to sell soap and other products, it homogenized cultural tastes, and created feelings of inadequacy in people whose lives didn't match the insipidly happy characters they saw on "Ozzie and Harriet" or "Leave It To Beaver."

It was, however, a very popular wasteland. Comedian Milton Berle's show was so loved that movie theaters in some towns closed down on Tuesday nights because everyone was home watching "Uncle Miltie." And in Toledo, Ohio, the city water commissioner discovered in 1954 that water consumption surged at certain times because so many people were using the toilet during commercials on popular TV shows.

Rock 'n roll

America had 13 million teenagers by the mid-1950s, and they had a lot of money to spend — an average of about $10 a week. One of the things they spent it on was their own music. It was a mix of blues and country that was as much about youthful rebellion as it was the sound, and it was called rock 'n roll, a term coined by a Cleveland radio personality named Alan Freed, who became its Pied Piper.

The backlash to it from adults was fierce. Ministers decried it as satanic, racists as "jungle music," and law enforcement officials as riot inciting. And the more adults squawked about it — surprise! — the more their kids wanted it. In 1954, "Shake, Rattle and Roll" by Bill Haley and the Comets sold more than one million records. Scores of rock stars came and went almost overnight. Others, such as Jerry Lee Lewis and Little Richard, were stars with more staying power.

An American king

And then there was Elvis. Born in Mississippi and raised in Tennessee by poor working-class parents, Elvis Presley became perhaps the most recognized personality in the world during the decade. In 1956 alone, he was selling $75,000 worth of records per day and a staggering 54 million people tuned in to see him on the Ed Sullivan television show.

One effect of the new music was to open up new audiences for African-American performers. Chuck Berry became the first black rock star to have a hit on the mainstream charts. More than 90 years after the end of slavery, music was one of the few fields that was open to black Americans.

Riding at the Back of the Bus

They had fought through two world wars and struggled through an economic disaster, and by the 1950s, many African Americans had had enough of fighting for nothing. Because of that, the decade witnessed a series of events that added up to the beginning of the civil rights movement.

Brown against the board

On May 17, 1954, the U.S. Supreme Court issued one of its most important decisions. In a case called *Brown v. the Board of Education of Topeka, Kansas,* the court ruled that the segregation of public schools was unconstitutional. It overturned an 1896 Supreme Court decision that had said schools could be segregated if the facilities that were offered different groups were equal (which of course they never were). "We conclude that in the field of public education, the doctrine of 'separate but equal' has no place," wrote Chief Justice Earl Warren.

What a doll

Ruth Handler went shopping in Switzerland in the mid-1950s and found gold. Handler, with her husband Elliot and his business partner, Harold Mattson, had started a toy company in 1945 that they named by combining Mattson's name and Elliot's to form "Mattel."

Ruth Handler purchased a German-produced doll named Lilli while on her Swiss shopping spree. Unlike most American dolls, which were modeled after babies, Lilli was modeled after babes — as in buxom, long-legged young women. Handler had seen her own daughter playing with similar-looking paper cutout dolls and thought a U.S. version of Lilli might catch on.

So in 1959, Mattel introduced a very grown-up looking doll with an impressive wardrobe, which, of course, was sold separately. The doll was a hit, and the company sold $500 million worth of the dolls and related products in the first decade after its introduction.

The line has added heaps of supporting characters in the ensuing 40 years, but the original mainstays have remained "Barbie" and "Ken," named after the Handler's own son and daughter, which makes doll collectors the world over glad they didn't name their kids Attila and Hortense.

The court followed its decision a year later with broad rules for desegregating America's schools, but they included no timetable. Some communities moved quickly. But others, mostly in the South, made it clear they were in no hurry to comply with the court's ruling. By 1957, only about 20 percent of Southern school districts had even begun the process.

In September 1957, a federal court ordered Central High School in Little Rock, Arkansas, desegregated. A white mob decided to block the admission of nine black students, and Arkansas Governor Orval Faubus refused to do anything about it. So a reluctant President Eisenhower sent in 1,000 federal troops and activated 10,000 members of the National Guard to protect the students and escort them to class.

In the same month, Congress passed a bill that authorized the attorney general to stop Southern elected officials from interfering with African Americans registering to vote, established a federal Civil Rights Commission, and created a civil rights enforcement division within the U.S. Justice Department. The sad fact, however, was that in many places in the South the laws went largely unenforced.

Boycotting the bus

Like a rock dropped in a still pond, the Supreme Court decision on school desegregation started ripples of change throughout the country. One of them hit Montgomery, Alabama, on Dec. 1, 1955. A 42-year-old African-American woman named Rosa Parks was tired after a long day working, and she was tired of being treated as a second-class human being. So Parks refused to get up from her seat on the bus when the driver demanded she give it to a white man. That was against the law, and Parks was arrested.

Her arrest sparked a boycott of the bus system by the black community. Facing the highly damaging boycott and a 1956 Supreme Court decision that declared segregation on public transportation unconstitutional, the Montgomery bus company dropped its racist seating plan in 1957.

More important than getting to ride in the front of the bus was the example the boycott set as to how effective organized demonstrations against segregation could be. And at least as important was the emergence on the national scene of the boycott's leader, an eloquent and charismatic son of a well-known Atlanta minister, and an admirer of the non-violent protest philosophies of India's Mohandas Gandhi. His name was Martin Luther King, Jr., and he was to become one of the most important men in America in the coming decade.

IT STARTED HERE

Fair ball

Branch Rickey needed an African American with some specific characteristics. He had to be smart, he had to be able to play baseball at the major league level — and he had to be able to keep his mouth shut.

Rickey, the general manager of the Brooklyn Dodgers, thought he had found him in John Roosevelt Robinson, a 28-year-old UCLA graduate and former Army officer whom Rickey had signed to play for Montreal (where it would be easier for a black ballplayer to break in) in the minor leagues in 1945. Robinson, known to his friends as "Jackie," had been a four-sport college star. And he was irritated when Rickey kept telling him about all the virulent hatred he would face as the first African-American player in the major leagues.

"Mr. Rickey, do you want a ballplayer who's afraid to fight back?" Robinson asked. "I want a player with guts enough *not* to fight back," Rickey replied.

On April 15, 1947, Robinson stepped to the plate for the first time in a major league game. By the end of the year, he was the National League's best rookie, and two years later, its most valuable player. Before he retired, he had led the Dodgers to six league championships. More important, Robinson opened the gates for thousands of African Americans in professional sports and inspired millions of Americans of all races with his dignity, courage, and refusal to lose.

Gee, Grandpa, What Else Happened?

July 7, 1946: Mother Frances Xavier Cabrini is canonized by the Roman Catholic Church as the first American citizen to become a saint. Cabrini established convents and orphanages in Europe and Latin America before dying in 1917.

Oct. 14, 1947: U.S. Air Force Captain Chuck Yeager, flying an experimental plane, becomes the first pilot to fly faster than the speed of sound.

Nov. 1, 1950: One of two Puerto Rican nationalists is killed in a gunfight with police after the two try to kill President Truman at the Washington residence where Truman is staying while the White House is being renovated. A policeman is also killed, but Truman is unhurt.

March 13, 1951: More than five million Americans tune in to watch televised hearings by the U.S. Senate Crime Investigating Committee. The committee, chaired by Senator Estes Kefauver of Tennessee, is looking into the existence of organized crime in America.

Oct. 5, 1953: The New York Yankees defeat the Brooklyn Dodgers in the World Series, winning an unprecedented fifth straight championship.

Aug. 12, 1955: The federal minimum wage is raised to $1 an hour.

Dec. 23, 1955: The Eisenhower Administration announces it has authorized sending a small force of military advisers to South Vietnam, to help that country in its civil war with North Vietnam.

1958: Americans buy 25 million circular pieces of plastic, called Hoola Hoops.

Nov. 2, 1959: A 33-year-old assistant English professor named Charles Van Doren admits he cheated on a popular TV quiz show called "Twenty-one," by being given the questions before the show. Other quiz show winners also admit they won games that were fixed to boost ratings.

May 1, 1960: The Soviet Union shoots down a U.S. spy plane over Soviet territory and captures its pilot, Captain Francis Gary Powers. The incident ruins chances of bettering U.S.-U.S.S.R. relations at a summit in Paris, especially after U.S. officials first claim Powers was flying a weather plane and just wandered off course. Powers is sentenced to ten years, but is traded in 1962 for a Soviet spy captured by the U.S.

SIDETRIP

Sput-what?

Frankly, it didn't look like much: a little blip of a light in the evening sky, appearing to be moving much slower than its 18,000 miles per hour.

But to Americans watching on October 5, 1957, the blip represented a terrible thought: The commies might someday rule the world from outer space. That's because the little blip was a Russian satellite called "Sputnik" (Russian for "fellow traveler"). It was the first such object and within a few weeks it was followed by Sputnik II.

Americans were shocked. Fears of super weapons orbiting above the U.S. competed with the feeling that a new day was dawning for humanity. During the next year, the U.S. launched four satellites of its own, and within two years, U.S. efforts to catch up with the Soviet Union in space would be in full gear. The Space Race had joined the Arms Race in the political Olympics between the Super Powers.

Chapter 21

Camelot to Watergate: 1961–1974

· ·

In This Chapter

▶ Electing and losing JFK

▶ Entering the war in Vietnam

▶ Trying to put an end to discrimination

▶ Establishing new rights

▶ Impeaching Nixon

▶ Timeline

· ·

*T*he decade of the 1960s began with a defeat for Richard Nixon and ended in victory for him. In between, America became mired in a war it never understood and saw its citizens take to the streets in the name of peace, justice, and racial rage.

By the mid-1970s, U.S. streets were clearing, Nixon had suffered the last, and worst, defeat of his career, and America was trying to figure out just what the heck had happened in the preceding 14 years.

Electing an Icon

He was young, rich, handsome, witty, married to an elegant and beautiful woman, and he looked good on the increasingly important medium of television. His opponent was middle class, jowly, whiny, married to a plain woman, and on television he looked like 50 miles of bad road.

Even so, Massachusetts Senator John F. Kennedy had won the presidency in 1960 over Vice President Richard Nixon by a very narrow margin — and only, some said, because his father, bootlegger-turned-tycoon Joseph Kennedy, had rigged the results in Illinois and Texas.

After eight years of the dull and fatherly Eisenhower, "Jack" and Jacqueline Kennedy excited the interest of the country. The administration was dubbed "Camelot," after the mythical realm of King Arthur. Kennedy — known to headline writers as JFK — gave off an aura of youth and vigor and shiny virtue. In truth, however, he was plagued with health problems from a bad back to venereal disease, was an insatiable womanizer, and didn't mind bending the truth when it suited his purposes.

Kennedy called on Americans to push on with a "new frontier" of challenges, and the first big challenge came very soon after he took office.

The Bay of Pigs

Cuba had been a thorn in the U.S. side since 1959, when dictator Fulgencio Batista was overthrown by a young communist named Fidel Castro. Castro soon became an ardent anti-American, ordering the takeover of U.S.-owned businesses in Cuba and establishing close ties with the Soviet Union.

Kennedy gave his approval to a scheme that centered on anti-Castro Cuban exiles being trained by the CIA for an invasion of the island. The idea was that the Cuban people would rally to the invaders' side and oust Castro. The invasion took place April 17, 1961, at the Bay of Pigs on Cuba's southern coast. It was a disaster. No one rushed to their side, and many of the invaders were captured and held for two years before being ransomed by the U.S. government.

The resulting embarrassment to America encouraged the Soviet Union to increase pressure in Europe by erecting a wall dividing East and West Berlin and resuming the testing of nuclear weapons. Kennedy, meanwhile, tried to counter the Soviet moves by renewing U.S. weapons testing, increasing foreign aid to Third World nations, and establishing the Peace Corps to export U.S. ideals, as well as technical aid. But the Russians weren't impressed and decided to push America to the brink of nuclear war.

The October crisis

During the summer of 1962, the Soviets began developing nuclear missile sites in Cuba. That meant they could easily strike targets over much of North and South America. When air reconnaissance photos confirmed the sites' presence on October 14, JFK had to make a tough choice: Destroy the sites and quite possibly trigger World War III or do nothing, and not only expose the country to nuclear destruction but in effect concede world domination to the U.S.S.R.

Patience

"I am prepared to wait for my answer until hell freezes over."

—Adlai Stevenson, U.S. ambassador to the UN, after demanding the U.S.S.R. delegate confirm or deny there were Soviet missiles in Cuba, October 25, 1962.

Kennedy decided to get tough. On October 22, 1963, he went on national television and announced the U.S. Navy would throw a blockade around Cuba and turn away any ships carrying materials that could be used at the missile sites. He also demanded the sites be dismantled. Then the world waited for the Russian reaction.

On October 26, Soviet leader Nikita Khrushchev sent a message suggesting the missiles would be removed if the U.S. promised not to invade Cuba. The crisis — perhaps the closest the world came to nuclear conflict during the Cold War — was over, and the payoffs were ample. The U.S. and U.S.S.R. installed a "hot line" between the two countries' leaders to help defuse future confrontations, and in July 1963, all of the major countries except China and France agreed to stop above-ground testing of nuclear weapons.

Dark day in Dallas

Even with his success in the Cuban missile crisis, Kennedy admitted he was generally frustrated by his first thousand days in office. Despite considerable public popularity, many of JFK's social and civil rights programs had made little progress in a Democrat-controlled but conservative Congress. Still, Kennedy was looking forward to running for a second term in 1964, and on November 22, 1963, he went to Texas to improve his political standing in that state.

While riding in an open car in a motorcade in Dallas, Kennedy was shot and killed by a sniper. A former Marine and one-time Soviet Union resident named Lee Harvey Oswald was arrested for the crime. Two days later, a national television audience watched in disbelief as Oswald himself was shot and killed by a Dallas nightclub owner named Jack Ruby, while Oswald was being moved to a different jail.

America was stunned. The age of Camelot was over. And a veteran politician from Texas named Lyndon B. Johnson was president of the United States.

Sending Troops to Vietnam

If John F. Kennedy represented a fresh new face in the White House, his successor, Lyndon Baines Johnson, was a classic example of the Old School of U.S. politics. A Texan, Johnson had served in both houses of Congress for more than 20 years before being elected as JFK's vice president in 1960 and was considered one of the most effective Senate leaders in history.

As president, Johnson inherited a host of problems, not the least of which was a growing mess in Southeast Asia, particularly Vietnam. Before World War II, Vietnam had been a French colony, and after the Japanese were defeated and driven out, it reverted to French control. But despite U.S. monetary aid, France was driven out of the country in 1954 by communist forces led by a man named Ho Chi Minh. The country was divided in two, with the communists controlling the northern half. Elections were scheduled for 1956 to reunite the two halves.

Only they never took place, mostly because South Vietnam dictator Ngo Dinh Diem was afraid he would lose. Diem was supported by the U.S., at least until 1963, when he became so unpopular he was assassinated with the U.S. government's unofficial blessing. At first, the support amounted to financial aid. Then U.S. military "advisors," who were not directly engaged in combat, were sent. But the pressure to do more mounted as the fighting dragged on, and by the time of Kennedy's assassination, he had sent 16,000 "advisors" to Vietnam.

Muhammad Ali

He was the most famous sports figure in the world, perhaps the most famous person, period, and if you didn't believe it, all you had to do was ask him. "I am," he would reply, "the Greatest."

Ali was born Cassius Clay in Louisville, Kentucky, in 1942. After a successful amateur boxing career, which included winning a gold medal at the 1960 Olympics, he turned pro. In 1964, Clay won the heavyweight championship and successfully defended it nine times over the next three years. Flamboyant, witty, charming, and arrogant, he was resented and disliked by many white Americans for not being humble enough.

He became even more controversial when he became a Black Muslim and changed his name.

Then in 1967, he was stripped of his title and sentenced to five years in prison for refusing to be drafted, on grounds of his religious beliefs. The Supreme Court eventually reversed the conviction and Ali won the title back in 1974 from George Foreman, defending it 10 more times before losing it in 1978 to Leon Spinks and then winning it for a third time in a return match with Spinks later that year.

Ali announced his retirement from the ring in 1979 (although he returned for two losing matches in 1980). The onset of Parkinson's disease has made it difficult for him to speak in recent years, but he managed an electrifying appearance as a torchbearer at the 1996 Olympics and remains one of the most recognized people in the world.

The Gulf of Tonkin

Shortly after taking office, Johnson ordered 5,000 more U.S. troops to Vietnam and made plans to send another 5,000. In August 1964, he announced that U.S. Navy ships had been attacked in international waters near the Gulf of Tonkin. Congress reacted by overwhelmingly approving a resolution that gave Johnson the power to "take all necessary measures" to protect U.S. forces. A few months later, LBJ ordered U.S. bombings of targets in North Vietnam. By March 1965, more than 100,000 U.S. troops were in the country. Within three years, the number had swelled to more than 500,000.

It was a lot of people to fight a war no one seemed to understand how to win. The U.S. had overwhelming military superiority. But it was mostly designed for fighting a conventional war, with big battles and conquered territories.

Vietnam was different. It was essentially a civil war, which meant it was sometimes confusing who was on whose side. The communists in the south were called the Vietcong, who were aided by North Vietnamese Army troops, referred to as the NVA. The dense jungle terrain made it difficult to locate and fight large concentrations of the enemy. There were conflicts between U.S. political leaders, who wanted to "contain" the war, and military leaders who wanted to expand it. Finally, the lack of clear objectives and declining public support demoralized many American soldiers.

The Tet Offensive

On January 31, 1968 — the Vietnamese New Year, called "Tet" — communist forces unleashed massive attacks on U.S. positions throughout Vietnam. The Tet Offensive, televised nightly in the U.S., shocked many Americans who had had the idea the U.S. was rather easily handling the enemy. In fact, U.S. forces eventually pushed the North Vietnamese forces back and inflicted huge casualties on them. But the impact the fighting had on U.S. public opinion was equally huge. Opposition to the war grew more heated and contributed mightily to LBJ's decision not to run for re-election in 1968.

Increasing Pressure in 'Nam and Escalating Fears at Home

With Johnson out of the 1968 race, Republican Richard Nixon narrowly defeated Johnson's vice president, Hubert Humphrey, and Alabama Governor George Wallace, an ardent segregationist who ran as an independent.

Nixon and his top foreign affairs advisor, Henry Kissinger, tried several tactics to extricate the U.S. from the war without just turning over South Vietnam to the communists. One tactic was to coerce the South Vietnamese government into taking more responsibility for the war. To force the issue, the U.S. began withdrawing some troops in 1969. At the same time, however, Nixon tried another tactic by ordering an increase in the bombing of North Vietnam, and also in the neighboring countries of Laos and Cambodia. In essence, he was trying to put pressure on both sides to stop the fighting.

In 1970, Nixon approved the invasion of Cambodia by U.S. troops who were pursuing North Vietnamese soldiers based there. The decision intensified opposition to the war, and massive antiwar demonstrations spread across the country. At Kent State University in Ohio, National Guard troops shot and killed four student demonstrators.

Anti-war fever grew even stronger in 1971, when the New York Times published what became known as the Pentagon Papers. The documents, leaked by a former Defense Department worker named Daniel Ellsberg, proved the government had lied about the war's conduct. Later that year, an Army lieutenant named William Calley was convicted of supervising the massacre of more than 100 unarmed civilians at a village called My Lai.

Despite the mounting opposition, Nixon easily won re-election in 1972, in part because of a politically inept opponent (U.S. Senator George McGovern of South Dakota), and in part because Kissinger announced a few weeks before the election that a peace settlement was not too far off.

After the election, however, Nixon ordered heavy bombing of North Vietnam's capital of Hanoi. But the bombing failed to break North Vietnamese resolve, and 15 U.S. bombers were shot down. On January 27, 1973, the U.S. and North Vietnam announced they had reached an agreement to end the fighting and would work to negotiate a settlement.

The peace treaty proved to be a face-saving sham, allowing U.S. troops to be withdrawn before the communists closed in. In April 1975, North Vietnamese troops overran South Vietnam and took over the entire country. America had suffered its first decisive defeat in a war, touching off a reassessment of its role in the world — and on how it would approach involvement in conflicts in the future.

Vietnam by the numbers

Number of Americans killed: 58,174. Number wounded: 304,000. Cost, 1950–1974: $150 billion. Number of U.S. troops stationed there at peak: 535,000. Average age of U.S. soldier killed: 23. Age of youngest killed: 16. Age of oldest killed: 62. Average number of days in combat by infantry solider in one year in Vietnam: 240.

Climbing the Mountain to Racial Freedom

While the civil rights movement began in the 1950s, it reached full steam in the 1960s, marked by several new tactics that proved effective in breaking down discrimination.

Enforcing their rights — African Americans

In February 1960, four African American students sat down at a segregated lunch counter in Greensboro, North Carolina, and refused to leave after they were denied service. The "sit in" became a strategy used across the country, and by the end of 1961, some 70,000 people had taken part in them. In May 1961, black and white activists began "freedom rides," traveling in small groups to the South to test local segregation laws (see Figure 21-1).

Figure 21-1:
Police removing demonstrators from a restaurant.

The inspirational leader of the movement was the Reverend Martin Luther King, Jr., a courageous and eloquent orator who founded the Southern Christian Leadership Conference and who won the 1964 Nobel Peace Prize for his civil rights work.

But not all African Americans were enamored of King's non-violent-demonstration approach. They also didn't believe equality could be attained through cooperation among the races. Leaders such as the Black Muslims'

Elijah Muhammad and Malcolm X warned African Americans not to expect nor seek help from whites. "If someone puts a hand on you," said Malcolm X, "send him to the cemetery."

Both approaches eventually put pressure on the federal government to act. President Kennedy and his brother Robert (who was also his attorney general) used federal troops and marshals to force the admission of black students to the state universities in Alabama and Mississippi. In June 1963, JFK proposed a bill that would ban racial discrimination in hotels, restaurants, and other public places and give the federal government more authority to clamp down on state and local agencies that dragged their feet in enforcing civil rights laws. Black organizers gathered 200,000 demonstrators for a march in Washington, D.C., to support the Kennedy proposal.

Kennedy's efforts were taken up by Lyndon Johnson, after Kennedy's assassination. Despite his Southern roots, LBJ was a committed liberal whose "Great Society" programs mirrored the New Deal of Franklin Roosevelt in the 1930s. In addition to providing more federal aid to America's down-and-outs, LBJ pushed through Congress the 1964 Civil Rights Act. It featured many of the same elements Kennedy had proposed. Johnson followed it with another bill in 1965 that strengthened federal safeguards for black voters' rights.

But events and emotions moved faster than politics. In early 1965, Malcolm X, who had softened his earlier opposition to interracial cooperation, was murdered by Black Muslim extremists who considered such talk traitorous. A few months later, a march led by Martin Luther King from Selma to Montgomery in Alabama was viciously attacked by state and local police, while a horrified national television audience watched.

Tired of waiting for an equal chance at the U.S. economic pie, many African Americans began demanding "affirmative action" programs in which employers would actively recruit minorities for jobs. "Black Power" became a rallying cry for thousands of young African Americans who had marched and demonstrated about all they cared to.

The anger broke out in a rash of race riots in the mid- and late 1960s. The first was in August 1965, in the Los Angeles community of Watts. Before it was over, six days of rioting had led to 34 deaths, 850 injuries, 3,000 arrests, and

---

Big dreams

"I have a dream that one day this nation will rise up, live out the true meaning of its creed . . . I have a dream that my four little children will one day live in a nation where they will not be judged by the color of their skin but by the content of their characters."

— Martin Luther King, Jr., August 28, 1963, before the Lincoln Memorial, Washington, D.C.

more than $200 million in damages. Over the next two years, riots spread to dozens of cities, including New York, Chicago, Newark, and Detroit, where 43 people were killed in July 1967.

Then things got worse. On April 4, 1968, Martin Luther King, Jr., was assassinated in Memphis, Tennessee. A white man named James Earl Ray was eventually arrested and convicted of the crime. Riots followed across the country, most notably in Washington, D.C.

The riots, in turn, triggered a backlash by many whites. George Wallace, a racist and ardent segregationist, got 13.5 percent of the vote in the 1968 presidential election, and much of the steam of the civil rights movement was gone by the time Richard Nixon moved into the White House.

Challenging the system — La Raza

African Americans weren't the only minority group on the move in the 1960s. Americans of Latin American descent had been treated as second-class citizens since the 1840s. While their numbers increased during and after World War II, mainly because thousands of Mexicans came to the country as a source of cheap labor, Latinos were largely ghettoized in inner-city "barrios" and rural areas of the Southwest and generally invisible in terms of the political process.

Between 1960 and 1970, however, the number of Latinos in the U.S. tripled, from three million to nine million, with perhaps another five million in the country illegally. Cubans came to Florida, Puerto Ricans to New York, and Mexicans to California. With the increase in numbers came an increased interest in better political, social, and economic treatment for "La Raza" ("the race"). Leaders, particularly among Mexican Americans, or "Chicanos," sprang up: Reies Lopez Tijerina in New Mexico, Rodolfo "Corky" Gonzales in Colorado, and Cesar Chavez in California.

Latinos began to pursue organized efforts to gain access to the educational and economic systems and fight racial stereotypes. Latin Americans were elected to municipal and state offices and gradually began to organize themselves into a formidable political force in some parts of the country.

Maintaining their culture — Native Americans

No minority group had been treated worse than American Indians or had been less able to do anything about it. They had lower average incomes, higher rates of alcoholism, and shorter life expectancies than any other ethnic group. And because their numbers were few, Indians had been largely ignored by the federal government since the turn of the century.

In the 1950s, federal laws and policies had tried to push Indians into white society and into abandoning traditional ways. But in the 1960s, some Indians began to push back. In 1961, the National Indian Youth Council was established, followed by the American Indian Movement in 1968. The efforts of these and other groups helped lead to the Indian Civil Rights Act in 1968, which granted U.S. rights to reservation Indians while allowing them to set their own laws according to tribal customs.

It would be nice to say that all the racial wrongs in America were made right by the tumultuous events of the 1960s. It would also be absurd. But it isn't absurd to say the period was an overall success in terms of civil rights. It established key new laws, instilled a sense of self-pride in minority groups, and served notice that the issue would not be swept under the rug. "Lord, we ain't what we ought to be," observed Martin Luther King. "We ain't what we wanna be. We ain't what we gonna be. But, thank God, we ain't what we were."

AMERICAN FACES

Cesar Chavez

His opponents accused him of "sour grapes," but to Cesar Chavez, it was merely a question of tactics.

Chavez was born in 1927 on a small family farm near Yuma, Arizona. During the Depression, his family lost the farm and were forced to move, becoming laborers on other people's farms in California and the Southwest. Chavez only occasionally attended school because the family moved so much, following the crops. After serving in the Navy during World War II, Chavez settled in San Jose, California, and became an official in a Latino community service organization.

In 1962, using his life savings, he founded the United Farm Workers (UFW), a union for a group that no other union was interested in. Chavez was an advocate of non-violence who believed the interests of the union should extend beyond

labor contracts to other areas of social justice for farm workers.

By the mid-1960s, Chavez and the UFW had begun to organize farm workers in earnest. When strikes failed to work, he began product boycotts, particularly against grapes. The aim of the boycotts was to get consumers not to buy the product until a fair labor agreement was in place. By the end of the 1970s, the UFW's membership was more than 70,000, the state of California had created a state board to mediate disputes between growers and workers, and for the first time, the nation's most downtrodden workers had union contracts. Chavez died in 1993. The following year, his work not only as a union leader, but also as a civil rights leader and humanitarian, was recognized when he was posthumously awarded the Presidential Medal of Freedom, the nation's highest civilian honor.

Entering a Generation in Revolt

Not all of the groups fighting the status quo were tied to each other by race or national origin. The war in Vietnam and the blooming civil rights movement triggered political activism among many young Americans, particularly on college campuses. Groups like Students for a Democratic Society appeared, and activities like draft card burnings became as common as pep rallies.

Draft dodging, drugs, and demonstrations

Because of opposition to the war, thousands of draft-age males fled to Canada and other countries rather than serve in the military. Their actions baffled many of their parents, whose generations had served in World War II and Korea, and helped widen the gap of misunderstanding between the age groups.

The gap was also evident in the younger generation's freer attitudes toward sex, public profanity, and hairstyles. More troubling, and longer lasting in terms of its impact, was the use of drugs by the "counterculture." The use of marijuana and hallucinogenics like LSD became commonplace. Most of it could be attributed to the excesses of youth. But it was also a disturbing preview of the plagues of drug use that would sweep over the country during the rest of the century.

Perhaps nowhere was the generation gap more visible then at the 1968 Democratic National Convention in Chicago. While mostly middle-aged and middle-class delegates debated an anti-war plank for the party platform, hundreds of mostly young and mostly poor demonstrators battled with club-swinging police in the streets outside the convention center. "The whole world is watching!" the demonstrators taunted. Ironically, many of those watching were so troubled by the sight of young people defying authority that they voted for Richard Nixon in 1968, and again in 1972. Nixon appealed to these voters, whom he called the "silent majority," because he spoke out strongly against the demonstrations.

Feminism

Draft cards weren't the only things being burned during the period. Women who resented their secondary roles in the workplace, the home, and the halls of government periodically burned their bras as a protest. They had plenty to protest. Women faced barriers in getting jobs and when they did find a job, they were paid far less than men doing the same work: In 1970 women earned 60 cents for every dollar paid a man. Married women were denied credit in their own names, even when they had jobs of their own.

The women's liberation movement gave birth to the National Organization of Women (NOW) in 1966, and by 1970 NOW was organizing women's rights demonstrations and winning court battles over equal pay for equal work. In 1972, Congress approved a constitutional provision called the Equal Rights Amendment, and sent it to the states for ratification. But a coalition of conservative and religious groups combined to fight the ERA, and in 1982 it was dead, three states short of the 38 needed for ratification.

As it turned out, the amendment hardly mattered, because many of the rights it would have provided were awarded in court decisions. One key decision came in 1973, when in *Roe v. Wade,* the Supreme Court essentially legalized abortion in the first three months of pregnancy. The ruling meant women now had a wider range of legal choices when faced with pregnancy. It also meant the beginning of an intense political, legal, social, and religious battle over abortion that continues today.

Gay days

The subject of homosexuality was so unspoken in America for most of its history that there were many Americans at the beginning of the twentieth century who had never heard of it or didn't believe it was real. In the 1960s, many psychiatrists believed homosexuality was a mental illness, and same-gender sex between consenting adults was still a crime in many states.

Harvey Milk

When the first openly gay elected official of any big U.S. city stepped in it, he really stepped in it. As a San Francisco county supervisor, Milk once pushed for a city ordinance to force dog owners to clean up after their pets in public places. Accompanied by reporters, he staged a stroll through a city park that ended with his foot in a pile of dog droppings, for the benefit of the cameras. The measure was approved.

Milk was born in 1930 in New York. He served in the Navy during the Korean War as a deep-sea diver, but was dishonorably discharged after his homosexuality was revealed. After a career as a Wall Street stockbroker, Milk moved to San Francisco's gay Castro Street district, opened a camera store, and began running for office as an openly gay candidate. He was finally elected, on the fourth try, in 1977.

In 1978, Milk and San Francisco Mayor George Moscone were shot to death at City Hall by a disgruntled former city official named Dan White. White received only a five-year sentence for the killings, triggering gay riots. But Milk's death also inspired many gay professionals to "come out of the closet," and encouraged other gays to run for office. It was something he would have found satisfying.

"If a bullet should enter my brain," he had said in a tape-recorded will, "let that bullet destroy every closet door."

That began to change in the late 1960s, however, as gay men and women began to assert themselves. In June 1969, New York City police busted a gay nightclub called the Stonewall and began arresting patrons. The bust sparked a riot in the predominantly gay community of Greenwich Village. Gay activist organizations like the Gay Liberation Front were started. But progress in changing anti-gay laws and homophobic attitudes has been slow and sporadic in the ensuing 30 years.

Problems in the White House

Vietnam and a whole bunch of unhappy people in the streets of America weren't the only problems Richard Nixon faced when he took over as president in early 1969. Inflation was running wild. Much of the problem was due to President Johnson's economic policy of "guns AND butter": paying for the war and at the same time expanding social programs.

The Nixon Administration

Nixon responded to the situation by cutting government spending and balancing the federal budget for 1969. He also rather reluctantly imposed wage and price freezes on the country. But he wasn't reluctant at all about dropping federal efforts to enforce school integration laws, since he had been elected with Southern support and was mindful that polls showed most Americans opposed forcing kids to take buses to schools in other neighborhoods to achieve racial balance.

Outside of Vietnam, Nixon enjoyed success in foreign policy. He went to China in early 1972, ending 20 years of diplomatic silence between the two countries and pursued a policy of "détente" (a French term for relaxing of tensions) with the Soviet Union.

These accomplishments, coupled with vague hints of looming peace in Vietnam and a backlash among voters Nixon called the "silent majority" against all the protesting, helped Nixon easily win re-election in 1972. In early 1973, the peace settlement with North Vietnam was announced. And despite Democratic majorities in Congress, Nixon was able to veto bills that challenged his authority in a number of areas. He took advantage of it to greatly expand the White House's power and cloak its actions from public scrutiny. And then an ex-FBI agent named James McCord wrote a letter to a judge, and the wheels of the Nixon White House began to come off.

Watergate

In a nutshell, here's what happened in the greatest presidential scandal in U.S. history (or second-greatest — see Chapter 23):

✔ On June 17, 1972, McCord and four other men working for the Committee to Re-Elect the President (or CREEP — really) broke into the Democratic Party's headquarters in the Watergate, a hotel/apartment house/office building in Washington, D.C. They got caught going through files and trying to plant listening devices. Five days later, Nixon denied any knowledge of it or any role in it by his administration.

✔ The burglars went to trial in 1973 and either pled guilty or were convicted. Before sentencing, McCord wrote a letter to Judge John Sirica, contending that high Republican and White House officials knew about the break-in and had paid the defendants to keep quiet or lie during the trial.

✔ Investigation of McCord's charges spread to a special Senate committee. John Dean, a White House lawyer, told the committee McCord was telling the truth, and that Nixon had known of the effort to cover up White House involvement.

✔ Eventually, all sorts of damaging stuff began to surface, including evidence that key documents linking Nixon to the coverup of the break-in had been destroyed, that the Nixon re-election committee had run a "dirty tricks" campaign against the Democrats, and that the administration had illegally wiretapped the phones of "enemies," such as journalists who had been critical of Nixon.

✔ In March 1974, former Attorney General John Mitchell and six top Nixon aides were indicted by a federal grand jury for trying to block the investigation. They were eventually convicted.

✔ While Nixon continued to deny any involvement, it was revealed he routinely made secret tapes of conversations in his office. Nixon refused to turn over the tapes at first, and when he did agree (after firing a special prosecutor he had appointed to look into the mess and seeing his new attorney general resign in protest), it turned out some of them were missing or had been destroyed. (They were also full of profanity, which greatly surprised people who had a whole different perception of Nixon.)

✔ In the summer of 1974, the House Judiciary Committee approved articles of impeachment against the president for obstructing justice.

The tapes clearly showed he had been part of the cover-up. On August 8, 1974, Nixon submitted a one-sentence letter of resignation, and then went on television and said, "I have always tried to do what is best for the nation." He was the first and, so far, only U.S. president to quit the job.

IN THEIR WORDS

"Four score and seven..."

Save the (expletive deleted) plan

"I don't give a shit what happens. I want you all to stonewall it, let them plead the Fifth Amendment, cover up or anything else if it'll save it — save the plan."

— Richard M. Nixon, discussing the Watergate cover-up with aides, March 22, 1973.

The Watergate scandal rocked the nation, already reeling from the Vietnam disaster, economic troubles, assassinations, and all the social unrest of the preceding 15 years. It fell to Nixon's successor, Vice President Gerald R. Ford, to try and bring back a sense of order and stability to the nation. And no one had voted for him to do it.

Gee, Grandpa, What Else Happened?

Feb. 20, 1962: A 40-year-old Marine Corps lieutenant named John Glenn becomes the first American to orbit the earth in space, making three trips around the globe before landing safely in the Atlantic.

July 28, 1963: Close to 50,000 music fans attend a folk music festival in Newport, Rhode Island. They listen to stars like Pete Seeger and Peter, Paul and Mary. But the real surprise is a 22-year-old singer/songwriter from Hibbing, Minnesota, with a nasal whine and songs that stir the soul. His name is Bob Dylan.

Aug. 24, 1964: The first Roman Catholic Mass said in English is performed by the Reverend Frederick R. McManus in St. Louis.

Aug. 1, 1966: A 25-year-old University of Texas honors student named Charles Whitman climbs a tower on the Austin campus and opens fire with a high-powered rifle. He kills 16 people and wounds 30 before he is killed by an off-duty policeman.

Jan. 15, 1967: The Green Bay Packers beat the Kansas City Chiefs 35–10 in the first Super Bowl in Los Angeles. Not a whole lot of people care: The stadium is only about two-thirds full.

Jan. 23, 1968: The U.S. Navy intelligence vessel *Pueblo* and its crew of 83 are seized by North Korea after it allegedly wanders into North Korean waters. The crew, minus one member who was killed, is released on December 23.

June 6, 1968: Senator Robert Kennedy of New York dies from an assassin's bullets in Los Angeles, hours after winning the California primary and all but clinching the Democratic presidential nomination.

April 22, 1970: Millions of Americans help clean up streets, parks, and beaches around the country on "Earth Day." The event, designed to heighten the public's environmental awareness, comes eight months after creation of the federal Environmental Protection Agency and five months after passage of the Clean Air Act.

June 29, 1972: The U.S. Supreme Court rules that the death penalty is unconstitutionally cruel and unusual punishment. The ruling overturns scores of death penalty sentences, and states scramble to revise death penalty laws that meet the court's guidelines.

May 8, 1973: A group comprised of American Indians and others end a 70-day occupation of Wounded Knee, on the Oglala Sioux reservation in South Dakota. The group had occupied the site, where an infamous massacre of Indians by federal troops took place in 1890, to protest federal Indian policies. The 120 remaining occupants surrender to federal agents.

SIDETRIP

Small steps and great leaps

It started with a challenge from John F. Kennedy and it ended with perhaps the greatest technological feat in human history: Man on the moon.

On May 25, 1961, Kennedy asked Congress for money to put a U.S. astronaut on the moon before the end of the decade. Congress agreed, and more than $1 billion was spent to get to the afternoon of July 20, 1969. At 1:17 p.m. (PDT), a craft carrying two men landed on the lunar surface. A few hours later, astronaut Neil A. Armstrong stepped out. "That's one small step for a man," he said, "one giant leap for mankind."

Armstrong was joined on the surface by Buzz Aldrin, while a third astronaut, Michael Collins, circled above in the mother ship, *Columbia*. A worldwide television audience estimated at one billion people watched from a quarter-million miles away.

Some lunar visit facts: Armstrong and Aldrin spent 21 hours on the surface, but only two hours, 15 minutes actually walking around and never ventured farther than 275 yards from their craft. They collected 46 pounds of rocks. And they left behind a plaque attached to the base of the landing craft (they got back to the Columbia in the top half of the two-stage lander.)

The plaque reads: "Here men from the planet Earth first set foot upon the moon, July 1969 A.D. We came in peace for all mankind."

Chapter 22

Hold the Malaise, or Ayatollah So: 1975–1992

● ●

In This Chapter

▶ Wading through Watergate

▶ Fueling a failing economy

▶ Smiling for the camera — and the country

▶ Thawing after the Cold War

▶ Timeline

● ●

*N*othing puts a damper on a country's attitude like a crooked president followed by a couple of relatively inept ones, and that's just what occurred in the 1970s. Throw in an oil crisis, a very unsettled economy, and a hostage situation in Iran, and we're not exactly talking about the Golden Age of America here.

In this era, a charismatic figure from, of all places, Hollywood, rides to the rescue, smiles a lot, and generally makes America feel better about itself by the end of the 1980s.

Wearing Someone Else's Shoes

No one voted for Vice President Gerald R. Ford when he became president of the United States on Aug. 8, 1974. Come to think of it, no one voted for him when he became vice president, either.

Ford was elected to Congress from Michigan in 1948, and re-elected every two years through 1972. In December 1973, President Nixon appointed Ford vice president after the incumbent vice president, Spiro T. Agnew, resigned. Agnew was a blustering eccentric who proved to be even a bigger crook than Nixon. Finding himself under investigation for extorting bribes from contractors while he was governor of Maryland, Agnew pleaded no contest to a charge of tax fraud, quit the vice presidency, and faded into richly deserved obscurity.

A month after becoming president when Nixon resigned in the wake of the Watergate scandal, Ford decided the country needed to put Watergate behind it. The best way to do that, Ford decided, was to pardon Nixon of any crimes he may have committed while in office. About 40 of Nixon's assistants weren't so lucky and were indicted for various offenses. Some of them, including Nixon's attorney general, John Mitchell, and Nixon's top aides, John Ehrlichman and John Haldeman, went to prison.

Doing the best he could

As an honest, hard-working, and amiable man, Ford did his best as president. Unfortunately, his best wasn't great. Although he had been a college football star and a leader in Congress, he developed an undeserved reputation as a not-too-coordinated, not-too-bright guy. Falling down a flight of airplane stairs, hitting a spectator with a ball during a golf tournament, and occasionally misspeaking didn't help. Lyndon Johnson joked that Ford had "played one too many games without his helmet."

Ford's pardon of Nixon angered many Americans who felt the former president should not have escaped facing the justice system. But even without the Watergate hangover, 1975 wasn't a great time to be president, for Ford or anyone.

In late April 1975, the communists completed their takeover in Vietnam. American diplomats scrambled onto escape helicopters from the roofs of buildings near the U.S. Embassy in Saigon, with the whole world watching from living room televisions. Most of the rest of Indochina had already fallen under communist control or fell soon after. President Eisenhower's "domino theory" had come true.

Whipping inflation

Even worse for Ford than the humiliation of the fall of Saigon, the U.S. economy was a mess. Inflation was soaring and the unemployment rate reached nine percent, the highest level since 1941. Ford's response included asking Americans to wear buttons that bore the acronym "WIN," for "whip inflation now." The buttons did not have much of an impact, however.

IN THEIR WORDS
"Four score and seven..."

Not on my shift

"I did not take the sacred oath of office to preside over the decline and fall of the United States of America."

— Gerald R. Ford, after assuming the presidency, August 1974.

First isn't always best

Videotape recorders have been around since the 1950s and were initially used by the television industry in place of film. But it wasn't until 1975 that the Japanese company Sony came up with a videotaping system for home use. It was called Betamax, it cost $1,260, and blank tapes were $25. Sony sold 30,000 of them in the United States.

The following year, the JVC company came out with its own system called VHS. Four more companies soon followed with their own VHS versions and prices dropped as competition increased. By 1982, prices were down to around $500 and a whole new business had been created: renting films on videotape.

Sadly for Sony's Beta, however, the video stores stocked more VHS tapes than Beta because there were more VHS machines being sold. By 1988, VHS machines controlled 95 percent of the U.S. market. And in 1998, the home Beta machine officially went the way of the dodo and the eight-track tape.

Despite the buttons' ineffectiveness to improve morale, Ford refused to take stronger measures. He neglected to address such issues as wage and price control and did little to lessen the country's growing dependence on foreign oil. Therefore, when oil-producing nations, mainly in the Middle East, dramatically jacked up oil prices — 400 percent in 1974 alone — the U.S. suffered a price increase on just about every other product as well.

The Nixon pardon, the humiliating end to Vietnam, and the staggering economy proved to be three strikes against Ford. After barely winning the Republican nomination over former California Governor Ronald Reagan, Ford lost the 1976 presidential election to Jimmy Carter, the former governor of Georgia. The way things turned out, Ford may have been the lucky one.

Good Intentions, Bad Results

America turned 200 in 1976 and for its bicentennial birthday it gave itself a new president. His name was James Earl Carter, but everyone called him Jimmy. He was a Naval Academy graduate, a nuclear engineer, a peanut farmer, and the former governor of Georgia. He ran for the presidency as a Washington outsider. Since U.S. voters were pretty sick of Washington insiders, they elected him in a close race over the incumbent Jerry Ford. Carter was the first candidate since 1932 to defeat an incumbent president. He was also the first president from the Deep South since the Civil War.

Ford had started his administration with the controversial pardoning of Richard Nixon and Carter started his with the controversial pardoning of Vietnam War draft evaders. There were other similarities. Both men seemed to have a tough time being consistent in their policy- and decision-making. And both had real troubles with the economy, because of runaway inflation and oil shortages.

Measuring misery

During the 1976 campaign, Carter added up the nation's unemployment rate and inflation level, called it a "misery index" and used it as an effective rhetorical weapon against Ford. Unfortunately for Carter, by the time he left office, the level of "misery" was higher than when he took over. The annual inflation rate — the change in the price of various consumer goods — went from 5 percent in 1970 to 14.5 percent in 1980. The price of gasoline went from about 40 cents a gallon to more than 70 cents. Part of the reason for both higher inflation and high oil prices was America's increasing dependence on foreign oil. Simply put, the country was using more oil — from running cars to making textiles — than it was producing.

In the early '70s, Arab oil-producing countries cut off supplies to the U.S. and other Western nations as a way of pressuring Israel to give back Arab territory it had taken during a 1967 war. When the embargo was lifted in 1974, the Western countries' oil reserves had dried up and the oil-producing countries could charge pretty much whatever they wanted for their product.

Higher oil prices helped fuel inflation, and inflation helped trigger higher interest rates. Companies couldn't afford to borrow money to expand and so unemployment rose. Carter tried various ways to combat the problems, including voluntary wage and price controls, but it didn't help much. Things got so bad, Carter went on national television to acknowledge that a "crisis of confidence" had struck the nation. The address became known as "the malaise speech," and to many people it made Carter appear to be a self-pitying crybaby.

Lust and found

"Christ set some almost impossible standards for us . . . I've looked on a lot of women with lust. I've committed adultery in my heart many times."

— Jimmy Carter, in a 1976 interview with Playboy Magazine.

A nuclear "oops"

One of the great hopes of weaning America from its dependence on foreign oil was nuclear power. Nuclear power is produced at plants like the one on the banks of the Susquehanna River in a bucolic area of Pennsylvania. It is called Three-Mile Island.

On March 28, 1979, one of the plant's thousands of valves went on the fritz. The malfunction caused temperatures in the plant's reactor chamber to climb to 5,000 degrees Fahrenheit, melting the lining of the reactor chamber before being stopped by the thick concrete floor.

Pregnant women and children were evacuated and as many as 60,000 other people voluntarily fled the area. As it turned out, only relatively low levels of radiation escaped and no claims of personal or property damage were ever proven.

But the accident effectively exploded the hopes of expanding nuclear power as an energy source in America. By the end of the twentieth century, nuclear power was a negligible source of energy in the U.S.

Befriending the enemy

On the foreign front, Carter had mixed results. He negotiated treaties to gradually transfer the Panama Canal territory to Panama. He reached agreement with the Soviet Union to restrict the development of nuclear arms, and furthered the restoration of relations with Communist China, which had been started by President Nixon.

Carter's biggest triumph was in engineering an historic peace agreement between Israel and Egypt, which had been at each other's throats for decades. At Camp David, the presidential retreat in Maryland, Carter brokered a deal in 1978 with Israeli Prime Minister Menachim Begin and Egyptian President Anwar Sadat. Sadat and Begin got the Nobel Peace Prize for their efforts; Carter got nothing but trouble in the form of multiple disasters involving Iran.

The United States had backed the shah of Iran since 1953, when the CIA helped him regain power in that country. When the shah was thrown out again in 1979 and replaced with a Muslim religious leader named the Ayatollah Ruhollah Khomeini, the U.S. allowed the shah to receive medical treatment in the U.S.

That angered Iranian mobs, who invaded the U.S. Embassy in the Iranian capital Teheran on Nov. 4, 1979. The mobs held the occupants of the Embassy hostage. Some hostages were allowed to leave, but 52 were kept as prisoners. In April 1980, Carter ordered a team of Marine commandos to Iran on a rescue mission. Because of a series of screwups and accidents involving the rescue aircraft, eight commandos were killed before the actual rescue even began, and the mission was called off.

Jesse Jackson

He could have been a professional athlete but became a preacher instead — and as a result became known as "the president of Black America."

Jackson was born in 1941, the illegitimate son of a South Carolina sharecropper. After a career as an all-state football player in high school, Jackson passed up a pro baseball contract and went to college instead. He also became active in the civil rights movement, and was with Martin Luther King, Jr., when King was assassinated in Memphis in 1968. In that same year, Jackson was ordained a Baptist minister.

Basing his work in Chicago, Jackson founded a program in 1971 called Operation PUSH (People United to Save Humanity). The program was designed to address problems facing inner-city youth. In 1986, he formed the National Rainbow Coalition, the aim of which was to bring together members of all races to address common goals. Jackson also ran for president in 1984 and 1988, generating enough support to become a major player in national Democratic Party politics and to be dubbed "president of Black America." He has also been something of a diplomat-without-portfolio, negotiating the release of hostages in Syria, Cuba, and Iraq.

Controversial, charismatic, and a gifted speaker, Jackson's major contributions as the twentieth century ended were as an inspirational advocate for human rights and as a bridge between grassroots organizations and traditional U.S. party politics.

Finally, after the shah died in July, negotiations for the hostages' release began. They ended with the hostages' being freed on Jan. 20, 1981, after 444 days in captivity. The day the hostages were freed was, coincidently, the last day of Carter's presidency.

There's a First Time for Everything

If you told someone in 1951 that Ronald Reagan would someday be president of the United States, they would have suggested you check into a rest home for the politically delusional. After all, the veteran actor had just starred in "Bedtime for Bonzo," in which his co-star was a chimpanzee. That qualified him for Congress, certainly, but hardly the White House.

In addition to being the first president to have starred in a movie with an ape, Reagan was also the first president to have been divorced, and at the age of 69, the oldest president when he took office. Reagan was born in Illinois in 1911, and after college became a sportscaster in Iowa. In 1937, a screen test led to Hollywood, and Reagan became a minor star, first in movies then in television. His taste for politics grew from serving two terms as president of the Screen Actors Guild, and as his politics became increasingly conservative, he found himself a favorite of the Republican Party's right wing. He ran for governor of California in 1966, defeating incumbent Pat Brown, and served two terms.

In 1976, he came in a strong second for the GOP presidential nomination, and then in 1980 swept both the nomination and the presidency over the unpopular Carter. His greatest campaign tactics turned out to be a single question: "Ask yourself, are you better off than you were four years ago?" — and not being Jimmy Carter.

As president, Reagan was essentially a cheerleader for a vision of America that counted on everyone trying not to be too different and not relying on government to do much about anything. He seemed to have an inexhaustible supply of both good and bad luck. He bounced back from being shot and seriously wounded after giving a speech at a Washington hotel in 1981, and in 1985 he won a bout with cancer. Despite his health problems, he managed an easy re-election victory in 1984 over Democrat Walter Mondale, who had been vice president under Jimmy Carter.

He greeted political setbacks with boundless good cheer and a joke or two. And no matter what else happened, Reagan's personal popularity stayed high — so much so that he became known as the "Teflon president": Like the non-stick coating used on pots and pans, nothing seemed to stick to him. But his nice-guy persona did not mean he was wishy-washy. When the country's air traffic controllers ignored federal law and went on strike in 1981, Reagan fired all 11,400 of them and refused to rehire them after the strike ended.

Buying into the "Reagan Revolution"

One of the fastest-growing portions of America's population during the 1980s didn't have a clue what Reagan was talking about when he laid out his vision of the country and probably wouldn't have liked it had they understood. They were immigrants from countries like Mexico, Cuba, Haiti, and Vietnam who came to the U.S. by the tens of thousands during the '80s. Many of them were counting on some form of government assistance to get started in their new lives in a new land.

But the people who had voted for Reagan knew exactly what he was talking about. Many of them were part of the "Sunbelt," the fast-growing states of the Southeast, Southwest, and West. As the region's population grew, so did its representation in Congress, and its political clout. (So powerful has the area become that every president elected between 1964 and 2000 was from a Southern or Western state.) In the West, in particular, Reagan's call for less government was in perfect harmony with the "Sagebrush Rebellion." The rebellion, which was mostly rhetorical, was a reaction to land use and environmental regulations and rules made in far-away Washington that were considered a threat to development of urban areas and resource-based industries, such as timber and mining. Reagan was the beneficiary of the growth in the Sunbelt's clout.

Laughing it off

"Honey, I forgot to duck." — Ronald Reagan to his wife, after being shot by an insane person, March 30, 1981. "Please tell me you're all Republicans."

—Reagan to doctors, as he was being wheeled into the operating room after the shooting.

Reagan also benefited from a revival in Christian evangelicalism that married itself to conservative politics in the late 1970s and 1980s. Conservative evangelicals — those who said they had been "born again" through a direct personal experience with Jesus Christ — were alarmed at what they saw as the country's moral laxity in the 1960s and early 1970s. America's real problems, they argued, could be traced to feminism, abortion, rising divorce rates, and homosexuality.

Groups like the Moral Majority, led by a Virginia-based television evangelist named Jerry Falwell, became powerful political forces in terms of raising money and mobilizing mass support — or opposition — for legislation and political candidates. Another "religious right" leader, Marion G. "Pat" Robertson founded the Christian Coalition and twice ran for president himself.

Finally, Reagan was supported by followers of a more secular cause — tax cutting. The high inflation of the 1970s caused many people's income and property values to rise — and also pushed them into higher tax brackets that ate up much of the increases. That naturally fueled taxpayer anger. In California, a cranky political gadfly named Howard Jarvis successfully pushed through an initiative that dramatically cut property tax rates and required state and local governments to drastically shift their way of financing government operations. The success of Proposition 13 led to similar efforts in other states. It also helped Reagan push through his own brand of tax cutting.

Paying for "Reaganomics"

Reagan figured that if you cut taxes on companies and the very wealthy and reduced regulations on business, they would invest more, the economy would expand, and everyone would benefit. Of course this approach would require cutting government services, which would most affect Americans on the bottom of the economic ladder. But the benefits would eventually "trickle down" from those on the top of the ladder to those on the bottom. At least in theory. So early in his administration, Reagan pushed through a package of massive tax cuts. And the economy got better. Unemployment dropped from 11 percent in 1982 to about 8 percent in 1983. Inflation dropped below 5 percent, and the Gross National Product rose.

AMERICAN FACES

Jim Bakker

He once spent $100 on cinnamon rolls so his hotel room would smell nice, which was okay because he was doing God's work — and had plenty of cash to spare.

Bakker was born in 1940 and grew up in a small town in Michigan. After high school, he attended a Bible college and became a minister. In the early 1970s, Bakker began a Christian puppet show on a local television station in Virginia. He developed a television ministry that became known as the PTL Club, which to followers stood for "praise the Lord" and to critics stood for "pass the loot."

There was plenty of that. With contributions from hundreds of thousands of his followers, Bakker and his wife Tammy Faye (who wore what seemed to be pounds of makeup and wept at the drop of a psalm) built "Heritage USA," a 2,300-acre Christian-themed resort, water park, and entertainment complex in South Carolina. In 1988, however, it was revealed that PTL had paid $265,000 to a former secretary named Jessica Hahn to keep her quiet about a sexual encounter she had had with Bakker eight years before.

The revelation was only one of many that followed over the next year. In 1989, Bakker was convicted of bilking more than 100,000 people of $158 million. He served five years in federal prison, and the scandal helped put the brakes to the momentum of the Christian Right.

REMEMBER

While Reaganistas were quick to point to the president's policies as a great deal, critics pointed in a different direction. Although Reagan had cut taxes, he and Congress had failed to cut government spending. In fact, he greatly increased spending on military programs. Because the government was spending far more than it was taking in, the national debt rose from about $900 billion in 1980 to a staggering $3 *trillion* in 1990. Moreover, most of the benefits of Reagan's trickle-down approach failed to trickle, priming the pump for another economic downturn after he left office.

Dealing with foreign affairs

As a true conservative, Reagan didn't much care for the Soviet Union or communists in general. He heated up the Cold War by, among other things, referring to the Soviets as amoral and irreligious. (Toward the end of his second term, however, it is true Reagan's anti-Soviet feelings began to soften, particularly after a moderate named Mikhail Gorbachev became Soviet leader.)

Reagan also irritated the Soviets by proposing a giant military program called the Strategic Defense Initiative (SDI), more popularly known as "Star Wars" after the popular science fiction film. Reagan's plan included missile-destroying lasers based on satellites in space. His vision never went anywhere, however, because Congress refused to go along with the program's enormous costs.

SIDETRIP

The *Challenger* tragedy

It was cold and windy at Cape Canaveral the morning of Jan. 28, 1986, but U.S. space program officials were determined to go ahead with the launch of the space shuttle *Challenger*. After all, the *Challenger* had already made nine successful trips into space and the National Aeronautics and Space Administration (NASA) had run 24 space shuttle missions without a major problem.

At 11:38 a.m. (EDT), NASA launched its 25th mission. At 11:40, it had its first major problem. As thousands of spectators watched in horror at the launch site and millions more watched on television, the shuttle exploded shortly after lifting off. All seven of the crewmembers were killed, including a Concord, NH, schoolteacher named Christa McAulliffe who was along for the ride as a way of increasing children's interest in the space program.

The cause of the explosion was later traced to a flaw in the rocket's booster system and led to a complete reevaluation of the shuttle and an examination of more than 1,000 of its parts. It took more than two years before the shuttle program was allowed to resume. In the 14 years following the *Challenger* disaster there were no more fatal accidents. One was enough.

Reagan also supported virtually any government that was anti-communist, including repressive regimes in Latin America, and was quick to respond to provocations by terrorist acts supported by Libya. But he did withdraw American peacekeeping troops from war-torn Lebanon after a 1983 terrorist attack killed 241 U.S. marines stationed there.

One of the anti-communist groups Reagan's administration supported was called the "contras" in Nicaragua, and it resulted in the biggest embarrassment of Reagan's presidency. In 1986, it was revealed the White House had approved the sale of weapons to Iran as part of a mostly unsuccessful effort to win release of some U.S. hostages in the Middle East.

It turned out that some of the money from the arms deal had been illegally siphoned off to the contras. Most of the blame for the scandal was pinned on an obscure Marine lieutenant colonel named Oliver North. But like other calamities, the Iran-Contra mess did little to harm Reagan's popularity or inflict any lasting damage on his administration. In fact, it didn't even hurt the election of his successor in the White House, a one-time Reagan political foe who had become Reagan's dutiful vice president. His name was George Bush.

Warming Up after the Cold War

On Nov. 9, 1989, the guards, who for decades had kept East Germans in the part of Germany controlled by communists and most everyone else out, were gone from their posts. Within weeks, so was the wall that had divided the city of Berlin. Within a year, East and West Germany, separated by the tensions of the Cold War since 1945, were reunited.

For all intents and purposes, the Cold War was over. For more than four decades, the ideological conflict between the Free World and the Communist World had influenced just about every aspect of U.S. life. The federal budget was built around the idea of defending the country against communism. Advances in science and medicine were often driven by the fervor to stay ahead of the communists. Schoolchildren were indoctrinated as to the evils of the communist menace and chided to do better than commie kids. Even international sporting events became intense political struggles.

But the boogey man began to deflate in 1979, when the Soviet Union intervened in a civil war in Afghanistan. Over the following decade, the Soviets poured thousands of troops and millions of rubles into what became the equivalent of their Vietnam. The difference was that the U.S. economy was strong enough and flexible enough to survive Vietnam, whereas the ponderous Soviet economy all but creaked to a halt.

Geraldine Ferraro

She was a self-made woman who forever made her mark in America's democratic process even though she came from the New York borough with the most undemocratic name of Queens.

Ferraro was born in 1935. Her father was an Italian immigrant who died when she was 8 years old. After graduating from college, Ferraro became an elementary school teacher while going to law school at night. After graduating from law school, she married and for the next 13 years was a housewife and mother. In 1974, she joined the Queens district attorney's office, and, in 1978, was elected to Congress.

As a congresswoman, Ferraro became an advocate for women's issues, particularly in providing women greater job training opportunities and ending gender discrimination in pension systems. In 1984, she was picked by Democratic presidential candidate Walter Mondale to be his running mate, making Ferraro the first woman to be part of the ticket for either of the two major political parties.

Mondale and Ferraro were clobbered, and it didn't help that a stink arose over allegations that her husband had done business with organized crime figures. Ferraro ran unsuccessfully for the U.S. Senate in 1992 and 1998. She was also a TV political talk show co-host, wrote three books, and became a business consultant. "We've come a long way since '84," she said in a 1999 interview. "That election really paved the way for women, and not just in politics."

P.S.: Through the end of the twentieth century, no woman had been on a Democratic or Republican national ticket since Ferraro.

Oil over the place

On March 24, 1989, Alaska's Prince William Sound was one of the most scenic and beautiful inlets in the world, teeming with birds, fish, and marine mammals. On March 25, 1989, it was a heart-breaking, stomach-turning mess: the site of the biggest oil spill in U.S. history.

It began when a giant tanker, the *Exxon Valdez*, hit a well-marked reef after picking up a load of crude oil at the town of Valdez. More than 11 million gallons of oil oozed into the sound and spread over hundreds of square miles. More than 250,000 birds were killed along with thousands of other animals.

It was quickly determined that the 984-foot ship's captain, Joseph Hazelwood, had been drinking before the accident. He was convicted the following year of negligence and sentenced to 1,000 hours of community service. He began the service in 1999, after nine years of appeals. Exxon spent $2.2 billion on cleanup efforts and paid another $900 million in a settlement to the state and federal government. As the twenty-first century began, there was still oil to be found on the shores of Prince William Sound.

In 1985, a remarkable man named Mikhail Gorbachev became the Soviet leader. Gorbachev realized that the old Soviet system could not continue to dominate Eastern Europe. In fact, it couldn't even continue to function as a country without some dramatic changes. He initiated two major concepts: *perestroika,* or changes in the Soviet economic structure, and *glasnost,* or opening the system to create more individual freedoms.

By the end of 1989, Soviet-dominated regimes in a half-dozen European countries, including East Germany, had collapsed and been replaced by more democratic governments. By the end of 1991, the Soviet Union itself had dissolved into a set of mostly autonomous republics.

The end of the Cold War and the collapse of the Soviet Union left the United States as the world's only true superpower. But it took no time at all for one of the planet's seemingly inexhaustible supply of thugs and bullies to test the U.S.'s will to live up to its role as the world's leader.

The Gulf War

If impressive resumes translated into leadership, they'd be carving George Bush's bust on Mt. Rushmore right now. After all, he was a Yale graduate, a World War II hero, an ambassador to China, a CIA director, and vice president under Reagan.

Bush was easily elected president in 1988 after waging a rather sleazy campaign against Democratic nominee Michael Dukakis. Voters were so turned off by the campaign and politics in general that the turnout was the lowest for a presidential election since 1924.

As president, Bush was hampered by several things. Democrats controlled both houses of Congress. Reagan's personal popularity was a hard act to follow. And Bush was simply not much of a leader, especially when it came to solving domestic problems.

His leadership was put to a stern test in 1990. On Aug. 2, the army of Iraq invaded and quickly took over the small neighboring country of Kuwait. Iraq was led by a brutal bozo named Saddam Hussein who proclaimed he was annexing Kuwait to Iraq and anyone who didn't like it could stuff it.

Bush chose not to stuff it. If you were a Bush supporter, his decision to intervene was based on his desire to defend the defenseless. If you were a bit more cynical, you'd be more likely to say it was to protect U.S. interests in Kuwait's oil production. Whatever the reason, in the weeks following the Iraqi invasion, Bush convinced other world leaders to establish a trade embargo on Iraq. Almost simultaneously, the U.S., Britain, France, Egypt, Saudi Arabia, and other countries began assembling a massive armed force in case the economic pressure didn't work.

TECHNICAL STUFF

Gulf War stats

About 540,000 U.S. troops were involved in the Gulf War. Of the 146 U.S. troops killed in action, it is estimated that about 25 percent were killed by "friendly fire" from allied troops. A total of 27,243 bronze stars for "heroic or meritorious achievement" were awarded during the seven-week war. After the war, about 90,000 troops complained of fatigue, skin rashes, headaches, and other symptoms. A decade later, no cause had been found for the syndrome, although possibilities ranged from allergic reactions to vaccinations to the use of nerve gas by Iraq. The war's estimated cost for the allies was put at $61.1 billion, $53.8 billion of which was paid by countries other than the U.S.

REMEMBER

When the economic pressure didn't work, the U.S. and its allies launched a gigantic aerial assault on Iraq on Jan. 16, 1991. After six weeks of massive bombardment, the allied forces sent in ground troops. The vaunted Iraqi military turned out to be made of papier-mâché. U.S. casualties were light, and about 100 hours after the ground war started, Iraq threw in the towel.

The victory, however, was not all that victorious. Kuwait was free, but the Iraqi dictator Saddam remained in power. Nine years after the war, the U.S. was still spending $2 billion a year to enforce a "no fly" zone over Northern Iraq, kept an armada of Navy ships in the area, and maintained a force of 25,000 troops in the region.

Back on the home front

If the Gulf War left a sour taste in the mouths of Americans who questioned its purpose, necessity, and results, things at home weren't much sweeter. For one thing, the economy was in the dumpster. The federal government, along with many individuals and corporations, had borrowed heavily in the 1980s causing the number of bankruptcies in the country to soar. The biggest mess was in the savings and loan industry.

IN THEIR WORDS

"Four score and seven..."

Good question

"People, I just want to say, you know, can we all get along? Can we just get along?"

— Rodney King, to reporters during the L.A. Riots, May 2, 1992

The Reagan Administration, in its quest to lessen the role of government, had pushed to loosen up regulations on savings and loan companies. The result was that many of them overextended credit and made stupid investments. Many of them collapsed. Tens of thousands of investors lost their savings and the federal government had to spend billions of dollars to bail many of the S&Ls out.

Not all the disharmony was economic. On March 3, 1992, a 25-year-old black man named Rodney King was pulled over for reckless driving by Los Angeles police. A witness happened to videotape several of the police officers beating King. Despite the videotaped evidence, an all-white jury acquitted the police. Los Angeles erupted in the worst U.S. domestic violence in more than a century. Before it was over, 53 people died, 4,000 were injured, 500 fires had been set, and more than $1 billion was lost in property damage (see Figure 22-1).

Figure 22-1: Aftermath of the Los Angeles riots.

All of this did not bode well for the incumbent president. Not only were Americans generally dissatisfied with the way things were, but Bush's troubles were also compounded by an eccentric Texan named Ross Perot. Perot was a billionaire who decided to run for president as a third party candidate and finance his own campaign. Despite his immense wealth, Perot ran as a populist, railing against the influence of special interests in the political process.

When the votes were counted, Perot had gathered an impressive 19 percent, the best showing by a third party candidate since Theodore Roosevelt in 1912. Bush finished second. The winner was a 46-year-old Democrat who had been elected governor of Arkansas five times.

His name was William Jefferson Clinton, and the name of his hometown said a lot about the feelings of the country as it as it headed down the homestretch of the twentieth century. The name of the town was Hope.

Gee, Grandpa, What Else Happened?

Sept. 5, 1975: Lynette "Squeaky" Fromme, a follower of the mass murderer Charlie Manson, points a gun at President Ford while Ford is visiting the state Capitol at Sacramento, Calif. The gun misfires. Less than three weeks later in

San Francisco, a sometime radical named Sara Jane Moore fires a gun at Ford from about 40 feet away. A bystander, Oliver Sipple, slaps Moore's arm as she fires, and the bullet misses.

Nov. 1, 1977: The federal minimum wage is raised to $2.65 an hour, with an increase to $3.35 an hour scheduled for 1981.

June 9, 1978: The Church of Jesus Christ of Latter Day Saints (Mormons) opens the church's priesthood to black males.

Feb. 2, 1980: The U.S. hockey team beats Finland 4–2 to win the Olympic gold medal. A few days earlier, the team had upset the vaunted Soviet team, making hockey fans of millions of Americans who didn't know a puck from a Zamboni.

Dec. 2, 1982: A retired dentist named Barney Clark has his heart replaced by a plastic and metal device — an artificial heart — in an operation at Salt Lake City.

Oct. 25, 1983: U.S. Marines invade and conquer the small Caribbean island nation of Grenada, after a communist-backed coup had taken place. President Reagan defends the action as necessary to protect about 1,000 Americans on the island.

Sept. 11, 1985: Pete Rose of the Cincinnati Reds gets the 4,192nd hit of his career, breaking Ty Cobb's record for hits in a career. At this point, Rose seems a sure bet for baseball's hall of fame. But in 2000, he was still out for allegedly wagering on baseball games while he was still a player and manager.

April 15, 1986: U.S. jets bomb targets in Libya in retaliation for Libya's suspected role in a terrorist bombing in Germany ten days before. Two U.S. pilots are killed, along with an unknown number of Libyans.

Oct. 19, 1987: The New York stock market plunges 508 points, or 22.6 percent of its total. The collapse wipes out $500 million in stock equity, the worst day in market history.

Aug. 24–26, 1992: Hurricane Andrew slams through South Florida, killing at least 15 people, destroying 85,000 homes, and causing more than $15 billion in damage. It is the most expensive natural disaster in U.S. history.

Chapter 23

The Future is Now: 1993–2000

● ●

In This Chapter

▶ Taking a look at President Clinton

▶ Handling terrorism on American soil

▶ Dealing with the outbreak of AIDS and the use of drugs

▶ Introducing e-mail, the Internet, and a global economy

▶ Viewing the new look of Americans

▶ Timeline

● ●

America was, toward the end of the twentieth century, on top of the world. Communism had crumbled. The economy, after a slow start, spent much of the decade in overdrive, sparked by revolutions in how we communicate and do business with each other and the rest of the world.

But the 1990s weren't all fun and games. Terrorism and violent confrontations between the government and domestic fringe groups came home to this country after having been regarded as events that were confined to foreign shores. And the president of the United States got caught with his zipper down.

Testing America: The Clinton Administration

Less than half the people who voted for a presidential candidate in 1992 voted for Bill Clinton, which shows there were a pretty fair number of people who disliked him or didn't trust him. At 46, he was the youngest president since John F. Kennedy. Like his fellow Democrat, Clinton could be charming and affable and had a weakness for women. Clinton was the first of the "baby boomer" generation — those born between 1946 and 1960 — to be president. He had avoided the draft during Vietnam and admitted that he smoked marijuana at least once. In short, he was a new kind of chief executive.

AMERICAN FACES

Hillary Rodham Clinton

She was the most powerful first lady in U.S. history — and maybe the most humiliated.

She was born Hillary Diane Rodham in 1947 in Chicago. Her father, a staunch Republican, owned a drapery-making business. After graduating from Wellesley College, Rodham enrolled at Yale Law School. There she met another law student named Bill Clinton. The two were married in 1975, and Clinton became attorney general, and then governor, of Arkansas. During her husband's time as a state elected official, Hillary Clinton had an active private law practice, as well as leading programs to reform the state's education system and other children's programs.

During the 1992 campaign, she helped defuse allegations about her husband's philandering by acknowledging it was true and then suggesting it was really none of America's business. Before and after the election, Clinton referred to his wife as the "co-president," and put her in charge of getting his health care reform plan through Congress. She also had influence on other administration policies.

When the Monica Lewinsky scandal broke, Rodham Clinton kept quiet, stood by her husband, and endured the embarrassment. And in 2000, she was elected a U.S. senator from New York, the first First Lady to win a major political office.

"She's a very unusual first lady, and she's been through a lot," observed former White House press secretary Mike McCurry in 1999. "But she's broken through a special kind of glass ceiling."

Presiding over a nation

REMEMBER

Clinton's first big battle as president was over his ambitious plan to reform the country's health care system. It was a system plagued by soaring costs, blindingly confusing programs, and increasing unavailability to the unemployed and the uninsured. As the baby boomers aged and needed more medical care, the strain on the system would only get worse.

Clinton put his wife, Hillary, in charge of getting his reforms through Congress. But her efforts were hampered when she became embroiled in a probe into the financial dealings of an Arkansas company called the Whitewater Development Corporation. The Whitewater probe led to Hillary Clinton becoming the first first lady to be subpoenaed in a criminal investigation. Coupled with her stubbornness in refusing to compromise with legislators, the scandal helped sink the president's health care reforms.

On the foreign front, Clinton was cautious. He did push through the North American Free Trade Agreement (NAFTA), which greatly reduced barriers between the U.S., Canada, and Mexico. But his biggest challenge came in what was the former country of Yugoslavia, which had split into smaller states after the collapse of Soviet dominance in Europe in the late 1980s. In one of the states, Bosnia, Serbian, Croatian, and Bosnian groups were fighting a civil war that threatened to spread. When diplomatic efforts failed, the U.S. and other nations sent in "peacekeeping" troops to enforce a fragile truce. Later in the decade, U.S. military forces and other countries also intervened when the former Yugoslavian state of Serbia invaded and terrorized Kosovo. The allied forces restored order, at least temporarily.

The failure of Clinton's health care reforms, plus a series of mini-scandals at the White House, combined with the clever political strategy of a Georgia congressman named Newt Gingrich, gave the Republicans control of both houses of Congress for the first time since 1946. Gingrich was elected House speaker.

Pushing the "Contract with America"

During the 1994 congressional campaign, Republicans had come up with a conservative litany of policies they said they would pursue if they came to power. They called it the "Contract with America," and after the election they began pushing an array of programs that were aimed at reducing federal spending on social programs, easing environmental rules, and cutting taxes and cutting government regulations on business and industry.

Clinton, sensing that the political mood of the country was shifting to the center, went along for the ride. In August 1996, he signed into law the Welfare Reform Act, which tightened up federal aid to those who wouldn't or couldn't work, and shifted more responsibility to the states. By the end of the decade, welfare rolls in much of the country had shrunk considerably. Well before the welfare bill, however, Clinton had shown his willingness to hug the middle. Shortly after taking office in 1993, he tried to end the ban on gays in the military. When a firestorm of opposition arose, he retreated to a "don't ask, don't tell" policy that said gays could serve in the military as long as they didn't tell anyone they were gay.

IN THEIR WORDS
"Four score and seven..."

I shall not tell a lie. . . .

"I want you to listen to me. I'm going to say this again. I did not have sexual relations with that woman, Miss Lewinsky. I never told anybody to lie a single time. Never. These allegations are false, and I need to go back to work for the American people."

— President Bill Clinton, January 21, 1998.

Bettor days

Americans have always been gamblers. Many of our ancestors gambled big-time just to get here in the first place. But chances are very few of them ever envisioned just how much legal U.S. gambling there would eventually be.

Fueled by relaxed moral views, more leisure time, and governments looking to raise money without raising taxes, legal gambling boomed in the last quarter of the twentieth century. In 1999, 37 states ran lotteries, 28 had casinos run by Native Americans, and only two — Utah and Hawaii — had no forms of legal wagering. It's estimated Americans bet $630 billion in 1998, which is more than they spent on groceries, movie tickets, and books combined.

Some of the biggest beneficiaries of all this betting were American Indians. Thanks to their status as sovereign nations and a 1988 congressional act, many — although by no means all — tribes were prospering from casinos they opened on tribal lands.

In 1999, a special federal gambling commission ended a two-year examination of the nation's gambling habits and made more than 70 recommendations to Congress and state legislatures, including urging a slowdown in the spread of more gambling. Few, however, were willing to bet on that happening.

But facing re-election in 1996, Clinton did not completely abandon the liberals who had voted for him in 1992. When the president and Congress could not agree on a federal budget, the government all but shut down in November 1995 and January 1996. The public largely blamed the Republicans in Congress, in part because Gingrich was viewed as something of a political weasel outside Washington. By 1998, the "Republican resurgence" was all but over, and Gingrich left Congress altogether.

The public's apathy toward the Republicans' "contract" combined with the fact that the economy was doing well. It was enough to allow Clinton to easily win re-election over Kansas Senator Bob Dole. One of Clinton's most ardent supporters in his re-election effort was a young White House intern named Monica Lewinsky.

Judging a president

Bill Clinton had had troubles with women before. During the 1992 presidential campaign, a nightclub singer named Gennifer Flowers claimed she and Clinton had a long affair while he was governor of Arkansas. Clinton first denied it, and then acknowledged that during his marriage he had committed adultery. As president, he was also unsuccessfully sued for allegedly sexually harassing a former Arkansas state employee named Paula Jones while he was governor.

Then in January 1998, it was revealed that an independent investigator named Kenneth Starr, appointed by Congress to look into the Whitewater real estate mess around Hillary Clinton, was also looking into a possible sexual relationship between Clinton and Monica Lewinsky. Lewinsky came to the White House in 1995 as a 21-year-old unpaid intern. She went on the White House payroll a few months later, but was transferred to the Pentagon after some Clinton aides thought she was getting too cozy with the president.

At first, Clinton and Lewinsky denied any hanky-panky. Clinton also adamantly denied he ever asked Lewinsky to lie about their relationship. As the months passed, however, the truth began to emerge. In a national TV address in August 1998, Clinton admitted to "a relationship with Miss Lewinsky that was not appropriate."

On October 8, the Republican-controlled House of Representatives voted to bring impeachment charges against Clinton, basically for fooling around with Lewinsky and then lying about it (although the formal charges were obstructing justice, tampering with witnesses, and lying under oath). He was impeached a few weeks later, the second president in U.S. history to be tried in the Senate.

But public polls showed that while most Americans were pretty disgusted with Clinton's morals, they didn't want to see him thrown out of office for them. The Senate agreed, and on February 12, 1999, it voted to acquit him.

Terrorism at Home

For most of the twentieth century, terrorism — using acts of violence to make a political point — was something most Americans regarded as a foreign pastime. But in the 1990s, the country found out just how small the world had become.

Not everyone thought terrorism was confined to the private sector. A small but fervent group of Americans believed the U.S. government was part of various international conspiracies bent on world domination. By 1997, right-wing paramilitary or survivalist groups had developed in every state. Some were led by Vietnam-era vets who felt betrayed by the government, others by religious fanatics, and still others by white supremacists.

Ruby Ridge

One such group formed in Idaho, about 40 miles from the Canadian border, at a place called Ruby Ridge. On August 21, 1992, U.S. marshals were watching a white supremacist named Randy Weaver when shots were fired. A marshal and Weaver's 14-year-old son were killed. The next day, an FBI sniper killed

Weaver's wife and wounded another man. At a subsequent trial, Weaver and another defendant were acquitted of all but one minor charge, and the government agreed to pay $3.1 million to the Weaver family for the incident. "Ruby Ridge" became a rallying cry for "militia" groups of all types.

Waco

By his own admission, Vernon Wayne Howell had an unhappy childhood, and by the time he was 22, he was still seeking something to belong to. So in 1981, he chose the Branch Davidians, a religious sect that in 1935 had settled about 10 miles outside of Waco, Texas. By 1990, Howell had changed his name to David Koresh and was head of the cult. Koresh called himself the messiah and took multiple wives from among his followers.

On February 28, 1993, federal agents looking for illegal weapons and explosives tried a surprise raid on the Branch Davidian compound. But Koresh had apparently been tipped off they were coming, and a gunfight erupted. Four agents and two cult members were killed, and a 51-day siege of the compound began.

On April 19, after negotiations with Koresh to surrender had stalled, federal agents attacked the compound and fired tear gas inside. A fire broke out and spread rapidly. When it was over, at least 82 people were dead, including 17 children. The government contended it had acted responsibly. Critics claimed it was at best a reckless mistake, and at worst, murder. One of the critics was a skinny 29-year-old former soldier named Timothy McVeigh.

AMERICAN FACES

Jimmy Buffett

Quick, name the only four authors who have topped the *New York Times* best-seller lists for both fiction and non-fiction? Right: John Steinbeck, William Styron, Ernest Hemingway — and Jimmy Buffett.

Buffett was born in 1946 in Mississippi. After spending some time in college, Buffett tried to become a country music star. But it soon became clear his musical mixture of rock, country, and Caribbean sounds didn't easily fit any one genre.

Neither did Buffett. While none of his records were smash hits, his concerts were consistently among the biggest draws in the country. He parlayed that popularity into a writing career that saw both a 1992 novel and a 1998 autobiography top the charts. He also wrote and produced a successful musical, opened a couple of popular restaurants, put out a line of clothing, and did it all while piloting his own seaplane.

"He calls me from time to time for advice," said billionaire investor Warren Buffett, his cousin, "but I should be calling him."

SIDETRIP

The People versus "The Juice"

It may have been unique in U.S. history: a national icon who was an accused double murderer.

Orenthal James Simpson — better known to his fans as "O.J." or "The Juice" — was a Hall-of-Fame football player who had been a successful movie actor and TV commercial spokesman. On June 12, 1994, Simpson's former wife, Nicole Brown Simpson, and her friend, Ronald Goldman, were brutally knifed to death in front of Nicole's Los Angeles condominium.

Simpson was a suspect and agreed to surrender to police. Instead, he led them on an incredible slow-motion, nationally televised chase along L.A. freeways before surrendering in the

driveway of his mansion. The evidence against Simpson seemed overwhelming. But after a trial that became an international media circus, Simpson was acquitted.

Critics claimed it was a result of a rich man being able to hire the best criminal defense attorneys in the country. Simpson lost a 1997 civil suit to the families of Nicole and Goldman and was ordered to pay $33.5 million for being responsible for their deaths.

"I'll never pay a dime of that verdict," Simpson said in a 2000 interview. "I didn't commit this crime. I don't believe I owe anything."

Oklahoma City

Not all of the mayhem of the 1990s involved government action. On February 26, 1993, the World Trade Center building in New York City was rocked by a bomb that killed six people. Members of a radical Islamic group were arrested and convicted of the crime.

But it was Waco that stuck in the mind of Timothy McVeigh. A Gulf War veteran, McVeigh believed the U.S. government had become part of an international totalitarian conspiracy. With a friend, Terry Nichols, McVeigh decided to do something about it.

On the morning of April 19, 1995, the nine-story Alfred P. Murrah Building, a federal office complex in Oklahoma City, was blasted by a powerful bomb (see Figure 23-1). The blast rained down concrete and glass for blocks around. A total of 168 people were killed, including 19 children who had been at the building's day care center. It was America's worst act of terrorism, and it stunned the nation. "This is why we live in Oklahoma," exclaimed a disbelieving woman. "Things like this don't happen here."

McVeigh and Nichols were arrested shortly after the bombing. At their trials, prosecutors charged the bomb — a mixture of fertilizer and fuel oil in a truck parked outside the building — had been set to mark the second anniversary of the Waco tragedy. McVeigh was sentenced to death in 1997, Nichols to life in prison.

Figure 23-1:
Result of the Oklahoma City bombing.

And in between the bombing and the sentencings, America was shook by yet another bombing, this one in a park in Atlanta during the 1996 Summer Olympics. Two people died and 111 injured.

The Unabomber

Other 1990s terrorists were more intellectual than McVeigh. Theodore Kaczynski was an eccentric hermit who had been a university math professor and had retreated to life in a tiny plywood shack in Montana. From there he mailed bombs to people he deemed were part of society's "evil" homage to technology. Over 18 years, Kaczynski mailed 16 bombs, killing three people, injuring 23, and triggering a massive manhunt. He became known as the "Unabomber," because his initial targets were universities and airlines.

Jesse Ventura

He may not have been the smartest governor Minnesota ever had, but it's safe to say that at 6'4" and 250 pounds, he could beat up most of America's other chief executives.

Born James Janos in Minneapolis in 1951, he attended community college, rode with a motorcycle gang in California, became a frogman/commando with the Navy SEALs in Vietnam — and then became a professional wrestler. As Jesse "the Body" Ventura, he was a popular "heel," or villain. After his career in the ring ended, he became a wrestling TV commentator, an action movie actor, a radio talk show host, and mayor of a Minneapolis suburb.

In 1998, he was the gubernatorial nominee of the Reform Party. No one gave him much of a chance to defeat Republican incumbent Norm Coleman or Democrat Hubert Humphrey III. But Ventura ran a populist campaign heavily leavened with candor and humor. On election night, he won 37 percent of the vote, which was enough to win in the three-man race. As governor, Ventura continued to gain national attention for his candid, and sometimes outrageous statements, and seemed to have a fast learning curve when it came to running the state.

And he had the hands-down best title of any governor for his autobiography. He called it "I Ain't Got Time to Bleed."

He was caught after he successfully demanded the *Washington Post* publish a long and rambling "manifesto" he had written. Kaczynski's brother recognized the thoughts as his brother's and contacted federal agents. Kaczynski was arrested and pled guilty in 1997.

Incidents like Oklahoma City and whackos like the Unabomber served notice on America that it was no longer an oasis of security in a dangerous world. If they needed another reminder, it came in 1995. Mindful of the possibility of a terrorist attack, Pennsylvania Avenue, the street in front of the White House, was closed to traffic.

Making Ourselves Sick

While the bombs and terrorism of the 1990s were scary, many more Americans were affected by different kinds of horrors: the twin plagues of AIDS and drugs.

Suffering from AIDS

First documented in 1981, AIDS (Acquired Immune Deficiency Syndrome) comes from the HIV virus, which in turn is spread by the exchange of bodily fluids, such as blood and semen. People could have the virus — be "HIV-positive" — and not have AIDS. Once the virus transmuted, however, death was a near certainty. Most of the early cases were among gay men, and there weren't all that many cases. "Only" 21,517 were reported in 1986.

SIDETRIP

Big Mac

Baseball had been the "National Pastime" for most of the century, but by the 1990s it was no longer the dominant pro sport. Football, basketball, and even hockey had made deep inroads into its popularity. Baseball had been wracked with labor strife in the decade and seemed to be populated with overpaid, selfish players and greedy team owners.

But on September 8, 1998, it's safe to say most sports-minded Americans were tuned into a baseball game in St. Louis between the hometown Cardinals and the Chicago Cubs. In the fourth inning, a tall, muscular 35-year-old first baseman for St. Louis named Mark McGwire hit the ball over the left field wall. It was his 62nd homerun of the season — a new major league record that broke the 37-year-old mark set by Roger Maris of the New York Yankees, and one of the most celebrated records in sports.

McGwire's feat was the highlight of a season that saw him battle back and forth with the Cubs' Sammy Sosa. Sosa finished the season with 66 homers; McGwire with 70. The race proved a big boost to baseball attendance, and the National Pastime was again on top of the sports world.

Still, AIDS was sobering on two levels besides the most important, which was the loss of life. Medical science had conquered many diseases by the end of the twentieth century and lessened the impact of many others. AIDS was a chilling reminder that man was still not master of his own medical fate.

The other level of AIDS's impact was political. Gays had made important strides in gaining the status of other minority groups. Some openly gay candidates had won elective office, and some states and cities had begun banning discrimination on the basis of sexual preference. But the spread of AIDS was seen by many homophobes as God's revenge against gays, and many people who previously considered themselves open-minded on the issue began to worry about contracting the disease from even casual contact with homosexuals.

As the disease spread from the gay community to intravenous drug users and heterosexuals, the numbers became epidemic. By the early 1990s, as many as 1.5 million Americans were believed to have the HIV virus, and 280,000 had died. But as the number of victims grew, so did public tolerance of the afflicted. Public sympathy was fueled in part by the revelations of public figures with the disease, such as basketball star Magic Johnson and Olympic diver Greg Louganis.

In 1997, the U.S. Supreme Court ruled that people with the HIV virus were covered by federal disability laws. And while no cure had been found by the end of the century, drug treatments had begun to show some success in staving off the disease and AIDS-prevention education programs had begun to reduce the number of new AIDS cases.

Toni Morrison

She turned to writing because of an unhappy marriage, and her husband's loss turned out to be the literary world's gain.

Chloe Anthony Wofford was born in Ohio in 1931 to an African-American family who had left the South to escape racism. Wofford grew up in a relatively racism-free environment. After graduating from college (where she took the name "Toni" because some people had trouble pronouncing her name), she became a university teacher. She married a young architect named Harold Morrison in 1958. But the marriage was an unhappy one, and she joined an amateur writing group to escape.

After getting a divorce, Morrison moved to New York and became a book editor. She also continued to write, and published her first novel, "The Bluest Eye," in 1970. Her fifth novel, "Beloved," won the 1988 Pulitzer Prize, and in 1993 she was given the Nobel Prize for Literature, the first African American woman to win the award.

"Tell us," she challenged black writers in her acceptance speech, "what it is to live at the edge of towns that cannot bear your company."

Morrison has told us that, and more.

Dealing with drugs

A much longer-lived malady than AIDS was America's drug habit. It was a habit that could be traced back to the addictions of Civil War veterans to laudanum and other painkillers used in the war.

But it really became epidemic in the 1980s and 1990s with the spread of "crack," a cheap, potent, and smokable form of cocaine, especially in the country's inner cities. The production and distribution of crack and other drugs became a multi-billion-dollar business, and America became the most lucrative market in the world for drug cartels in Asia and Central and South America. A 1997 national survey found 77 million Americans said they had used an illegal drug at least once.

The blossoming drug trade triggered deadly turf wars in U.S. cities as rival gangs battled for control of the local drug markets. Not since the gang wars of Prohibition had American streets seen so much gunfire — and this time it was with automatic weapons that sprayed bullets all over the place and killed many innocent bystanders.

By 1990, more people were being sent to U.S. jails and prisons for drug-related offenses than for any other crime. The war on drugs ground on through the 1990s, and when the use of crack declined, the use of methamphetamine, or "crank," grew. By the end of the decade, a new drug called "ecstasy" had made an appearance, and the U.S. justice system had made little lasting impact on America's addictions.

Creating a World of Change

The last decade of the twentieth century saw America, and the rest of the world, undergo some pretty revolutionary changes. One of the biggest was in the development of technology, particularly in computers. The speed of their development was staggering. A theory put forward in 1975 by Gordon Moore, a pioneer in computer technology, was that silicon chips — the souls of computers — would double in complexity every two years, and it turned out to be even faster. As the chips got more complex, their uses grew, and as their uses grew, their prices dropped. In 1994, a computer sophisticated enough to do high-speed, three-dimensional graphics for things like military flight simulators cost $300,000. In 2000, better computers than that were available in kids' video game systems for $400.

Many of the advances were in communications, and sharing information became as big a business as manufacturing a product. The number of cellular phones in the country, for example, jumped from less than 10 million in 1990 to more than 100 million in 2000.

Entering the e-mail revolution

In the early 1960s, some American scientists began kicking around the idea of a computer system, using research computers called "nodes," that could continue to function even in the event of a nuclear war. That possibility was of keen interest to the Pentagon, which financed much of the work.

The result, in late 1969, was the birth of the Internet, which led to "e-mail," which led to a communications revolution. By the late 1990s, virtually every part of the world was linked to every other part. Americans alone sent an estimated 2.2 billion e-mail messages *per day,* or about seven times the number of pieces of first-class mail. By the end of 2000, it was estimated e-mail messages had replaced 25 percent of what was now referred to as "snail mail."

But the Internet, which gave birth to a network of information sources called the World Wide Web, did far more than make it easier to check in on Grandma or chat with Uncle Louie in the old country. It allowed businesses to reduce their costs and be more efficient by instantly knowing how much inventory they needed to keep on hand, how much of a product they needed to make, and who could supply them with the raw materials and parts they needed.

Retail customers could comparison-shop in businesses across the country and around the world — and they did. "Online" shopping for the Christmas holidays in 1999 was estimated at $7.3 billion. In 2000, it was expected to be $12.5 billion.

A pawn for Deep Blue

Garry Kasparov didn't offer to shake hands with his opponent after winning the chess match four games to two in February 1996. It wasn't just Kasparov's well-known arrogance — his opponent had no arms. Kasparov, the world chess champion since 1985, had been beaten by IBMRS/6000SP, a computer christened "Deep Blue" by its IBM Corporation designers.

The win was called a victory for man over machine, in an age seemingly dominated by machines that could do nearly everything better than humans. Kasparov readily agreed to a rematch the following year.

It was a bad move for the grandmaster. On May 11, 1997, Kasparov stormed out of a small room in New York City after being soundly thrashed by the computer, which had been tweaked and tuned since the first match. Deep Blue could execute 200 million possible moves in a second.

Kasparov did prove, however, that there are some things machines still can't match up to humans on: After its loss, the machine didn't whine or complain nearly as much as the defeated man did after his.

The computer revolution had impacts far beyond shopping and business. It led to amazing advances in medicine and biological research. And it led to a very real reduction in the time and space between America and the rest of the world, creating a true "global economy."

Trading under a global economy

The global economy — an economy that closely tied together the production and consumer patterns of many nations — was created not only by the development of information-sharing technologies and computers, but by many countries dropping their trade barriers and opening their markets to the rest of the world.

One of the effects of the global economy was the creation of a wave of "mega mergers" among big corporations from different countries: Daimler Benz of Germany with Chrysler in automobiles, British Petroleum of England with Amoco in oil. The bigger companies promised, and often delivered, more efficiencies, better products, and lower prices.

But there were drawbacks. The intertwining of economies meant America was more affected by downturns in other parts of the world. Products from other parts of the world were often more attractive to American consumers than their U.S.-made counterparts, and the country's trade deficit steadily rose — from $155 billion in 1997 to $299 billion just two years later.

And many U.S. companies exported jobs as well as products, by transferring their manufacturing operations to countries where the cost of labor was much lower. In Thailand, for example, a worker might be paid $2 for a nine-hour day making footwear, or a worker in Haiti might be paid $2.50 a day to make shirts. But while critics complained it was exploiting foreign workers, the companies responded that the wages were fair by Third World standards and helped the countries build their own manufacturing bases.

The global economy did seem to favor the top of the economic food chain. The top 1 percent of income earners saw their incomes grow an additional 31 percent between 1991 and 1997, while the bottom 90 percent's income grew just 3 percent. And it was so easy to spend money, Americans did it with enthusiasm. Savings rates dropped to almost nothing by the end of the decade, leaving many Americans in a precarious position when and if the economy went into a tailspin.

There were few signs of that happening, however, as the century ended. In 1997, the average U.S. family's annual income passed $40,000 for the first time. The number of people below the poverty level set by the federal government fell to 11.8 percent, the lowest since 1979, and the poverty rates among African- and Asian-Americans fell to their lowest levels ever. Even Congress couldn't spend fast enough to keep up with the sparkling economy. The federal budget went from having an annual deficit of $300 billion at the beginning of the decade to a surplus of $123 billion at the end.

Getting a New Look

America entered the twenty-first century with a lot more gray around the temples than it had 100 years earlier. The number of Americans over the age of 65 more than doubled from 1960 to the mid 1990s, and the number past the age of 85 more than tripled.

Even as people were living longer, the birthrate in the 1980s and 1990s declined, and the oldest of the baby boomers were entering their 50s. The result of this "graying of America" was a growing political concern with medical care, Social Security, and other "senior" issues. The growth in their numbers also gave seniors more political clout as a group.

But gray wasn't the only color America was turning. Immigration had generally declined from 1910 to 1970. But in the 1970s, there were four million legal immigrants, and six million more in the 1980s. Millions more came illegally. Most of the newcomers were from Asia or Latin America. In the nation's most populous state, California, more than half the residents were non-white in 1999.

As usual, when there was a surge in immigration, there was an outcry from some quarters that the new immigrants would prove a drain on the country's social service resources and the economy. Actually, a 1997 study by the National Academy of Sciences found that the impact of immigrants on the economy wasn't all that big a deal either way.

But at least one group of new immigrants was being welcomed with open arms. In October 2000, Congress overwhelmingly approved a bill that would almost double the number of legal immigrants who had skills in high technology fields.

Gee, Grandpa, What Else Happened?

June–July 1993: A series of drenching storms strike the Midwest, killing 50 people and leaving 70,000 homeless over nine states. Eight million acres are flooded, and damage is put at $12 billion.

Aug. 8, 1993: Four U.S. soldiers are killed in the African nation of Somalia after their jeep runs over a land mine. The soldiers are part of a multi-national peacekeeping force in the country. The deaths bring the total number of U.S. troops who have died there so far to 12.

Jan. 17, 1994: A pre-dawn earthquake rumbles through the Los Angeles area, killing 61, collapsing freeways, and damaging or destroying 45,000 residences.

Aug. 11, 1994: Major league baseball players go on strike, causing cancellation of the World Series for the first time since it began in 1903.

Oct. 16, 1995: Hundreds of thousands of African American men gather in Washington D.C. for the "Million Man March." The event is organized by Nation of Islam leader Louis Farrakhan, who challenges black men to be more responsible fathers and community members.

Nov. 19, 1997: A 29-year-old seamstress in Des Moines, Iowa, named Bobbi McCaughey gives birth to seven children: four boys and three girls. The septuplets are the second known set to be born alive, and the first to all survive their first month.

Feb. 26, 1998: Television talk show hostess Oprah Winfrey prevails in a lawsuit brought against her by Texas cattle ranchers. The ranchers alleged Winfrey damaged their business by saying on her show that an outbreak of Mad Cow Disease in Britain "just stopped me cold from eating another burger."

April 20, 1999: Two teenaged boys enter a high school in Littleton, Colorado, with guns and explosives. They kill 12 students and a teacher before killing themselves. It is the worst of several tragedies that center on guns and kids during the year.

Aug. 27, 1999: Scientists report that for the first time ever, water in liquid form has been found in an object from outer space, a meteorite discovered in Texas. They are not sued by Texas cattle ranchers.

Jan 1, 2000: Despite widespread fears that computers would be unable to read the date correctly and crash — the "Y2K effect" — America and the rest of the world slides into the new year with only minor problems. The U.S. Commerce Department estimates more than $100 billion was spent from 1995 to 1999 to fix the problem.

June 7, 2000: A federal judge orders the breakup of giant technology company Microsoft, saying it can't be trusted to obey U.S. anti-trust laws. The order, which is appealed, sends shock waves through the high-tech world.

Part V
The Part of Tens

The 5th Wave — By Rich Tennant

"Oh, will you take that thing off before you embarrass someone!"

In this part . . .

Americans love lists, from best baseball players to best ice cream flavors. Part of the reason is because we love to argue, and there's nothing like a list of someone else's choices to engender a debate.

So here's a part to take to cocktail parties, gatherings of relatives, or the office water cooler. It has the ten best and ten worst presidents, ten historical events that never really happened, ten inventions that changed life as we know it, and ten events that had an impact on American culture. Who says so? Me. You can make up your own lists.

Chapter 24

The 10 Best — and 10 Worst — Presidents

. . . .

Here's something to inform, amuse, or irritate you: The author's choices for the 10 brightest lights and 10 dimmest bulbs to occupy the White House as chief executives.

The Best

Here are the 10 best presidents, starting with the very best and ending with the really good:

1. **Abraham Lincoln:** He saved the country. Period.

2. **Franklin D. Roosevelt:** He faced two major crises, the Depression and World War II, and handled both of them.

3. **George Washington:** Being first is never easy, and he set a great example.

4. **Thomas Jefferson:** A man of boundless talent.

5. **Theodore Roosevelt:** At times both tireless and tiresome, he got things done.

6. **Andrew Jackson:** Like Teddy Roosevelt, he suppressed a personal impulse for excess to accomplish much in a tumultuous time.

7. **Woodrow Wilson:** Cranky, stubborn, and idealistic, he followed his own advice: "The president is at liberty . . . to be as big a man as he can."

8. **Harry Truman:** Coming after FDR was a very tough act to follow, and he more than held his own.

9. **James K. Polk:** Hey, this guy did everything he said he would do, and then had the good sense to get out.

10. **John Adams:** It's tough being second, too. Adams sacrificed his career, and the life of his political party, to keep the country out of war.

The Worst

Now, here are the 10 worst presidents, starting with the very worst and ending with the merely bad:

1. **William Henry Harrison:** During his inaugural address, Harrison promised to let Congress direct the government. Then he died a month after taking office. You can't do much less.

2. **Richard Nixon:** He disgraced the office, and would be No. 1 on this list except that he actually had some far-sighted environmental and foreign policies.

3. **James Buchanan:** Totally unqualified for the job and proved it.

4. **Warren G. Harding:** A nice guy and a terrible president.

5. **Ulysses S. Grant:** A great general and a terrible president.

6. **Zachary Taylor:** Never voted, had no vision or agenda. Biggest accomplishment may have been dying 16 months after taking office.

7. **Millard Fillmore:** Only became president because Taylor died. So unimpressive his own party refused to nominate him at the next election.

8. **Calvin Coolidge:** He would have made a great eighteenth century French king: He hated changes in the status quo and liked wearing silly hats.

9. **Franklin Pierce:** Unwittingly did his best to make it harder to find a peaceful solution to the issue of slavery by repeatedly making bad decisions.

10. **Jimmy Carter:** One of the country's best ex-presidents.

Chapter 25

Ten Historical Events That Probably Never Happened

• •

*P*art of the charm of U.S. history is that many of the images it conjures up are based on things that never really happened. Many historians are appalled at the acceptance of myths as fact by so many Americans. Many historians should relax. History, after all, is our shared heritage and our collective memories, and if we are a bit fuzzy about some of the details, hey, that's what we have historians for. Still, it is interesting to look at how some fictions have become facts, such as:

The Pilgrims Landed on Plymouth Rock

Not unless they had really long legs. Most scholars put the Pilgrims' landing in 1620 about 10 miles north of the lumpy scrap of stone known as Plymouth Rock. Moreover, chances are the rock was well above the high-tide line when the English expatriates got here. But in 1741, the legend was started by a 95-year-old man who said his dad told him about it. In 1769, the "event" became an annual celebration in New England. By 1835, French visitor Alexis De Tocqueville reported pieces of the rock were being venerated in different American cities, and it was well established as an American icon. Today, what's left of the rock is preserved in a state park near the mouth of Plymouth Harbor.

Paul Revere Warned Everyone in Lexington and Concord that "The British Are Coming! The British Are Coming!"

If he had, it would have confused the heck out of everyone, since most colonists thought of themselves as British too. Actually, Revere did ride to Lexington and warned John Hancock and Sam Adams that British soldiers were coming to arrest them. Revere was then captured by the British on his way to Concord, but they let him go after they heard shots and decided to retreat to Boston. The Revere legend was born when Henry Wadsworth Longfellow wrote a popular, albeit inaccurate, poem about it in 1863. Longfellow left out that Revere was accused of cowardice and insubordination during the Revolutionary War. Revere was court-martialed, but acquitted, and became a successful businessman. But he was by no means a national hero until Longfellow's poem appeared.

The "Liberty Bell" Cracked When It Rang Out for Independence on July 4, 1776

Maybe, just maybe, it rang on July 8, 1776, but not July 4. The bell arrived in Philadelphia from England in 1752, was installed in Independence Hall in 1753 — and promptly cracked. It was melted down and recast, but sounded awful. So it was melted down again, and re-recast. It may have been rung on July 8, 1776, when the Declaration of Independence was read in public, but there is no record of it anywhere. In 1847, a guy named George Lippard wrote a fictional account of how some old bellman rang the bell so hard on July 4, 1776, it cracked. Actually, the bell did crack again, and was silenced for good, on Washington's Birthday in 1846. No matter. The Lippard story struck a chord in the public's imagination and became part of American folklore.

Betsy Ross Sewed the First American Flag

The legend of Betsy Ross and the original Stars and Stripes in 1776 first surfaced in 1870, when one of her grandsons, William J. Canby, recounted a story he said his grandma had told him. According to Canby, George Washington and several others visited Ross at her upholstery shop in Philadelphia and showed her a crude drawing of a flag, which she then produced. Although Ross did make some flags during the period, there is absolutely no record the Canby story was true, and some evidence exists that the flag was not designed until 1780 by a guy named Francis Hopkinson. But Canby and his relatives did such a great public relations job for Grandma, her home in Philly is now an historical site. Trouble is, there is also great doubt that the home actually ever housed Betsy Ross.

Davy Crockett Died Fighting at the Alamo

It's a basic tenet of popular American history: Davy Crockett, icon of Texas independence, mythic hero for millions of baby boomers and merchandising gold mine for Walt Disney, died swinging his rifle at the gates of the Alamo on March 6, 1836. Trouble is, there is some evidence he didn't. Contemporary accounts of the event, including a diary purportedly written by a Mexican army officer who was there, say that Crockett and at least six other Alamo defenders surrendered and then were brutally executed on the personal orders of Mexican General Antonio Lopez de Santa Anna. Defenders of the Crockett legacy insist the diary attributed to a Jose Enrique de la Peña is a fake and contest other evidence that its account is the right one. If it is a fake, however, it's an expensive one: The diary was auctioned off in 1998 for $350,000.

Indians Learned the Practice of Scalping from Europeans

At some point in the twentieth century, it became generally accepted that American Indians learned the practice of taking the scalps of their foes from Europeans, specifically the British. But the facts don't seem to back up the assertion. Archeological and anthropological evidence indicates scalping existed among some tribes before Europeans even visited the New World, and the word "scalp" does not appear as a verb in English books until the late seventeenth century. But it is possible Europeans spread the practice to tribes that did not previously scalp. And there is no doubt Europeans embraced the practice, paying bounties for scalps of enemies. P.S.: Being scalped didn't necessarily mean being killed. There are more than a few instances of scalped people surviving, and not all of them were U.S. Marines at boot camp.

Billy the Kid Killed 21 Men Before He Was 21 Years Old

Like most stories about the Bad Men of the Old West, that's a gross exaggeration. Born Henry McCarty, the desperado who became known as "Billy the Kid" killed four men for sure and may have had a hand in the deaths of six more. The real champion killer of the Old West was probably John Wesley Hardin, a Texas bad man who shot and killed at least 24 men, and perhaps as many as 40, by the time he was 24. He once killed a man for snoring too loud in the next room at a hotel by shooting him through the wall. P.S.: Like Wild Bill Hickock, Hardin was shot from behind and killed while playing poker.

Lincoln Said "You can't fool all the people all the time. . . ."

One of the most famous quotes attributed to Abraham Lincoln is this: "If you once forfeit the confidence of your fellow citizens, you can never regain their respect. You can fool all the people some of the time and some of the people all the time, but you can't fool all the people all the time." But there's no record that he ever really said it. In fact, the quote wasn't even attributed to him until more than 40 years after he died, when some people said they thought they heard him say something like it in 1858 in Illinois. He also never said, "If I knew what brand he used, I'd send every general a barrel," in response to complaints about General U.S. Grant's drinking. But it's a good line.

Teddy Roosevelt Led the "Rough Riders'" Cavalry Charge that Won the Battle of San Juan Hill

Actually, the Rough Riders didn't ride much of anything while fighting in Cuba during the Spanish American War, because they left most of their horses in Florida by mistake. In addition, the Rough Riders were only a few hundred men out of more than 8,000 U.S. soldiers who took part in the battle. In fact, about 1,200 African Americans, known then as "Buffalo Soldiers," had as much to do with the victory as the Rough Riders. But Roosevelt's own account of the battle became so popular, it helped push him along the road to the White House.

John F. Kennedy Wrote "Profiles in Courage," for Which He Was Awarded a Pulitzer Prize in 1957

It's true that Kennedy, then a U.S. senator from Massachusetts, won a Pulitzer for *Profiles in Courage,* a small book about senators who had performed a courageous act while in office. It's also true the book won him national attention and cemented his standing among liberals in the Democratic Party. But it's questionable whether he wrote it, or at least wrote it by himself. There is evidence it was actually written by one of his speechwriters, Theodore Sorenson. It's also probable that *Why England Slept,* an earlier best-selling book on the causes of World War II credited to Kennedy, was at least partly the work of someone else.

Chapter 26

Ten Inventions That Changed Life as We Know It

. . . .

*B*uild a better mousetrap, goes the old saying, and the world will beat a path to your door. But just how good a mousetrap do we need? And who wants the world messing up your lawn beating paths to your door?

No matter. There are things that come along in life that make a difference. Some foster big changes, some so small we don't even really notice them. Here, in more or less chronological order, are ten inventions that changed American life. Some more than others.

Safety Pin (1849)

A New York mechanic named Walter Hunt owed a friend $15. Being an inventive man (he had invented America's first sewing machine, but refused to patent it because he thought it would throw people out of work), Hunt began fiddling with a piece of brass wire, coiling it at the center and shielding the point. In 1849, he patented his invention, but then sold the rights for $400. Which left him $385 ahead.

Elevator (1854)

Elisha Otis was a Vermont man who had to move some stuff upstairs at his boss' bed factory. He could use an elevator — they had been around for decades — but elevators had the unfortunate habit of frequently crashing to the first floor. So Otis came up with a brake system. He demonstrated his invention at an exposition in New York in 1854 — and revolutionized urban life by making it far easier to make buildings taller.

Blue Jeans (1873)

Jacob Davis was a Reno, Nevada, tailor with customers who were tough on their pants, even though the pants were made of denim. Davis came up with the idea of putting metal rivets at areas of stress. Great idea, but Davis lacked the $68 he needed to file patent papers. So he called on a successful San Francisco businessman named Levi Strauss and offered to share the patent. They received their patent in 1873 — and the rest is fashion history.

Plastic (1909)

Leo Baekeland was a Belgian-born chemist who made his first million by inventing a photographic paper that could use artificial light to be developed. Then he turned his attention to coming up with a new substance for insulating electrical coils and wires. In 1909, he introduced the first fully synthetic plastic, called Bakelite. Hundreds of variations have been invented since, and it's hard to imagine a world without plastic.

Brassiere (1914)

Women had been trying to figure out what to do with their bosoms, in a fashion sense, for thousands of years, but New York socialite Mary Phelps Jacob still wasn't satisfied. Faced with having to wear something under her new sheer evening gown, she fashioned two handkerchiefs, a cord, and some ribbon into the first modern bra. Jacob received a patent in 1914. Stock prices for corset companies were never the same.

Television (1927)

Philo Farnsworth was mowing an Idaho wheat field in 1920 when he came up with an idea: Scan a picture in horizontal lines, like the rows of wheat, with an electron beam, and reproduce it somewhere else. By 1927, he had patented his idea, and two years later was head of the Farnsworth Television and Radio Corporation. Television made its official debut at the New York World's Fair in 1939, but Farnsworth was too involved in legal fights over his baby to enjoy it. He died in 1971, dispirited and forgotten. Television survived.

Remote Control (1950)

What's TV without a remote? The first remote controls were developed in World War II by the German navy to control motorboats that could ram enemy ships. After the war, the Zenith Corporation developed a unit called "Lazy Bones." It was connected to the TV by a cable, but people kept tripping over it. In 1956, company engineers developed a unit using ultrasonic waves, and 20 years later, an infrared beam unit. And you wonder why the upholstery is wearing out on the couch.

The Pill (1960)

If you were an ancient Egyptian and wanted to practice birth control, you used a mixture of crocodile dung and fermented dough. But that wasn't appealing to Katherine McCormick, the fabulously wealthy heiress to the McCormick mechanical reaper fortune. She forked over about $2 million in the 1950s to finance research into a contraceptive that was safe, easy to use, and effective. In 1960, such a pill was approved by the Food and Drug Administration. It gave women more control over their reproductive lives than ever before.

The Internet (1969)

In the 1960s, some American scientists began kicking around the idea of a communications system using central research computers called "nodes" that could continue to function even through a nuclear war. That interested the Pentagon, which then financed more research. In late 1969, four universities connected via computer, and the Internet was born. America now sends out more than two billion e-mail messages a day.

Post-It Notes (1980)

Okay, it's not the greatest invention since, well, sliced bread, but you have to admit they are handy. They were invented by a 3M Company research scientist named Spencer Silver, who was trying to develop a super strong adhesive and came up with a weak one instead. A few years later, a colleague of Silver's named Arthur Fry stuck some of Silver's glue to the back of some markers that kept falling out of his church hymnal. Voilà! Losing telephone messages got a little harder to do.

Chapter 27

Ten Events That Defined American Culture

• •

"**I**nvention" isn't the only important word to begin with the letter "i." There are also "innovation" and "inspiration." And of course, "important." Here's a list of ten important innovations or inspirations in various cultural fields that have had their impact on American life.

The Publication of Poor Richard's Almanack (1732)

Benjamin Franklin was 26 years old when he began "Poor Richard's Almanack" in 1732, under the name Richard Saunders. He would continue it every year until 1758, liberally borrowing maxims and proverbs from lots of other people. No matter. It became a huge best seller, and the first American book besides the Bible to give Americans something in common from a literary standpoint.

The Performance of "The Black Crook" (1866)

Americans had been singing and dancing on stage in comic operas since the 1780s. But it wasn't until the opening of "The Black Crook" at Niblo's Garden in New York City that song and dance were married to melodrama, giving birth to the American musical. The cast included a chorus and dancing girls who showed their legs.

The Opening of the Home Life Insurance Building (1884)

There was a whole lot of construction in Chicago following the great fire of 1871. It included the first big building to be erected on a skeleton of steel girders, which gave it more strength and allowed it to be ten stories high. Designed by architect William L. Jenney, it opened the door, with the invention of the elevator brake, to the skyscrapers of the twentieth century.

The Copyright Act (1909)

This law gave authors, publishers, and composers control over their work, and the rights to compensation if others wanted to use it. Over the rest of the century, the law has been extended to other creations, including paintings, movies, and computer programs. It helped make the arts a more attractive way to make a living.

Jazz (1920s)

Born from the slave songs of the South, jazz hit its stride in the 1920s and influenced nearly every form of music to come along since: swing, bop, rock, fusion, and even classical. Jazz also influenced the culture in other ways, such as clothing styles and language.

Abstract Expressionism (1950s)

This was the first major art movement to begin in the United States. It featured violent color patterns and motion over subject. Its leader was Jackson Pollock, who discarded easel and palette, laid his canvas on the floor, and dripped or poured paint on it.

Elvis Presley (1956)

He was the king of rock and roll, and in 1956 he ascended to the throne. Presley had three number one hits, outraged adults, and thrilled teens with his pelvic gyrations on national television and became a cultural icon virtually overnight. Every rock idol who came after him was compared to the King.

The Establishment of the NEA (1965)

While other countries had long histories of government support of the arts, America didn't get into the act until the establishment of the National Endowment for the Arts. Over the past 36 years, the NEA has provided support for a wide range of artistic efforts, some of them intensely controversial. It has also sponsored exhibits from around the world.

Woodstock (1969)

It was supposed to be just a three-day music festival in rural New York. Instead it became one of the biggest "happenings" in world history. More than 400,000 people braved driving rainstorms to dance, play, and listen to music. Three people died; two were born. Most important, the festival opened the eyes of many older Americans who had felt they had nothing to learn from the "peace and love" mantra of the Flower Children.

"Deep Throat" (1972)

It was pretty much like every other porn movie: inane plot, bad puns, and wooden acting. But "Deep Throat" somehow was seen as chic by Middle America. It played in "legitimate" theaters, attracted couples instead of just men, and paved the way for greater acceptance of sex in the cinema, and society in general.

Part VI
Appendixes

In this part . . .

A nation's greatness can be measured by the words it lives by, and Americans have put together some pretty great words over the past few hundred years. Here are four documents that are among the most important, not only in U.S. history but in the history of the world: the Preamble to the United States Constitution, the Bill of Rights, the Declaration of Independence, and the Gettysburg Address.

They're here as reference tools, sure. But take a moment or two to read them, and you may find they are a lot more than that. For a nation and its people, they're words to live by.

Appendix A

Preamble to the United States Constitution

● ●

*W*e *the People* of the United States, in Order to form a more perfect Union, establish Justice, insure domestic Tranquility, provide for the common defense, promote the general Welfare, and secure the Blessings of Liberty to ourselves and our Posterity, do ordain and establish this Constitution for the United States of America.

Appendix B

The Bill of Rights: Amendments 1–10 of the Constitution

• •

*T*he Conventions of a number of the States having, at the time of adopting the Constitution, expressed a desire, in order to prevent misconstruction or abuse of its powers, that further declaratory and restrictive clauses should be added, and as extending the ground of public confidence in the Government will best insure the beneficent ends of its institution;

Resolved, by the Senate and House of Representatives of the United States of America, in Congress assembled, two-thirds of both Houses concurring, that the following articles be proposed to the Legislatures of the several States, as amendments to the Constitution of the United States; all or any of which articles, when ratified by three-fourths of the said Legislatures, to be valid to all intents and purposes as part of the said Constitution, namely:

Amendment 1

Congress shall make no law respecting an establishment of religion, or prohibiting the free exercise thereof; or abridging the freedom of speech, or of the press; or the right of the people peaceably to assemble, and to petition the government for a redress of grievances.

Amendment II

A well regulated militia, being necessary to the security of a free state, the right of the people to keep and bear arms, shall not be infringed.

Amendment III

No soldier shall, in time of peace be quartered in any house, without the consent of the owner, nor in time of war, but in a manner to be prescribed by law.

Amendment IV

The right of the people to be secure in their persons, houses, papers, and effects, against unreasonable searches and seizures, shall not be violated, and no warrants shall issue, but upon probable cause, supported by oath or affirmation, and particularly describing the place to be searched, and the persons or things to be seized.

Amendment V

No person shall be held to answer for a capital, or otherwise infamous crime, unless on a presentment or indictment of a grand jury, except in cases arising in the land or naval forces, or in the militia, when in actual service in time of war or public danger; nor shall any person be subject for the same offense to be twice put in jeopardy of life or limb; nor shall be compelled in any criminal case to be a witness against himself, nor be deprived of life, liberty, or property, without due process of law; nor shall private property be taken for public use, without just compensation.

Amendment VI

In all criminal prosecutions, the accused shall enjoy the right to a speedy and public trial, by an impartial jury of the state and district wherein the crime shall have been committed, which district shall have been previously ascertained by law, and to be informed of the nature and cause of the accusation; to be confronted with the witnesses against him; to have compulsory process for obtaining witnesses in his favor, and to have the assistance of counsel for his defense.

Amendment VII

In suits at common law, where the value in controversy shall exceed twenty dollars, the right of trial by jury shall be preserved, and no fact tried by a jury, shall be otherwise reexamined in any court of the United States, than according to the rules of the common law.

Amendment VIII

Excessive bail shall not be required, nor excessive fines imposed, nor cruel and unusual punishments inflicted.

Amendment IX

The enumeration in the Constitution, of certain rights, shall not be construed to deny or disparage others retained by the people.

Amendment X

The powers not delegated to the United States by the Constitution, nor prohibited by it to the states, are reserved to the states respectively, or to the people.

Appendix C

The Declaration of Independence

*I*N CONGRESS, July 4, 1776.

The unanimous Declaration of the thirteen united States of America,

When in the Course of human events, it becomes necessary for one people to dissolve the political bands which have connected them with another, and to assume among the powers of the earth, the separate and equal station to which the Laws of Nature and of Nature's God entitle them, a decent respect to the opinions of mankind requires that they should declare the causes which impel them to the separation.

We hold these truths to be self-evident, that all men are created equal, that they are endowed by their Creator with certain unalienable Rights, that among these are Life, Liberty and the pursuit of Happiness. —That to secure these rights, Governments are instituted among Men, deriving their just powers from the consent of the governed, —That whenever any Form of Government becomes destructive of these ends, it is the Right of the People to alter or to abolish it, and to institute new Government, laying its foundation on such principles and organizing its powers in such form, as to them shall seem most likely to effect their Safety and Happiness. Prudence, indeed, will dictate that Governments long established should not be changed for light and transient causes; and accordingly all experience hath shewn, that mankind are more disposed to suffer, while evils are sufferable, than to right themselves by abolishing the forms to which they are accustomed. But when a long train of abuses and usurpations, pursuing invariably the same Object evinces a design to reduce them under absolute Despotism, it is their right, it is their duty, to throw off such Government, and to provide new Guards for their future security. —Such has been the patient sufferance of these Colonies; and such is now the necessity which constrains them to alter their former Systems of Government. The history of the present King of Great Britain is a history of repeated injuries and usurpations, all having in direct object the establishment of an absolute Tyranny over these States. To prove this, let Facts be submitted to a candid world.

He has refused his Assent to Laws, the most wholesome and necessary for the public good. He has forbidden his Governors to pass Laws of immediate and pressing importance, unless suspended in their operation till his Assent should be obtained; and when so suspended, he has utterly neglected to attend to them. He has refused to pass other Laws for the accommodation of large districts of people, unless those people would relinquish the right of Representation in the Legislature, a right inestimable to them and formidable to tyrants only. He has called together legislative bodies at places unusual, uncomfortable, and distant from the depository of their public Records, for the sole purpose of fatiguing them into compliance with his measures. He has dissolved Representative Houses repeatedly, for opposing with manly firmness his invasions on the rights of the people. He has refused for a long time, after such dissolutions, to cause others to be elected; whereby the Legislative powers, incapable of Annihilation, have returned to the People at large for their exercise; the State remaining in the mean time exposed to all the dangers of invasion from without, and convulsions within.

He has endeavoured to prevent the population of these States; for that purpose obstructing the Laws for Naturalization of Foreigners; refusing to pass others to encourage their migrations hither, and raising the conditions of new Appropriations of Lands. He has obstructed the Administration of Justice, by refusing his Assent to Laws for establishing Judiciary powers. He has made Judges dependent on his Will alone, for the tenure of their offices, and the amount and payment of their salaries.

He has erected a multitude of New Offices, and sent hither swarms of Officers to harrass our people, and eat out their substance. He has kept among us, in times of peace, Standing Armies without the Consent of our legislatures. He has affected to render the Military independent of and superior to the Civil power. He has combined with others to subject us to a jurisdiction foreign to our constitution, and unacknowledged by our laws; giving his Assent to their Acts of pretended Legislation:

For Quartering large bodies of armed troops among us: For protecting them, by a mock Trial, from punishment for any Murders which they should commit on the Inhabitants of these States: For cutting off our Trade with all parts of the world: For imposing Taxes on us without our Consent: For depriving us in many cases, of the benefits of Trial by Jury: For transporting us beyond Seas to be tried for pretended offences: For abolishing the free System of English Laws in a neighbouring Province, establishing therein an Arbitrary government, and enlarging its Boundaries so as to render it at once an example and fit instrument for introducing the same absolute rule into these Colonies: For taking away our Charters, abolishing our most valuable Laws, and altering fundamentally the Forms of our Governments: For suspending our own Legislatures, and declaring themselves invested with power to legislate for us in all cases whatsoever.

He has abdicated Government here, by declaring us out of his Protection and waging War against us. He has plundered our seas, ravaged our Coasts, burnt our towns, and destroyed the lives of our people. He is at this time transporting large Armies of foreign Mercenaries to compleat the works of death, desolation and tyranny, already begun with circumstances of Cruelty & perfidy scarcely paralleled in the most barbarous ages, and totally unworthy the Head of a civilized nation.

He has constrained our fellow Citizens taken Captive on the high Seas to bear Arms against their Country, to become the executioners of their friends and Brethren, or to fall themselves by their Hands. He has excited domestic insurrections amongst us, and has endeavoured to bring on the inhabitants of our frontiers, the merciless Indian Savages, whose known rule of warfare, is an undistinguished destruction of all ages, sexes and conditions.

In every stage of these Oppressions We have Petitioned for Redress in the most humble terms: Our repeated Petitions have been answered only by repeated injury. A Prince whose character is thus marked by every act which may define a Tyrant, is unfit to be the ruler of a free people.

Nor have We been wanting in attentions to our Brittish brethren. We have warned them from time to time of attempts by their legislature to extend an unwarrantable jurisdiction over us. We have reminded them of the circumstances of our emigration and settlement here. We have appealed to their native justice and magnanimity, and we have conjured them by the ties of our common kindred to disavow these usurpations, which, would inevitably interrupt our connections and correspondence. They too have been deaf to the voice of justice and of consanguinity. We must, therefore, acquiesce in the necessity, which denounces our Separation, and hold them, as we hold the rest of mankind, Enemies in War, in Peace Friends.

We, therefore, the Representatives of the united States of America, in General Congress, Assembled, appealing to the Supreme Judge of the world for the rectitude of our intentions, do, in the Name, and by Authority of the good People of these Colonies, solemnly publish and declare, That these United Colonies are, and of Right ought to be Free and Independent States; that they are Absolved from all Allegiance to the British Crown, and that all political connection between them and the State of Great Britain, is and ought to be totally dissolved; and that as Free and Independent States, they have full Power to levy War, conclude Peace, contract Alliances, establish Commerce, and to do all other Acts and Things which Independent States may of right do. And for the support of this Declaration, with a firm reliance on the protection of divine Providence, we mutually pledge to each other our Lives, our Fortunes and our sacred Honor.

(Signed) John Hancock, Button Gwinnett, Lyman Hall,George Walton, William Hooper, Joseph Hewes, John Penn, Edward Rutledge, Thomas Heyward, Jr., Thomas Lynch, Jr., Arthur Middleton, Samuel Chase, William Paca, Thomas Stone, Charles Carroll of Carrollton, George Wythe, Richard Henry Lee, Thomas Jefferson, Benjamin Harrison, Thomas Nelson, Jr., Francis Lightfoot Lee, Carter Braxton, Robert Morris, Benjamin Rush, Benjamin Franklin, John Morton, George Clymer, James Smith, George Taylor, James Wilson, George Ross, Caesar Rodney, George Read, Thomas McKean, William Floyd, Philip Livingston, Francis Lewis, Lewis Morris, Richard Stockton, John Witherspoon, Francis Hopkinson, John Hart, Abraham Clark, Josiah Bartlett, William Whipple, Samuel Adams, John Adams, Robert Treat Paine, Elbridge Gerry, Stephen Hopkins, William Ellery, Roger Sherman, Samuel Huntington, William Williams, Oliver Wolcott, Matthew Thornton

Appendix D

The Gettysburg Address

● ●

"*F*ourscore and seven years ago our fathers brought forth on this continent a new nation, conceived in liberty and dedicated to the proposition that all men are created equal.

Now we are engaged in a great civil war, testing whether that nation or any nation so conceived and so dedicated can long endure. We are met on a great battlefield of that war. We have come to dedicate a portion of that field as a final resting-place for those who here gave their lives that that nation might live. It is altogether fitting and proper that we should do this.

But in a larger sense, we cannot dedicate, we cannot consecrate, we cannot hallow this ground. The brave men, living and dead who struggled here have consecrated it far above our poor power to add or detract. The world will little note nor long remember what we say here, but it can never forget what they did here.

It is for us the living rather to be dedicated here to the unfinished work which they who fought here have thus far so nobly advanced. It is rather for us to be here dedicated to the great task remaining before us — that from these honored dead we take increased devotion to that cause for which they gave the last full measure of devotion — that we here highly resolve that these dead shall not have died in vain, that this nation under God shall have a new birth of freedom, and that government of the people, by the people, for the people shall not perish from the earth." — President Abraham Lincoln

Index

• *A* •

abolitionists
  colonial, 37
  Garrison, William Lloyd, 146
  John Brown, 162
  Stowe, Harriet Beecher, 154
  Sumner, Charles, 160
abortion legalized, 306
abstract expressionism, 356
Acoma, 19
Acquired Immune Deficiency
  Syndrome (AIDS),
  335–336
Adams, John, 64–65, 345, 367
  death, 132
  defeated in1800, 100
  elected President, 91
  elected to Congress, 131
  foreign policy, 95
  judgeships filled, 101
  vice president, 90
  XYZ Affair, 95
Adams, John Quincy
  elected President, 131
  immigration issue, 122
  tariff, 132
  Treaty of Ghent, 116
Adams, Samuel, 63, 65,
  347, 367
Afghanistan, 321
African Americans
  Brown v. the Board of
    Education, 291
  Buffalo Soldiers, 350
  desegregation, 291–292,
    301–302
  Great Depression era, 248
  Great Migration, 223
  Harlem Renaissance, 239
  Jim Crow laws, 202

  lynchings, 202, 248
  NAACP, 227
  Plessy vs. Ferguson, 202
  Reconstruction era, 182,
    185, 187
  right to vote, 187
  riots, race, 302
  World War II service, 268
aging of population, 340
Agnew, Spiro T., 311
Agricultural Adjustment Act
  (AAA), 254
agriculture
  1920s, 236
  American Indian, 11, 15
  colonial, 58
  cotton, 125–126, 178
  expansion westward, 198
  Great Depression, 246
  mechanization, 140
  sharecropping, 183
  slavery for, 126
  soil depletion, 102
  sugarcane, 28, 126
  tobacco, 35
AIDS (Acquired Immune
  Deficiency Syndrome),
  335–336
airplanes, 222, 242, 264
Alamo, 144
Albany Congress (1754), 53
Albuquerque founded, 55
alcohol
  excise tax, first, 92
  post-revolutionary
    consumption, 86
  Prohibition, 240–241
Alexander VI, Pope, 30
Ali, Muhammad, 298
Alien and Sedition Acts,
  93–94
Allen, Ethan, 79, 86

amendments to Constitution.
  See specific amendments
American Academy of Arts
  and Sciences, 84
American Colonization
  Society, 128
American Expeditionary
  Force (AEF), 226
American Federation of
  Labor (AFL), 209,
  220, 250
American Indian Movement
  (AIM), 304
American Indians
  agriculture, 11, 15
  Anasazi, 12
  Bering Strait passage
    theory, 9–11
  Cherokee, 84, 124, 142
  citizenship ordered, 249
  civil rights movement,
    303–304
  Clovis culture, 11
  colonial relations with, 44
  disease, role of, 29
  enslavement of, 27
  Five Civilized Tribes, 15, 142
  Great Plains, 14, 199–200
  Hispaniola, 27
  Indian Removal Act, 142
  Iroquois League, 14
  migration to America, 9–11
  Mound Builders, 12–13
  Northeast, 14
  Northwest, 13
  Ogallala Sioux, 192
  Oglala Sioux, 310
  Ottawa tribe, 55
  Pawtuxet tribe, 39
  Pequots, 45
  population estimates, 13

American Indians *(continued)*
  Proclamation of 1763, 61
  scalping, 349
  Seminoles, 142
  Sioux, 199–200, 202
  Southeast, 15, 142
  Southwest, 14
  Tecumseh, 112–114
  tribes, number of, 13
  Wounded Knee, 201, 310
American Party, 156
Amherst, Jeffrey, 54–55
Anasazi, 12
Anthony, Susan B., 159
Anti-imperialist League, 216
Antietam, 172, 177
Appleseed, Johnny, 104
Appomatox Courthouse, 178
Arkansas, 328
Armour, Phillip, 152
arms embargo, 263
arms, right to bear, 363
Armstrong, Neil A., 310
army. *See* U.S. Army
Arnold, Benedict, 73, 81
Arthur, Chester A., 211
Articles of Confederation, 76,
    85–86
assembly, freedom to, 363
Atlanta Olympics
    bombing, 334
atomic bomb, 274–275
attorney, right to an, 364
Audubon, John James, 117
Austin, Moses, 132, 143
automobile, 221

• *B* •

baby boom, 288
baby boomers, 327–328, 340
Baja California, 46
Bakker, Jim, 319
Balboa, Vasco Nunez de, 25
Bank of the United States,
    120, 138

banks
  Bank of the United States,
      120, 138
  Emergency Banking Act, 253
  failures, Great
      Depression, 246
  Glass-Stegall Banking
      Act, 254
  national, 92
  savings and loan
      bailout, 324
  state-chartered, 120
Barbary States, 107
Barbie dolls, 291
Barker, Ma, 258
Bartlett, Josiah, 367
baseball, 158, 242, 260, 293,
    335, 341
basketball, 205
battles. *See specific battles by
    place name*
Bay of Pigs, 296
Beckley, John James, 108
Bell, John, 162
Bering Strait passage theory,
    9–11
Berlin Airlift, 281
Berry, Chuck, 291
bicentennial, 313
Biddle, Nicholas, 139
Bill of Rights, 89, 363
Billy the Kid, 349
Black Codes, 185
Black Crook, the, 355
Black Hawk, Chief, 142
Black Muslims. *See* Nation of
    Islam
Black, Shirley Temple, 258
Blackwell, Elizabeth, 188
Bladensburg, Battle of, 115
Bloomer, Amelia, 164
Bonaparte, Napoleon, 103
Bonhomme Richard, 82
Bonus Army, 248
Boone, Daniel, 67–68
Booth, John Wilkes, 179
bootleggers, 240

Boquet, Henry, 55
Bosnia, 329
Boston
  Bunker Hill, Battle of, 79
  established, 40
  Intolerable Acts, 64
  Paul Revere, 348
Boston Massacre, 63–64
Boston Tea Party, 63–64
Bow, Clara, 238
boxing, 298
boycott
  First Continental
      Congress, 65
  Montgomery busses, 292
  Stamp Act, 62
Boylston, Zabdiel, 55
Braddock, Edward, 54
Bradford, Andrew, 55
Bradford, William, 39
Branch Davidians, 332
Braxton, Carter, 367
Breckenridge, John, 162
Britain
  army of, 69
  colonial policies, 59–60
  disadvantages in
      Revolution, 70
  impressment of sailors,
      95, 108
  invasion of D.C., 115, 117
  reasons for emmigration
      from, 33–34
British East India
    Company, 64
Brooklyn Bridge, 213
Brooks, Preston, 160
Brown University, 67
Brown v. the Board of
    Education, 291
Brown, John, 162
Bruce, Blanche Kelso, 183
Bryan, William Jennings,
    211–212, 232–233
Buchanan, James, 161,
    163, 346
buffalo, 200

Buffalo Soldiers, 350
Buffett, Jimmy, 332
Bulge, Battle of the, 272
Bull Moose Party, 225, 228
Bull Run, 176
Bunker Hill, Battle of, 79
Burgoyne, Johnny, 81
Burnside, Ambrose, 175
Burr, Aaron, 100, 107
Bush, George, 321, 323–325
Byrd, Richard, 244

• C •

Cabot, John, 25
Cabrini, Frances Xavier, 293
Cahokia, 12
Calhoun, John C., 112, 131,
  136–137, 154
California
  capture by U.S., 149
  Gold Rush, 150–153
  Great Depression era, 248
  immigration, 340
  Proposition 13, 318
  Serra, Junipero, 67
  statehood, 154
Calley, William, 300
Calvert, George, 43
Cambodia, 300
Camp David, 315
Canada, 328
  border dispute, 149
  coveted by U.S., 112
  invasion of, 81
  War of 1812, 114
canals, 124
capital of U.S.A., locations, 89
Capone, Al, 240, 244
Carnegie, Andrew, 207, 216
Caroll, Charles, 367
carpetbaggers, 186–187
Carter, Jimmy, 313–314,
  316, 346
Cartier, Jacques, 26

Cassidy, Butch, 214
Castro, Fidel, 296–297
cattle drives, 196, 198
cellular phones, 337
Centennial Exhibition, 199
Central Intelligence Agency
  (CIA), 283, 323
Challenger tragedy, 320
Chambers, Whittaker, 284
Champlain, Samuel de, 26
Chancellorsville, 177
Chapman, John, 104
Charleston, 182
Charleston, surrender of, 82
Chase, Samuel, 102, 367
Chattanooga, Battle of, 177
Chavez, Cesar, 303–304
Cherokee, 84, 124, 142
Chesapeake incident, 108
Chesebrough, Robert A., 208
chess, 338
Chicago, 210, 240, 244,
  305, 356
Chickamauga, 177
China, 307
  Korean War, 283
chocolate, 32
Christian Coalition, 318
Christian Right, 318–319
Churchill, Winston, 270
Civic Works Administration
  (CWA), 253
civil rights
  American Indians, 303–304
  Brown v. the Board of
    Education, 291
  desegregation, 291–292,
    301–302
  Fair Employment Practices
    Commission, 267
  Fourteenth Amendment, 185
  gay rights, 306, 329, 336
  Nineteenth Amendment, 223
  Plessy vs. Ferguson, 202
Civil Rights Act, 302

Civil Rights Commission, 292
Civil War
  Antietam, 172, 177
  Appomatox Courthouse, 178
  armies, 172–173
  arms, 171
  blockade, naval, 174
  Bull Run, 176
  casualties, 173
  Chancellorsville, 177
  Chattanooga, 177
  Chickamauga, 177
  destruction from, 181–182
  Fort Sumter, 176
  Gettysburg, 168, 177
  North's advantages, 169,
    178–179
  secession of states, 163, 165
  Sherman's March, 175
  Shiloh, 177
  slavery during, 171
  South's advantages, 170
  South's disadvantages,
    178–179
  strategies, 170
  Vicksburg, 177
  Wilderness, Battle of
    the, 177
Civilian Conservation Corps
  (CCC), 253
Clark, Abraham, 367
Clark, William, 105–106
Clay, Henry, 112, 116, 128,
  138, 145, 154
  Bank of the United
    States, 138
  secretary of state, 131
Cleveland, Grover, 211–212
Clinton, De Witt, 118
Clinton, Hillary, 328, 331
Clinton, William (Bill), 325,
  327, 329–331
Clovis culture, 11
Clymer, George, 367
Coca-Cola, 206

cocaine, 337
Cochrane, Elizabeth, 210
Cold War, 279
  Berlin Airlift, 281
  Cuba, 296–297
  ending of, 321, 323
  Greek revolution, 280–281
  Korean War, 282–283
  Reagan era, 319
  Truman Doctrine, 281
  Turkish revolution, 280–281
  Vietnam, 283
Columbus, Christopher,
  22–24
commerce. *See* tariffs; trade
common law, 364
Common Sense, 74
communism, 231,
  281–282, 284
Compromise of 1850, 153–154
computers, 337–338
Concord, Battle of, 67, 347
Confederate States of
  America, 166, 170
Congress. *See also*
    Contintental Congress
  impeachment of Andrew
    Johnson, 188
  New Deal legislation, 253
  Radical Republican control,
    184–185, 187–188
  Republican control in
    1990s, 329
  Seventeenth
    Amendment, 219
Congress of Industrial
    Organizations (CIO), 250
consent of the governed, 365
Constitution of U.S.
  Bill of Rights, 89, 363
  compromises in, 88
  convention for, 87
  Eighth Amendment, 364
  Fifteenth Amendment, 187
  Fifth Amendment, 364
  First Amendment, 363
  Fourteenth Amendment, 185

Fourth Amendment, 364
Ninth Amendment, 364
Preamble, 361
provisions of, 88
ratification contest, 88, 89
Second Amendment, 363
Seventh Amendment, 364
Sixth Amendment, 364
Tenth Amendment, 364
Third Amendment, 363
Thirteenth Amendment, 184
Continental Army, 70
Continental Congress
  First, 65–66
  Second, 72
continentals (currency), 71
Contract with America, 329
Coolidge, Calvin, 234–235,
  245–346
Copperheads, 169
Copyright Act of 1909, 356
Coral Sea, Battle of, 273
Cornwallis, General Charles,
  82–83
Coronado, Francisco, 26
corporations, 318
  British East India
    Company, 64
  Dutch West Indies
    Company, 44
  globalization, 339
  Standard Oil Company, 190,
    208–209
  Virginia Company, 34
Corrupt Bargain, The, 131
cotton, 118, 125–126, 178, 183
cotton gin, 125
Coughlin, Charles E., 257
cowboy, 197
crack cocaine, 337
Crazy Horse, 202
Credit Mobilier Construction
    Company, 207
Crockett, Davy, 143, 348
cruel and unusual
    punishments, 364
Cuba, 212, 296–297, 350
Cuban Missile Crisis, 296

Cumberland Road, 118
currency
  bank-issued, 120
  continentals, 71
  silver ratio, 212
  state issued, 86
Custer, George Armstrong,
  192, 200–201

• *D* •

D-Day, 272
Darrow, Clarence, 232
Darwin's theory of
  evolution, 232
Davis, Jefferson, 166
Dawes, William, 66
de Kalb, Johann, 78
de las Casas, Bartolome,
  23, 29
de Onate, Juan, 26
de Soto, Hernando, 26
Dean, John, 308
death penalty, 310
debt, U.S.
  first funding of, 92
  Reagan era, 319
  surplus under Clinton, 340
  World War II, 265
Declaration of Independence,
  75–76, 348, 365
Deep Blue, 338
Deep Throat, 357
Democratic Party
  1968 Convention, 305
  early, 133
Democratic Republicans, 91
Dewey, George, 213
Dewey, Thomas, 282
Diem, Ngo Dinh, 298
diet
  1920s, 237
  19th century, 142
  McDonald's, 289
  Pure Food and Drug Act, 219
  World War II soldiers, 269
Dillinger, John, 258–259
diners, 191

discrimination, racial, 127
District of Columbia invaded
    by British, 115
Dole, Bob, 330
Domino Theory, 284, 312
Doolittle, James, 272
double jeopardy, 364
Douglas, Helen Gahagan, 285
Douglas, Stephen A., 154,
    160, 162
Douglass, Frederick, 192
draft
    Clinton, William, 327
    Vietnam, 305
    Vietnam evaders
        pardoned, 314
    World War II, 263
Drake, Francis, 26
Dread Scott Decision, 161
drugs, recreational, 305, 337
DuBois, W.E.B., 227
due process of law, 364
Dukakis, Michael, 323
Dust Bowl, 246
Dutch colonies, 44
Dutch West Indies
    Company, 44
Dylan, Bob, 309

e-mail, 338
Earhart, Amelia, 260
Eastman, Crystal, 223
Eaton, John, 136
ecstasy, 337
Edwards, Jonathan, 52–53
eight-hour day, 210, 243
Eighteenth Amendment, 219
Eighth Amendment, 364
Eisenhower, Dwight D., 271,
    283–285, 292, 294
El Alamein, 271
Electoral College, 89
electricity introduced, 209
Ellery, William, 367
Ellsberg, Daniel, 300

Emancipation Proclamation,
    171–172
Embargo Act, 108–109
Emergency Banking Act, 253
Emergency Quota Act, 231
England. *See* Britain
enumeration of rights, 364
Equal Rights Amendment, 306
Ericsson, Leif, 16
Erie Canal, 124
Eriksdottir, Freydis, 17
establishment of religion, 363
evangelicalism, 318
Exxon Valdez, 322

Fair Labor Standards Act, 254
Falwell, Jerry, 318
Farrakhan, Louis, 341
Faubus, Orval, 292
Federal Bureau of
    Investigation (FBI),
    259, 331
Federal Emergency Relief Act
    (FERA), 253
Federal Reserve, 219
Federalist Papers, 89
Federalists, 90, 93–94, 100
feminism, 305. *See also*
    women's rights
Ferraro, Geraldine, 322
Fifteenth Amendment, 187
Fifth Amendment, 364
Fillmore, Millard, 154, 157, 346
First Amendment, 363
First Continental Congress,
    65–66
Fisk, James, 190
Five Civilized Tribes, 15
flag, United States, 84, 348
flappers, 241
floods of 1993, 340
Florida, 32, 54
Flowers, Gennifer, 330
Floyd, Pretty Boy, 258
Floyd, William, 367

football, 227, 260, 309
Ford, Gerald R., 311–313, 325
Ford, Henry, 221
foreign aid, 261
Fort McHenry, 115
Fort Necessity, 53
Fort Sumter, 163, 176
Fort Ticonderoga, 79
Foster, Stephen, 164
Fourteen Points, 229
Fourteenth Amendment, 185
Fourth Amendment, 364
France. *See also* New France
    Revolutionary War, role in,
        76–77
    World War II, 263
    XYZ Affair, 95
Franklin, Benjamin, 53, 58, 77,
    87, 96, 355, 367
Freedman's Bureau, 182
freedom of the press, 93, 363
Fremont, John C., 152, 161
French and Indian War,
    53–54, 59
French Revolution, 94–95
Fromme, Lynette
    (Squeaky), 325
Fugitive Slave Law, 154
Fulton, Robert, 110
fundamentalism, 232

G.I. Bill of Rights, 287
Gage, Thomas, 66
Gallatin, Albert, 101
Galveston hurricane, 227
gambling, 330
gang wars, 337
Garfield, James A., 211
Garrison, William Lloyd, 146
Garvey, Marcus, 234
gay rights, 306, 329, 336
George III, 70, 365–366
German immigrants, 156
Gerry, Elbridge, 87, 367
Gershwin, George, 244

Gettysburg, 168, 177
Gettysburg Address, 168, 369
Ghent, Treaty of, 116
Gingrich, Newt, 329–330
Glass-Stegall Banking Act, 254
Glenn, John, 309
global economy, 339
Goddard, Robert, 244
Gold Rush, 150–153
Good Neighbor Policy, 262
Gorbachev, Mikhail, 323
grand juries, 364
Grant, Ulysses S., 148, 174,
    346, 350
  Appomattox
    Courthouse, 178
  elected President, 189
  re-elected President, 190
  Shiloh, Battle of, 177
  Vicksburg, 177
Great Awakening, 52–53
Great Depression, 245–247,
    250, 253–254, 257–258
Great Migration, 223
Great Plains
  American Indian tribes, 14
  Dust Bowl, 246
  Indian Wars, 199–200
Great Society, 302
Greeley, Horace, 190
Greene, Nathanael, 79, 82
Grenada, 326
Grenville, George, 61
grog, 50
Guadalcanal, Battle of, 273
Guadalupe Hidalgo, Treaty
    of, 149
Guam, 215
Guatemala, 283
Guilford Courthouse, Battle
    of, 82
Gulf of Tonkin Resolution, 299
Gulf War, 323–324
gunboat diplomacy, 218
Gwinnett, Button, 367

• **H** •

Haiti, 218
Haitian revolution, 104
Hall, Lyman, 367
Hamilton, Alexander
  constitutional
    convention, 87
  debt funding plan, 92
  duel with Burr, 107
  election of 1800, 100
  Federalist Papers, 89
  treasurer of U.S., 90
Hancock, John, 59, 76,
    347, 367
Hanna, Mark, 211, 216
Hardin, John Wesley, 349
Harding, James, 346
Harding, Warren G., 234
Harlem Renaissance, 239
Harpers Ferry, 162
Harrison, Benjamin, 211, 367
Harrison, William Henry,
    113–114, 145, 346
Hart, John, 367
Harvard University, 46
Havemeyer, Henry O., 208
Hawaii, 118, 212, 263
Hawkins, Sir John, 24
Hayes, Rutherford B.,
    190–191, 211
Haymarket Square, 210
Hayne, Robert, 137
health care reform, 328
Henry, Patrick, 65
Herjolfsson, Bjarni, 16
Hessians, 74, 81
Hewes, Joseph, 367
Heyward, Thomas, 367
Hickok, James Butler (Wild
    Bill), 213, 349
Hindenburg explosion, 260
Hiroshima, 274
Hispaniola, 27
Hiss, Alger, 284
Hitler, Adolf, 262–263, 270–272

HIV virus, 335–336
hockey, 326
Holocaust, 271
Home Life Insurance
    Building, 356
Homeowners Loan Act, 254
homosexuality, 306, 329, 335
Hooker, Joseph, 175
Hooper, William, 367
Hoover, Herbert, 235, 247, 251
Hoover, J. Edgar, 231
Hoovervilles, 247
Hopkins, Harry, 255
Hopkins, Stephen, 367
Hopkinson, Francis, 348, 367
House of Burgesses, 36
House Un-American
    Activities Committee
    (HUAC), 284
Houston, Sam, 143
Howe, William, 79
Hudson, Henry, 26
Humphrey, Hubert, 299
Huntington, Colis P., 190
Huntington, Samuel, 367
Hurricane Andrew, 326
Hussein, Saddam, 323–324
Hutchinson, Anne, 43
Hylton v. United States, 96

 • **I** •

Ice Age, 10
immigration
  1886 to 1915, 203–204
  1980s, 317
  1990s, 340
  19th century, 121
  Chinese, 203
  colonial era, 58
  Emergency Quota Act, 231
  Japanese, 262
  Latin American, 303–304
  Mexican, 249, 268
  mid-19th century, 155–156
imperialism, 216–218

impressment, 367
income, distribution of, 339
Indian Civil Rights Act, 304
Indian Removal Act, 142
Indians. *See* American
    Indians
industrialization, 205, 209,
    220, 264–265
inflation, 287, 312, 314, 318
initiatives, 219
International Workers of the
    World (IWW), 221–222
Internet, 338
Intolerable Acts, 64
Iran, 283, 315
Iraq, 323–324
Irish immigrants, 156
iron curtain, 280
Iroquois League, 14
Irving, Washington, 117
Isabella, Queen of Spain,
    22–23
isolationism, 262
Israel, 315

● *J* ●

Jackson, Andrew, 345
    Bank of the United
        States, 138
    Battle of New Orleans, 116
    childhood, 134
    defeat in 1820, 131
    duels, 110
    Eaton affair, 136
    elected president, 131–132
    inauguration, 133–134
    Indian policy, 141
    nullification, 137
    re-election, 138
    spoils system, 135
    Texas policy, 144
Jackson, Jesse, 316
Jackson, Thomas J.
    (Stonewall), 170, 177
James I, 34, 38, 43
Jamestown, 34–37

Japan, 164, 262–263, 268,
    272–274
Japanese-Americans
    imprisoned, 269
Jay, John, 65, 90, 96
    Federalist Papers, 89
    treaty with Britain, 95
jazz, 239, 356
Jefferson, Thomas, 67,
    345, 367
    death, 132
    Declaration of
        Independence written,
        75–76
    elected President, 100
    elected Vice President, 91
    Embargo Act, 108–109
    First Inaugural Address, 100
    presidency, 101
    Sally Hemmings affair, 101
    secretary of state, 90
Jenkins, Edward, 50
Jenney, William L., 356
Jim Crow laws, 202, 223
Johnson, Andrew, 184–189
Johnson, Lyndon B., 251,
    297–299
Jones, John Paul, 82
Jones, Paula, 330
Joseph, Chief, 201
jury trials, 364, 366

● *K* ●

Kaczynski, Theodore, 334
Kaiser, Henry J., 266
Kamehameha the Great, 118
Kansas-Nebraska Act, 161
Karlsefni, 17
Kasparov, Garry, 338
Kefauver, Estes, 293
Kellogg-Briand Pact, 261
Kennedy, John F., 99, 290,
    295–298, 302, 310, 350
Kennedy, Robert, 302, 310
Kent State massacre, 300
Key, Francis Scott, 115

Khomeini, Ayatollah
    Ruhollah, 315
Khrushchev, Nikita, 297
Kidd, William, 46
King George's War, 50
King William's War, 49
King, Martin Luther, 292,
    301–302
King, Rodney, 324–325
King, Rufus, 130
Kinsey, Alfred C., 288
Kissinger, Henry, 300
Kitty Hawk, North
    Carolina, 222
Knights of Labor, 209
Know Nothing Party, 156
Knox, Henry, 90
Korea, 309
Korean War, 282–283
Koresh, David, 332
Kosovo, 329
Ku Klux Klan (KKK), 180, 189,
    232, 234
Kuwait, 323–324

● *L* ●

La Raza, 303
La Salle, Sieur de, 48
labor unions, 209–210, 220,
    222, 243, 250–251,
    265, 304
Lacota. *See* Sioux
Lafitte, Jean, 132
Land Ordinance of 1785, 86
Laos, 300
Latin American relations, 262
Lawrence strike, 220
League of Nations, 230
Lebanon, 321
Lee, Francis Lightfoot, 367
Lee, Richard Henry, 75, 367
Lee, Robert E., 148, 162, 170,
    174, 177–178
Leif Ericsson, 16
Lend-Lease Act, 263
Levitt, William J., 288

Lewinsky, Monica, 328, 330–331
Lewis, Francis, 367
Lewis, John L., 250
Lewis, Meriwether, 105–106
Lewis, Sinclair, 260
Lexington, Battle of, 66
Leyete Gulf, Battle of, 273
Liberia, 127
Liberty Bell, 348
Library of Congress, 108
Libya, 326
Lincoln, Abraham, 345
  assassination of, 179
  begins presidency, 165, 167
  character of, 167
  Douglas debates, 162
  election, 162–163
  Emancipation
     Proclamation, 171–172
  Gettysburg Address, 168, 369
  habeus corpus
     suspended, 169
  opposes Mexican War, 150
  re-election, 169
  slavery, view of, 183
Lincoln, Benjamin, 82
Lindbergh, Charles, 242–243, 247, 263
Lippard, George, 348
Little Big Horn, 200
Livingston, Philip, 367
Lodge, Henry Cabot, 230
Long, Huey, 256–257
Longfellow, Henry
     Wadsworth, 348
Los Alamos, New Mexico, 274
Los Angeles, 84, 325, 333, 341
Los Angeles, Battle of, 268
Louisiana, 256
Louisiana Purchase, 104
Louisiana territory, 48, 56, 103, 105
Lowell, Francis Cabot, 118
Lowell, James Russell, 150
Loyalists. *See* Tories

Ludlow massacre, 220
Lusitania, sinking of, 225
Lynch, Charles, 84
Lynch, Thomas, 367
Lyon, Matthew, 94

• *M* •

MacArthur, Douglas, 273, 282
Macdonough, Thomas, 116
Mad Cow Disease, 341
Madison, James, 111
  Bill of Rights by, 89
  constitutional convention, at, 87
  elected president, 111
  Federalist Papers, 89
  Marbury v. Madison, 101
  re-elected, 118
  trade bans, 112
Magellan, Ferdinand, 25
Mah Jong craze, 239
Maine, state of, 128
Maine, the, 213
Malcolm X, 302
Manhattan Project, 274
manifest destiny, 147
Mann, Horace, 141
manufacturing
  1920s, 235
  cotton cloth, 118
  early 19th century, 123
  shift to third world, 339
  World War II, 264–265
Marbury v. Madison, 101–102
Marshall Plan, 281
Marshall, John, 102–103, 123
Maryland, 37, 43
Massachusetts
  Intolerable Acts, 64
  slavery abolished in, 84
Massachusetts Bay Colony, 40
Masterson, William Barclay
     (Bat), 197
Mattel, 291
Maverick, Samuel A., 149
Maya empire, 19

Mayflower, 38
Mayflower Compact, 39
McCarthy, Joseph, 286
McCarty, Henry, 349
McCaughey septuplets, 341
McClellan, George B., 167, 169
McCord, James, 307–308
McCormick's reaper, 140
McDonald's, 289
McGovern, George, 300
McGwire, Mark, 335
McKean, Thomas, 367
McKinley, William, 211–212, 216
McPherson, Aimee
     Semple, 233
McVeigh, Timothy, 332–333
Meade, General, 177
Meat Inspection Act, 219
medicine
  19th century, 122
  AIDS, 335–336
  health care reform, 328
Memorial Day Massacre, 251
Merrimac, 174
Metacom, 45
methamphetamine, 337
Mexican War, 148–149
Mexico, 218, 328
Microsoft, 341
Middleton, Arthur, 367
Midway, Battle of, 273
militia, 331–332, 363
Milk, Harvey, 306
Million Man March, 341
minimum wage, 236, 254, 294, 326
mining, 195–196
Minnesota, 334
missionaries
  Serra, Junipero, 67
  Spanish, 29, 46
Missouri compromise, 128
Mitchell, John, 308, 312
molasses, 28
Mondale, Walter, 317

Monitor, 174
monopolies, 209
Monroe Doctrine, 129–130
Monroe, James
    elected president, 119
    Louisiana territory
        treaty, 104
    presidency, 130
    re-election, 130
    slavery, 127
Monroe, Rose, 267
Montreal, 54, 81
moon hoax, 135
moon landing, 310
Moore, Gordon, 337
Moral Majority, 318
Moran, George, 240, 244
Morgan, J. P., 207
Mormons, 157. *See also*
    Smith, Joseph
Morris, Lewis, 367
Morris, Robert, 367
Morrison, Toni, 336
Morse, Samuel F.B., 141
Morton, John, 367
Mosby, John Singleton, 175
Moscone, George, 306
Mott, Lucretia, 159
Mound Builders, 12–13
movies, 237, 242
Mt. Rushmore, 262
muckrakers, 220
Muhammad, Elijah, 260, 302
musicals, 355
Mussolini, Benito, 262, 271
My Lai, 300

Nagasaki, 275
Napoleon, 112
Nat Turner's rebellion, 139
Nathan, Hale, 83
Nation of Islam, 260, 298,
    302, 341

National Association for the
    Advancement of Colored
    People (NAACP),
    227, 268
National Endowment for the
    Arts (NEA), 357
National Industrial Recovery
    Act (NIRA), 254
National Organization of
    Women (NOW), 306
National Recovery
    Administration
    (NRA), 254
National Republican
    Party, 138
nationalism, 120
Native Americans. *See*
    American Indians
Nativists, 156
NATO (North Atlantic Treaty
    Organization), 281
Navidad, 23
navy. *See* U.S. Navy
NEA (National Endowment
    for the Arts), 357
Nelson, Thomas, 367
New Amsterdam, 44, 45
New Deal, 252–255
New France, 30, 48–50, 53–54
New Jersey, founding of, 44
New Mexico, 46
New Orleans, Battle of, 116
New York State
    founding of, 44
    invaded in 1814, 116
    Revolutionary War in, 81
    slavery legalized, 37
New York stock exchange, 96
newspaper, first, 84
Nicaragua, 218, 321
Nichols, Terry, 333
Nimitz, Chester, 273
Nineteenth Amendment, 223
Ninth Amendment, 364
Nixon, Richard M., 284–285,
    290, 295, 299–300, 305,
    307–309, 312, 346

North American Free Trade
    Agreement (NAFTA), 328
North, Lord, 64, 66, 70, 83
Northwest Ordinance, 86
Nova Scotia, 50
nuclear power, 315
nullification, 137

O'Daniel, W. Lee, 251
O.K. Corral, 213
Oak Ridge, Tennessee, 274
Office of Price Administration
    (OPA), 265
Ogallala Sioux, 192
Oglala Sioux, 310
oil, 192, 208–209, 323
oil embargo, 314
Oklahoma, 198
Oklahoma City Bombing, 333
Oliver Wolcott, 367
Opechencanough, Chief, 45
Oppenheimer, J. Robert, 274
Osceola, Chief, 142
Oswald, Lee Harvey, 297
Otis, James, 59
Ottawa tribe, 55

● *P* ●

Paca, William, 367
Paine, Robert Treat, 367
Paine, Thomas, 74–75
Palmer, A. Mitchell, 231
Panama Canal, 217–218, 315
Panic of 1819, 121
Panic of 1837, 145
Parks, Rosa, 292
Parliament, 60–61
Patton, George S., 272
Pawtuxet tribe, 39
Pearl Harbor, 263
Penn, John, 367
Penn, William, 43

Pennsylvania
  founding of, 43
  oil discovered, 164
Pentagon Papers, 300
Pequots, 45
Perot, Ross, 325
Perry, Matthew, 164
Perry, Oliver Hazard, 114
Pershing, John, 226
petition, freedom to, 363
Philadelphia, 348
Philip, King, 45
Philippines, 213, 215, 272–273
Phips, William, 41
Pierce, Franklin, 346
Pike, Zebulon, 110
Pilgrims, 38–39, 347
Pinckney, Thomas, 91
pirates, 107, 132
Pitt, William, 54, 62
Plessy vs. Ferguson, 202
Plymouth, 39
Plymouth Rock, 347
Pocahontas, 35–36
Point Four Program, 281
polio, 286
Polk, James K., 145, 147,
  149, 345
Pollock, Jackson, 356
Pontiac, Chief, 55
Poor Richard's
  Almanack, 355
population
  1930, 260
  American Indian, 13
  baby boom, 288
  census of 1800, 102
  censuses of 1810 and
    1820, 121
  Civil War, 155
  colonial, 47, 57–58
  slaves, 58, 126
population, aging of, 340
Populism, 212
pornography, 357

Portugal
  division of world, 30
  explorations by, 22
powers not delegated, 364
Powers, Gary, 294
Powhatan, 35–36
Prescott, Samuel, 66
Presley, Elvis, 290, 356
press, freedom. *See* freedom
  of the press
primary elections, 219
Princeton, Battle of, 81
privateers, 31
Proclamation of 1763, 61
Profiles in Courage, 350
Progressives, 218–219,
  221, 225
Prohibition, 219, 240–241
Protestantism, 34
public land, sale of, 122, 139
public schools, 134, 141
public works debate, 124
Pueblo seized, 309
Puerto Rico, 215, 293
Pulaski, Casimir, 78
Pulitzer, Joseph, 210
Pure Food and Drug Act, 219
Puritans, 40–41

• Q •

Quakers, 40, 43
quartering of soldiers,
  363, 366
Quebec, 48, 54, 81
Quebec Act, 65
Queen Anne's War, 50

• R •

Radical Republicans,
  184–185, 187–188
radio, 238, 242
railroads
  early, 140
  expansion of, 206–207

public land donated to, 206
  robber barons, 207
  transcontinental, 160, 192
Rainbow Coalition, 316
Raleigh, Walter, 26, 31
Randolph, Edmund, 90
Randy Weaver, 331
Rankin, Jeanette
  Pickering, 224
Ray, James Earl, 303
Read, George, 367
Reagan, Ronald, 313,
  316–319, 321
recall elections, 219
Reconstruction
  carpetbaggers, 186
  ending of, 191
  KKK, 186
  military governance, 187
  Radical Republicans,
    184–185, 187–188
Red Cloud, Chief, 192
Red Scare, 231
referenda, 219
Reform Party, 334
religious freedom, 363
Remus, George, 241
Repressive Acts, 64
Republican Party
  Contract with America, 329
  creation of, 161
  Radicals, 184–185, 187–188
Republicans, Jeffersonian, 91,
  93–94, 101–102
Revenue Acts, 61
Revere, Paul, 64, 66, 347
Revolution of 1800, 99
Revolutionary War, 79
  American disadvantages, 70
  Army, U.S., 70–71
  British disadvantages, 70
  Bunker Hill, Battle of, 79
  Charleston, surrender of, 82
  Fort Ticonderoga, 79
  France's role in, 76–77
  Guilford Courthouse, Battle
    of, 82

invasion of Canada, 81
Naval battles, 82
peace treaty, 83
Princeton, Battle of, 81
Saratoga, Battle of, 81
Trenton, Battle of, 81
Yorktown, surrender of, 83
Rhode Island, founding of,
42–43
Rickey, Branch, 293
right to bear arms, 363
riots, race, 302
Roanoke, Virginia, 31, 44
Robertson, Pat, 318
Robinson, Jackie, 293
rock 'n roll, 290, 356
Rockefeller, John D., 190,
208–209
rockets, 244
Rodney, Caesar, 367
Roe v. Wade, 306
Rolfe, John, 35–36
Rommel, Erwin, 271
Roosevelt, Eleanor, 252
Roosevelt, Franklin D.,
252–256, 262–263, 265,
270, 272, 345
Roosevelt, Theodore, 216,
218, 225, 228, 345
Rosenbergs, 285
Rosie the Riveter, 267
Ross, Betsy, 348
Ross, George, 367
Rough Riders, 350
Ruby Ridge, 331
Ruby, Jack, 297
rum, 28, 50
Rush, Benjamin, 367
Ruth, George Herman
(Babe), 242
Rutledge, Edward, 367

● **S** ●

Sacajawea, 106
Sagebrush Rebellion, 317
Salk, Jonas, 286

San Francisco, 83, 306
San Francisco
earthquake, 227
Sanger, Margaret, 225, 228
Santa Anna, General, 143,
149, 349
Santa Fe, founding of, 46
Saratoga, Battle of, 77, 81
savings and loan bailout, 324
scalawags, 186
scalping, 349
Schuckburg, Richard, 56
Scopes trial, 232–233
Scott, Winfield, 148, 170
Scottsboro boys, 249
searches and seizures, 364
secession, 163, 165
Second Amendment, 363
Second Continental
Congress, 72
Securities Exchange
Commission (SEC), 254
segregation, 202
self-incrimination, 364
Seminole war, 142
Separatists, 38
Sequoyah, 124
Serapis, 82
Serbia, 329
Serra, Junipero, 67
Seventeenth Amendment, 219
Seventh Amendment, 364
Seward, William, 167
sharecropping, 183, 248
Sheridan, Philip, 199
Sherman, Roger, 367
Sherman, William T., 175, 192
Shiloh, Battle of, 177
Simpson, Orenthal James, 333
Sinclair, Upton, 218
Sioux, 199, 200, 202
Sixth Amendment, 364
skyscraper, first, 356
slavery
American Indian, 27
Civil War era, 171

Compromise of 1850,
153–154
conditions of, 159–160
Fugitive Slave Law, 154
international trade
abolished, 88
Jamestown, 36
Massachusetts, abolished
in, 84
Mexico, abolition in, 143
Nat Turner's rebellion, 139
population growth, 58, 126
relation to agriculture, 126
Revolutionary War
period, 78
Sommersett case, 67
Spanish, 28–29
Thirteenth Amendment, 184
three-fifths rule, 88, 127
trade, early, 37
value of slaves, 126
Slidell, James, 147
smallpox, 30, 32, 55, 84
Smith, Al, 235
Smith, James, 367
Smith, John, 35–36
Smith, Joseph, 132, 146
Social Security, 254, 257
Somalia, 341
Sommersett case, 67
Sons of Liberty, 62–63
Sorenson, Theodore, 350
Sosa, Sammy, 335
South Carolina
Charleston, 182
Fort Sumter, 163
nullification, 138
Soviet Union. *See* Union of
Soviet Socialist
Republics
space race, 294, 309–310, 320
Spanish-American War,
212–213, 350
speech, freedom of, 363
spoils system, 135
Sputnik, 294
Squanto, 39

St. Brendan the Navigator, 18
St. Valentine's Day Massacre, 240, 244
Stalin, Joseph, 263, 270
Stamp Act, 61
Standard Oil Company, 190, 208–209, 219
Standish, Miles, 39
Stanton, Edwin, 167
Stanton, Elizabeth Cady, 159
Star Wars, 319
Star-Spangled Banner, The, 116
Starr, Kenneth, 331
states' rights, 137, 364
Statue of Liberty, 214
steel manufacturing, 207
Stephens, Alexander, 184
Stevens, Thaddeus, 185, 187
stock market crash, 243, 245
Stockton, Richard, 367
Stone, Thomas, 367
Stonewall riot, 307
Stowe, Harriet Beecher, 154
Strategic Defense Initiative (SDI), 319
Students for a Democratic Society (SDS), 305
suburbanization, 288
sugarcane, 28, 126, 208
Sumner, Charles, 160, 187
Superman, 256
Supreme Court
  Brown v. the Board of Education, 291
  Marbury v. Madison, 101–102
  minimum wage laws struck down, 236
  packing attempt, 255
  Plessy vs. Ferguson, 202
  state law first struck down, 118
  supreme justice, first, 103
Swain, Louisa, 192
syphilis, 31

• T •

Taft, William Howard, 225
tailoring, 121
Tammany Hall, 190
Tarbell, Ida, 218
tariffs
  Abominations, Tariff of, 132, 138
  established, 92
  increased in 1920s, 235
  War of 1812, 121
Tarleton, Banastre, 77
taxation. See also tariffs
  colonial, 59–60
  excise, on whiskey, 92
  gambling, 330
  income tax, 179, 221, 276
  limits on state power, 123
  Reagan tax cuts, 318
  Revenue Acts, 61
  Stamp Act, 61
  Townshend Act, 62, 64
Taylor, George, 367
Taylor, Zachary, 148, 153–154, 346
tea, tax on, 62, 64
Tecumseh, 112–114
telegraph, 141
telephone invented, 209
television, 244, 289–290
Temple, Shirley, 258
Tennessee Valley Authority Act (TVA), 254
Tenskwatawa, 113
Tenth Amendment, 364
terrorism, 331
Tet Offensive, 299
Texas
  Alamo, 348
  American settlements in, 143
  independence, 144
  oil discovered, 32
  statehood, 144
  Waco, 332

Thames River, Battle of, 114
Theodore Roosevelt, 350
Third Amendment, 363
Thirteenth Amendment, 184
Thomas, George H., 177
Thoreau, Henry David, 150
Thornton, Matthew, 367
Three-Mile Island, 315
Thurmond, Strom, 282
Tilden, Samuel B., 190
timber industry, 59
Tippecanoe, Battle of, 113
Tisquantum, 39
Titanic sinks, 227
tobacco, 24, 35, 102
Tories, 70, 77
Townsend, Frances E., 257
Townshend Act, 62, 64
trade. See also tariffs
  bans by Madison, 112
  Congress's power over, 88
  global, 339
  NAFTA, 328
trade deficit, 339
Trail of Tears, 142
trans-Atlantic cable, 141
Treaty of Ghent, 116
Treaty of Guadalupe Hidalgo, 149
Treaty of Paris, 54
Treaty of Versailles, 230
Trenton, Battle of, 81
trials, speedy, 364
Triangle Shirtwaist Factory fire, 220
Tripoli, war with, 107
Truman, Harry, 272, 281–282, 285, 293, 345
trusts, 209
Truth in Securities Act, 254
Tubman, Harriet, 180
Turner, Nat, 139
Tuskegee Institute, 202
Tweed, William M., 190
Tyler, John, 145

• U •

U.S. Army
  argument against, 87
  Civil War era, 172–173
  homosexuals in, 329
  Revolutionary War era,
    70–71
  World War I, 226
U.S. Marines
  Grenada, 326
  Iran rescue mission, 315
  Lebanon, 321
  Nicaragua invaded, 218
  Tripoli war, 107
U.S. Navy
  agreement to limit size, 261
  Algiers, fight against, 132
  Civil War era, 174
  Pueblo seized, 309
  Revolutionary War era, 82
  Tripoli war, 107
  War of 1812, 113–115
  World War II, 263, 273–274
Unabomber, 334
unalienable Rights, 365
Uncle Sam, 114
Uncle Tom's Cabin, 154
Underground Railroad,
    161, 180
Union of Soviet Socialist
    Republics, 279–281, 294,
    296–297, 321
Union Pacific, 207
Union Party, 162, 169
United Auto Workers (UAW),
    250
United Farm Workers
    (UFW), 304
United Nations (UN)
  created, 280
  Korean War, 282
urbanization, 155, 204–205
Utah, 157

• V •

Valentino, Rudolph, 242
Van Buren, Martin, 144
Vaseline, 208
Ventura, Jesse, 334
Vernon, Edward, 50
Verranzano, Giovanni, 25
Vicksburg, 177
videotape recorders, 313
Vietnam, 283, 294, 298–300,
    305, 312
Vikings, 16–18
Villa, Pancho, 218, 225
Virginia
  colonial laws, 46
  House of Burgesses, 36
  Jamestown, 34–37
  Roanoke, 26, 31, 44
Virginia Company, 34
Von Stueben, Frederick, 78

• W •

Waco, Texas, 332
Wallace, George, 299, 303
Wallace, Henry, 282
Walton, George, 367
War Hawks, 112
War of 1812, 111, 113–117
War of the Worlds panic, 259
warrants, search, 364
Warren, Earl, 291
Warren, Mercy Otis, 109
Washington, Booker T.,
    202, 227
Washington, George, 345
  appointed to commander in
    chief, 72
  character of, 73
  constitutional convention,
    role at, 87
  death of, 96
  elected President, 89
  faults of, 72
  flag, U.S., 348

French and Indian War,
    53–54
  retirement, 91
  Revolutionary War
    strategy, 79
  surveyor, 56
  victory at Yorktown, 83
  Whiskey Rebellion, 93
Watergate, 308
Watts riot, 302
Webster, Daniel, 137, 154
Webster, Noah, 91
Welfare Reform Act, 329
Wells, Orson, 259
West, settlement of, 158,
    195–196, 198
Whigs, 138, 145, 161
Whipple, William, 367
Whiskey Rebellion, 93
whiskey, tax on, 92
White House, burning of, 117
White, Dan, 306
Whitewater, 328
Whitney, Eli, 125
Wilderness, Battle of the, 177
Williams, Roger, 42–43
Williams, William, 367
Wilson, James, 367
Wilson, Sam, 114
Wilson, Woodrow, 225,
    229–230, 345
Winfrey, Oprah, 341
Winthrop, John, 40
witch trials, Salem, 41
Witherspoon, John, 367
Wolfe, James, 54
women's rights, 222
  1920s, 241
  1960s, 305
  abortion legalized, 306
  admission to medical
    schools, 188
  admitted to college, 146
  birth control, 225, 228
  Equal Rights
    Amendment, 306
  Nineteenth Amendment, 223

women's rights *(continued)*
  Seneca Falls, 158–159
  World War II, 266–267
  Wyoming suffrage, 192
Woodstock, 357
Woolworth, Frank W., 204
working conditions, 220
Works Projects
      Administration
      (WPA), 254
World Trade Center
      bombing, 333
World War I, 226
World War II
  allied strategy, 270
  atomic bomb, 274–275
  beginning, 263
  bombing campaign, 270
  D-Day, 272
  El Alamein, 271
  financing, 265
  manufacturing, 264–265
  Pacific campaign, 272–274
  Pearl Harbor, 263
  preparations, 263–264
  submarines, 270
  U.S. Navy, 270, 273–274
  women during, 266–267
World Wide Web, 338
Wounded Knee, 201, 310
wrestling, 334
Wright brothers, 222
Wyoming, 192
Wythe, George, 367

XYZ Affair, 95

Y2K scare, 341
Yalta, 270
Yankee Doodle, 56
Yeager, Charles, 293
Yorktown, surrender of, 83
Young, Brigham, 157
Yugoslavia, 329

YOUR ONLINE RESOURCE

Discover Dummies Online!

The Dummies Web Site is your fun and friendly online resource for the latest information about *For Dummies*® books and your favorite topics. The Web site is the place to communicate with us, exchange ideas with other *For Dummies* readers, chat with authors, and have fun!

Ten Fun and Useful Things You Can Do at www.dummies.com

1. Win free *For Dummies* books and more!
2. Register your book and be entered in a prize drawing.
3. Meet your favorite authors through the IDG Books Worldwide Author Chat Series.
4. Exchange helpful information with other *For Dummies* readers.
5. Discover other great *For Dummies* books you must have!
6. Purchase Dummieswear® exclusively from our Web site.
7. Buy *For Dummies* books online.
8. Talk to us. Make comments, ask questions, get answers!
9. Download free software.
10. Find additional useful resources from authors.

Link directly to these ten fun and useful things at
http://www.dummies.com/10useful

For other technology titles from IDG Books Worldwide, go to
www.idgbooks.com

Not on the Web yet? It's easy to get started with *Dummies 101*®: *The Internet For Windows*® *98* or *The Internet For Dummies*® at local retailers everywhere.

Find other *For Dummies* books on these topics:
Business • Career • Databases • Food & Beverage • Games • Gardening • Graphics • Hardware
Health & Fitness • Internet and the World Wide Web • Networking • Office Suites
Operating Systems • Personal Finance • Pets • Programming • Recreation • Sports
Spreadsheets • Teacher Resources • Test Prep • Word Processing

The IDG Books Worldwide logo is a registered trademark under exclusive license to IDG Books Worldwide, Inc., from International Data Group, Inc. Dummies.com and the ...For Dummies logo are trademarks, and Dummies Man, For Dummies, Dummieswear, and Dummies 101 are registered trademarks of IDG Books Worldwide, Inc. All other trademarks are the property of their respective owners.

IDG BOOKS WORLDWIDE BOOK REGISTRATION

We want to hear from you!

Visit **http://my2cents.dummies.com** to register this book and tell us how you liked it!

- ✔ Get entered in our monthly prize giveaway.

- ✔ Give us feedback about this book — tell us what you like best, what you like least, or maybe what you'd like to ask the author and us to change!

- ✔ Let us know any other *For Dummies*® topics that interest you.

Your feedback helps us determine what books to publish, tells us what coverage to add as we revise our books, and lets us know whether we're meeting your needs as a *For Dummies* reader. You're our most valuable resource, and what you have to say is important to us!

Not on the Web yet? It's easy to get started with *Dummies 101*®: *The Internet For Windows*® *98* or *The Internet For Dummies*® at local retailers everywhere.

Or let us know what you think by sending us a letter at the following address:

For Dummies Book Registration
Dummies Press
10475 Crosspoint Blvd.
Indianapolis, IN 46256

BESTSELLING BOOK SERIES